TESTIMONY OF A DEATH

THELMA TODD: MYSTERY, MEDIA AND MYTH IN 1935 LOS ANGELES

By

Marshall Croddy
and
Patrick Jenning

Copyright © 2012 by Patrick Dennis Jenning and Marshall Lee Croddy

All rights reserved

November 2019 revision

ISBN 9-781530-498475

Bay City Press

5 Varsity Circle

Rancho Mirage, CA 92270

www.baycitypress.com

NOTE:

All quotations in this book indicating the spoken words of the witnesses involved in the Todd mystery are directly from printed sources. No dialogue has been invented.

For Coral and Dorathy

ACKNOWLEDGMENTS

This is a book long in process. Many years ago, Dorathy Croddy, the mother of one of the authors, spoke of her long dead friend, the beautiful Thelma, and warned her children of the dangers of automobiles in closed spaces. Through the years, the authors wondered about the fate of the beautiful woman, a star of their favorite comedies, who died mysteriously one night long ago. However, it was not until a cold winter in 1983, far away from the warm Castellammare coast, when Pam, the wife of the other author, decided to search the faded papers for the real story and began in earnest an answer to the puzzle of Todd's death.

Through many years of research, we have had the help and support of numerous individuals and many who graciously granted interviews and/or shared their personal memories. All the following contributed much to this book: Pamela Jenning, Keri Doggett, William Todd, Scott MacQueen, Richard Bann, Jack and Mary Sauer, Lina Basquette, Michael Rhodes, Cole Johnson, Dave and Ali Stevenson, Dean Ward, A. T. Nelson, Robert Hanlon, Alex Gordon, Rudolph Schafer, Phyllis and Grant Cooper, Judge Arthur Baldanado, Dr. Joseph Choi, Katherine La Hue, Marie and William Clark, Corey Clark, Jake Jacoby, Jack Halstead, Coy Watson, Delmar Watson, Robert Shuler III, Willie Wilkerson, John Reynolds, Don Gallery, Emily Tortia, Leonard Maltin, Mark Wannamaker, Jeffrey Elliott, Catherine Rohrer, Terry Allen, Debra Dresbach, Bruce Campbell, Hynda Rudd, Juliet Begley, Morita Aspen, Rob Starr, and Robert Lacey.

We also wish to gratefully acknowledge the collections of the following institutions and their librarians, archivists, and staff whose knowledge, dedication and kindness so aided us in our research. They include the U.C.L.A Research Library, Library of the Academy of Motion Picture Arts and Sciences, University of Southern California Digital Library, Chicago Public Library, Los Angeles Public Library, Santa Monica Public Library, Library of Congress, New York Public Library and its eastside Annex, Culver City Library, Garland County Public Library, Garland County Historical Society, Los Angeles County Library System, Los Angeles Natural History Museum, Los Angeles Police Department, Los Angeles County Coroner's Office, Los Angeles County Office of the District Attorney, Los Angeles County Archive, Dayton,

Ohio Public Library, Bison Archives, Federal Bureau of Investigation, Lawrence, Massachusetts Public Library, and Eddie Brandt Saturday Matinee.

Finally, we want to give special recognition to Coral Suter, who gave so much of her heart to this book and made such crucial contributions to the project. We remember Coral for her beauty, the fierce brilliance of her intellect, and the uncommon kindness of her soul.

TABLE OF CONTENTS

INTRODUCTION	i
ONE: Monday Morning	1
TWO: The Queen of the Lot	5
THREE: Monday Afternoon	15
FOUR: Tuesday	21
FIVE: Wednesday Morning	31
SIX: Wednesday Afternoon	41
SEVEN: The First Week Ends	54
EIGHT: The Public Clamor	62
NINE: Gentlemen From Other Towns	72
TEN: West Takes the Stand	83
ELEVEN: Murder, Suicide, or Accident	89
TWELVE: The Reporters	109
THIRTEEN: The Publicists	118
FOURTEEN: The Making of a Legend	126

FIFTEEN: The Patina of Mystery	134
SIXTEEN: Frauds and Slanders	142
SEVENTEEN: Keeping the Lid On	154
EIGHTEEN: The Big Fix	160
NINETEEN: The Case Against Roland West	168
TWENTY: The Mystery of Roland West	179
TWENTY-ONE: The Prince of Darkness	203
TWENTY-TWO: Let the Evidence Show	213
TWENTY-THREE: The Cause of Death	222
TWENTY-FOUR: The Sightings	230
TWENTY-FIVE: Suicide?	242
TWENTY-SIX: An Accidental Conclusion	248
BIBLIOGRAPHY	261
INDEX	270
NOTES	276

INTRODUCTION

Who doesn't love a mystery? All the more when the solution is hidden in time or controversy. History is full of such conundrums: the death of Napoleon; the assassinations of Lincoln and Kennedy; the identity of Jack the Ripper; the disappearances of Amelia Earhart and Jimmy Hoffa; the fate of DB Cooper; the Borden murders. Within an almost timeless netherworld of intrigue, Kings and Queens, Czars and Czarinas, pretenders and heirs apparent, the famous and infamous move to their real or apparent fates at Mayerling or Yekaterinburg or over the South Pacific. In their wakes, the ripples of mystery, rather than dissipating with time, seem to strengthen, assuming archetypal form: he didn't commit suicide, he was murdered; she didn't die, she escaped; it wasn't a lone gunman, but was a conspiracy at the highest level.

Enduring mysteries share one common feature. All excite the public's imagination when the event first occurs, whether because of the nature of the act or because it involved a famous person. Often, the event that becomes the mystery serves as a milestone in the lives of ordinary people—where were you when you heard Kennedy had been shot or Marilyn Monroe found dead? While most present unique challenges to the institutions charged with investigating or interpreting the event—the police, the press and the court—many grow in mystery over time. These events can escape the confines of the original solution aided by obsessed amateurs who clumsily wield the weapons of science and history, muddying and deepening the mystery as they try to resolve it.

Once the great mysteries centered on the deaths of royals and aristocrats, but beginning in the 1920s the deaths of Hollywood celebrities often became the focus. Perhaps because of the nature of their profession, the deaths of actors tend toward the mysterious. Courted by the camera, they achieve apparent immortality, their youth preserved by film, lighting, makeup and cosmetic surgery, their personalities enhanced by the persona of every character they play. Youthful death is antithetical to their profession and leaves their fans with a feeling of betrayal, especially when the death tends towards the ridiculous rather than the sublime. We do not want to believe them capable of succumbing to the garden variety of deaths that come to many of us, through falls and car accidents, heart attacks or rapidly developing illness, or the random violence of the street. Perhaps because they seemed to live outside the monotony of life and the limitations that hamper most of us, we want to believe their deaths also implied some greater significance. Larger in their lives, they must also be larger in their deaths.

Thelma Todd's death in 1935 became one of Hollywood's famous mysteries because she was a beautiful and popular young comedienne. The mystery has endured not so much because Todd's reputation has endured but because the riddle of her death is so complete. Murder, suicide, or accident, the trio of causes that every coroner must face with every corpse, was not determined definitively at the time or since. This is not to say that her death hasn't generated a number of detectives and at least an equal number of solutions. But nobody has come forth with an explanation of the actress' death that compels belief, or one that, at the minimum, is not loaded with egregious factual and interpretative errors.

At one point, it was the purpose of the authors of this book to offer just such a theory, one that would close the Todd case forever. As our research progressed, however, it became clear that the Todd mystery is nearly perfect. None of the primary explanations, murder, suicide, or accident, and none of the specific theories (Murder: by whom? Suicide: why? Accident: how?) is decisive. With the deaths of most of the participants in the events surrounding Todd's death and the weakening memories of those who still live, the possibility of finding the answer to the Todd riddle has become more and more elusive. However frustrating, the mystery of Thelma Todd's death, when understood in terms of the context in which it occurred, offers a remarkable insight into a time and place that have been slowly buried beneath layer upon layer of myth.

The context of Todd's death is multifold: on one hand, it is the motion picture business in its Golden Age, on the other it is Los Angeles at a time when the city tottered on the verge of its greatness. The first implies and is characterized by legends and pleasant distortions; the second suggests a gritty reality that lies beneath the myths. For various reasons, Los Angeles has been seen popularly through Hollywood's filters. To understand what happened when Thelma Todd died, it is necessary to remove those filters and to gaze directly on the city itself, as it was in 1935, the year of her death.

In that year, while the movie industry was in what was later characterized as its Golden Age, Southern California itself was suffering like the rest of the nation through the Great Depression. To some extent, this period was simply a pause after decades of incredible growth, and not much of a pause at that. During the first three decades of the century, Los Angeles grew from a small city of 100,000 persons to a bustling metropolis of over 1.2 million. Another 2.2 million lived outside the city in the small towns and unincorporated areas of the coastal plain. During the thirties, the area's population would grow by a more modest but still impressive 25%, topping four and a quarter million by 1940.

Along with the population boom came dramatic changes in the landscape. The bean and grass fields disappeared as more and more families chose to live in single-family homes in housing tracts. The small towns quickly melded together in one vast urban landscape, which included even the hillsides near Hollywood and along the coast. In a few years, the next great boom would occur as the area's industry geared up for war production, bringing with it the first major smog infusions for which the city would soon be infamous. Nevertheless, in 1935, residents still called the pollutants that obscured the mountains on the long cloudless summer days "haze"–not smog or smoke. The area's warm dry air had long been the best selling point for this arid land that rose gently from the sea to the eastern mountains and foothills. While industries came and went–cattle, oranges, beans, and wheat–the land itself was the enduring commerce of the region. If you could get the buyers to look at it, it sold itself; the trick was to get the buyers, who were thousands of miles away, to come and look.

Promotion of the area's natural beauty was the direct goal of many of the local civic organizations and the chief byproduct of many of its industries, from oranges to movies. At the same time, suppression of information that might alienate potential buyers, many of whom hailed from the Midwest and were searching for a more temperate Iowa or Ohio or Missouri, was crucial. The rowdy element of the nineteenth century frontier town, for years as violent and wild as the legendary cattle and mining towns of the old west, lived on in abundant gambling dens and bordellos that were protected by the police and ignored by the press. The interests of the homegrown crime organizations thus coalesced with those of business groups, the one eager to profit from vice and the other wanting to keep the region attractive to migrants from the colder climates–at least those with money in their pockets. Both relied on the cooperation of politicians, police and the press to "keep the lid on" the local crime business, in other words, to keep it out of the news and out of the general knowledge of the population. This policy allowed politicians to boast that LA was, in the parlance of the times, the "White Spot" of the nation, free from crime, radical labor, and the foreign immigrant hordes that beset the eastern metropolises. It was not true, but it was a myth that sold. To keep on working, it had to be maintained. Those who protested against the protection of vice were quieted quickly and effectively. Some were compromised; others were simply bought.

Nevertheless, as time went on and the population increased, the agitation for reform grew more intense while the reformers became more adamant. Outside criminal interests, seeing a profitable new venue, maneuvered to take over the homegrown operation. It was becoming more and more difficult to "keep the lid" on; all that was needed was an event that would blow it off completely and expose the set-up that the combination of politicians, police, newspapers and businessmen had maintained for so many years. When that event came, it would bring down a mayor, a police chief, and most of the top cops in the LAPD and lead to the emergence of another city hundreds of miles across the desert devoted to the pleasures that Los Angeles had determined to deny its citizens.

In the pages that follow, we hope that the mystery of Thelma Todd's death will again unfold as it originally did in late 1935, with its manifold allusions to this unique time and place and its corresponding intimations of many times and places.

We also hope to elucidate the process by which the Todd mystery evolved over time, fueled by confusion over the original context and record, sensationalism, and, in some cases, outright fabrication. In this sense, the case of Thelma Todd's death serves as a cautionary tale. In today's celebrity-transfixed culture, with a 24-hour news cycle and unfettered electronic media overload, the distortions that evolved over 75 years since the Todd death now spring up overnight.

Finally, we will return to our original purpose in our long quest: solving the mystery of Thelma Todd's death, or at least, the mystery about the mystery of her tragic death.

The headings had lost their original brightness, the blackness of the print having turned almost green, the paper was yellowed and the photographs looked faded and confused, lacking light and shade . . . . [T]he bigger and more extended the heading, the greater the sense of futility and absurdity it gave, announcements of events that had lost their importance and significance by the evening of the very day on which they had appeared, now, with their noisy incomprehensibility, were repugnant not only to the memory but to the imagination as well. The most absurd headings . . . were those that included underneath the news a comment of a more or less tendentious kind; with their mixture of graphic vivaciousness and complete absence of echo they were reminiscent of the extravagant bawlings of a madman that deafen but do not affect the feelings. This, then, was the past . . . this uproar now silent, this fury spent, to which the very stuff of the journal, the yellowed paper that soon would break up and fall into dust, lent a quality of shabbiness and vulgarity. The past was made up of violence, of error, of deceit, of frivolity, of falsehood . . . and these were the only things that men had thought worthy of being published, day by day, and by which they recommended themselves to the memory of posterity. Life, in its normality and its profundity, was absent from these pages; yet what was he himself looking for . . . but the testimony of a crime.

— Alberto Moravia, *The Conformist*, translated by Angus Davidson

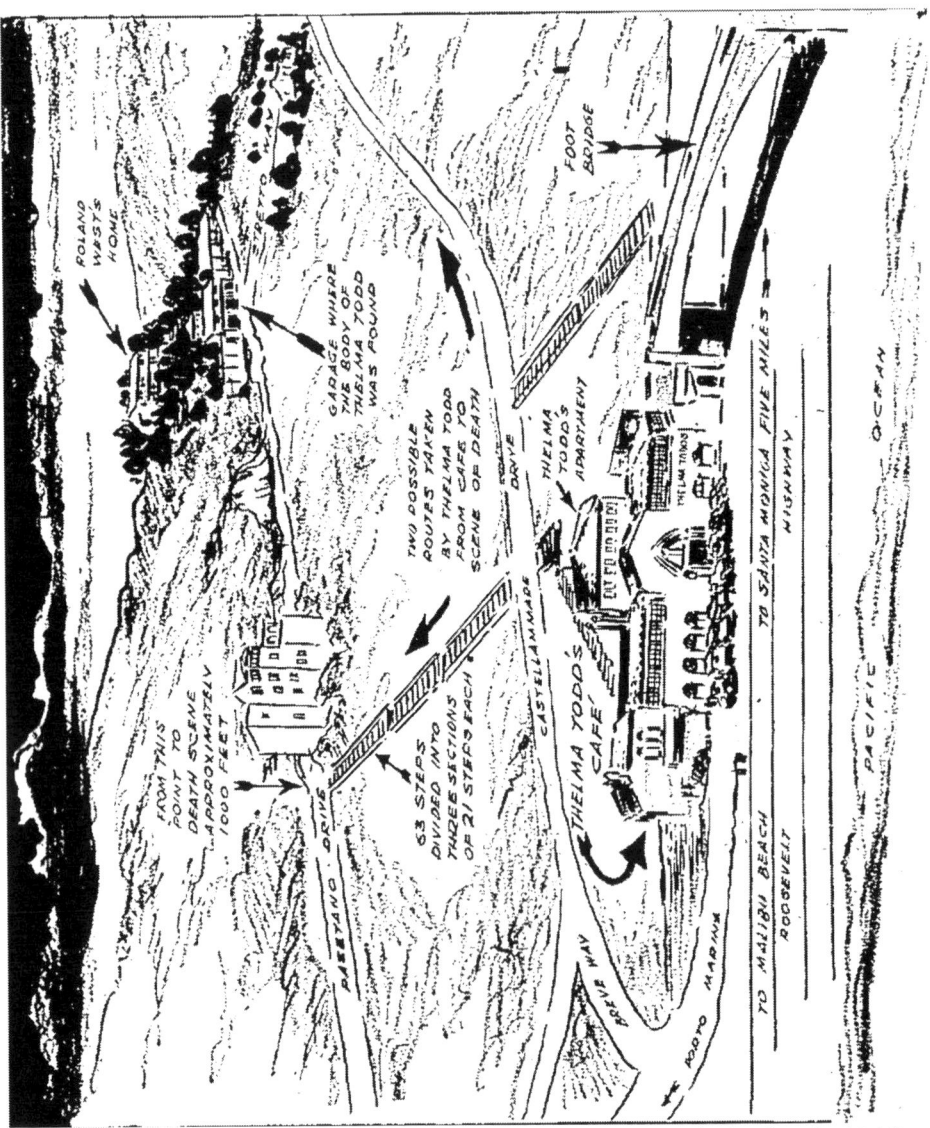

The Cafe Building and Castillo Del Mar in 1935. Todd's apartment is incorrectly placed on the third floor of the building. Actually, it was directly above her name on the right side of the building in the diagram. Artist: Athol Ewing, *Los Angeles Times Staff*. Copyright © 1935. *Los Angeles Times*. Reprinted with Permission.

ONE: MONDAY MORNING

My daughter's been murdered!
— Alice Todd[1]

She lay on her left side behind the steering wheel of the expensive phaeton, a mink coat snug about her shoulders, her head drooping over the edge of the seat. The gorgeous face, half covered by a tousle of blonde locks, was sunk into the cushion. From the way her arms hugged her chest, the hands cupped near her face, Detective Clark understood why at first the maid thought she was sleeping. The legs, however, told a different story. Clad in silk stockings, they twisted unnaturally from the center of the seat toward the driver's side of the floor. One foot rested next to the automobile's foot pedals, its pink lacquered toenails glistening through blue sandals. This was no ordinary slumber.[2]

Clark felt her body. It was cold and stiff. She appeared to have been dead for some time. A slim platinum brooch, tied at the side in a bow and scattered with tiny sapphires and diamonds, pinned a wilted and faded flower to her dark blue evening gown.[3]

The detective stepped back from the body and surveyed the death scene. The interior of the garage was still deep in shadows, its chilly air traced by a faint scent of mildew and engine oil. The automobile was backed into the right hand stall, the bumper pressed firmly against an old suitcase and a couple of tires, the radiator glittering in the noonday sun that poured through the open garage door. To the right, nearest the driver's side, a desk, a day bed couch and several steamer trunks were piled against the cement wall. A stall for a second automobile was to the left, presently empty. A narrow shelf with a few old jars and cans stretched along the wall on the rear of the garage.

Nothing out of the ordinary. Nothing to explain, at least at first glance, the dead woman lying on the car seat.[4]

Clark looked at her again. He recognized her, of course. With her classic features, blonde, curly hair, and flawless complexion, she was one of Hollywood's most famous beauties, a veteran of dozens of comedy shorts with ZaSu Pitts and Patsy Kelly and many dramatic and comedic features, including films with the Marx brothers and Laurel and Hardy. Los Angeles also knew her as the proprietor of a swank restaurant and bar several hundred steep yards down the hill from the garage, Thelma Todd's

Sidewalk Café. During the last eighteen months, it had become a watering hole for residents of the Malibu movie colony, beachgoers and the few locals of the sparsely inhabited neighborhood. The beautiful and vibrant Miss Todd, who often served as hostess herself, was its main attraction.

Clark moved along the hood of the car, inspecting its shiny metal. His partner from the West Los Angeles Division, Detective A. S. Roselli, watched from outside the garage. Standing next to Roselli was the man who had ushered the detectives into the garage a few minutes before, introducing himself as Mr. West, Roland West. It was his garage: he owned the estate on the hillside above and the restaurant building on the highway down the hill. Short, stocky, and somewhat bandy-legged, West was dressed in a gray, pin stripe jacket and dove gray trousers. Clark regarded him for a moment and then asked what he knew about the dead woman.[5]

West explained he learned of the tragedy from Miss Todd's maid, Mae Whitehead, who found the body when she arrived at the garage around 10:15 that morning, intending to swap her own automobile for the phaeton, which she would then drive down the hill to the restaurant building along the highway. Clark glanced at the young black woman who stood in the sunlight outside the garage, gazing morosely at the ocean. Whitehead had first contacted the café's treasurer, Mr. Smith, who in turn buzzed West on the house phone, West recalled. West paused, as if stricken by the memory: later he would remark that the phone buzzed heavily over and over, with a terrible insistence. He had never known it to ring like that.

He had dressed quickly and then hurried downstairs to climb into Whitehead's car. Normally, it took just a minute to reach the garage, but the distraught maid missed a turn and had to circle back by another street.[6] When at last they reached the garage, West rushed into the garage while Whitehead remained in the car. He found Thelma slumped behind the steering wheel, just as Mae had described her. He touched her face. There were a few drops of blood around her mouth. He wiped them off with his handkerchief.

West ordered Whitehead to drive up the hill to the upper tier of the estate to fetch the Schafers, Rudolph, the restaurant's manager, and his wife, Alberta, West's sister-in-law. A few minutes later, the couple came down the steps to the right of the garage. At West's direction, Schafer took West's own automobile, a Hupmobile parked in the now vacant stall next to the phaeton, to get a doctor and the police. Then West sent Whitehead to call Todd's mother.[7]

With his sister-in-law looking on, West, a former moving picture director of mystery films, made a rudimentary investigation of the death scene. He noticed the car's ignition button was in the "on" position,[8] and a robe customarily kept in the trunk was missing.[9] It appeared to him that Todd, whom he had not seen since Saturday evening, had fallen asleep while running the engine of her car, perhaps for warmth.

Clark had to agree that it didn't look like foul play. The actress' clothing was not disarranged and dust on the passenger side and rear of the front seat was undisturbed.[10] There were no weapons in the garage, no signs of violence at all; only a little blood around the mouth and nose of the deceased that could have been caused when, overcome by carbon monoxide, the actress collapsed and her face struck the steering wheel.[11] Robbery and murder did not seem likely. A thief would not have left her fur and jewelry, particularly the three expensive-looking platinum rings adorning her hands. And the thin white evening purse on the seat beside her could not have held much more than its present contents: four handkerchiefs, a cigarette case, lipstick and a small white coin purse with a single Yale door key inside.[12]

There were questions that needed to be answered, however. West pointed out that the gas gauge on the dashboard showed three gallons left in the tank. If Miss Todd was unconscious or already dead, why did the engine stop with gas remaining in the tank? And what was she doing in the garage in the first place, several hundred yards above her apartment on the coastal highway? There was no note, but one couldn't completely rule out suicide.

Clark walked out onto the narrow hillside street. Somehow, a photographer for one of the local papers had learned of the death and was already on the scene, busily unpacking his gear outside the garage door.[13] Clark ordered a uniformed officer to close the garage doors and keep everybody out.

A second uniformed officer was leaning against the side of a prowl car, watching Roselli, who was beginning to question the black maid near the side of the road. Clark told him to locate a phone. It was time to call Central.[14]

Downtown, they liked to think they knew how to handle cases like this. This one would make them jump.

An hour later, a caravan of squad and unmarked cars, sirens wailing, swept down Roosevelt Highway, rounded the café building at the bottom of the hill and steered up the narrow, curving streets, cutting their sirens as they approached the garage. Thelma Todd's friends and relatives, who had arrived during the past hour to find the uniformed policeman barring the garage, backed off the street to let them pass.[15] The police cars parked at odd angles along the narrow strip of asphalt, their doors opening to emit a small band of uniformed officers, nattily dressed detectives,[16] reporters and cameramen. As they congregated before the heavy wooden doors, a middle-aged, thickset man in a dark suit stepped out from one of the cars and brushed past them. He exchanged a few words with Detective Clark and then pointed at the garage door with his right forefinger. The uniformed officer quickly opened it.

With news photographers in tow, Homicide Captain Hubert J. Wallis entered the garage and peered into the driver's side of the automobile. A pudgy former London bobby[17] in his early fifties who wore round, horn-rimmed glasses and spread thinning hair ineffectually over a bald crown, he had survived three decades of political upheaval to rise to Chief of the Los Angeles Police Department's Homicide Squad. Bending over, he lightly touched the nape of the dead woman's neck. The newspaper photographers pressed forward.

Wallis held the pose for several seconds as the flashbulbs popped.

During his career, he had seen many dead bodies, including some famous ones. But he had never been photographed with one this beautiful.

TWO: THE QUEEN OF THE LOT

> By now, Thelma Todd's death has become a Case, an impersonal, irrelevant thing all but obscuring the girl, the woman, who is dead. But those who mourn her knew her to be the possessor of many extraordinary qualities. Most of all, she was–although I dislike the word–regular.
> – Philip K. Scheuner

The scene surrounding the exotic figure crumpled in the front seat of a luxury motorcar, dressed in the finery of her last Hollywood outing, marked a nightmarish end to a charmed and public life.[1]

For eight years, Thelma Todd's beauty, wit and vivacity had graced Southern California, where she swirled on the glamor circuit of the movie capital in its golden age. She danced with abandon at the Trocadero and the Mocambo, the chic nightclubs of the Hollywood set. She mugged for the camera in the exclusive booths of the Brown Derby, usually in the company of a handsome or distinguished man. She met her former husband under the famous palms surrounding the floor of the Coconut Grove. Shopping trips with girlfriends inevitably led to lunch at the Vendome, Musso and Franks, Perinos or the Bullock Wilshire's tea room. Loving speed, she drove her Lincoln phaeton convertible with the pedal to the floor, her platinum curls blowing in the wind.

At private parties in the Hollywood set, she was always in demand.

"Thelma was widely known and welcome at many hilarious Hollywood parties," the *Washington Post* recalled. "She was often called 'Hot Toddy.' It was she who won a bet once during prohibition by bringing six bottles of premium Scotch whisky past customs agents by sewing them inside her mink coat and then wearing nothing but an extremely daring Cleopatra costume underneath the coat. She dazzled them by opening it swiftly. They told her to go home and put some clothes on."[2]

Thelma charmed all castes in the film industry, from the moguls, producers and actors down to the stagehands. She was known as the "queen of the lot" at the Hal Roach studio. Casually chewing gum or schmoozing with Pip the Pup, the canine star of the Little Rascals series, Todd's lack of affectation was as evident as her extraordinary beauty.[3] Columnist Philip Scheuner wrote several days after her death, "I have heard her (half-mischievously, I always suspected) adopting a distinctly Boston Back Bay accent among her ritzier friends; and again, indulging in the saltiest give-and-take with the crew on a comedy set. It is they who will miss her most of all, the grips, the props, the assistant assistants, and the guys who take the fall for the guys who don't. Toddy spoke their language." Hal Roach himself commented, "She was a favorite with everyone on the lot, from the lowliest employee to the highest. She apparently was always joyous and seemed to thoroughly enjoy her work." Dorothy Granger, her co-star in several shorts, remembered her years later: "She had a wonderful sense of humor. She'd just start to laugh—for no reason! And sometimes we'd have to shoot seven or eight times before she'd simmer down enough. It got so that we'd just start to look at each other, and we'd start giggling!"[4]

That morning, however, the Roach studio sets fell quiet as Stan Laurel, Oliver Hardy, Charley Chase, ZaSu Pitts and the other Roach studio stars collected in small groups to recall their friend. Even on this dark day, amid the shock of her death, her fellow comedians could not help but recall her usual gaiety and sense of humor. "Thelma's just kidding us," a disbelieving Patsy Kelly exclaimed before she realized that it was not a Todd prank and collapsed in grief. It was the second tragedy to touch Todd's co-star since she arrived in Hollywood; two years earlier, she survived drowning when a car she was riding in backed off the Venice Pier into the ocean, killing the driver, nightclub entertainer and female impersonator, Jean Malin.[5]

Despite the pranks on and off the screen, Thelma had a quiet, intellectual side. She played the piano, wrote poetry and occasional pieces for the newspapers, and studied at least three languages at various times in her life. Intelligent as well as exuberant, she was fiercely protective of her privacy, especially in matters of romance, and distrustful of Hollywood and the mores of the studio powers.

"She safeguards real emotion with a crystal hardness allied with a sardonic wit," noted one writer.

"Her reserve is such a contrast to the natural effusiveness of actors," another commented.[6]

She was close to her mother, who came with her to Hollywood, where they shared a small apartment for several years. Only a few weeks before, her mother wrote to her relatives of her daughter's homesickness as the holidays approached. The two of them cooked a Thanksgiving dinner together.

In some ways, she was still a small town girl. In Lawrence, a mill town on the Merrimack River in northeastern Massachusetts, she was the darling of the town, the girl who made good. "Nowhere . . . did the sad happening create a greater stir and more general and sincere sorrow than back here in Lawrence, among the home folks who knew and loved her best," the *Lawrence Evening Tribune*, observed on her death. "All along they had watched with interest the progress to filmland heights of the girl whose achievements and acts reflected creditably at all times on her native city . . . ." The paper recalled Thelma as "the little home town girl who went out and made good in a great big way, without ever losing the fine qualities that endeared her to them in the days of her youth."[7]

She was of the third generation of Todds in Lawrence. Her father, John, was born in Ireland on August 22, 1871 and emigrated with his parents at twelve.[8] He attended public schools, worked as a textile bleacher at the Farwell Bleachers Company and lived briefly in New York City and Boston before he and a partner established a carpet and upholstery-cleaning firm named Farley and Todd Co. A few years later, Todd brought his younger brother, Adam, into the business, henceforth known as the Todd Brothers.[9]

Her mother, Alice Edwards, was a Canadian who had moved to Lawrence, where she met John shortly after he started in the carpet business.[10] The couple had two children. The first, William, born in 1903, died at seven when a flywheel broke into pieces at a creamery in New Hampshire, where the family was visiting Alice's relatives. Thelma was born on July 29, 1906.

On the strength of the Todd Brothers' moderate success, the Todds lived comfortably, moving from Thelma's birth home on Broadway in Lawrence to a new wooden-frame home at 592 Andover Street when she was twenty.[11] While John Todd achieved some prominence in local politics, serving as the Commissioner of Public Health and Charities, Alderman, and, from 1915 to 1925, Assistant Superintendent of Streets, Thelma attended local public schools in Lawrence. In high school, she was a popular girl who served as a gossip correspondent for the school newspaper, the Lawrence High School Bulletin. She wore her golden hair long, and though prone to chubbiness, her beauty was striking. Combined with intelligence and a generous nature, she was a popular figure with Lawrence's younger set. Years later, her younger cousin would recall puzzling over the commotion she invariably caused whenever she passed down the street. The same commotion would cost her a Christmas vacation job at a local Five and Dime when she was fifteen. The store manager discovered the boys gathered around her counter were more interested in Thelma than in spending money.[12]

Thelma arrived in Hollywood at about the time the industry was putting its final touches on what would be known as the "studio system." In fact, her career had been founded on one of the earliest attempts at systematizing in the industry. After winning several local beauty contests, she caught the attention of a local theater magnate by the name of Napoleon L. Demara, operator of the Empire and several local vaudeville houses.[13] Demara contacted Paramount talent spotters after Thelma modeled at several fashion revues at his theater. Jesse Lasky, owner of Famous Players-Lasky Corporation, which evolved into Paramount Studios, signed her to a contract stipulating she would enter the Paramount College at Astoria and, after graduating, journey west to Paramount's Hollywood studio.[14]

The Paramount College was Lasky's brainchild. He believed Paramount was "using up our natural resources of star personalities faster than new ones could be developed," creating a need to cultivate systematically the many "attractive, photogenic" but unskilled young people who were eager and available. The school would train them to act. Years later, Lasky recounted how the studio selected the first and only class of the innovative school:

> We selected twenty-four talented boys and girls from all over the country, using our scattered film exchanges for the weeding-out process on the basis of photographs, school standing, amateur dramatic activities, etc. We paid their transportation and living expenses in New York during six months of courses in dramatics, make-up, costuming, etiquette, and the various skills such as riding, fencing, dancing, swimming, and automobile driving which were all-important to a player in the silent pictures.[15]

The training also involved some advanced arts of movie-making, including "scenario construction and interpretation, direction, stage lighting, photography and applied psychology."[16] The regime was strict, both on and off the set, undoubtedly to the dislike of the exuberant young actors. "They treated us like children," Thelma complained several years later, "We had to be in bed by ten o'clock. My wildest dissipation was to go out dancing 'til 4 o'clock and that happened only two or three times."[17]

After six months of training, twelve of the original sixteen[18] students attended a graduation dinner held at the Ritz-Carlton Hotel on March 2, 1926.[19] Most received single year studio contracts with Paramount, but Thelma's was more inclusive, stretching over five years, with a beginning salary of $75 a week that increased on a sliding scale to $500 in the fifth year.[20] It was a great deal of money for a young woman.

The students also garnered roles in *Fascinating Youth*, a film comedy about a group of New York youths who run a winter hotel in the Adirondacks. The parts were tailored to fit the talents of the Paramount graduates, Thelma being cast as one Lorraine Lane. Director Sam Wood used the film as part of the students' instruction, photographing rehearsals to allow the young actors to correct performance flaws before the final takes.[21] Although the film no longer exists and the reviews of the time do not detail Lorraine's character, the *Lawrence Evening Tribune*, by no means an objective source, assured its readers that Thelma acquitted herself of the role "in a most accomplished way."

To boost the picture, Thelma appeared in person at several movie houses in New York and New England, dancing an Argentine tango with co-star Greg Blackton for the enthusiastic audiences. The day following her appearance before an overflowing audience at the local Palace Theater, the Lawrence paper applauded her performance and the "smart" talk she gave after the show, adding that the young actress had lost the excess weight evident in her screen persona.[22]

With the rest of the cast of *Fascinating Youth,* Thelma toured the Midwest and South, promoting the film with personal appearances while filming scenes for a second picture in the larger cities they visited.[23] The tour was scheduled to last thirteen weeks, dipping as far south as Dallas, and eventually delivering the troupe to Hollywood, where they were to become part of Paramount's studio stock.[24] In late July, however, word reached Thelma in Memphis that her father had succumbed to a heart attack in New York City, where he and his wife had moved while she attended the nearby Astoria school. Thelma returned to Lawrence for the funeral. The tour finished its final weeks while she and her family grieved at home.

Despite the experiences of attending the special school for actors and appearing in a feature-length movie, Thelma was still not committed to an acting career. After graduating from Lawrence High School in 1923, she had attended Lowell Normal School, where she trained to be a teacher, one of the few professions open to a young woman in the somewhat impoverished mill town.[25] "I expected to go back to teaching even after attending the School. I had no burning ambitions," she told a magazine interviewer several years later. A scarcity of teaching jobs, however, may have prompted her to consider other careers. As time went on, she would become more dedicated to a film career. "I began to get ambitious. To worry if I wasn't given a good part, if someone else got that bit I had my eye on."[26]

During the next two years, she made films with Paramount in both New York and Hollywood. From the front porch of the bungalow apartment on Fountain Avenue she shared with her mother, Thelma could see the Italianate and Spanish estates of the motion picture rich rising along the twisting roads of the Hollywood Hills. Moving picture and real estate money were also spurring a building boom in nearby Beverly Hills and Holmby Hills. Along the shoreline northwest of Santa Monica was the famous Gold Coast, site of Marion Davis' Ocean House and other private palaces. Soon, further along the coast, would be the Malibu movie colony.

More modest homes were sprouting up throughout the city and its satellites as hundreds of thousands of refugees from eastern winters arrived each year. Soon the entire coastal plain would be one big city, but in the late twenties bean fields and orange groves still demarcated the numerous towns and neighborhoods. The air was clear and on most days you could see the mountains to the east above the burgeoning skyline of downtown. It was a great time to be in LA. In her early twenties, beautiful and charming, Thelma made the most of it, toting a flask full of whisky in her purse, escaping her mother's sharp eye by borrowing a friend's car for assignations with young men.[27]

Although her role and performances were unremarkable, Thelma readily found movie work, playing opposite some of the stars of the time, including Gary Cooper, William Powell, Walter Pidgeon, Richard Dix, and Ed Wynn. In February 1928, her work in *Vamping Venus*, one of two films she made while on loan from Paramount, impressed First National Pictures executives, who purchased her contract.[28] (Years later, Thelma herself claimed Paramount lost interest in her when she refused sexual favors to an unnamed studio executive.)[29] During the next eighteen months, she was featured in no less than eight films for First National, mostly for producer Richard A. Rowland. Her contract allowed her to work occasionally for other studios, including Columbia and United Artists. It was for the latter that she worked in the silent version of the eventual classic, *Hell's Angels*.[30] Thelma had the part of the leading lady, but other commitments forced her withdrawal from the cast when the production was delayed. Jean Harlow, then a novice, replaced her, launching her own career with the role when the film was remade as a talky.[31]

Thelma's First National films were unexceptional. By 1929, although a steadily employed film actress for three years, she herself observed that she had not "done anything big and exciting."[32] Portrayed by the press as stylish, intelligent, and reserved in a way unusual for actresses, she described herself as "living in hopes. Despite rumors she was engaged to another aspiring actor from Lawrence, James Ford, and another that she was planning to marry screenwriter Charles Furthmann,[33] she denied matrimonial plans, dating some of Hollywood's leading bachelors, including Harvey Priester, film editor Al Hall, and Ivan Lebedeff, who had fallen for her in Lawrence before either came to Hollywood.[34]

In late April 1929, Thelma began working for the Hal Roach Studios. In her first role at the studio, she played in Laurel and Hardy's first talky short, "Unaccustomed As We Are." The script involved the usual series of misadventures in Laurel and Hardy shorts, with Thelma playing a helpful neighbor who unwittingly puts Oliver in a difficult position with his wife. It was a good role for her: partially unclothed, she showed off both her beauty and her talents for slapstick, and the Roach studio was appreciative. She had already signed a five-year contract with Roach and the Victor Talking Machine Company, which gained rights for the same period to record her singing voice.[35] Although her vocal career did not develop,[36] she would enjoy a great deal of success as a Roach comedienne.

For the next two years, she appeared with Charley Chase, Harry Langdon, Edgar Kennedy, Anita Garvin, Dorothy Granger, and Laurel and Hardy in a number of shorts filmed on the Roach lot. Roach then paired her with ZaSu Pitts to create "the female Laurel and Hardy." With Pitts and, later, Patsy Kelly, she made over five dozen comedy shorts between June 1931 and her death.

Like other comedy duos, the Pitts-Todd and later the Kelly-Todd teams tried to develop a dynamic between the comedic pair spanning from one short to the next. Opposite Pitts, the perennially bewildered and bumbling young woman, Thelma was the wiser friend who got them out of trouble; with Kelly, who took on a street-wise and assertive persona, Thelma was dreamy and dilettantish. Although often uneven, the shorts were popular and profitable for the Roach studios.[37]

Although her sixty-one Roach studio comedy shorts were the bread-and-butter of the remainder of Thelma's career, she continued to work in dramas for other studios. She appeared in *Her Man*, a 1930 Pathe production starring Helen Twelvetrees, and *The Hot Heiress*, a 1931 First National production. She also had secondary roles in several Tiffany studio productions in 1931. In the same year, she played Ivy Archer in the original film version of Dashiell Hammett's *The Maltese Falcon*.

Thelma's most ambitious foray into drama came in 1931, when she played the female romantic lead opposite Chester Morris in Roland West's *Corsair*. West convinced her to adopt the stage name of Alison Loyd for this film,[38] explaining to the press that the change was made so "no taint of comedy might cling to her skirts." (On hearing this, Roach retorted that henceforth Thelma would go by the stage name of Susan Dinkleberry in his comedies, so that no taint of drama would cling to her petticoat.) *Corsair* was the story of a young man who turns his back on a business career and takes up rum running. Neither a critical nor a financial success, the film failed to vault Thelma into the front ranks of dramatic actresses, as West hoped. Thelma returned to comedy shorts, occasional minor dramas, and a handful of comedy features with the Marx Brothers and Laurel and Hardy.

Although it failed to propel her dramatic career, *Corsair* marked a turning point in Thelma's life. During the filming on Catalina Island, she and West grew fond of each other.[39] West was already married to silent screen star Jewel Carmen, however. According to Louella Parsons, writing at the time of Thelma's death, West, believing his infatuation with Thelma was unrequited and unwilling to hurt Jewel, decided to take to the sea to "get [my feelings for Thelma] ... out of my system."[40] He and Jewel set off on a series of cruises in his yacht *Joyita*, to Alaska and Mexico.[41] In the meantime, Thelma, reportedly disappointed by the failure of her romance with West, continued to play the field until, in early spring of 1932, she met a handsome young man who had just arrived from New York City with aspirations to become an actor or a filmland talent agent.[42]

Pasquale "Pat" DiCicco was the son of the man they called "The Broccoli King" back in his hometown of New York City. His father was a Long Island truck farmer who had pioneered the planting and marketing of the vegetable on a large scale in the United States.[43] Pat came to Los Angeles, according to one report, to make money on his own.[44]

DiCicco and Thelma surprised their friends and the film community by eloping to Prescott, Arizona on July 10. When they returned, they repeated their marriage vows at the Hollywood Baptist Church. For a short while, they were one of Hollywood's brightest couples, but their marriage would last only 18 months. Rumors of problems reached the press early in the spring of 1933 as Thelma left on a trip to England.[45] In September 1933, Thelma wrote DiCicco out of her will.[46] They separated in February 1934 and divorced on March 2.

At the divorce trial, Thelma testified DiCicco was surly to her, had treated her "in a rude manner" and "quarreled with her for no reason at all."[47] She also claimed he mistreated her friends. Later, both Thelma and DiCicco attributed their divorce to conflicting careers; Thelma would write a short piece in the newspaper advising readers that Hollywood and marriage did not always mix.[48] She had not even had time to visit DiCicco's family home on Long Island.[49] She did not mention in court what she told relatives—that she believed DiCicco was unfaithful to her.[50] Nor did she mention the intemperate and violent behavior DiCicco's next wife, Gloria Vanderbilt, would record later.[51]

Although DiCicco told his family after their divorce that Thelma still wanted to patch up their relationship, by late August 1934 she had moved on. She was associated with West and his Castellammare café, then named Joya San Iguiel, and renting a home at 17925 Tramonto Drive on the hill above the café, not far from West's Castillo Del Mar. There she lived until the summer of 1935 when she moved down to the second floor of the restaurant. By then it was known as Thelma Todd's Sidewalk Café.[52]

Thelma still pursued her acting career. During 1934 and 1935, she made eighteen shorts with Patsy Kelly. She also appeared in eleven feature films, including *Two for Tonight*, with Bing Crosby and Joan Bennet, in which she had the female lead. However, she recognized her film career might soon end. The restaurant business offered a practical career, perhaps in the same way teaching had years before.[53] Undoubtedly, West, who had already given up directing to open a restaurant, influenced her thinking.

As the afternoon's vigil continued, news of Todd's death spread rapidly to the pressrooms of Los Angeles dailies and radio stations as well as to the lots and executive offices of the movie industry.[54] Within hours, radio broadcasts and afternoon newspapers across the nation were headlining the tragedy. For a nation still in the doldrums of an economic depression, the news of the death of a famous and glamorous star—one whom life seemed to have favored at every step—brought home the often learned lessons of mortality. So it had been several years before with the murder of the Lindbergh baby and, earlier that same year, with those of Wiley Post and Will Rogers.

At the death scene, reporters scribbled notes and took photographs as the detectives from the Los Angeles Police Department performed their grim work in the dark garage. A small group of Thelma Todd's friends huddled on the street and spoke in low, halting voices as they tried to make sense of the tragedy. Occasionally, a sedan or touring car maneuvered around the small but growing throng to park haphazardly on the twisting road fronting the garage. As the day wore on and the investigation began to settle into a pace, cameramen fiddled idly with their equipment while reporters and Miss Todd's friends recited the depressing facts of the mystery over and over.[55]

A few of this diverse group, drawn from the nooks and crannies of Todd's life, knew each other well, sometimes from long associations. Others had never met. West, related by marriage to Rudolph Schafer and his wife, had spent many years working with Charles Smith, the restaurant's elderly bookkeeper. Mae Whitehead and Robert Anderson, a young bar boy at the restaurant, had worked in the café building for months. Another familiar face in the neighborhood was that of Florian "Jack" Sauer. That morning, West called Sauer, a Castellammare neighbor and owner of the Pacific Palisades service station that serviced Todd's Lincoln, to ask him to get a doctor. Sauer brought Dr. Phil Sampson, a Santa Monica physician, carefully observing West's stricture to tell no one about the tragedy.[56]

Mrs. Alice Todd–Thelma's mother–was also present. Driven to the garage by Harvey Priester, scion of a prominent Hollywood family and Todd's former boyfriend, the 56-year-old widow was beside herself with grief. She had already suffered the deaths of Thelma's older brother and father. Thelma was all she had left of her family and now she too was gone. Priester tried to comfort her, but his own grief weighed heavily. He could not bring himself to enter the garage.[57]

Among the last to arrive was Pasquale "Pat" DiCicco, Todd's ex-husband. Divorced from Todd for nearly two years, he still felt compelled to rush to the garage as soon as heard the grim news that morning at the Paramount studio lot, where he had been plying his trade as an actors' agent.[58] A cameraman caught him as he talked quietly with Mae Whitehead. Smoking a cigarette and dressed in a gray speckled jacket, black pleated trousers, a polka-dot tie and a fedora, he gazed forlornly at the rough pavement beneath his feet.[59]

Within this assembly, Roland West took center stage. Forced by circumstances to greet each arrival, answer police questions and acquaint them with the scene, he also had to contend with his own grief. At one point, visibly overcome, he sat slumped on the running board of the phaeton, his head buried in his hands.[60] At 2:00 p.m., when the authorities removed Todd's body from the car, his ordeal intensified. As attendants gingerly lifted the sheet-covered corpse and angled it out the phaeton's right side door, West hovered in the background, and then stooped to steady the awaiting stretcher that was already in the sure grasp of a burly detective. Later that afternoon, he was better composed and attired. He had changed from the gray pinstriped suit coat and light pants thrown on when he first learned of Todd's death that morning to a navy blue blazer, sharply creased gray trousers and white shoes. He seemed dwarfed by the tall homicide detectives as he answered questions about Todd and his actions of the previous Saturday.[61]

West's solitary villa, towering above the assembly of investigators and mourners, provided an appropriately Gothic backdrop for the tragic scene. Constructed in the Spanish eclectic style popular with the motion picture nouveau riche, with elements of classic, Italian, Moorish, and medieval architecture, its martially inspired facade rose circle of bone, Wagner lifted the brain from the actress' skull. In it, one reporter would later remark, was "stilled the secret of her death."[12]

Back at the garage, the detectives continued their investigation of the death scene. A few examined Todd's powerful automobile, the massive 12 cylinder chocolate brown and white 1932 Lincoln phaeton. Several "covered" the car for fingerprints,[13] while others checked under its hood for evidence. Two officers from the West LA station drained a gallon of gas from the tank after noting that the ignition was in the "on" position and that the automobile's battery was dead. As Wallis observed, "the motor had been running and stopped,"[14] allowing the ignition switch to drain the battery. After clutch starting the phaeton, they drove it down the hill and back,[15] a small cloud of fumes spewing behind them.[16] It was apparent that the engine had not run out of fuel.

Meanwhile, other detectives tried to determine why Todd was in the garage in the first place. They soon learned that Todd's chauffeur, Ernest Peters, was the last known person to see her alive. Early Sunday morning, thirty hours before Mae Whitehead discovered her body, Peters brought Todd home to the café building from the Trocadero Restaurant, a favorite nightspot of the movie set. At the "Troc", she had been the guest of honor at a party thrown by Mr. and Mrs. Stanley Lupino and their actress daughter, Ida. By questioning Peters and other witnesses, including Whitehead, West and movie theater impresario Sid Grauman, the police quickly determined the broad outline of Todd's movements on Saturday.

Todd had spent most of Saturday shopping for Christmas with her mother. At I. Magnin's on Hollywood Boulevard, she had picked up some handkerchiefs. After visiting her dentist nearby, the two women went to Barker Brothers in downtown Los Angeles, where Thelma purchased bookends, a cigarette box, a relish tray, and a clock. Sometime that afternoon, they stopped for gas at the Muller Brothers' Service Station on Sunset Boulevard, where Thelma purchased 10 gallons of gasoline and fed her phaeton another quart of oil.[17] It was late in the afternoon when she and her mother returned to the Sidewalk Café.

In her apartment above the café, Thelma chatted with her mother as she dressed for the Trocadero party. Around 8:00 p.m., both left the café in Peter's limousine. For most of the drive, the women sat quietly, speaking of matters of no great importance: Christmas plans, a visit Thelma planned to pay Alice the next Tuesday, the party for Thelma at the Trocadero. On Wilshire, Thelma unexpectedly asked Peters to stop at a florist's shop, handing him a dollar to buy a pink camellia, which she pinned to the left shoulder of her dress with a brooch.

As they neared the Trocadero, Thelma debated whether to go straight in or see her mother to the latter's apartment a few blocks away. "She intended to drive home with me," recalled Alice later, "but when we reached the Trocadero she asked the doorman whether the guests at the Lupino party had assembled. He replied, 'Yes,' and she then said she thought she had better stay." As Peters and her mother pulled off towards her mother's apartment, Thelma entered the elegant nightclub alone.[18]

Architecturally, the Café Trocadero was a cross between a roadhouse and a farmhouse. Capped by a small cupola, the building sprawled down the hillside where Sunset Plaza Drive meets Sunset Boulevard. Before *Hollywood Reporter* publisher Billy Wilkerson bought it in 1934, it had housed a notorious gambling club, La Boheme. Its roomy cellar seemed perfect storage for Wilkerson's newly legal liquor stash. He remodeled the inside, installing square-bubble Deco windows to face the street, skirted the roof with a wide, striped awning and, in September, opened his French café, commonly referred to by a nickname, the Troc.

Wilkerson envisioned that, complemented by nearby gambling casinos, with their hint of the demimonde, the restaurant would provide an arena in which the film capital's officially sanctioned glamor could blossom. Located on the county strip it was not hampered by Los Angeles' blue laws, which prohibited dancing after 2:00 a.m. on every day except Sunday, when it was banned altogether. For film personalities, it offered valuable publicity through its connection to Wilkerson's weekly newspaper.

The restaurant quickly became one of Hollywood's hot spots. Mogul Joe Schenck rhumba'd at the first of the restaurant's opening parties and tangoed through the second. Ida Lupino had also been seen at both, while actor George Raft, with Bugsy Siegal's moll Virginia Hill, and Pat DiCicco, with starlet Sally Blane, settled for the public opening a few days later. During the year following its opening, everyone who had made it or wanted to make it in Hollywood and could afford dinner and the right clothes ascended its three cement steps, tipped the tuxedoed doorman and passed through the portals to the main lobby, a long hall papered with blown-up photos of Paris, to be greeted by hatcheck girls in white aprons. Beneath a two-foot Eiffel Tower at the east end, stairs led down to the French Grill, a cocktail lounge with a country kitchen look. There amidst the oak paneling and 70,000 well-displayed bottles of vintage wines and rare spirits, the Lupino party had gathered that evening near the gleaming copper bar.[19]

The Lupinos, their guests, and Thelma remained in the bar until a little after ten, when, sixteen to twenty guests having arrived, they trooped upstairs to dinner. In the elegant main dining room, whose cream-colored walls were embellished by gold traces in the molding, tables with silk-covered chairs surrounded a cozy dance floor. There the party enjoyed a sumptuous five-course dinner, Thelma sitting at the head of the table, an empty chair to her right.

According to guests at the party and other diners at the restaurant, the comedienne was in high spirits most of the evening. Harvey Priester told reporters the fun-loving actress was "gayer than usual Saturday night."[20] Fred Keating, a magician, M.C. and

RKO bit player, remarked, "I was struck by her wit and charm. She seemed to be more vivacious than when I knew her before." "Often during the evening," reported hatcheck girls Anita Hammond, Maxine Marshall and Loretta Jones, "Miss Todd would say in a jovial mood, 'I resent it,' but she was always in a happy frame of mind and we thought she was merely using a modern phrase in a jocular manner."

She danced throughout the evening, several times with Stanley Lupino, who tried to interest her in starring in a new film he expected to make soon. "No one could have been in better spirits or more brilliant and sparkling than Thelma," Lupino declared. "She was the life of the party. There was nothing in her manner to indicate that anything was worrying her."[21] Impresario Sid Grauman, who stopped at the Trocadero with producer Richard Rowland for a bite to eat, recalled that Thelma's gaiety continued into the early morning hours. When she left his table— after asking him to call the café to let West know she was on her way home—Grauman recalled, "She was still the happy laughing girl she had been, as far as I could observe, all evening."[22]

Nevertheless, according to dance instructor Arthur Prince, her mood changed after she left Grauman's table. In the middle of a tango, Thelma told Prince that she was tired and wanted to go home.

"Whether someone said something, I don't know," Prince told officers who interviewed him Monday afternoon, "But Thelma suddenly turned deeply despondent. "She was totally different. All her gaiety had evaporated. She seemed terribly depressed."[23]

Prince's wife accompanied her to the coat checkroom where Thelma suddenly began to deride the motion picture industry. "Don't let Hollywood change you," she advised Mrs. Prince. "Stay just the same; don't take any stock in what people tell you; go your own way. Hollywood is full of unhappiness: don't let it get you." After she gathered her wrap, Prince escorted her to the front entrance of the Trocadero.

Outside, Peters was waiting in his limousine. He had been there since a little before nine, after taking Thelma's mother to her apartment.[24] Peters expected Todd to leave the party before 2:00 a.m., since she had mentioned an appointment at the café at 1:55 that morning; it was now 3:00.

Peters noticed that Todd seemed "cold sober."[25] However, he also detected something odd in her mood. "She was very quiet, which for her was strange. On other evenings, she liked for me to run back the window between us and we'd chat on the way up the coast. But she didn't say anything much this time. I wouldn't call her glum, but I'd say she had something on her mind."[26] On Todd's instructions, he drove fast to Castellammare, exceeding seventy miles an hour for a time and running the boulevard stops.

What did Thelma have on her mind? That, it soon became clear that Monday afternoon, was a key question. For some reason, she did not enter her apartment after Peters left her at the Sidewalk Café. Instead, she climbed hundreds of yards up the hillside to the garage, where her body would be found Monday morning.

Roland West had his theory of what happened to her. When she reached her apartment door that night, he surmised, she found it deadbolted from the inside; he himself had slid the bolt into place an hour before when he came through the door after walking her dog. The single key her maid placed in the purse—and which Captain Clark found when he inventoried the items in the purse on Monday—could open the door lock, but not move the deadbolt. Finding the door deadbolted, Thelma, "a very considerate girl" who would not want to disturb anybody's sleep,[27] West reasoned, climbed the hill to the garage to await the porters who opened the Café around 6:00 a.m. After sitting for some time in the front seat of the phaeton with the garage doors closed, she started the engine, either to heat the garage's chilly morning air or to warm the motor for a drive to her mother's apartment on Fountain Avenue in Hollywood. As West would remark ruefully several days later, "she would never think of little details"[28]—such as the fact that the while the engine warmed poisonous gas was flooding the garage.

This plausible theory raised as many questions as it answered. Why did Whitehead put only the single key in Todd's purse? Why did West deadbolt the door to her apartment when he knew she was on her way home? Was Thelma so considerate that she would endure the frigid December coastal weather in an automobile just to avoid awakening West? And just what was the nature of the relationship between Todd and West, who had such ready access to her apartment?

Despite these questions, West's theory received a powerful endorsement that afternoon. On learning of the tragedy, Joseph Schenck, head of United Artists and a longtime power in motion pictures whose influence spanned the Los Angeles social and political elites,[29] rushed from his house in Palm Springs to West's side. They were old friends and business associates -- West had directed and produced pictures for Schenck and his actress wife, Norma Talmadge. The two men conferred privately, and afterward Schenck emerged to declare to reporters there was "absolutely no doubt" that Todd's death was accidental.[30]

As the evening closed over the city, law enforcement officials were confident that her death was unintentional. At 4:45 in the afternoon, Bruce Clark completed Los Angeles Police Department's Form R-144, "Dead Body Found" report. As he expected, the Coroner's office confirmed the actress died from carbon monoxide poisoning. Although Clark noted a "small amount of blood from mouth and nose" of the deceased, he added there were "no other visible bruises."[31] Nothing at the scene of death indicated a struggle or suggested foul play.

However tragic or puzzling, Todd's death appeared the result of nothing more than a series of misadventures.

According to Ford, the phone call occurred sometime between 4:00 and 4:30, probably closer to the latter. She also claimed she told her brother-in-law, George Baker, that the actress was on her way.[5] Baker, an assistant director at Hal Roach studios, was a close friend of Thelma's. Around 7:00, worried she had not arrived, he called her apartment. He spoke to a man who told him he had not seen Thelma all day.[6]

The three detectives returned to Central Homicide that evening with a problem. The possibility Todd did not die early Sunday morning threatened to unravel the knot police investigators had almost tied around the case. Roland West had suggested a workable accident scenario; now its premise, that Todd died Sunday morning while running her automobile in the closed garage, was in question. If Thelma died Sunday morning, it was reasonable to suppose she turned on the engine of her phaeton either to warm the garage or to prepare to drive. If she did not die Sunday morning, if she lived at least long enough to make the phone call to Mrs. Ford, then one had to ask anew why she was found in the garage the next day, and what had induced her to run the phaeton with the garage doors closed. Accidental death under such circumstances was harder to conceive.

What was a problem for the police, however, was an opportunity for the press. Reporters pounced on Mrs. Ford's statements, which turned a good story into a sensational one, scrutinizing and speculating in print about each new item of evidence like so many armchair sleuths. There was a long tradition of detective work among LA reporters on the police beat; often, they doubled as ancillary cops, carrying guns and working hand-in-glove with investigators.[7] But in this case, some reporters found themselves marching in a different direction than the police -- towards a murder theory.

The *Los Angeles Daily News'* Vincent Mahoney laid out the mystery succinctly, even prophetically:[8]

> Thelma Todd of Hollywood, until a few hours ago one of the most classically beautiful women alive, was found dead yesterday morning in a hill-side garage near her home in Pacific Palisades—dead under circumstances that raised a mystery that may never be solved.
>
> Crumpled in the front seat of her luxurious automobile in mink coat and blue-and-silver evening gown, her fine Roman profile unmarked and still beautiful, though she had been dead several hours, the actress was found shortly after 10 o'clock by her mulatto maid, Mae Whitehead.
>
> The only mark on her face was a touch of blood about the lips.

> Although police at first believed Miss Todd died early Sunday morning, Mrs. Wallace Ford, wife of the film actor, last night informed detectives she had talked to the blond actress as late as 4 pm Sunday
>
> . . .
>
> In official and other quarters, including immediate family, were found those committed to three opinions regarding her death:
> 1. Murder
> 2. Accident
> 3. Suicide
>
> There was early evidence for each theory, creating as profound a three-cornered puzzle as has faced investigators here in many years.

Mahoney noted Captain Wallis had stated that the case was "virtually closed," the death being either an accident or a suicide. The journalist, however, found problems with both theories. Thelma was known as a gay, positive, successful person, not morbidly depressive. Her mother expounded, "She had not been ill. She was intelligent. She had no reason to end her life." Her café was doing well and she was busy planning a New Year's party and buying presents for Christmas. Furthermore, what the reporter called "a transaction of complete vanity" demonstrated her "intention-to-live . . . she had had a tooth removed, and was wearing a temporary shell while another was made."[9]

Nor did the accident theory sit well with the *Daily News* reporter. "If accidental, death could only have arisen . . . from a set of circumstances so extraordinary as almost to bar belief," he declared. Thelma had to be ignorant of the common knowledge that it was dangerous to run an automobile in a closed garage. The expensive phaeton had to die off by itself after being warmed. Assuming she started the car to warm herself, as the police suggested, she must have remembered that a running automobile would warm the garage while forgetting it would also poison the atmosphere. If she was cold, why didn't she put on the gloves found beside her on the car seat? "For that matter," the reporter cried with incredulity, "why did she climb the hill from her café, above which was her flat . . .? For the lack of a forgotten key?"

> To have died by accident she would have had to climb a hill in her rich evening clothes; pull open a heavy garage door; then close the door so that no light entered (and no <u>light</u> was turned on); place herself in the dark on the front seat of her $3000 Lincoln sports phaeton; turn on the ignition and start the engine; faint so that her face was bruised, her nose and mouth bloodied, a gold cap be knocked from the top of a tooth that had been capped the day before-- AND THEN SLUMP DOWN IN SUCH A WAY THAT SHE KILLED THE ENGINE OF THE CAR AFTER SHE WAS DEAD.

Mahoney stated his own theory of the case in a curious digression:[10]

> In the greatly successful picture of last spring, "Border Town," Bette Davis, leading woman, inaugurated, so far as Hollywood was concerned, the garage murder. She tricked her husband into his garage, the doors of which closed by a photo-electric mechanism, seated him, at the wheel, stupid with whisky, started the motor and passed by the photo-electric "eye," closing the doors and killing him with carbon monoxide.

Other journals echoed *Daily News*' doubts about the LAPD's accident theory. The *Los Angeles Examiner* headlined Todd's death, devoting four pages to photographs and articles. The paper opined that Mrs. Ford's revelations contradicted the evidence developed by the police investigation.[11] Its sister Hearst paper, the *Evening Herald and Express*, soon to surpass the *Daily News* in its flamboyant coverage of the events surrounding Todd's death, declared, "The key to Thelma Todd's death mystery lies behind two garage doors—heavy wooden doors crossed with steel that creak when moved like the doors of a morgue."

While granting Todd was well enough and strong enough to climb the hill to the garage, the paper asked [12]

> Why, if she were cold enough in her fur coat to turn on the auto engine for warmth, did she not put on her gloves that were found beside her body … And could another hand have turned off the ignition of the car after she was dead and then turned it on again after the motor stopped to establish an appearance of suicide?

With the press questioning their apparently hasty conclusions, the police scrambled Tuesday morning to reexamine the evidence. After conferring with investigators Sketchley, Joe Taylor, William Clark, Eddie Romero, Joe Whitehead, and Gene Bechtel, Wallis told reporters he planned to interview the principal witnesses in the case himself that afternoon at Alice Todd's apartment on Fountain Avenue.[13] Meanwhile, other detectives ran down other aspects of the case, which included checking the stories of some of the witnesses.[14]

Taylor went to question Martha Ford, who continued to insist the woman she talked to Sunday afternoon was Thelma.[15] However, while sticking to her claim that Thelma said she was "still in evening clothes"[16] and that she was bringing a guest[17] to Ford's party, Ford admitted initial confusion about the caller.

"I thought she had said, 'Velma.' I asked 'Velma who?' And she replied, 'No, no, this is Thelma, Thelma Todd. You know, Toddy, your hot toddy. Get ahold of yourself, Toots.'"[18]

The caller did not tell Ford where she was phoning from, only that she would reach her home via Ventura Boulevard. Mrs. Ford believed the call came from Santa Monica, however. When Thelma said she would arrive in 30 minutes, Ford remarked, "That's fast traveling from Santa Monica to Laurel Canyon, Toddy."[19]

Detectives questioned some of her guests to corroborate her claim. Warren Stokes recalled Mrs. Ford told him "a little after 4 o'clock Sunday afternoon that Thelma was coming over with 'someone who would surprise us all'."[20] Two other guests, Eddie Gargan, who arrived at the party just as Ford received the call, and Peter Hancock, confirmed Ford's statement that she turned to them and said, "That's great. Toddy's coming—now the party can commence."[21] The guests put the time at 4:10.[22]

Detective Taylor was not convinced. He suspected an impersonator made the phone call, either from Santa Monica or on an extension phone in the Ford residence.[23] Phone company records for Todd's apartment revealed only one call to the Ford residence over the weekend: 11:27 Saturday morning, when, on Thelma's instructions, Mae Whitehead phoned Mrs. Ford to accept her invitation to the cocktail party.[24]

Through the press, the detectives called on anybody who saw Todd on Sunday to come forward.[25] But even before their plea was printed, new claims arose that Todd was alive on Sunday. An unidentified caller told police Captain Blaine Steed he saw Miss Todd driving alone down Hollywood Boulevard shortly before noon on Sunday.[26] A second more substantial report came from W. F. Persson, owner of a cigar store at Eighth and Figueroa streets in downtown Los Angeles. Described by one newspaper as "a middle-aged, serious appearing" man, Persson told police Miss Todd entered his cigar store at 9:00 a.m. Sunday morning. In a "low, cultured voice," she asked him to dial a telephone number on the store's pay phone. "I was afraid she would collapse," he reported. "She had a haggard, ghastly look, as if she had gone for a long time without sleep and was under some terrific mental strain." Persson was waiting on a customer and did not overhear the woman's conversation in its entirety, but he believed she made an appointment with the person she called. He contacted the police after he recognized Todd from a photograph in a news story about her death.[27]

With several witnesses claiming Todd was alive after Sunday morning, the autopsy results became more critical. Shortly after 12:00 p.m., Coroner Nance announced his findings. Todd died from carbon monoxide poisoning from the phaeton's fumes, he declared. Her blood contained 75% monoxide saturation, an indisputably lethal amount. Despite the claims of other partygoers at the Trocadero that she drank little that night, her brain contained .13% alcohol, an amount that indicated the actress drank considerably before she died. Coroner Nance speculated that she was very intoxicated Sunday morning. "There undoubtedly had been a higher alcoholic content, but a large portion probably was eliminated by oxidation between the time she left the Hollywood party and the time of death," he remarked. "Indications were found that there had been sufficient alcohol to stupefy her." The coroner reasoned not only would inebriation have impaired her judgment, desensitizing her to the danger of starting the phaeton in the closed garage, it might have also accelerated the poisoning process. "Increased heart action caused by the alcohol would have pumped the monoxide poison through her blood in a few minutes," he observed.[28]

Nance rejected speculation that Thelma had suffered a heart attack. Her heart appeared strong, showing no chronic ailment that may have caused death. The blood on Todd's face proved that it did not fail. "Miss Todd bled from the nose before death overtook her," he observed, "Whether she collapsed due to an alcoholic condition, the effects of carbon monoxide from which she dies, or a combination of the two, her heart was going for several minutes before she died." The Coroner was unsure why Todd bled and lost her temporary tooth, but he repeated speculation that her face may have struck the steering wheel of the car as she lost consciousness. He found no other marks on the actress' body.[29]

Autopsy Surgeon Wagner found Thelma's other vital organs normal. Her stomach was partially filled with undigested food that normally would require six to eight hours to digest. Considering that other guests at the Trocadero reported Thelma dined between 11:30 and midnight Sunday morning, and factoring in the retarding effects of alcohol on digestion, the Coroner declared the undigested food in her stomach indicated she died around 6 a.m. Sunday morning. 3[30]

As for other evidence of the time of Thelma's death, Coroner Nance was not specific. He told reporters "climatic conditions at the place of death—a high, cold wind and low temperature—probably preserved the body after death, eliminating the conditions from which an autopsy surgeon can accurately estimate the time of death." Death occurred from 12 to 30 hours before the discovery of the body, between 4:30 Sunday morning and 10:30 Sunday night. Analysis of Todd's stomach and vital organs would continue, Autopsy Surgeon Wagner said. Although he and Nance were convinced she died from carbon monoxide, they would run tests to check for poison over the next few days.[31] In addition, Nance announced a Coroner's Inquest for Wednesday morning at 9:30 to clear up the "many mysterious circumstances connected with this case."[32]

Among the mysterious circumstances of the case were reports Todd recently was the victim of extortion demands. Several papers recalled that, beginning in February 1935, the actress received threatening notes signed with drawings of the Ace of Hearts, Spades, and Diamonds. The notes demanded $10,000 and threatened "to wreck that Santa Monica café of yours" or to "lay you out"[33] unless the money was paid. Named by the notes as a go-between was Abe Lyman, an orchestra leader and former beau of Miss Todd, who quickly denied any knowledge of the affair to FBI agents.[34] Threatening phone calls to the café from "The Ace" followed the notes. Lyman also received several notes, one of which demanded he use the code term "All is Well" on his next national radio broadcast to signal he would cooperate with the extortionists; else, Todd would be kidnapped and held for ransom. Although he complied, Lyman received a subsequent note complaining that he had "failed" the extortionists and warning him Todd would soon be seized.[35]

The FBI assigned two agents to guard Todd. At the time, she was living in a rented house on the hill above the Sidewalk Café. The agents watched the house and trailed her whenever she went out. After a while, the agents' intrusion on her privacy began to annoy her. She also grew more and more resentful of living in fear of kidnapping and extortion, a fear she shared with many in the Hollywood community, especially since the murder of the Lindbergh baby. Threats of extortion and kidnapping were so rampant at the time that the Lindberghs themselves would leave the country within two weeks of Todd's death.[36]

Todd decided to act on her own. She agreed to meet the extortionist, setting up a rendezvous on Hollywood Boulevard. In her purse, she carried a .22 revolver. Outside Warner's theater, the man told her to drive to a remote spot, but Thelma refused to follow his orders. She tried again to trap him when the threats continued, again arranging a meeting on Hollywood Boulevard, with the .22 in her purse. But once again, she was instructed to go to a remote location and refused to do so.[37]

In August 1935, the FBI arrested Harry Schimanski, the 34-year-old landlord of an Astoria, New York apartment building and booked him on charges of sending Todd the notes. Schimanski protested his innocence and, on October 31, pled not guilty to the charges. Somebody else also believed him innocent. A Long Island reporter who had followed the Todd extortion story when he lived in Los Angeles that spring received several anonymous letters and phone calls from a man who claimed that the real extortionist was still at large.[38] The reporter, sensing the real culprit was the caller himself, arranged to meet him, bringing in tow two FBI agents, who seized the extortionist at the rendezvous.[39]

The man turned out to be Schimanski's 26-year-old tenant Edward Schiffert, a drugstore handyman[40] described by his parents as mentally unsound.[41] Schiffert confessed he made the threats in order to get publicity for Todd. The FBI suspected he and Schimanski might have been in cahoots, but they soon dropped the case against the landlord, though they continued to suspect him for some time.[42] Coincidentally, on the day of Todd's death, Schiffert was committed indefinitely to Manhattan State Hospital after psychiatrists stated he had developed a "fantasy love affair" with the actress, whom he had seen only on the screen. The handyman first sent Todd love letters, but later switched to threats and demands for money.[43]

Although Schiffert had been in custody since November 7, rumors abounded that Todd received additional notes in the weeks before her death, including one threatening her for failing to pay gambling losses.[44] When Captain Wallis and other detectives questioned the key witnesses at Alice Todd's apartment, a statement by chauffeur Ernest Peters raised anew the possibility Todd may have been the victim of an extortion racket. "Miss Todd was afraid that, because she had been the target of extortion notes, she might be slain or kidnapped by gangsters," Peters told Wallis. "She had told me to drive at top speed and not to make boulevard stops. I drove between 65 and 70 miles an hour."[45]

Despite Peters' statement and a report of a "strange coupe," usually driven by a woman, patrolling the area of the Sidewalk Café in the weeks preceding Todd's death,[46] Wallis continued to focus on accident as its cause.

The key element in his developing theory was Roland West's ambiguous, if not obfuscatory, account of his relationship with Todd and the living arrangements in the building. While he acknowledged he slept in a room with ready access to Todd's apartment, he continued to describe himself as merely her business partner.[47] There were rumors, however, that his relationship with Todd went much deeper; perhaps, it was easy to surmise, there was also much more to his deadbolting of the side door and failure to search for Todd Sunday than he was willing to admit.

Wallis did not hesitate to point to lover's pique as a factor in Todd's tragic death. It was clear that, in his statements to police, West was more candid than he had been when talking to reporters. To the latter, he described Todd as "very considerate" in explaining why she would have gone to the garage to sleep; but he told police she was also a very stubborn and independent girl who refused to comply with his demand that she come home early. "West said that Miss Todd had been 'stepping,'" Wallis told reporters. "Saturday night, before she went out, he told her that she must be in by 2 o'clock or he would lock her out. West said that he did not answer the dog's whining because he was hurt and proud and that the same hurt pride prevented him from making inquiries all day Sunday of Mrs. Todd or anyone else who might have known where Miss Todd was."[48] Wallis drew some blunt conclusions from his Tuesday interview of West: "It is my opinion that Miss Todd and West had a tiff Saturday night when she left for the party at the Trocadero. I believe he told her to be home at 2 o'clock or he would lock her out."[49]

Despite his blunt talk about the friction between Todd and West, Wallis continued to insist Todd died accidentally.[50] Reporters were not so sure and even some of the detectives had their doubts. They agreed that there was little physical or psychological evidence for suicide, but they were troubled by many aspects of the case,[51] including West's puzzling statements. Certainly, if Todd died from foul play, one person with the opportunity to murder her was West himself. His statements implied he might have also had the classic lover's motive: jealousy.[52] The extortion notes Todd had received suggested other suspects. Although the confessed author of the notes was in a mental institution, it was possible other players entered the game once the extortion notes became public.

Other reports were coming to police, however, that pointed to another suspect, should a murderer be wanted. The newspapers referred to him as a "sportsman and artists' agent."[53] In 1935, he was still struggling to make it as an agent, although one of his clients was Cesar Romero.[54] He supplemented his income as a stage dancer, giving ballroom exhibitions.[55] He also had a bit part in a 1934 Universal film called *Night Life of the Gods*.[56] He was handsome and fun loving and successful with the ladies.

Pasquale "Pat" DiCicco, Thelma Todd's former husband, was at the garage Monday morning. Blocked by a policeman from entering the garage through one of its sliding doors, he slipped into it by the other. Glimpsing the body of his former wife, he returned immediately to sit in his car, overwhelmed.[57] "It seemed so unreal that Thelma's life had been so suddenly ended I wanted to see the proof with my own eyes," he explained to one reporter.[58] He wanted to make it clear that this need for realization, and not a lingering or reborn relationship, propelled him to the garage. "Until last Friday, I hadn't seen Thelma for a year," he declared. "Friday, at lunch, I saw Thelma at the Vendome. We spoke for a moment, quite briefly, and that was the last I saw of her."[59]

Rumors were reaching police, however, that he and Thelma had reconciled and even were considering remarriage. The police wanted to ask him about his relationship with his ex-wife and about reports of his activities at the Trocadero Saturday night. Restaurant guests claimed that DiCicco was to have escorted Thelma to her party, but instead dined at another table with actress Margaret Lindsay. Reportedly, he and Todd quarreled briefly when she danced by his table with Stanley Lupino.[60]

They would have to wait to talk with DiCicco, however. Tuesday evening, he boarded the TWA Sky Chief for New Jersey, intending to spend the holidays at his family's farm on Long Island.[61] As George Rochester, foreman of the Grand Jury would comment later that week, "his sudden departure . . . raised questions only he could explain."[62]

FIVE: WEDNESDAY MORNING

> We must know exactly what time [Todd] left the Trocadero and what time she arrived at her home and what time she entered the garage. And we must know why she went to the garage. We expect the inquest to disclose why she was locked out of her apartment and why there should have been necessary any arrangements whereby Roland West was to let her in.
>
> — Hubert Wallis, Homicide Captain, LAPD[1]

The Coroner's Inquest into the death of Thelma Todd began at 9:30 a.m. Wednesday morning, December 18, in Room 102 of the Hall of Justice in downtown Los Angeles.[2] A massive granite structure in the classical tradition, it was one the first buildings constructed as part of the new civic center proclaiming and celebrating Los Angeles' emergence as one of the nation's great cities. Its austere lower nine stories served as the base of an elaborate temple facade of polished columns three stories high. Inside, the entrance foyer of golden walls, massive Ionic columns, and a coffered ceiling projected a suitably intimidating impression of transcendent order.[3]

Other impressive buildings recently had been constructed nearby. A block away was City Hall, the formal seat of power in the municipal government. Also not far were other seats of power in the city. Nearby stood the *Los Angeles Times* building, where publisher Harry Chandler promulgated his reactionary convictions in an office linked, according to rumors, via private phone line to a cubby office in the City Hall for private conferences with the mayor.[4] And, gracing Grand Avenue was the Biltmore Hotel, the place where many of the local underworld and political fixers maintained suites.

Illuminated by twin wrought-iron chandeliers and smelling faintly of formaldehyde from the nearby morgue,[5] the cramped coroner's hearing room was packed that morning with witnesses and officials, including several investigators from the District Attorney's office seated in the front row, and W. P. Hendry, chief of police at Metro-Goldwyn-Mayer studios.[6] Several hundred spectators, part of the largest crowd ever to attend a Coroner's Jury, thronged the corridors outside the room, spilling onto the sidewalk. A few managed to elbow their way into the hearing room to squeeze against the back wall.[7]

At the front of the room, seated at an elevated desk beneath a simple round black wall clock, County Coroner Frank Nance, a bespectacled man in his fifties, presided over the inquest. A witness box abutted his desk to his left, beyond which sat a jury of nine hapless pedestrians who happened to be passing by the Hall of Justice that morning when the coroner sent out his deputy to impress a panel of jurors.[8]

Normally Nance delegated the task of conducting Coroner's Jury Inquests to one of his deputies, but this time he had decided to conduct the inquest himself.[9] Facing him from behind a plain oak table were the deputy coroners and Deputy District Attorneys George Johnson and O. R. Emerson. In the ensuing weeks, Johnson would take a key role in investigating the Todd death; today his role would be to assist Nance in questioning the witnesses.

Although the papers listed over a dozen persons who would testify, only eight did. These eight provided the jury with a cross-section of the case. Conspicuously absent were Sid Grauman, Stanley and Constance Lupino and their daughter, Ida, whom the press had identified as potential witnesses. Alice Todd, the dead star's mother, was scheduled to testify, but broke down and was escorted from the hearing room by Harvey Priester.[10]

When he returned, Priester was first to take the witness stand.[11] The son of two of the earliest residents of Hollywood, he had ventured into real estate and construction and even ran a gas station for a few years before becoming an insurance agent with a large clientele, especially among the movie set. He was good-looking and had been linked romantically to both Todd and Claire Windsor.[12]

Priester attended the Trocadero party Saturday night. After asking a series of questions to establish basic facts about Thelma and her finances, Nance and Deputy DA Johnson quizzed him closely on his impressions of Thelma that night. He had an eye for detail, especially where she was concerned. He recalled that she wore "a blue gown with sort of glittering material and bright blue shoes," "a couple of clasps in either side of her hair," "a diamond engagement ring . . . [and] a little flower like a camellia."[13] He had not observed her drinking as closely, however. He remembered only that she had a drink before dinner and champagne with her meal. Still, he stated firmly, when he last saw her, shortly before he left the Trocadero between two-thirty and three, she was not intoxicated.[14]

After Priester, Mae Whitehead, Miss Todd's personal maid, who had found her dead body, took the stand. Dressed in black and wearing a gardenia on her shoulder, Whitehead, a tall young woman in her late twenties, struggled to hold back her tears.[15] In a low voice, she replied tersely and, at times, somewhat evasively, to questions about Saturday evening, when she dressed Todd for the Trocadero and Monday morning, when she found her body.[16]

Whitehead explained it was her practice to stop at the garage each morning before heading to the café. She routinely exchanged her own car for Miss Todd's Lincoln phaeton, driving the latter down to the café. That morning she reached the garage shortly before 10:30. Both doors were closed, but not locked.[17] Carrying in her left arm some bundles she intended to put on the passenger seat, she slid open the rightmost garage door with her right hand, exposing the front grill of the phaeton, which was backed into the garage.[18] Moving towards the passenger door, she was startled to see her mistress asleep behind the steering wheel.[19] The blonde actress was slumped over, Whitehead recalled, but not quite lying down; her head drooped to the left onto her chest, bare arms resting in her lap.[20] She was wearing the same clothes Whitehead had helped dress her in Saturday night. On the seat next to her, Whitehead noticed the white evening bag in which, thirty-six hours earlier, she had placed thirty-five cents and a single key to the exterior door of her mistress' apartment.[21]

Rounding the front grill of the phaeton, Whitehead found the driver's door slightly ajar. She bent over to examine her mistress more closely. A small smudge of blood was under Todd's nose.[22] Whitehead realized suddenly that Thelma was not sleeping. She was dead.[23]

Deputy DA Johnson pressed Whitehead for details of the position of Todd's body when she found her, showing her a photograph of Todd's body. As she gazed at the photograph, Whitehead reacted immediately. "She wasn't lying down that way when I saw her," she exclaimed. "She was more upright, just with her head down."

"This picture indicates that she was slumped over towards the left," Johnson observed.

"She was slumped over towards the left," Whitehead replied, looking carefully at the photograph, "But not that far."

"You don't know whether she had been moved after you first saw her?" Coroner Nance asked.

"No," Whitehead replied.

"You were not there all the time?"

"No."

"But the impression you got, she was sitting back of this wheel in the normal position of a person who was about to start the car or drive?" inquired Nance.

"Yes."

Todd's chauffeur, Ernest Peters, followed Whitehead on the stand. Peters, a gaunt man dressed in a business suit and wearing round, wire frame glasses, testified he had known Todd for three years. During the past year, he had driven for her about five times.

Peters recounted chauffeuring Todd and her mother to the Trocadero Saturday night, including an unplanned stop at a florist's on Wilshire Boulevard, where Todd gave him a dollar to purchase a camellia, which she pinned to her dress. They arrived at the Café Trocadero Restaurant at 8:25. He then took Alice Todd to her apartment, not my best friend."

"You have been associated with her for how long?"

"I have known her for four years," West replied. "I have been associated with her in business about two years."

"Are you interested with her in this café business?" Nance asked.

"Only that I am financially back of the café."

"Now you say that you live at the café," Nance went on.

"I live at the café," West agreed.

"Now what are the apartments at the café–the living apartments? How are they arranged?"

"Well," West began, "There is this one main room (and the outside one is always Miss Todd's) and that is as large as this court room and it is divided off with pillars. And whenever I sleep at the café I went into the back room and there are folding doors which are locked. And outside the lobby is all private and couches out there and places to sleep."

"How many entrances to those apartments?" Nance asked.

"The main entrance is through a room which has never been opened and occupied as a ladies' boudoir. And going from there is the main room to the main apartment."

"One entrance that went through the café?" Nance asked.

"Not through the café, the café is on the left."

"Is there **any** entrance through the café?"

"There is no such entrance through the café."

Nance considered West's words for a few seconds. Earlier, when Mae Whitehead had testified about the layout of Todd's apartment, she stated that one entered it either from the outside, after coming up the stairway from the highway, or through a door which opened out into a hallway leading to an interior set of stairs which descended to the café. Now West seemed to contradict her.[36]

"Were you there last Saturday evening or that apartment"? Nance asked.

"I was there and escorted Miss Todd and her mother to the car," West replied.

"Did you have any conversation with her before that about what she was intending to do that evening?"

"I knew what she was intending to do and had been invited by her to go along."

"Will you please relate, in your own way, what that conversation was and what happened?"

"Well," West began, "She said, 'Can you go tonight?' and I said, 'Not Saturday night, because we are very busy.' And she had been busy buying Christmas presents and was rather tired. And I said–in a joking manner in front of her mother and everyone else up there and the chauffeur–I said, 'Be home by two o'clock.' And she said, 'I will be here at two five.' And every time I said that she would open the door and laugh. And I said two o'clock and she said two five."

"Was it all in fun or in good spirits?" Nance inquired.

"Well," West responded, "I think you can ask the chauffeur or mother."

"But as far as you are concerned?"

"As far as I was concerned, it was laughing," West replied. "And I said 'Be home at two o'clock,' and she said, 'Two five.' And it was joking, as everyone would notice."

"Did you say, 'If you are not home at two o'clock I will lock you out?'" the coroner asked bluntly.

"No," West replied firmly. "I said, 'After two o'clock the outside door is locked.'"

"What did you mean by that?"

"Well, we have heard people around there and I had bars put up at the window."

"Prowlers?"

"Prowlers," West affirmed. "The manager told me that. And I had bars put on the window, especially after she got those messages," he continued, evidently referring to the threatening letters Todd received months before from the "Ace of Spades."

"She would never go to that door on Saturday night," West insisted, and explained that Todd carried three keys to the building and its apartment, but did not normally carry one to the outside door of the apartment—at least not on Saturday nights. He knew she didn't carry a key to the outside door because one time before she tried to enter the apartment through the outside door and, finding it locked, roused him by rapping on the window.

"I had been very tired that night and I thought I dreamed that the pane was broken and looked up and the curtain was moving. And she said 'The door is locked,' and I said, 'Why haven't you got the other keys?' And I got up and got in a bathrobe and let her in and went back to my place. That was an experience to let her know she could get in that door," West reflected.

"Mr. Peters has stated he left her there at the doorway where he was accustomed to leaving her and the maid said she had a key—described it as a Yale key," Nance recalled. "Was that key sufficient to let her into that apartment?"

"That particular key, it wouldn't," West replied. "I put the lock on that door myself Saturday night. It is put on every night either by myself or the manager."

"How did you expect her to get in under those circumstances?" Nance demanded.

"I didn't know until Monday morning that she didn't have her keys," West rejoined. "The maid told me she only had one key to the outside door."

"She didn't have the other keys," Nance observed. "Let's see what they look like."

A clerk came forward with an envelope, from which he took a ring of keys to hand to West. West held up one of the keys for Nance and the jurors to see. "There is the pass key that Miss Todd had to the main door. I thought she had these keys," he indicated two other keys on a ring. "She had other keys like to the ladies' boudoir that I haven't got. And if I had known she didn't have that one key, I would have stayed up and waited for her."

"Where did you go?" Nance asked.

"I didn't go anywhere. I was at the café until closing time, which I imagine was about two o'clock, when I received a message from Mr. Grauman."

"Where were you when you received the message?"

"I was in the cocktail lounge."

"At the café?"

West nodded. "And one of the cashiers called me and I went into the main dining room and talked to Mr. Grauman."

"What was the message?" Nance asked.

"That Miss Todd was talking to the Skouras boys and said she was leaving immediately."

"What time was that?"

"That was about five minutes to two. And I talked to Sid and I said, 'When are you coming down,' and so forth and said nothing else. Said 'bring your mother down,' and that was about the amount of the message."

"Did you remain there at the café then?"

"After a got the message, I went upstairs and got the dog and [went] through the side door and took him for his walk and then brought him back and locked that door. Bolted it. The other door was bolted, the main door, the way we always use. And went into my room, closed the apartment, locked it and took the dog in with me and covered him up."

"Now," Nance continued, "did you hear any sound after that?"

"I fell asleep... I would not know... I imagine, about two thirty. I was awakened about three thirty by the dog whining and he never whines—he has a habit of whining when he gets uncovered. And I look over to see, to cover him up and he was all covered. And I looked at the clock and it was exactly three thirty. Whether that clock was right or not, I don't know. It was a table clock. And I called out to see if Miss Todd was home and received no answer. But I heard the water running in the building and figured that—there was nobody up—I figured that she had come in from the outside the regular way and gone to bed. And the dog was quiet and I went to sleep."

"How long did the dog whine?" Nance asked.

"As soon as I waked up he whined," West replied.

"Didn't bark?"

"No. No bark."

"And you didn't get up?"

"No, but when he whines, I knew he would know her."

"Did it occur to you there was a double lock on that door?" Nance asked.

"I didn't know she didn't have a key to the main door," West protested. "I didn't know what keys she had! I never knew that until Monday morning."

"When you retired, you assumed she had a key to get into the apartment?"

"Yes."

"How far is this garage from the café, Mr. West?"

West considered the question for a moment. "There are two ways to get to the garage, one steps and one a walkway. Miss Todd used to take the steps. She never wanted to walk, but if we ever come home and knew there was no one to take the car up, sometimes she would take the steps and I would take the walk down." He turned in his chair and looked out the window. "The garage was as a far as that building," he said, pointing out the window.

All eyes in the court followed his finger towards a structure several hundred yards away.

"The Federal building?" Nance asked.

"Back of the Old Gold sign."

Nance gazed at the building for a few seconds appraisingly. "Would there be any way to get assistance on finding herself locked out, anyone around there where she could get assistance that time of the morning?" he asked finally.

"Miss Todd is very considerate and she knew she could arouse me," he insisted. "And if she got in at three thirty or four o'clock and knew she didn't have her keys, knowing that she didn't have her key she might have walked up there because I made that remark to her and said, 'If you don't come home you can always go to your mother's.' But she never did, but she could always rouse me very easily."

"Had she ever gone to the garage that way?" asked Nance.

"Never."

"Ever been locked out that way before?"

"Yes, when she broke the pane of glass to wake me up."

"She could have done the same thing that night if she wanted to?" Nance asked.

"You could not keep Miss Todd out of any place if she wanted to get in," West replied emphatically.

"Do you know why she went to the garage?"

West collected himself. "I don't know whether she ever came to the apartment," he paused, pointing to the map of the café building on the bulletin board, "Because when you come up these stairs, as the chauffeur will tell you, you walk this far and continue twenty-five feet and go up the stairs and go around to the garage or continue on around to this door."

"On that particular occasion," Nance asked, "or any time recently, had you noticed she was at all moody or unhappy about anything?"

"Miss Todd was never unhappy," West insisted. "She had everything to be happy about. Everything."

"Was she making immediate plans for things that were pleasant?"

"Yes, she was finishing a Roach contract and Mr. Schenck told her in front of me that as soon as she was finished he was ready to sign her up. She has her mother she was taking care of, and has her café, and has everything, in fact."

"Did she appear to be in good health?"

"Fine."

"Never complained of any . . ."

"Yes, she used to have fainting spells," interrupted West.

"Fainting?"

"Yes."

"She wasn't accustomed to vigorous exercise?"

"She never walked. You never could get her to walk."

"It is quite a climb up to that garage for a person who is not accustomed to exercise." Nance suggested.

"It is a climb for anyone." West agreed.

"The mink coat that she was wearing–you knew that?"

"Very well."

"It is very heavy?"

"Yes, very heavy."

"And if one has been at a dancing party and exercising that way several hours in the evening and has to climb a hill that would be rather fatiguing for one not used to exercising?"

"The chauffeur told me she was very tired when she got out of the car," West replied. "He had never seen her that way so she must have been tired before she even started to climb."

"Do you know of any reason in the world why this death occurred and the way it did, can you give us any help as to what occurred?"

"Well, the only help . . . ," West began, and then paused. He seemed to puzzle over the question for a second. "Perhaps she had tried that door, didn't want to waken anybody, may have thought she would go to the car, stay there until the porters come in the morning, which is six o'clock. And say she went there at three thirty or four. She may have got chilled and started the car and may have thought she would drive down to her mother's. Started the car and warmed it up and then open the doors. She would never think of little details . . . . "

SIX: WEDNESDAY AFTERNOON

> Deliberate upon the evidence that has been presented to you and determine how, when and where the deceased came to her death and whether her death was homicidal, suicidal, accidental, or natural.
>
> — Coroner Frank Nance[1]

After lunch, West returned to the stand. Johnson asked him to go over some of the same areas that Nance had addressed, in particular, his motive for bolting Todd's apartment door.

"She never come in that door on Saturday nights," West explained, "Because it was always bolted when the maid left on Saturday night. It might sometimes be bolted at eight o'clock at night. And if the dog was taken out he was taken out that door, because that is a dead entrance. And if the dog was taken out at two o'clock in the morning, they would take him out by that door and bolt it again."

"When did you bolt that door that Saturday night?" Johnson asked.

"I bolted the door when I brought the dog in."

"About two thirty?" Johnson asked.

"About two fifteen," West specified.

West explained that he then went to bed only to be awakened shortly afterward by Todd's dog.

"I heard the dog whining at 3:30. That was what the clock said on the table."

"You mean you were awakened and then went to sleep again?" Johnson inquired.

"I went to sleep," West began. "First, I got up and examined the dog to see if he was uncovered—he always whines when he is uncovered—and I covered him up and lay there a few minutes and heard the water running in the other lady's boudoir and figured it was Miss Todd."

"What is there in the way of partitions, or doorways, if anything, between the bedroom you were occupying and the apartment of Miss Todd?" Johnson asked.

"There is double doors with locks on both sides."

"Sliding doors?"

"Sliding doors," West declared. "Solid wooden doors."

"Were those doors locked that night?"

"Those doors were locked."

"From your side?"

"From my side."

"And is there any way of communicating, that is, talking, from the quarters that you are occupying, with Miss Todd over in her quarters, except by opening those doors?"

"No," West replied. "Only by talking loudly you could hear through those doors if you pull the drapes back."

When Johnson asked about the following morning, Sunday, the day Todd was missing from the café, West explained that he awoke sometime between 9:00 and 11:00 and checked for Miss Todd.

"I went out to see, opened the door, rapped, went out," he began.

Johnson interrupted him. "You mean went out where?"

"Out into the big room," West explained, "Like this court room and saw she wasn't there. And then I went into the lady's boudoir, opened with my pass key and examined the huge couch in there because she had slept on that couch. And there was what I considered an impression on that couch. Thought she had slept there because nobody else could have done that. Then I figured she had got up and went to her mother's."

"Got up and gone to her mother's?"

"Gone to her mother's."

"Did you make any investigation as to her clothing or what clothing she had left or taken?" Johnson asked.

"No," West replied, "Because she had so many clothes that I could not tell. I don't think anyone could tell."

West recounted that he then picked up his newspaper and read it before ringing for breakfast. It was past noon before he went downstairs to the café.[2] Bob Anderson, the young bartender who took care of Miss Todd's phaeton, was behind the bar. West asked him which car Thelma had used–the phaeton or his Hupmobile. "Mr. West," Anderson replied, "we are so busy I haven't had time to go up there today."

After speaking to Anderson, West remained in the café all afternoon, chatting with automobile dealer Robert Cooper, who was selling him a car for his wife, Jewel. Cooper left around 2:00 in the afternoon, just before the arrival of West's mother, who visited him every Sunday afternoon. West and his mother went upstairs to the apartment. His mother asked about Thelma. West told her she had gone to visit her own mother.[3]

Late that afternoon, after his mother departed, West went upstairs to rest. "I was very nervous," West remembered, "Nervous for some reason, I don't know why." Around 6:00, the phone rang. It was one of the Skouras brothers, calling for Thelma. At the Trocadero the previous night, she had invited him to dine with his family at her café that evening. "Miss Todd isn't here, but we are expecting her any minute," West told him. The Skourases decided to come on anyway, and West called down to the café to speak with Schafer. He told the café manager about Thelma's guests, asked that they receive the best of service, and mentioned that he expected Thelma back "any moment." "And the reason I said 'any moment,'" West explained, "I knew she went out with an evening dress, I couldn't see any other way she could have any clothes if she went to her mother's, and I think it was about 6:30." [4]

A few minutes later, the phone rang again. This time George Baker was on the line, calling from Martha Ford's house to inquire on Todd's whereabouts.

"I said, 'Miss Todd will be here in a little while.' And he said, 'Will you deliver a message to call up North Hollywood?' And I said, 'What is the message?' And he said, 'I am calling for Martha Ford, and Miss Ford wants to have her call her up.' And I said, 'I will tell her.' And then I looked at the time and it was seven o'clock."

Still convinced that Todd would arrive shortly, West went downstairs. The Skouras party arrived soon afterward. West, who knew one of the several Skouras brothers through Joseph Schenck, greeted them. That Thelma was not at the café surprised the Skourases, since she bet them Saturday night that they would not come down to her restaurant for dinner the following evening. Before departing sometime after 11:00, the Skourases came over to his table again to express their surprise that Todd had not returned. West told them he could not get over it himself.[5]

"Did you make any inquiry anywhere regarding the whereabouts of Miss Todd?" Johnson asked.

"No; I never did that," West admitted.

"Did you leave the café—I mean, the building there itself—that day at all, Sunday?"

"Never left the building."

"Make any further inquiry, of Bob or anyone else, as to the cars in the garage?"

"Not me."

"You didn't make any inquiry of anybody?" Johnson demanded.

"I would not." West replied.

"Well, you didn't."

"I didn't," West agreed.

After the Skourases left, West retired to his apartment, where he lay awake until about 5:00 a.m., Monday, before falling asleep. Around 10:00, the house phone, buzzing insistently, awakened him to the news of Todd's death.

Johnson quizzed West closely on his actions of Monday morning. Once again, West recited his observations: the ignition switch in the on position, the gas remaining in the tank, the dust on the side of the seat. He recounted his observations with a haunted, obsessed insistence on details, as if he were reliving his impressions of that terrible morning as he spoke of it on the witness chair. "I came to the garage and rushed in the door and there was Miss Todd lying over there. I put my hand onto her face and there was blood and I wiped it off on my handkerchief, drop, and then I sent Mae to go up, she could not go through the garage, and I said, 'Stay in the car and go around and get Mr. Schafer and his wife as quick as you can.' And she sent them down and they came down and opened the door from the inside and then I told Schafer, I said, 'You go get the police and get a doctor.' And he jumped in the car and I said. 'Mae, you go down and get the mother.' I went in the car—I think the door, I don't know how I got this thought, that the door had been closed, but I found out now, I think the mother told me later, the door was open in the car. And I looked over there and I saw the switch and Mrs. Schafer was over there, and I walked up and down the place and went on the other side and looked to see how much gas was in the tank and it was almost empty. And I know from the position that she was trying to get out of that car. I know that because otherwise she would not have turned in the way she did and the door would not have been open. She was trying to get out of that car."

That Todd was trying to escape from the poisonous garage was evidently important to West; he insisted on it a few seconds later, stating, "I know now positive she was trying to get out of the door." Despite widespread suspicion that Todd had been murdered and that he had done the deed, West seemed more concerned with the possibility that Todd committed suicide. The open door was evidence to him that she had not wanted to die.

So far, West had sidestepped suggestions in the courtroom that day that he was involved romantically with Todd, implying there was nothing more than business and friendship between them. He spoke matter-of-factly about their business arrangement, telling the jury

> I put up the building, I own the building, I put the equipment in that building, and the reason I put the equipment in, it cost so much I would not ask anybody to put equipment in to carry out my ideas, but Miss Todd carried out my ideas and run that place according to my ideas, but she had the finest and best equipment of any place in this city.[6]

Despite his insistence that solid wooden doors separated his sleeping area from Todd's, the coroner and deputies apparently were not persuaded by West's depiction of a relationship of platonic innocence. This became clear as Johnson turned his questioning towards the links between Todd, West, and DiCicco. Already, the subject of Todd and DiCicco's relationship and their rumored confrontation at the Trocadero had come up when Harvey Priester was on the stand. Deputy DA Johnson had questioned Priester closely on an engagement ring that Todd wore to the restaurant. Priester admitted that he had noticed it, but did not know if it signaled anything about impending marriage plans for the actress. Nor did the insurance man know anything about the alleged quarrel between Thelma and DiCicco at the latter's table. As far as he knew, the romantic relationship between them was over even though the former couple remained friends; Todd had told him that she was "through with [DiCicco] absolutely." Perhaps it was West who had given Todd the engagement ring.

"Mr. West, were you engaged to marry Miss Todd?" Johnson asked the former director.

"No," West replied.

"Were you acquainted with her former husband, Mr. DiCicco?"

"No, I never met him."

"Had you ever discussed with her, her relations or her feelings toward him?"

"Well, I have known Miss Todd a good many years," West observed. "I knew her before she married Mr. DiCicco; she was a great friend of mine."

"My question is, had you ever discussed with her or had she discussed with you her situation with Mr. DiCicco?"

"No."

"Never at all?"

"Only that she got a divorce from him."

"Do you know of any intention or contemplation she had of remarrying him again," Johnson asked.

West appeared taken back. "Oh, no," he replied.

"Did you ever know of anything of that kind?" Johnson persisted.

"I knew that could not be," West contended.

"Well, she and he were friendly, were they not?" Johnson suggested.

"She was friendly with everyone," West rejoined. "She loved everyone. She liked everyone."

"Your relations with Miss Todd were more or less intimate, were they not? Johnson asked."

"She was my best friend," West stated calmly, then corrected himself. "One of my best friends, I should say."

"Did you have any suggestion for her or otherwise that she might contemplate leaving you and resuming marriage relations or otherwise with her former husband?" Johnson asked.

"Leaving me?" West gasped, straightening up in his chair.[7]

"Yes."

"I could not have any such thought," he declared.

"Nothing like that had ever been suggested?"

"I could not have such thought or she would not have such thought," West insisted. "There could not be anything like that. She was my partner, also."

West's testimony that day, like much of what he and others would say about the death of Thelma Todd in the coming weeks, confused as much as it clarified the issues surrounding the tragedy. West himself would allow as much several weeks later, as he readied himself to testify before the Grand Jury, blaming the shock and strain of Todd's death for his lack of coherence.[8] While the trauma of her death may have contributed to his confusion, his perplexing descriptions of the café building's living quarters and his puzzling explanations of his behavior Sunday appeared to reflect other causes. Many wondered whether West was hiding something.

Earlier in the day, West named another person who might shed light on the mysterious death, the café's treasurer, Charles Smith. Smith had been an associate of West since the early movie days[9] as a screenwriter and theatrical manager and now lived in a small apartment above the garage. According to West, Smith had gone home around 2:30 a.m. that morning and had not gone to sleep until an hour later. While Smith was not in court that day, West had asked him already if he had noticed any activity, but Smith had told him he had not heard a sound.

"You feel if you were upstairs over that garage in Mr. Smith's apartment, you would hear the car running downstairs?" Nance asked West.

"I believe when the car started it would waken anyone because that car, when it started, would make more noise than breaking a pane of glass."

His depiction of the loud noise the phaeton made when starting prompted a tactful rejoinder from the next witness, Robert Anderson, the café's young bartender, who regularly shuttled Miss Todd's car up and down from the hillside garage. Anderson explained that normally the engine started quietly, but it could be noisy if one set the throttle wide open. Presumably, that was what he did Saturday morning when West, lying awake in his bed, heard him fire it up.[10]

Shortly after the café closed, Anderson drove the phaeton up the hill from the front of the café and backed it into the garage. Miss Todd, he explained, always headed the car front in when she parked in the garage, but he backed it in to make it easy for her to drive out. As usual, that night he made a point to push the ignition button off and turn the key in the ignition lock so there was no drain on the battery: on one occasion, another restaurant employee left the ignition on and the battery was dead the following day. He then left the key in the switch and closed the garage door.[11]

Robert Cooper, the automobile salesman who visited West at the café Sunday afternoon, also testified about the Lincoln phaeton. Cooper seemed a little uncomfortable with his presence before the inquest and quickly explained that it had come about accidentally. He had been at police headquarters the day before, trying to sell an automobile to the Homicide Squad, when he noticed a group of reporters crowded around a nearby desk. He asked the detectives what was going on. One remarked that the journalists were trying to solve the Thelma Todd mystery. Cooper let on that he knew Miss Todd and her automobile and got a subpoena for his trouble.[12]

Already, newspapers had quoted his observations that the automobile produced carbon monoxide rapidly and got only five miles to the gallon.[13] He had also been cited, along with unnamed others, as the source for the information that Todd never had much gas in the tank.

Cooper revealed the automobile had a "blow-by" condition caused by a slight deformity in its cylinder walls. During compression, the engine oil at the top of the cylinders was forced past or "blown-by" the pistons. Some of this oil could have gotten into the plugs while the engine idled, causing them to foul and kill the engine.[14]

Later that afternoon, Martha Ford testified about the phone call she claimed she received from Thelma Sunday afternoon. Ford was a hit with reporters sitting in the audience. One described her as a "beautiful, blue-eyed blonde, attired in a stunning black dress" while another noted that this "striking ash-blond" was both "self-possessed" and "highly intelligent."[15] Her mental acuity and stability were key to the credibility of the strange tale she had told police.

Ford testified she had last seen Todd three or four weeks earlier near the Broadway Department Store in Hollywood. While she had not spoken with Todd on the telephone for over a month, during the past several months they had talked two or three times by phone—enough for her to assure the Inquest that she could not have been mistaken the woman who she spoke with over the phone late Sunday afternoon was Thelma.[16]

The phone rang around 4:10 Sunday afternoon as she entertained the first few party guests at her home at 3528 Laurel Canyon Boulevard. Mrs. Ford picked it up herself on one of the three extensions in her home.[17]

"Hello, this is Thelma," the caller said.

At first, Ford thought the voice said the name of another girl friend, Velma. "When are you kids coming out?" she asked.

"Who do you think this is?" the caller asked.

"Velma," replied Ford.

"No, it is 'Hot Toddy' Toddy," the voice on the other end responded.

"I don't know the exact sequence, whether one thing was first or the other," Ford told the jury, "but the substance of the conversation was she said 'What are you wearing at the party?' and I said, 'I am wearing hostess pajamas.' And she said she had on an evening gown and I said, 'Whatever you are wearing will be all right.' And she said she was bringing someone with her and I asked if it was a girl friend and she said no, and I asked who it was and she wouldn't tell me. She said, 'I want to have the fun of seeing your face when I come in the door.' And she mentioned something about going through a short cut or something like that and I said if you know about it, all right, there is such a place, and she said, 'I will take a chance,' and she spoke of the address being wrong, and she said, 'I will be there in half an hour.' And I said, 'All the lights will be on and you can't miss the house because there will be plenty of cars there.' And said she, 'O.K.'"[18] As she had already told the police, George Baker, her brother-in-law, grew worried when Todd failed to arrive and called the Sidewalk Café sometime between 6:30 and 7:00 p.m.[19]

Once Ford finished her narrative, Coroner Nance appeared to try to shake her from her story by focusing on the physical evidence that appeared to contradict her account or at least make it seem improbable. "Did you suppose she would probably wear the same gown to your party Sunday afternoon as she wore Saturday night?" he asked.

"Well, it would have depended on the dress," Ford replied calmly. "Cocktail dresses and dinner dresses are sometimes very much alike."

What about the faded camellia found pinned to Todd's dress, which Detective Bruce Clark would later describe as "a very faded flower . . . [that] looked like it had been dead for at least a couple of days" and Deputy Coroner Russel Monroe would observe was "much too withered" to wear to a party?[20]

"Did you suppose if she had purchased a camellia on Saturday evening on her way to the Trocadero, she would have that same faded camellia on her dress Sunday afternoon at four o'clock?" Nance demanded.

"I should not think so," Ford replied. "I think it would be mussed up."

"And you think if she was found dead in the same gown with that camellia, you still feel she talked to you Sunday afternoon?" challenged Nance.

Ford did not budge. "I know she talked to me Sunday afternoon," she insisted. "I am as sure as any human being could be."[21]

Whatever other evidence might suggest, Ford knew what she had heard.

The evidence that most directly contradicted Ford's claims and supported the police theory came next through the testimony of Autopsy Surgeon A. F. Wagner, who presented the scientific evidence behind his estimate of Sunday morning as the time of Todd's death. Wagner began his testimony by reading his official report:

> I performed an autopsy on Thelma Todd December 17, 1935, at Los Angeles County Coroner's Mortuary and found the exterior of the body presenting a red discoloration and on examination of the blood I found it to contain seventy-five to eighty per cent of carbon monoxide saturation. On opening the head, the brain showed a scarlet red color of the blood and the organs of the body were similarly colored. On opening the body I found all the vital organs normal, that is, free from organic disease. There were no marks of violence anywhere upon or within the body. A superficial contusion on the lower lip did not penetrate beneath the skin. The cause of death was carbon monoxide poisoning.[22]

On Nance's request, Wagner explained the deadly process of carbon monoxide poisoning.

> The poison is drawn in, a little of it, by each breath, and it accumulates in the body until finally the blood is practically saturated. In the living body, however, it never becomes saturated, that is, it don't take up as much carbon monoxide gas as it would outside of the body, so that when we have the blood saturated, we call that one hundred percent. When we test the blood for the amount of carbon monoxide it has in it after we do any autopsy, that is expressed in terms of that one hundred per cent. If we get above seventy per cent, that is fatal. Some can take in more before they die. It goes as high as eighty and ninety per cent, but that is about the limit. It is merely—it takes some time, too, out in a garage where the motor would be running and generating some of the carbon monoxide, it would take a few hours before there would be sufficient carbon monoxide in the blood to cause death.[23]

Death by carbon monoxide poisoning, Wagner told the court, "is the same as asphyxiation":

> It is an internal or blood asphyxiation. Besides keeping oxygen out, it also keeps the oxygen from the tissues. The carbon monoxide takes the place of the oxygen in the hemoglobin of the blood, so the final result is an asphyxiation. Carbon monoxide retains its hold upon the hemoglobin, which the carbon dioxide does not do.[24]

The blood of the victim becomes bright red, coloring the organs which it suffuses, Wagner explained. Death occurs when the brain, denied oxygen, fails, and all processes it controls, such as breathing, terminate.

The effects of monoxide are insidious. "The victims become drowsy at first," he testified, and are unlikely to know that they are exposed to the gas. While hemorrhaging is not associated with carbon monoxide poisoning, a small bit of blood-stained froth may "bubble up" through the nostrils and mouths of the victims after because of congestion in the mucous membrane. "The blood that was seen around this case had not significance other than just the poisoning of the gas," Wagner averred. "It did not mean that it was due to any bruise or any fall or any violence at all."[25] While he could not state categorically that all the blood found about Todd's face was due to frothing, Wagner had not found any significant bruising to account for the blood, only "a superficial contusion on the lower lip [that] did not penetrate beneath the skin." This Wagner attributed to the lip "coming in contact with a hard object."[26]

On the critical issue of time of death, Wagner was careful:

> [M]any elements enter into it [the time of death calculation]. When the weather is quite cold, as it was on that night . . . a body won't show the post-mortem effects

you would get in the daytime or in the warmer weather. She had been dead some time, some hours. As close as I think anybody can get at it, at least, by observation of the body itself, she could have been dead anywhere from twelve to thirty hours. My best judgment was it was about eighteen hours.[27]

Wagner explained that these estimates, based on the "gross appearance of her body," were timed backwards from the autopsy examination, which began sometime between 4:30 and 5:00 Monday evening. That meant that the physical evidence of Todd's body indicated a time of death between 10:30 a.m. Sunday and 4:30 a.m. Monday, with 10:30 p.m. or 11:00 a.m. Sunday the most likely time.[28]

Nevertheless, the history of the case—developed from the statements and testimony of the witnesses—also had to be considered. One key element in the minds of the Coroner and his Autopsy Surgeon was the food that filled half of Todd's stomach. Wagner testified the stomach empties itself under normal circumstances within six hours, though excitement or alcoholic beverages can delay the process. As Priester testified that Todd finished her dinner before midnight Saturday, the fact that Todd's stomach was found half-full indicated a time of death in the early hours of Sunday morning. And the fact that she was found dead in the same clothing she wore to the Trocadero argued against the likelihood that she went somewhere else to eat after returning to Castellammare that morning.[29]

Asked to take into account the testimony of the witnesses as well as the condition of the body, Wagner estimated the time of death as "some time Sunday morning, anywhere from five to six o'clock on to eight o'clock." The doctor noted Detective Clark testified that rigor mortis had set in the body when he first came on the scene. "If that is the case," he observed, ". . . she must have been dead quite some time for rigor mortis to develop the way it did." Although rigor usually develops after about six hours from death, in carbon monoxide poisoning cases it takes a bit longer, Wagner explained. "My best judgment, from all facts taken into consideration, she died some time Sunday morning," he concluded.[30]

Of course, in determining the time of death as occurring in the early morning, Sunday, he effectively rejected Ford's testimony.

After the coroner's jurors had heard all the witnesses in the case, the nine jurors retired to the jury room. They deliberated for an hour and twenty minutes, a length of time one newspaper called "unprecedented."[31] Observers, like reporter Mahoney, who sensed manipulation and orchestration in the questions posed by the authorities, no doubt expected they would return a verdict in line with the accident theory promulgated by the Los Angeles Police Department. However, they split on the verdict. Five concluded tentatively that the death was accidental, but the other four voted for a straightforward "open" verdict indicating they were unable to determine the cause of death.[32] On the single page, pre-printed form entitled "Verdict of Coroner's Jury," they wrote that death was caused by "carbon monoxide poisoning" but avoided deciding the critical time of death issue by assigning the "16th day of December 1935" as the day she died. This date was the Monday on which her body was found, rather than the Sunday on which Dr. Wagner placed her death. They also recommended a "further investigation to be made in this case, by the proper authorities." Considering the contradictory and confusing evidence presented to them, the jury's tentative conclusion may have been the most honest one they could make. To know what really happened to Thelma Todd would require many more days and weeks, and even then, the matter would be in doubt.[33]

While Roland West's testimony furnished the headlines for Wednesday evening and Thursday morning newspaper editions his estranged wife, Jewel Carmen, had a story of her own to tell that would propel the Todd mystery further along its confusing track. Carmen had been a leading lady in the silent films of the late 'teens and twenties, playing opposite Douglas Fairbanks in three films in 1916, a credulous young beauty who one movie journalist dubbed "a queen of blondes."[34] When questioned about Todd's death Tuesday evening by police detectives William Clark and Edward Romero,[35] she recalled an incident on Catalina Island several years before.

> One day when Miss Todd was in bathing in the ocean she had a fainting spell which she ascribed to the condition of her heart. She was asked why she smoked and sometimes drank if her heart was in that condition and she replied that physicians had told her that she had only five or six years to live any way and that she might as well have what fun she could.[36]

Later, Carmen told Louella Parsons "You had only to see the puffy shadows under her eyes to know that she suffered from a heart affliction. She told me of dizzy spells and as soon as I heard that her body had been found in the garage, I was sure she had suffered one of her heart attacks and probably died before she could get out of the car."[37]

As to her own activities over the weekend, Carmen recounted that she spent Saturday night at home, then left her apartment with two friends around 11 a.m. Sunday to visit Mt. Wilson, returning late that evening.

That, at least, was her story Tuesday evening. On Wednesday, following the dramatic testimony of the Coroner's Inquest, Carmen telephoned police to reveal she had something more to tell them.

"I was evasive when I talked to you last night," she confessed to detectives Blaine Steed and Thad Brown. "I want to tell everything I know now. I saw Thelma Todd with a man of dark complexion whom I did not recognize about 11 p.m. Sunday."[38]

"I was returning from the San Fernando Valley, and was traveling east on Hollywood Boulevard, when I saw a chocolate-colored phaeton which I immediately recognized as belonging to Miss Todd.

"I stepped on the gas and drew as close as possible. Sitting next to the driver was Thelma Todd. I recognized her from a smart hat I knew she wore and also her golden curls."[39]

To disprove any suspicion that she had concocted her story during the last two days, Carmen cited her friend, Mrs. Sonia Ardell. Mrs. Ardell called her Monday around 3 p.m. to tell her of the discovery of Thelma's body. "Why I saw her just before midnight last night!" Carmen said she had exclaimed.[40] Why hadn't Carmen told the police this before? Because, she told Steed and Brown, "some newspaper men were at police headquarters."[41]

In addition to revising her account of her activities Sunday night to include sighting the supposedly dead actress, Carmen also changed her tune when discussing her relationship with West. When questioned Tuesday night, she denied reports she and West were separated, though she admitted three months had gone by since she last visited Castellammare.[42] Wednesday evening she admitted they no longer lived together. "I haven't talked to Mr. West for a long, long time," she admitted. "I entertain only the friendliest feelings for him and I believe he thinks the same of me. I have always known of Mr. West's feeling for Miss Todd. We have discussed the matter many times. Mr. West was a gentleman at all times. We have been separated for more than two years yet there has been no talk of a divorce. I understand Mr. West and Mr. West understands me."[43]

Jewel had been on site on Catalina Island in the summer of 1931 for the filming of *Corsair*. From her own comments to reporters in 1935, it appeared she got along well with Todd from the start, although it is not clear how much she knew then of her husband's interest in the young actress. After the filming of *Corsair*, she and West departed on their cruise, West endeavoring, secretly one must suppose, to get Thelma out of his mind. By the time they returned, Carmen had lost whatever love she might have had for the sea, even when it was several hundred feet below. "I came home a physical wreck," she would tell Louella Parsons. "No woman used to the comforts of life could endure the hardships of such a voyage. After I returned, I felt I couldn't stand the sound of the ocean. It was too nerve-wracking and so I left our home and tried to rest my nerves which were in a terrible state after two years and a half away from civilization."[44] Part of the problem was Castellammare's isolation: Jewel was used to society, friends, and the city. She had never liked the remote Castillo Del Mar, especially after her return from the sea.[45]

Jewel's departure from Castillo Del Mar was also a separation from Roland, as she would aver some years later in a divorce action, specifying that it took place on March 1, 1934. By December 1935, she was living at 317 South Ardmore with her spiritualist consultant, Mother Grey.[46]

At least one detail of Carmen's account seemed questionable: her claim that Todd was wearing a hat when she saw her Sunday night.[47] Todd had not worn a hat at the Trocadero Saturday night and was not wearing one when found Monday morning. While claiming she could not possibly have been mistaken about the identity of the woman she saw in the automobile Sunday night, Carmen wavered on her contention that the woman was wearing a hat. "Although I am not sure about Miss Todd wearing a hat," she admitted, "I just get the impression that she was wearing a pert little hat, cocked over her right eye."[48] The windshields that protected the rear seat of the phaeton, which Carmen claimed to have ridden in herself as a "bosom friend" of Thelma's, were up, she observed further.[49]

Carmen admitted her description of the man with Todd was sketchy, as she caught just a "fleeting glimpse" of him: he was "tall and dark," and was wearing "a checked, pepper-and-salt effect top coat and hat,"[50] "a foreign-looking man."[51] He was driving the automobile, while Todd "was sitting well over on her own side of the front seat." Carmen observed, "The couple in the car appeared to be very serious. I didn't notice any attempt at conversation. The man didn't look at his companion all the time the car was in my sight." She turned behind the car onto Vine Street but continued on her way to her apartment on South Ardmore when the phaeton turned west on Santa Monica Boulevard.[52]

The reaction of law enforcement officials and reporters to Carmen's statements ranged from perplexity to dismissal. The police detectives expressed doubts about her story almost immediately, but District Attorney Buron Fitts, whose office was expanding its role in the case, decided to interview her.[53] Certainly, as the *Daily News* observed, it would have been an extraordinary coincidence that she, "of all the thousands of persons who could have, saw Miss Todd driving down Hollywood boulevard at 11:00 o'clock Sunday night...."[54]

Whatever else was true about Carmen's statement, which, like many of the issues surrounding Todd's death, would become more problematic as days and weeks passed, it was clear the Todd mystery was deepening. The set of factors identified on Monday had quickly been supplemented on Tuesday; new issues had arisen on Wednesday at the Coroner's Inquest, and Wednesday evening brought more new reports and claims. Indeed, as the focus of the investigation shifted from the Coroner's Inquest to the Grand Jury, a new element added to the mystery: rumors of underworld involvement in the Sidewalk Café operation and possibly in Todd's death as well.

SEVEN: THE FIRST WEEK ENDS

So far, nothing conclusive has been brought forward to show that this may have been a murder but it is obvious that the whole picture is far from clear . . .
— District Attorney Buron Fitts[1]

Shortly after the Coroner's Jury revealed its ambivalent verdict Wednesday afternoon, Los Angeles County Grand Jury foreman Rochester announced a Grand Jury investigation of Todd's death that would pursue a "totally new angle."[2] Rochester refused to divulge details of the new investigation, but indicated it would include additional questioning of witnesses about Todd's activities at the Trocadero Saturday night.[3] Already, he had directed that the contents of Todd's stomach be analyzed further to detect poisons or drugs.[4]

The Grand Jury foreman also told reporters of rumors of possible underworld involvement in Todd's death. According to his sources, gamblers had tried to set up gaming resorts near Todd's café. One report even claimed underworld figures threatened Todd after she refused to allow them to open an exclusive gambling parlor for wealthy society and film figures on the café's second floor.[5] According to another rumor, however, a gaming club was already scheduled to open New Year's Eve, less than two weeks away. Still, café manager Schafer insisted that Todd refused vehemently to allow gaming equipment in her café.[6]

When Rochester finished speaking, District Attorney Buron Fitts announced his office would conduct its own investigation of the case separately from the Grand Jury inquiry. Observing, "Some witnesses have not been as helpful as they might have been," Fitts declared that twenty subpoenas would be issued. DA investigators Tom Cavett, Jess Winn and Lloyd Yarrow were already assigned to the case, along with Deputy District Attorneys Johnson and Eugene Blalock. One of their priorities would be to ferret out the facts behind the gambling rumors: Tom Cavett would concentrate on this angle by questioning "big shots" in the Santa Monica area.[7]

By the following day, three separate but cooperative investigations into the actress' death were in full swing. District Attorney Fitts conferred with his investigators and deputies to plan the DA Office's strategy. LAPD Chief of Detectives Joe Taylor took charge of the police investigation, ordering the re-questioning of West, Smith, Schafer, Anderson, and Mae Whitehead, then drove to the café with Detective Eddie Romero to retrace Todd's alleged walk from the café to the garage.[8]

Meanwhile, the Grand Jury's Criminal Complaints Committee met in special session to discuss the case with several deputy district attorneys, Coroner Nance and Autopsy Surgeon Wagner. Informed by Nance and Wagner that Todd's vital organs had been removed, the committee decided not to interfere with the cremation scheduled that afternoon. After the meeting, Foreman Rochester promised the jury would call before it all the important figures of the case as well as all Trocadero employees on duty the night of the party.[9]

One aspect of the mystery that intrigued both the Grand Jury foreman and the District Attorney was the identity of the guest Todd intended to take to Ford's Christmas party. According to Mae Whitehead, when Todd instructed her to call the Ford home Saturday to accept the party invitation, she also asked her to obtain permission to bring a guest. Although Whitehead did not know who this person was, her testimony paralleled and to some extent corroborated that of Martha Ford. If there was anything to Ford's testimony, one had to ask who would so surprise or scandalize Ford that she would "drop dead" when she opened the door and found him or her standing next to Thelma?[10]

One person who would fit the bill among Thelma's friends was ex-husband Pat DiCicco. Rochester revealed he had enlisted the help of the NYPD to serve a summons on DiCicco.[11] "We have asked DiCicco to come back, hoping he may assist us in arriving at the facts," Rochester explained, and went on to caution reporters:

> We are not pointing the finger of suspicion at anyone. We are anxious to learn from Mr. DiCicco, for whom a subpoena has been issued, whether there was anything in Miss Todd's life that might lead him to believe she was murdered.[12]

The message of the telegram Rochester sent to DiCicco, however, was curt.[13] "Your hasty departure raises numerous questions concerning your wife's death," it observed, then asked that he return to Los Angeles to appear before the Grand Jury the following Monday.[14] DiCicco, who had been staying at the Hotel Delmonico in New York City, was now at his family's farm at Smithtown on Long Island.[15] He had already blasted the investigation, calling it "absurd" and the work of politicians eager for headlines. Like the police, he believed the death an accident.[16]

Despite his annoyance with the inquiry, DiCicco was willing to cooperate. On receiving Rochester's telegram, he responded by telegraph the following day.[17] On Saturday, he spoke via telephone with Rochester, who granted him permission to stay in New York until after Christmas and to return to Los Angeles by airplane on Friday.[18]

Rochester also announced the Grand Jury was subpoenaing DiCicco's Saturday evening companion, the beautiful film actress, Margaret Lindsay. Miss Lindsay, whose birth name was Margaret Keis, was a twenty-five-year-old Iowan who had come to Los

Angeles by way of a stage career in England. In addition to three 1935 Jimmy Cagney films, *Devil Dogs of the Air, G-Men*, and *Frisco Kid*, she had recently co-starred with Bette Davis and Paul Muni in *Bordertown*. Because this film included a scene in which an automobile running in a closed garage serves as a murder weapon, the *Daily News* compared it to Todd's mysterious death. Her latest film, *Personal Maids Secret*, was currently featured at the Hollywood and Downtown theaters. According to Deputy District Attorney Blalock, the investigators wanted to ask her about the events at the Trocadero—particularly, anything that might have led her to suspect Todd planned a rendezvous later that night.[19]

In light of Ernie Peters' claim that Todd told him she had an appointment at 1:55 that morning and rumors DiCicco and Todd were thinking of remarrying, investigators wondered whether Lindsay suspected the former couple planned a late-night rendezvous.[20]

While the investigation continued, the friends, relatives, and fans of Thelma Todd went about the sorrowful task of bidding farewell to the beloved actress. Patsy Kelly, her movie partner and close friend, watched over her body at Pierce Brothers funeral parlor, a mission revival building on West Washington Boulevard. Another of Todd's close friends, Dorothy Callahan, sat with her. The following morning, at 8:00, the casket was opened for public viewing. Dressed in blue satin pajamas with a high neck, Thelma lay in an orchid-colored casket, her shoulders and face uncovered, with a corsage of pink camellias and lilies of the valley clasped in one of her hands. A single blonde curl fell over her right eye. A blanket of white roses and lilies of the valley spread over the lower, closed half of the casket, and a barricade flowers from her friends and relatives separated the casket from the passing mourners. Prominent among the floral displays was a large wreath of white roses and green ferns from Roland West, crossed by a white ribbon and imprinted with "Alison," the stage name he had bestowed on Thelma when he tried to transform her career from comedy to drama in *Corsair*. Other floral tributes came from Harvey Priester, Charlie Chaplin, Stan Laurel and Oliver Hardy, and several persons connected with gambling circles, Eddie Mannix, Frank and Vic Orsatti. A photograph of Thelma sat on a table in the middle of the room.[21]

The police worried Todd's funeral might provoke a riot like that which attended Rudolph Valentino's in New York several years before, but the mourners, numbering 10-12,000 and predominantly young and female, were quiet and orderly, shuffling past the bier over a period of five hours. The funeral services themselves took place at 3:30 in the afternoon at Forest Lawn's Wee Kirk of the Heather chapel. Approximately 200 of Todd's friends listened to Harold L. Proppe, reverend of the Hollywood Baptist Church, where Todd and her mother attended services, describe her as "one of the most genuine persons alive."

Among the guests were some who already figured in the mystery of her death and some who were yet to do so. Roland West escorted her mother, while Harvey Priester, who had taken care of the funeral arrangements, directed the morticians. Also attending were Sid Grauman, Hal Roach, Mr. and Mrs. Stanley Lupino and their daughter, Ida, Sally Eilers, Patsy Kelly, the Oliver Hardys and Stan Laurels, Ivan Lebedeff, ZaSu Pitts, Charley Chase, Thelma Dodge, Joseph Schenck, Mr. and Mrs. Wallace Ford, Rudolph Schafer and his wife, Mr. and Mrs. Eddie Mannix, Charles Smith, Zeppo Marx, Mae Whitehead, Ronald Button and his wife, and a surprise mourner, Los Angeles political boss Kent Kane Parrot. After the services, as Jack Luden stood by on the request of her mother, Thelma's body was cremated and her ashes delivered to her mother.[22]

While the funeral was over, the mystery of Todd's death continued. New issues and questions would arise with each edition of the local presses; problems earlier resolved would become entangled and perplexing again; new angles would appear as the investigators chipped away at the old. "It may take us two weeks to dispose of this case, which is not one puzzle, but a score of puzzles," Grand Jury foreman Rochester would proclaim the following Monday. However accurate was his conception of the mystery, his optimism would prove unwarranted.

Already problems that had seemed laid to rest were being resurrected. Although Detective Bruce Clark declared during his Coroner's Jury testimony that Thelma's shoes showed scuffing from her climb up the hillside, Deputy District Attorney Johnson emerged from a meeting with Rochester to announce he was dissatisfied with the police examination of the slippers.[23] Some observers judged that Todd's slippers should have shown more wear from a climb up the hill from her apartment; that they did not was evidence she had not made the climb. And, as Johnson argued, "If she didn't walk to the garage how did she get there?"[24]

To resolve the matter and to test the effects of a climb up the hill to the garage from Todd's apartment on a woman of Todd's age and build, Rochester and Johnson arranged for a woman "operative" of approximately Todd's height, weight, and age, dressed in an evening gown and wearing "satin silver slippers," to reenact the purported death walk.[25] Unfortunately, the results of this test, inconsistently reported in the newspapers at the time, resolved nothing; the issue of the shoes would puzzle the press and public for weeks, then decades.

The death walk reenactment was only one of several experiments performed after the Coroner's Inquest. On Sunday, Investigators Cavett, Joe Whitehead and Police Chemist Pinker began a series of tests at the garage to determine the answers to several questions. How quickly did the phaeton produce carbon monoxide? How long would it run in the closed garage? Could the engine be heard in the upstairs apartment where Smith lived? Was the automobile moved after Robert Anderson backed it into the garage Sunday morning?

The first issue, the time it would take the phaeton to produce a lethal quantity of carbon monoxide, had been addressed already on Friday when police placed two lovebirds in the garage, started the automobile, and closed the garage doors. The lovebirds having done their duty, the investigators evidently felt the need for a more accurate measurement of the phaeton's exhaust. This time, with reporters looking on, Detective Lieutenant Whitehead climbed behind the wheel of the phaeton with a watch in his hand. Police Chemist Ray Pinker closed the garage door and Whitehead started the engine. After a minute, Whitehead pounded at the door, coughing and clamoring for air, his eyes watering and nostrils stinging. "I was nearly fainting," he told reporters later. "The engine was running at only idling speed but gases filled the garage almost instantly." After letting him out, Pinker (a man "familiar with gases," according to the *Los Angeles Times*) sniffed the garage air and proclaimed, "It would just about do it now."[26]

This test seemed to prove the phaeton produced a lethal amount of carbon monoxide rapidly. At least this was the spin the newspapers, undoubtedly on the authority of the investigators, put on the results, ignoring the fact that carbon monoxide is an odorless gas.[27] It was hard to argue with the proposition that the exhaust of the phaeton's 12-cylinder engine would put out a deadly quantity of gas if given enough time. But would its engine run long enough in a closed garage to produce a fatal amount of noxious gas?

Complicating this question was a problem first raised by Jewel Carmen when she spoke with police. "Water has carried off some of the ceiling plaster," West's estranged wife reported, "Leaving holes in the ceiling." The holes made the garage "entirely too well ventilated," for Thelma to have died there from carbon monoxide. At the Coroner's inquest, West confirmed the ceiling damage. However, the following day, Charles Smith, the tenant in the upstairs apartment, told reporters that though a section of plaster had been removed to prevent dampness the "hole" did not go clear through the ceiling.[28] Additionally, according to Carmen, the garage had "extra ventilating pipes" which "would have kept the place clear of gas—even with an auto motor running and the doors closed."[29]

Another problem the detectives had to solve was why, having run long enough to lull Todd to her death, the automobile's engine stopped with several gallons yet remaining in its tank. To do so, they conducted a series of simple experiments, starting the engine, closing the garage doors, and letting the engine idle until it stalled. On the first trial, starting cold, the motor ran for 2 minutes and 40 seconds. Joe Whitehead opened the garage door to let in air, then closed it again and restarted the engine. This time, it ran for 4 minutes and 55 seconds. On the third attempt, with the door closed, the motor, thoroughly warmed with its throttle slightly advanced, ran 46 minutes and 40 seconds.[30]

If, as the investigators maintained, the phaeton's engine could produce a lethal amount of carbon monoxide in just two minutes, there was little question the automobile was deadly over a longer span. Even without a driver to pump the accelerator, it ran well past the two-minute mark on its first try. In addition, the tests proved empirically that the automobile could run long enough to kill its occupant and then shut off by itself, with fuel yet remaining in the tank. Why it would suddenly stop was still a matter of some conjecture, however. The police investigators argued that, by filling the interior of the garage with carbon monoxide, the motor eventually starved itself of oxygen.[31] However, Autopsy Surgeon Wagner disputed this view, observing the garage was not air-tight—as the police later themselves demonstrated with a candle that wavered in the slight draft flowing from the bottom to the top of the doors.[32]

After consulting with mechanics on the characteristics of the phaeton, the press advanced another possibility. According to the *Daily News*, the automobile

> [i]s equipped with a brake booster which operates off the intake of the carburetor. When the emergency brake is set, air from the carburetor is utilized to keep a constant pressure and a set brake might have milked the carburetor of too much air to continue mixing.[33]

In addition, Todd's phaeton had its "blow-by" problem: the cylinders were "out of round," permitting oil to blow by the pistons. At idle, compression of the piston within the chamber could jet oil on the engine, possibly even into the car's floorboards. As Robert Cooper testified before the Coroner's Jury, the same process could result in oil being forced into the spark plugs, which would then foul, stalling the automobile.[34]

Roland West had raised a third issue for the investigators in his Coroner's Jury testimony when he pointed out that Charles Smith, the café's elderly bookkeeper, lived with his wife in the apartment above the garage. Why hadn't Smith heard the noisy automobile starting up, West wondered when the windows of the apartment were open? Although Bob Anderson, who took care of the car, corrected West's assertion that the automobile "would waken anyone" when starting, it seemed a point worth pursuing, especially when linked with Jewel Carmen's comments on the broken plaster in the garage's ceiling which may have admitted fumes into the apartment as well as noise.

To resolve the issue, police chemist Ray Pinker and Smith stood directly above the car in the latter's living room while a detective started and then idled the motor in the garage below them. Though the garage doors were open, the two men heard a whine and then nothing more. Only when the detective raced the engine was "the vaguest of sounds" perceptible. The noise was clearly not loud enough to awaken a man. "The wind and sea that night would have drowned out the engine," the apartment's elderly tenant observed, "even going fast."[35] As for exhaust fumes entering the apartment, the investigators found no openings in the garage's ceiling that might have leaked fumes.[36]

Finally, the various reports of sightings of Miss Todd prompted the detectives to examine the exhaust marks on the rear wall of the garage. After Robert Anderson parked the car in the same position that he had Sunday morning, a detective fired up the automobile's engine. The black marks produced by the car's large exhaust pipe, which spread out to a three- or four-inch flat end, looked identical to those already on the wall. Inexplicably, the investigators proclaimed the experiment proved that the phaeton had not moved since the bartender parked it in the garage Sunday.[37]

While examining the death scene on Friday, DA Investigator Tom Cavett noticed dried blood on the running board of the phaeton that LAPD detectives had overlooked. About three inches in diameter, the blotch was beyond the spot where Miss Todd's head had hung. Unlike the blood already found—around her mouth, on the car seat eight inches inside the door and on the metal strip of the inner front door panel of the automobile—it was difficult to see how this blotch could have stained the running board unless at some point Todd had been outside the car after she started to bleed. Cavett speculated Todd tried to escape from the automobile and flee the garage in her death struggle, but slumped back into the driver's seat as the monoxide overcame her. This scenario would explain not only the blotch of blood but also the fact that the driver's side door of the automobile was partly ajar when Mae Whitehead found her body.[38]

Captain Wallis immediately ordered that scrapings from the new blood stain be included in chemical tests on other blood spots in the garage. According to the *Los Angeles Times*, the tests were based on the "known fact that monoxide cannot get into the free blood . . . but only into blood as it courses through the lungs." If scrapings from blood found on the front seat and running board showed traces of monoxide, then Thelma bled while under the influence of the gas. Clean samples would raise the specter of foul play: they would indicate injuries suffered before the actress inhaled the phaeton's noxious exhaust.[39]

As straightforward as the test seemed, reports of results were surprisingly muddled. Several Los Angeles newspapers stated on the afternoon of the 26th that no traces of monoxide were found on the bloodstain. However, they cautioned readers that, according to Autopsy Surgeon Wagner, the "results of the analysis were inconclusive from a scientific standpoint as a negative result would be possible whether or not she died in the car." However, the following morning the *Los Angeles Times* reported Captain Wallis claimed the tests results indicated carbon monoxide was in the blotch found on the running board. It would be several weeks before the full report of the findings were released.[40]

However ambiguous the results of the various tests conducted in the garage, it was clear the investigators, chemists, and lab technicians expected and perhaps hoped they would support the accidental death by monoxide scenario. Still, while the tests were underway, there were more signs Todd's death was not accidental. The most dramatic of these came from the Trocadero's headwaiter, who served the Lupino party and the Grauman table where Todd visited and afterward called Roland West to inform him she was about to leave the Trocadero. The headwaiter, Alex Hounie, complained he had received several threats in the last few days. The first came by postcard to the Trocadero on Thursday, the 19th. Words cut from newspapers and pasted to the postcard ordered Hounie, addressed simply as "Mr. Alex/café employee," to "WITHHELD [sic] TESTIMONY OR KIDNAP TRIP." At eleven p.m. that night, as he drove home along Sunset Boulevard, two men in another car forced his automobile to the curb at Sweetzer Avenue. "You've had your warning!" one of them shouted before they sped away. Hounie tried to follow to get the car's license plate, but lost the car in traffic.[41]

The threats against Hounie baffled police, who pointed out that nothing in the testimony he was scheduled to give the Grand Jury the following week, which mainly revolved around Todd's dinner and drinking at the Trocadero, was significant enough to incriminate anybody.[42] One newspaper speculated the threats might have arisen from Hounie's pending testimony in another case, which involved "a matter that certain persons would wish kept quiet."[43] Nevertheless, deputies from the Los Angeles County Sheriff's Office guarded the terrified waiters' West Hollywood home and an armed escort accompanied him to his two places of employment, the Vendome Café and the Café Trocadero.

The threats drew the attention of federal authorities as well. After United States District Attorney Peirson M. Hall and John Harold Hanson, the new head of the United States Department of Justice in Southern California, reviewed the case, they assigned their "crack sleuth," Elton Billings, to look into reports that Todd received two extortion notes shortly before her death.[44]

Unfortunately, neither the federal investigators nor the sheriff's deputies were able to scare off the threateners, who continued to plague Hounie even after he offered his meager testimony before the Grand Jury. On the day before Christmas, he received another warning, this time by telephone. There was no question as to the purpose of this latest threat. The anonymous caller warned Hounie to "stay out of that Thelma Todd case." If he didn't, he would be killed.[45]

EIGHT: THE PUBLIC CLAMOR

> Like moths flitting around bright lights at night, there are invariably unpredictable people who find themselves bewitched by the white glare of publicity illuminating famous people involved in front-page news stories.
> — Florabel Muir[1]

As if the claims of Martha Ford, W.F. Persson, and Jewel Carmen were not troubling enough, the investigators found themselves besieged by new reports the dead actress cavorted about town Sunday afternoon and evening. An anonymous caller told police he had seen Todd driving in Hollywood Sunday afternoon.[2] A Santa Monica city official and his 21-year-old son also claimed they spotted Thelma Todd in her phaeton with a short, slight blond girl driving west on Wilshire Boulevard Sunday around 5 p.m.[3] More substantive was the claim by Sara Kane Carter, described by one paper as a "40-year-old, serious-looking widow":[4]

> I saw Thelma Todd a few minutes after 4 o'clock, Sunday afternoon. She walked into the Laurel Drug Company store at the northeast corner of Laurel Canyon and Sunset boulevards and she went right into the pay phone booth and talked over the telephone for five or six minutes. Thelma ... I call her that because I was a fan of hers and had seen her many times, in person and in pictures—was wearing a brown fur coat and a bluish evening gown with a metallic silver sheen. Her blonde curls were especially striking. I had left my home at 8181 Utica Drive in Laurel Canyon at 10 minutes to 4, and I'm positive it was a few minutes after I saw Thelma. I've seen lots of screen stars in that store in the six years I've lived in Laurel Canyon ... . I've seen Thelma Todd there and other places enough to be positive it was she.[5]

After observing Todd, Carter said she exclaimed, "These Californians wear evening dress at the strangest times, don't they?" to two nearby store clerks.[6]

Carter's story placed Todd at the Laurel Drug Store at approximately 4:05, roughly the same time Martha Ford received her mysterious phone call. Investigators noted the Ford caller's question about a "short cut" via Ventura Boulevard to her Laurel Canyon home made sense if the phone call originated from Laurel and Sunset. From that point, a driver might want to know whether to take Laurel Canyon Boulevard or the Cahuenga pass and Ventura Boulevard.[7]

The proprietor of a Christmas tree lot at the corner of Euclid and Wilshire in Santa Monica and his employee also claimed to have spotted Todd on Sunday. On Friday, December 20, J. E. Cummings and the lot's security guard, Arthur San Juan, told Santa Monica police detectives John Grier and J.E. Edwards that Todd, dressed in a blue gown, visited their lot early Monday morning in the company of a young man. The pair picked out a tree and ordered it sprayed silver and then drove off, promising to pick the tree up later. They never returned, however. Cummings and San Juan described the young man in her company as about twenty-six years old, with a dark complexion, black hair and heavy black eyebrows. Fashionably dressed, he wore a longhair overcoat on top of a brown suit and sported a navy blue hat. The police showed the two men a photograph of Todd. They identified her as their customer.[8]

On Tuesday, the 24th, Cummings and San Juan contacted the Santa Monica police again. This time they complained they had been threatened. Cummings told police he was on the lot Monday night with his finance, Helen San Juan, Arthur's sister, when two men pulled up across the street in a dark-colored sedan. While one man stood by the car, the other asked Cummings what he remembered about seeing Todd.

"Listen, fellow, you know you shouldn't bother so much about nothing," the man told him after Cummings finished speaking. "There's been too much talking about it [the Todd case] and if I were you I wouldn't have much more to do with it."

Shortly before midnight the same night, Arthur San Juan was asleep in a parked car. Two men in dark overcoats covered the car doors. One reached into the driver's side and banged San Juan's head against the seat. "Are you Cummings?" he demanded of San Juan and called him a liar when he replied in the negative. Drawing a pistol from his pocket, he warned San Juan to keep his mouth shut about the Todd case. The two men then left in an automobile with covered license plates. After hearing of the threats, the Santa Monica police placed a guard at the lot.[9]

These reports were the most credible of the many that flooded authorities during the first weeks of the Todd investigation. By Christmas, they had checked numerous claims—including several anonymous telephone calls—that Todd had been sighted after Sunday morning, often in the company of a "dark-haired man." The investigators claimed most too insubstantial to bother with and the rest a waste of time.[10]

Overall, the authorities dismissed the sightings, some of which came after the details of the case became public.[11] Indeed, they seemed almost eager to do so. For instance, Deputy District Attorney Johnson assiduously pursued the rumor that another 1932 Lincoln phaeton with a blonde woman and a dark man cruised about Hollywood on Sunday. If true, this rumor would dispose of many of the sighting claims wholesale. However, investigators learned the automobile in question was not driven that Sunday in the places where Todd's car was spotted.[12]

While the investigators could ignore many of the Sunday Todd sightings, those of Carmen, Ford, and Persson were not so easily dismissed. They would get further attention the following week during the Grand Jury investigation. Cigar storeowner Persson would repeat his claim that a haggard, exhausted woman he identified as Todd entered his cigar store at Eighth and Figueroa around 9:00 a.m. Sunday morning to use the telephone.[13] According to Persson, the woman was not wearing a hat but was dressed in a dust-covered "blue sequined dinner gown" and dirty "high heel blue shoes." Her bearing was unsteady, a condition he attributed to either alcohol, drugs, or a hangover.

According to Persson, the woman handed him a nickel and asked him to dial a phone number for her. Although he could not remember the alphabetic prefix of the phone number other than to guess it was either GL (Gladstone) or PR (Prospect), he recalled the following digits as 7771. As he dialed, the woman slumped against the counter with a "dazed, fixed look." "Miss Todd seemed to be struggling with some sorrow and laboring under some stress of mind," the storeowner recalled. He handed her the phone as it began to ring. While she talked in the booth, a dark, heavy-set, middle-aged man stalked up and down the alley outside, carrying a fur coat.

After the woman finished her conversation, she asked another customer—a man Persson could not identify—to dial a second number, this time without giving Persson a nickel payment for the call. A few minutes later, the man from the alley came into the cigar store. Unlike the woman, he seemed very much at ease. Smiling, he handed her the fur coat. The couple then left the store and walked over to the steps of a nearby church. There they sat for about a half hour.[14]

Persson admitted he had never seen the actress in person before Sunday, but insisted he recognized her from fan magazines in his store. Other pedestrians in the neighborhood also reported seeing the heavy-set man and the blonde woman sitting on the church steps.[15] In addition, two cigar store customers, Robert E. Fisher and Harold Wollcott, were also ready to testify.

Because of the close match between Todd's death garments and Persson's description of the clothing the blonde woman wore, Grand Jury Foreman Rochester had Todd's clothing and another evening dress brought out to test whether the two cigar store customers could identify the correct one before the Grand Jury.[16] The results proved somewhat mixed. Wollcott demurred a bit, observing only that Todd's shimmering evening gown "looked like" the one worn by the mysterious young woman. Fisher, however, was more certain. "Yes, I think that's the dress," he told the jury, according to an unidentified source, adding theatrically "I think that's the dress worn by a beautiful blonde woman I saw making a telephone call in a cigar store at Eight and Figueroa at 9 o'clock on Sunday morning, December 15. And I think the woman who wore it was Thelma Todd." After identifying the young woman as Todd from a photograph of the actress, Fisher admitted he was "not sure about [Todd's] shoes. They are a little different . . . from those worn by the woman in the cigar store," he noted, "But, of course, I didn't observe her shoes very closely."[17]

Jewel Carmen would also testify before the Grand Jury. Reportedly overwhelmed by grief over Todd's death and the stress brought on by questions from reporters and investigators, Carmen was under a physician's care on Friday, December 20, refusing all visitors and phone calls. However, one reporter succeeded in talking to a woman at her household, who told him the ex-actress had recanted her statement about seeing Todd. "Miss Carmen thought at the time it was Thelma, but she knows now she was mistaken," the woman explained. "The police were wrong in quoting her as having said she followed the car." Although the woman did not reveal her identity, she claimed she could speak for Miss Carmen. Before the Grand Jury, however, Carmen repeated the story she told police, though she admitted she could not positively identify the woman in the automobile as Todd.[18]

The Grand Jury would also hear Martha Ford, who repeated the testimony she gave before the Coroner's Jury. "Nothing in the world could change my story," she told one reporter.[19] Despite her doggedness, her initial mistaking of the caller for another friend named Velma taxed her credibility. Apparently mindful of the problem, Ford told a reporter she had spoken with Velma since the party and confirmed Velma did not call her on the day of the party.[20]

However, comments by Mae Whitehead and several other witnesses that Thelma abhorred the nickname "Hot Toddy," which Ford claimed Todd used when she called on Sunday, tended to discredit her story. "I never heard her use such a name, either Hot Toddy or Toddy, but I do know that she objected to its use," Todd's maid told the Grand Jury. "She became very angry when one of her friends called her that in a joking manner." The deputy district attorney checked the point with several other witnesses as they appeared to testify and was told repeatedly the same thing: Thelma Todd did not like to be called "Hot Toddy."[21]

As for Sara Kane Carter, the woman who claimed she saw Thelma Todd in a drugstore on Laurel Canyon Boulevard, the DA and the Grand Jury did not even call her to appear. However, both the authorities and the *Daily News* checked the automatic tape attached to the phone at the Laurel Drug store and found no record of a call to the Ford home.[22] In case Todd stopped somewhere else to place the call to the Ford home, the phone company checked the tapes of other public phones in the area, but again came up empty-handed.[23]

As reports of post-Sunday morning sightings of Todd poured in, the more sensationalistic papers began to play up the responses of the city's supernaturalist community to her death. Los Angeles was already famous for its lunatic fringe of faith healers, psychics, and illuminati, and it was too much to expect they would refrain from dancing on the stage built on the death of a famous actress. One of the chief benefactors of Todd's death was an astrologist named Mahion Norvell, who in December of the previous year had predicted, "A mysterious and sensational tragedy . . . will result in the death of a well known blonde actress." Norvell, a slim, dark man in his late twenties, was said to be filmland's favorite fortune-teller, with a list of clients that "reads like a movie colony directory."[24]

Norvell had described the death at the time as "surrounded by a drinking party." The astrologer claimed after Todd's death that he had known she would die in late 1935, but, as a matter of policy, he had not revealed her identity at that time. Norvell's other predictions for 1935, a separation, divorce, and quick remarriage for Clark Gable, a divorce for Jean Harlow, and romance for Mae West had also in part proven true, so he was undoubtedly eager to offer his prognostications for 1936. Among them was a prediction of war between Russia and Japan in 1936 and that in 1940 the United States would engage in a "short, deadly conflict."[25]

Hollywood's penchant for spiritualists and seers had already entered the Todd case by way of Mother Grey, Jewel Carmen's live-in spiritualist. It was not surprising that Todd herself was linked to Southern California's community of mystics, or that the spiritualist in question had material aspirations as well. On December 21, one newspaper reported the dead actress had been a client of Joe Alperson, alias Prince Omwah, a "starry-robed West Hollywood seer," who, like Norvell, had a large following among the Hollywood set. While he was on trial for an alleged threat on the life of spiritual investigator Dr. U. L. di Ghillini, three women claimed Alperson, whose other, probably more fitting pseudonym was "Spike," had bilked them for over $3,000 under the guise of collecting donations for a spiritualistic temple. According to reports heard by Detective Lieutenant Merle Swan of the LAPD bunco squad, Thelma was also out $8,000 to the mystic. Bert Wallis, however, announced he was not investigating Alperson in connection with Todd's death.[26]

Inevitably, the psychics offered solutions to the Todd mystery. One woman claimed the actress was murdered by a "gorilla man" whose face the psychic discovered in Bert Wallis's ear when she turned upside down a published photo of him examining Todd's corpse. The *Herald Express* was either impressed or amused enough to feature this story on the front-page of their 12/20/35 edition complete with an upside down close-up of Wallis' ear.[27]

Another connection to the spiritualist community was more to the point. A numerologist named Patricia D'Este, who also claimed ties to many film stars, reported a conversation she had with the actress three weeks before her death at Attorney A. Ronald Button's home during a party honoring Jack Warner. Her account cast a light on Todd's state of mind at the time:

> I was reading on the porch for each of the guests as they came to me. Miss Todd was one of those who came. I told her: 'You have a brilliant future, but you have had a hard time to attain the position you occupy. You deserve a great deal of credit.'
>
> I nearly fell out of my chair at her next words. She said to me: 'I don't want

any future—I don't want to live any more.'

I thought for a minute she must be joking.

But she was not smiling. She gazed at me calmly, seemingly emotionless. Her eyes were clear. I repeated to her that her future was 'bright.'

'I don't care whether my future is bright,' she said. Then without anything further along this line, she asked me 'Will I marry this year?'

'You will if that is your desire,' I told her.

'Will I be happy if I do marry?' was her next question.

'I cannot answer that question unless you give me the name of the man,' I told her. She did not answer. She refused to give me any name.

'Will I go to Europe?' was her next question. I told her she would take a trip, but whether it was over water, I did not know.

. . . .

Thelma Todd was smiling when she came to me. She was smiling when she shook my hand and left. But she said one strange thing just before she walked away. She looked directly at me and said, 'You have a tooth in your mouth that needs to come out. It is affecting your eyes.'

'I'll see to it at once,' I told her, although I did not have a bad tooth, that I know of. 'Send me the bill,' she said, as she smiled and walked away.[28]

D'Este also reported Todd inquired whether she should remain in the business she was in or make a change. "I told her," D'Este reported, "that she might make a change about the first of the year, or possibly a little before the first of the year."[29]

Besides adding an aura of fatalism to the Todd mystery, D'Este's story suggested there might have been another side to the optimistic and cheerful portrait invariably painted by Thelma's friends, one more anxious and troubled.

A few days later, another mystic entered the mystery with even more fanfare than had D'Este. A. R. Blanchard, an "elderly, gray-haired man," who described himself as a Spiritualist, visited the Hall of Justice on the day after Christmas to proclaim he knew the solution to the mysterious death. Although he wanted to speak only with Grand Jury Foreman Rochester, Blanchard was first accosted by Deputy DA Johnson and DA investigators Winn and Yarrow, who met with him for a half hour. Although Rochester left the building without seeing him, the elderly medium haunted the Hall of Justice corridors the next day, pressing invitations to a séance featuring the spirit of the late comedienne into the hands of Grand Jury witnesses.[30]

It was clear the mystery fascinated the public, and not just the fringe personalities who pressed into its limelight. "From coast to coast, 'Thelma Todd' and the bizarre circumstances of her weird death seemingly furnishes the chief topic of conversation— in homes, business offices, street corner chats, on trolley cars—almost everywhere," observed one reporter, who noted the comedienne was never as well known during her life. Another reporter had overheard debates about the cause of her death outside the Pierce Brothers funeral home as her body lay in state; most thought it was murder.[31] Little of the public discourse about her death made it to print, one noteworthy exception being a letter to the editor warning of a cover-up similar to that in the William Desmond Taylor case.[32] Yet many citizens with theories on the case felt compelled to put them on paper and send them to authorities; DA Fitts claimed "crank" letters offering solutions to the case had inundated his office and the Homicide Squad. One letter writer from Pennsylvania even expressed his suspicions about Todd's death in a letter to J. Edgar Hoover. Hoover wrote back, disclaiming any authority over the case.[33]

The mystery was a boon for the newspapers. The *Herald Express* noted the story sold over 46,000 copies of its Monday evening edition, a significant figure even if it was lower than two other major news stories of the last decade, the airplane crash and death of Will Rogers and Wiley Post (110,000 extra copies) and the capture of William Hickman, a notorious child-killer (165,000 papers). The front-page treatment the story continued to receive, often accompanied by blaring headlines and promises of upcoming sensations, attested it was a winner for the local journals.

At the café, which reopened for business on Thursday, December 19, the public's interest in the mystery was apparent in the scores of souvenir hunters, who stole napkins, sugar bowls, silverware, and, especially, sugar cubes wrapped with paper featuring a picture of Thelma. One enterprising collector even tried to chip away a brick on the exterior wall of the café. Unfortunately for West and restaurant manager Schafer, the souvenir hunters displaced regular customers, causing cash receipts for the business to fall off. A reporter described some of them when the Grand Jurors visited

> . . . the radio was pouring the saccharine strains of "Lover, Come Back to Me," through a muted sound system. And in the bar the curious trippers who flock to the Sidewalk Cafe daily and ask questions like: "Where was Thelma murdered?" were milling around and plying a shrugging bartender with endless queries There was a giggling red-haired girl, whose really radiant beauty was marred a bit by just a touch too much of drink, and her gray-haired squire who seemed a trifle ill at ease.

the café two weeks later, on January 3:[34]

> There were several women, fat and round and soft as soggy dumplings, who were annoyed because they couldn't go upstairs and watch the grand jury at work. There were a couple of bluejackets, who strolled in with a girl friend, and the boys apparently hadn't been reading the papers, for one of them asked:
> "Say, does Thelma Todd ever come around this joint?"

Sightseers also cruised by the garage on Posetano, stopping to pose for photographs before the closed doors. One man explored a "deserted mountain cabin" in the hills behind the restaurant and found a napkin and saucer from the café and a small amount of Canned Heat, a wood alcohol jelly from which desperate drinkers commonly extracted a juice during prohibition. After turning over his findings to Capt. Blaine Steed, the man, Howard Ross of Hollywood, declared his theory: "She was kidnapped and held in that mountain cabin until her abductors forced her to die by carbon monoxide." The investigators were unpersuaded.[35]

The newspapers' view of the mystery is easier to establish. Ranging from hyperbolic incantations of the mysterious elements to sober recapitulations of the facts, the news stories conveyed bewilderment and fascination with the developing drama. "Unexplained hours. Vitally important minutes. Strange lapses," intoned Hearst's *Los Angeles Examiner* with characteristic melodrama. "Across the face of the Thelma Todd mystery, the hands of a clock loom significantly. And those hands are entangled in the stray skeins of discrepancy, which characterize the amazing case."[36] The *Examiner's* sister journal, *the Los Angeles Herald and Express*, featured a photograph of several investigators standing before the death garage. "WHAT HAPPENED BEHIND THESE DOORS?" was inscribed overhead. The article declared that the mystery involved "as notable a cast of characters as has been assembled for any real life drama for many a day."[37]

As the Grand Jury prepared to investigate the death for evidence of murder, the newspapers speculated brazenly on the possibilities as they tried to arrange the evidence of the case in reasonable patterns. *The Los Angeles Herald and Express* wrote[38]

> Picture Thelma Todd, weary from the long night of the gay party, the dancing, the champagne drinking, the ride to and from the party, slumped resting in the car.
>
> Picture some angry person who found her there in the dark, low in spirits, low in vitality. A sudden blow. A fainting woman, a woman who would not forget when she awoke in the bright of day.
>
> A cunning thought. A motor started suddenly. A garage door closed. A woman still unconscious. The lurking slayer outside, watching and waiting for that sneaking death to come.
>
> But some stir of consciousness returns. A pathetic, weak cry, an effort to arise, a door latch turned and a door partly opened. The woman is trying to escape. The slayer slips in, strikes again, the struggling form wilts. Death comes this time. The poison wins.

Less sinister death scenarios were also aired. Capt. Don Wilkie, described as a "former ace of the United States secret service," speculated that Todd had slept in the garage as a prank, arose late the next afternoon after twelve hours sleep, called Mrs. Ford, then returned to the garage to start the engine of the phaeton, "intending to back out and force the unlocked swinging garage door open, as she went." But, exhausted by the climb up and down the hill, she had breathed too deeply the carbon monoxide fumes and perished.

Wilkie's theory was full of holes, not the least of which, as the editor of the paper dutifully pointed out, was that the doors did not swing but slid, and the automobile was backed, not headed, into the garage. Overall, it was a sloppy effort to resolve the mystery's confusing and contradictory facts.[39]

With so much contradictory evidence, it was easier simply to note the issues of the mystery, a strategy used by several papers. Under the heading, "25 Unanswered Todd Questions Are Asked," the *Evening Herald and Express* ticked off some the major issues:

When did Thelma die?

Where did she go after Chauffeur Ernest Peters deposited her in the doorway of her cafe at 3:30 a.m. Sunday?

Why did she not attempt to awaken Roland West, her partner, if she were locked out?

If she went immediately to the garage where her body was found, why did not Charles Smith, watchman, sleeping directly over the garage, awaken if the motor of her car was started, as police believe?

If she went to the garage because she was cold, why did she get into her open car instead of West's sedan?

Did Martha Ford really hear the voice of Miss Todd at 4:10 p.m. Sunday?

If it were Miss Todd's voice, where was she?

Where had she been since 3:30 a.m.?

What prevented her from appearing at Mrs. Ford's cocktail party in half an hour, as she supposedly promised in the telephone call? Who was the mysterious guest she promised to bring in the telephone call? Who was the promised to bring that would "surprise" everyone?

What was his or her connection with the case?

Where was Miss Todd going at 11 p.m. Sunday night when Mrs. Roland West said she saw her?

What time did she leave the Trocadero party—3:15 a.m. as Chauffeur Ernest Peters claimed or earlier, as others believed?

Why did she delay her departure from the night club when she asked Sid Grauman, theater owner, to telephone West at 1:55 a.m. that she was leaving immediately?

Why was .13 of 1 per cent alcohol found in her brain when Peters claimed she was entirely sober during the ride home?

Why had she failed to turn over two new extortion notes to federal agents?

Why did she make a telephone call from the Trocadero ladies' room at 11:45 p.m. Saturday evening and to whom?

What connection is there with "gambling interests" that reportedly sought to establish gaming at her Sidewalk café?

Why did her mother, Mrs. Alice Todd, cry out "My daughter has been murdered!" when informed of her death?

Why did Miss Todd refuse to allow Peters to accompany her to the door as he usually did when he deposited her outside the café?

Why did Mrs. West wait three days before informing authorities she had seen Miss Todd at 11 p.m. Sunday night?

Why was West so astounded when asked at the coroner's inquest if he knew that Miss Todd intended remarrying her former husband, Pasquele DiCicco?

These were not all the good questions, nor were all these questions good ones. Some reflected the reporters' own confusion more than actual difficulties of the case. Nevertheless, after five days of investigation, the list—and others like it in competing journals—indexed the mystery's growing complexity. And there was more to come.

NINE: GENTLEMEN FROM OTHER TOWNS

> ... facing the crime sleuths was another riddle, the tangle skein of loves which whirled their way about the scintillating film actress.[1]
>
> —Los Angeles Herald Express

The initial session of the Grand Jury Inquest into Thelma Todd's death took place on the fifth floor of the Hall of Justice building Monday morning, December 23. A small eager crowd of movie fans loitered in the corridors, hoping to glimpse the motion picture personalities as they arrived to testify. Reporters and photographers also prowled the hallways, popping flashbulbs as over two dozen subpoenaed witnesses arrived and departed.

First to testify was Margaret Lindsay, DiCicco's date at the Trocadero Saturday night. Decked in a dark blue serge suit and a silver fox fur, her dark hair covered by a small black hat, Lindsay appeared calm despite rumors that distress over Todd's death had driven her into seclusion over the weekend. Pausing at the door of the jury room, she flashed a broad grin at the appreciative photographers.

Sid Grauman, jaunty in a brown suit, arrived soon afterward. While he waited to testify, the theater impresario charmed reporters while lamenting the circumstances that made him, a key witness just because he "did a favor for a lovely girl."[2]

Several of the witnesses were less amiable. Martha Ford, smartly dressed and self-assured, was ready to reproach those who doubted her tale of the Sunday afternoon phone call. Ernie Peters, Todd's chauffeur, refused to pose for photographers and snarled he was "telling the truth and that's all and that's that." Roland West also shunned reporters and photographers. Grim and silent in a large polo coat, he paced the corridors with his brother-in-law, Rudolf Schafer. West's wife, Jewel Carmen, complained to reporters she was not feeling well. Her physician entreated the jury unsuccessfully to take her testimony immediately because of her fragile mental condition. For a while, her eyes clouded and her face pale, she and West huddled together in a corner of the hallway, holding hands and whispering. Eventually, she departed without testifying, having been instructed to return on Friday.[3]

In addition to the film luminaries answering the Grand Jury summons that Monday morning, eight bartenders and waiters from the Trocadero appeared. The DA deputies and jury members wanted to question them about Todd's meal Saturday night, including her drinks. Ernie Peters, Charles Smith, and Mae Whitehead would follow them in the afternoon.

Grand Jury Foreman Rochester predicted the Grand Jury's investigation into Todd's death would prove "the most exhaustive investigation" of the 1935 jury's tenure. Four sessions were planned around the Christmas holiday on Wednesday and two more the following week, on Monday and Tuesday, with probable night sessions. The early sessions would focus on witnesses who found the body or could help establish the time of death, including those who claimed to have talked with or seen Todd after Sunday morning. Although one newspaper predicted Pat DiCicco, still in New York for the holidays, would figure most prominently in the jury's investigation, Rochester himself touted Roland West as the investigation's star witness.[4]

The jury was scheduled to hear testimony at 10:00, but in preparation for the first session foreman George Rochester scheduled a preliminary 9:30 a.m. meeting. The nineteen jurors were a good cross-section of well-to-do Southern California society, reflecting the ventures and vocations of the community at large. Of its three women, one was in business, one in social work, and one a clubwoman. Among the sixteen men were three bankers, four real estate men, a financier, an inventor, and an undertaker. The foreman, George Rochester, an Atlanta, Georgia native, worked on newspapers in Idaho and Oregon before alighting in California in the 1920s. He purchased the *Long Beach Argus* in 1928, and added three other community newspapers in Paramount, Riverside, and Ventura to his small empire over the next few years.[5]

At the 9:30 meeting, the jurors received a typewritten 100 page police report prepared under the direction of Bert Wallis. The report, replete with details of the police investigation, concluded the "preponderance of evidence" indicated accident as the cause of Todd's death, the result of a series of tragic blunders that began when West locked her apartment door. Still, as Deputy District Attorney George Johnson observed, the jury would focus its investigation on the possibility that Todd was murdered. "The Grand Jury will look for murder," Johnson noted, "If murder was not possible, the Grand Jury would not be interested."[6]

Johnson's point was a critical one. In practice, the Grand Jury's activities fell broadly into two areas: investigating possible criminal behavior and conditions, such as widespread graft or organized crime, and determining whether sufficient evidence existed of a specific crime to indict a suspect for trial in Superior Court. While the jury could extend its mandate as it saw fit—notwithstanding the restraining influence of the District Attorney's office—its involvement in the Todd case was unusual. Normally, the district attorney would have brought before it the name of a specific suspect in a specific crime. In the Todd case, not only was there no identified suspect, there was no clear evidence of a crime.

The Grand Jury's investigation amounted to a search for a corpus delicti, the elements or body of a crime, initiated in part in response to the recommendation of the

Coroner's Jury that further inquiry be made into Todd's death. Ultimately, the jury was limited to determining whether Todd died as the result of a criminal act. If it found she died at the hands of another, it could take the next step and determine who appeared to have killed her and issue appropriate indictments. On the other hand, if it could not determine that another person had a hand in her death, its inquiry would conclude without further action. In such a case, it did not matter whether the jurors decided Todd was a suicide or the victim of a tragic accident, or whether they could not decide how she died. In any of these cases, it would come to the same thing: no crime had been committed and no indictment would be issued.

The findings of the jury would also have a direct impact on the public's knowledge of the testimony offered during its sessions. Without an indictment, no transcript of the proceedings, official or otherwise, would be made from the tape record of the court stenographer. In such a case, it was likely that all the public and press were ever to know about the testimony behind the jury room's closed doors would come from the witnesses, who were not sworn to secrecy, or the loose tongues of the jury members.

As it turned out, the witnesses, the Deputy District Attorneys and the jurors were all loquacious. They spoke at length with reporters outside the Grand Jury room, describing in detail the testimony that took place beyond the closed doors. Nor was foreman Rochester circumspect in his capacity as spokesman for the jury. He readily offered his observations and conclusions as the inquest progressed, and his dramatic claims that gamblers had been moving in on the Sidewalk Café and that strong evidence existed that Todd was the victim of a "monoxide murder" would set the tenor for many more sensational revelations to come.[7]

While the Grand Jury was in session late in the afternoon, an unexpected witness appeared in the hall outside, creating the day's big sensation. Ida Lupino, the beautiful young English actress, who, with her parents, hosted the party for Todd at the Trocadero Saturday, arrived at the Hall of Justice, clasping the arm of her father, Stanley. Although expected to testify eventually about Todd's activities at the Trocadero, Miss Lupino was not scheduled to testify Monday, and her appearance came as a surprise to the small crowd of reporters staking out the hallways. As it turned out, the Grand Jury room was not her destination. Instead, after talking with DA Deputies Blalock and Johnson, she and her father were escorted to the offices of the DA himself, Buron Fitts.[8]

After the meeting, the Lupinos spoke with reporters about the reason for her unexpected appearance.[9] Ida explained she had come to tell the investigators of a puzzling interaction she had with Todd at the Trocadero. Early Saturday evening, she recalled, she and Thelma "slipped off" together for a confidential chat.

"Well, Ida, what are you doing about your love life?" Thelma asked Ida coyly.

"I'm not doing anything at all," Lupino replied, "I'm too busy working right now at the studio." She then asked Thelma about her own love life.

"I'm in the midst of the most marvelous romance I've ever had with a San Francisco business man who is just too grand for words," Thelma gushed, adding "You know what gentlemen those San Franciscans are!"

"I remarked jokingly that I supposed I'd have to go to San Francisco to find a real gentleman," Ida recalled later, "And she said, 'You really should sometime, my dear.'"[10] Sensing Todd was reluctant to name the gentleman in question, Ida did not press for his name, but felt certain this love affair was behind Thelma's gaiety and happiness. Her father also recalled overhearing the conversation and characterized it to reporters as "half-joking."[11]

The disclosure of a mysterious love interest in the deceased actress' life caused an immediate sensation among reporters and investigators. Who was this mysterious "gentleman from San Francisco?" Was he the person who would cause Ford to "drop dead" with surprise or astonishment when Thelma arrived with him at the Ford party? Was he also be the last person to have seen her alive? Deputy DAs Blalock and Johnson joined Rochester in declaring it essential that they identify and talk with Thelma's secret love interest. Investigators were immediately assigned to concentrate on the gentleman from San Francisco angle.[12]

The best sources for information on Todd's romantic affairs were her close friends and relatives, but they were not entirely helpful. Alice Todd claimed she knew nothing about a San Francisco man in Thelma's life, although she conceded her daughter might have kept the man a secret from her. None of Thelma's confidantes could name him either, but ZaSu Pitts, her former partner in comedy shorts, recalled her interest in a man from "up north" a few years before. A report that she and her husband, actor's agent J. L. Woodall, lunched with Thelma and the unidentified man on the Saturday before her death brought a swift denial from the comedienne. While she confirmed she and Todd met Woodall at Perino's Restaurant for lunch after shopping together on Wednesday, the 11th, there was no fourth to their party.[13]

Somehow, the investigators learned the gentleman from San Francisco was a "wealthy sportsman of the middle-aged playboy type" currently in town for the opening of the Santa Anita race track.[14] Although they did not know his name, they pleaded for him to do the "gentlemanly" thing and reveal himself.[15]

The rumors of a secret love in Thelma's life piqued the interest of investigators. Those who claimed to have seen her on Sunday linked at least three mysterious figures to Todd. W. F. Persson and customers of his cigar store claimed a dark, heavy-set, middle-aged man joined the woman he identified as Todd after she left his store. J. E. Cummings said he saw her with a "young, handsome, foreign-appearing man" at the Santa Monica Christmas tree lot where he worked. Jewel Carmen told police of seeing her with a "tall and dark . . . foreign-appearing man" as they drove Todd's Lincoln through Hollywood.[16]   Was one of these men—if they were different men—Todd's gentleman friend from San Francisco?

Could he be the person whom Thelma telephoned from the Trocadero? According to Anita Hammond, a hatcheck girl at the restaurant, Thelma placed a telephone call from the women's restroom at 11:45 Saturday night. Hammond described her as "exceedingly anxious" her conversation not be overheard.[17]

In checking the Trocadero's telephone records, Claude Peters, the chief investigative agent for the Southern California Telephone Company, discovered one long distance call made Saturday night from the restaurant to New York. Investigators from the District Attorney's office quickly contacted the New York State Attorney's office to help trace the call to identify both the caller and the recipient. Although newspapers assured their readers that authorities would identify quickly the person who received the call, they never released a name.[18]

According to the *Los Angeles Times*, New York authorities were also asked to check the movements of a "close man friend of Miss Todd" who flew to New York after Todd's death and was presently staying in a hotel there. As this request occurred on the day after Pat DiCicco returned from Long Island, the investigators apparently were not referring to him, unless they wanted to check his past movements rather than monitor his present ones. Possibly, the unidentified man was A. Ronald Button, Todd's attorney, who had arrived in New York the day before. In its following edition, the newspaper described his questioning "on some matters that have developed in the [Grand Jury] testimony."[19]

Investigators also checked the records of Thelma's apartment phone for a call to the northern California city. Finding nothing and speculating she might have placed her calls from outside the apartment in deference to Roland West's feelings, they also examined the records of some of her favorite haunts, such as Perino's. Again, they came up empty-handed.

Perhaps the actress' own hand would reveal her mysterious lover. Grand Jury Foreman Rochester announced on December 28 that he learned from a telephone caller, whom he did not identify, of a journal Todd kept of her financial and personal affairs. He quickly ordered a search for the diary. Investigators questioned several of Todd's close friends, including Roland West, Ida Lupino, ZaSu Pitts, and Catherine Hunter, but could not find a diary or to confirm Todd kept one. Shortly after the start of the New Year, the press speculated the diary was in a safe deposit box at a Hollywood bank, sealed since the day she died. However, the officer from the County Treasurer's office in charge of auditing the box, E. R. Whitcomb, found only annuities, stocks and bonds.[20]

As the search for the gentleman from San Francisco continued, the parallel quest for Todd's alleged mystery guest took a bizarre turn. A bit actor named Charles Duke York, who worked with Thelma in *Two for Tonight*, a Bing Crosby vehicle, and in another unreleased Todd/Kelly film, told police that he and former middleweight wrestling champion Patrick Finnegan of Springfield, Ohio (known professionally as Lord Lansdowne) were to be Thelma's mystery guests at the Ford party. Repeating his story to Chief Deputy District Attorney Robert P. Stewart and Grand Jury foreman Rochester, York claimed that, when they dined together the Thursday night before her death, Thelma asked him and Lansdowne to accompany her to Ford's party. The two men would pretend to be English nobleman, the Duke of York and Lord Lansdowne, a stunt they often played for friends. While the press thronged about them, the two aspiring actors, propped with tuxedos and monocles, struck their poses for photographers while York explained the stunt:

> I was going to wear a starched shirtfront with a ribbon across the front and cock a monocle in one eye. Lord Lansdowne, one of my close personal friends, was going to dress similarly.... Everything was all arranged. Thelma, I understand, had called Mrs. Ford the previous Wednesday and told her she was bringing a couple of guests who she would not name. On Sunday, the day before Miss Todd was found dead, I called repeatedly and tried to get her. I never succeeded in locating her. The following day I read that she had been found dead.[21]

The pair explained they had not come forward before because they feared "it would have appeared a mere effort to get publicity." They were doing so now only because York received an anonymous phone call from a woman commanding him to tell what he knew about the Todd case.[22] York also suggested, "A man who has figured in the death investigation might try to 'break' him in motion picture work if he talked."

After hearing York's story, police contacted an unnamed Hollywood "film magnate" and gained assurances the actor's career would not suffer because he talked to police. Told of York's concerns, West scoffed "I haven't any power to injure anyone in the motion picture business and he needn't worry about it."[23] As for York's and Lansdowne's claim, West would have none of it. "I don't believe a word of York's story," he told reporters in the waiting area outside of the Grand Jury room, where he had been cooling his heels for several days. He rejected York's assertion that York called Todd's apartment repeatedly Sunday, claiming only three telephone calls reached the café Sunday, none of which were from York.

> I was home all day Sunday when York asserts he repeatedly tried to reach Miss Todd. There were only three telephone calls received. Each has been checked from its origin and not one was from York. I wish he would let us know from what telephone he made those calls.[24]

Bristling with contempt, West declared he knew whom Todd planned to take to Ford's cocktail party but would reveal the person only to the Grand Jury. That she planned to take a guest in the first place seemed unimportant to him. "She nearly always took someone with her to parties," West explained.

> It was her habit, if someone called and asked her to attend some affair, she would always say, "Yes; but I want to bring a guest. Sometimes it would be me. Sometimes it would be her mother. Sometimes it would be someone else altogether.[25]

However, when, as he entered the Grand Jury room several days later, West "laughingly" told the press the mystery guest was "nobody at all." "Miss Todd went places alone–it was to be the case at Mrs. Ford's party," West explained. "She always went everywhere alone. And that explains why there was a vacant place next to her at the Trocadero . . . . Her friends always understood she would go places alone, but they always set an extra place in case she should bring someone."[26] Testifying before the Grand Jury, he admitted he was "only talking" when he declared he would reveal the name of Thelma's mystery guest. "I really can't name anyone, I know, however, that it was Miss Todd's custom to ask if she could bring a guest to social affairs, just in case she wanted to be accompanied by an escort."[27]

The issue of Todd's escort would be muddled further when Miss Lupino testified shortly after the start of the New Year. She was misquoted, she told the jury and the press: Thelma did not say the gentleman was *from* San Francisco, but that he was *in* San Francisco, on business. She recalled Thelma told her she "did so want to bring him to the party tonight but he is in San Francisco and won't be back for several days."[28]

Ultimately, whether the man was "from San Francisco" or "in San Francisco" did not matter. Neither the police nor the district attorney's investigators ever revealed, if they in fact discovered, the identity of the man with whom Thelma was having "the most marvelous romance" of her life. Perhaps he did not even exist; flickering about the blonde actress were several rumored lovers, at least in ambition if not in fact. The gentleman from San Francisco, if he existed at all, was only the most elusive of her purported suitors. The comedienne had been linked to various figures in and out of the film industry since she arrived in Hollywood ten years before, but in few cases were the romantic links publicized. A few, like the gentleman from San Francisco, were shadowy, nameless figures. There was a rich Arabian gentleman from an eastern city, for instance, who allegedly gave her a diamond bracelet. Who this was and whether he existed at all was an open question–her close friend and co-actress, Patsy Kelly, denied knowing anything about the Arab or the bracelet.[29] When his time before the Grand Jury came, Harvey Priester, himself a suitor for Thelma's affections, spoke of several men who were in love with her, some "desperately" so.[30] As interviewers noted, the actress herself normally refrained from discussing her love life.[31]

The precise detail Lupino furnished to the papers at the time ("You know what gentlemen those San Franciscans are!") makes it difficult to believe the press simply misunderstood her. Despite the young actress' later revision of the published account of her earlier statements to the press, other rumors of a San Francisco gentleman in Thelma's life had already reached the newspapers before Lupino arrived at the Hall of Justice Monday afternoon. On the morning of Lupino's disclosure, The *Los Angeles Examiner* reported that "[i]t is known that some months ago Miss Todd was keenly interested in a San Francisco man and had made trips there to see him."[32] Indeed, Thelma's involvement with a San Francisco man, a banker by trade, was reported by her close friend Catherine Hunter in an article in *Photoplay* almost four years before.[33]

As for York and Lansdowne, their fear, real or pretended, of being viewed as publicity hounds was apparently justified. Grand Jury foreman Rochester did not bother to subpoena them and dismissed their testimony out of hand. "Nothing to it," he declared, "Their stories don't make sense."[34] After a day or two of headlines, the two men and their claims faded from the news—except for reports of Lansdowne's loss in a wrestling match at the Hollywood Palladium on the final day of the year.[35] Deputy DA Johnson was apparently referring to them and spiritualist Blanchard when he grumbled the case was "a publicity band-wagon" and "a hodge-podge of honest evidence and obvious faking." The difficulty, as the Deputy DA pointed out, was in "trying to sift the one from the other."[36]

The only indisputable love of Thelma Todd's life, past or present, was Pat DiCicco, her former husband. While DiCicco took pains to deny it, gossip reaching the investigators and newspaper reporters suggested their romance had rekindled over the past months. Along with reports that he and Todd quarreled at the Trocadero the night of her death, his sudden trip to New York the day after her body was discovered and his resemblance to the dark-complected, dark-haired man seen with Todd on Sunday, the rumors made DiCicco a favorite with feature writers, not quite a suspect but certainly suspicious.

Accounts of DiCicco and Todd's encounter at the Trocadero were little more than a murmur in the background of the booming headlines until Ida Lupino spoke to reporters Monday afternoon after her interview with the District Attorney. In her "clipped, precise, British accent," Miss Lupino told reporters she saw DiCicco by accident at the Trocadero on the Thursday before Todd's death.[37] DiCicco had heard she was giving a party and wanted to know why he wasn't invited.[38] When Lupino explained the party was in honor of Todd and his presence might be embarrassing, he advised her he and Todd were "pals" and it would "be swell" if he came. He promised to let her know either the following day or on Saturday if he was coming.[39]

Afterward, Lupino called Todd to let her know her former husband wanted to come to the party.[40] Thelma, she recalled, was "extremely pleased" to hear DiCicco was coming and, although she did not want to come to the restaurant in his company, as it "wouldn't look quite right," she suggested he sit next to her. "We regarded him as her escort," Ida observed.[41] DiCicco called her Saturday to ask when the party was and what he should wear. Now certain of his attendance, she arranged the seating so that DiCicco would sit next to his former wife.[42]

The chair beside Todd remained vacant that evening, however. DiCicco, a regular at the Trocadero, was at the restaurant, but he was with Margaret Lindsay. When he learned the Lupino party was forming downstairs in the French Grill cocktail lounge, DiCicco told Lindsay he didn't want to see Todd, so the couple remained at a table near the small dance floor in the restaurant's main dining room.[43] Later, after the Todd party climbed the stairs to have dinner, Todd danced by the table with Stanley Lupino. Todd stopped to introduce the British actor. Then she eyed DiCicco critically.

"Fancy seeing you here," she quipped. "You're a nice guy. You said you couldn't make this party, and here you are."

DiCicco protested he sent a message to the Lupinos explaining he wouldn't be able to attend the party—a claim Ida would later deny emphatically.[44]

"I think you had better write Mrs. Lupino a note expressing your regret, anyway," Thelma replied. "And I think you should apologize to Ida."[45]

According to Lindsay, there was "no hint of anger" in the conversation between Todd and DiCicco.[46] Other unnamed witnesses heard it differently, claiming Todd and DiCicco were at the point of an argument, but Stanley Lupino managed to draw Thelma away.[47] At first, Ida Lupino and her father also played down the encounter at DiCicco's table, noting Miss Todd took DiCicco's absence at her table "naturally enough"[48] and that the former couple seemed on good terms.[49] However, testifying before the Grand Jury shortly after the start of the New Year, Ida would claim Todd "bawled out" DiCicco—although, by her own account, she was not an immediate witness to the event.

While in New York, DiCicco denied rumors he and Thelma were considering remarriage, asserting they had seen each other "only about five times and never alone" since their divorce. Their divorce was an "amicable agreement," he contended, and "as dignified as that of any couple in Hollywood."[50]

Although DiCicco received permission from foreman Rochester to delay his return to Los Angeles until after Christmas, the press and the investigators continued to monitor his activities in New York. After leaving Newark Airport in the evening of the 26th, his flight was expected at 8:00 a.m. on the following morning. A blizzard in the Midwest delayed it until 3:35 that afternoon, however. On the way, the plane stopped off at Kansas City, where DiCicco reiterated he believed Todd's death was accidental. "I'm going voluntarily to testify," DiCicco told local reporters, "But if I had known anything that might have had any bearing on the case I'd have offered it before this."[51]

A light rain was falling as DiCicco, impeccably groomed and dressed in a hat and beige overcoat, descended the steps from the TWA Sky Chief to the runway of the Grand Central Air Terminal in Glendale.[52] His cousin, Albert Cubby Broccoli, a jeweler and the future producer of the James Bond films of the sixties, awaited him.[53] So did E. P. Davis, an investigator from the District Attorney's office, carrying a summons for that afternoon's Grand Jury session.

DiCicco, doubtlessly exhausted from traveling, was incensed by the subpoena.[54] He declared later,

> I don't see why it was found necessary to subpoena and escort me to the grand jury. I have returned voluntarily, with no more than a mild suggestion from the District Attorney's office that I might help the inquiry, and I think this subpoena business is unfair. I wired District Attorney Buron Fitts from New York as soon as I read that there was some demand for my services to help the Grand Jury. I got no answer. I had to telephone Rochester before I could get definite word to come, and even then he said that it was "all right with him" if I did. I came voluntarily, and with the intention of doing all I can to help.[55]

Davis tried to smooth things over by explaining the summons was only issued because of the tardiness of the plane and the Grand Jury's desire to hear DiCicco that afternoon.[56]

Before leaving for downtown, DiCicco contradicted Margaret Lindsay's statement that he told her he lunched with Thelma several days before her death. He explained that he and Todd, who was with a girl friend, sat at separate tables at the Vendome Café on Thursday. The two exchanged greetings, he maintained, nothing more. As to rumors of reconciliation between him and Todd, he declared there was nothing to them.[57]

Later in the afternoon, accompanied by Davis, DiCicco arrived at the Hall of Justice. Roland West sat on a bench outside the jury room at the time, talking with reporters. He glanced up as DiCicco passed. The two men looked at each other for a moment, but made no sign of recognition. Then DiCicco entered the jury chambers.

Before the jurors, the former husband of the dead actress told the jurors he solicited an invitation to her Trocadero party as a joke and "never seriously thought of accepting." Somewhat contradictorily—or perhaps the contradiction was just between the various reports filtering to reporters from the secret Grand Jury testimony—he explained he'd been uncertain Miss Lindsay would be in town Saturday night, but when he learned she would, he called the Lupino household with his regrets. Somehow, he maintained, the message failed to reach the Lupinos.[58]

After he and Lindsay left the Trocadero, he took the actress home and then went to his own. He had no plans for seeing Thelma the following day and was neither the mystery guest of Ford's party nor the dark, handsome foreigner seen with Todd on Sunday.

Given the ballyhoo of the past weeks, DiCicco's testimony was anticlimactic. After his flights to and from New York and several weeks of excited speculation in the press, his testimony disappointed both the reporters and the jurors, who observed he furnished "nothing of value."[59] Although the press would speculate repeatedly during the next week that the jury would recall him, especially when Ida Lupino's testimony seemed to contradict his own on several points,[60] DiCicco would not be subjected to further interrogation. Nonetheless, the investigators and the press continued to focus on Todd's romantic life.

Roland West, who journalists paired with DiCicco as the "two men who played the most important roles in Thelma Todd's life"[61], had been waiting for most of the week in the corridor outside the Grand Jury room. Now it was his turn to testify.

TEN: WEST TAKES THE STAND

> Ten years from now, five years from now, someone will not be able to break out with a new solution of the so-called "Todd Mystery"– if there is a mystery–because then the authorities can pin such a party down to face facts.
> – Roland West[1]

"Thelma Todd's death was the greatest shock of my life," Roland West told reporters as he waited outside the Grand Jury room. He struggled to control his emotions. "For three days after her death I could hardly talk. My mouth dried up, my throat burned, yet police detectives and investigators plied me with questions. They have taken five statements from me so far. Now I am to be the last witness at this inquiry. That is all right with me. I don't think anyone knew Thelma Todd better than I did."

West paused, collecting himself. "She was a keen, witty, powerful personality," he went on with evident admiration. "We were partners. If she wanted to buy her lunch, she bought it. I bought mine."

"Would you believe it?" he asked, looking from face to face. "I never bought Thelma Todd anything–no jewelry, no clothes, no presents. The only flowers I ever got Thelma were the flowers they put on her casket."

West looked away and was silent for some time.

"Thelma Todd was ready to start a new phase of her career, and she had everything to live for–money, position, beauty," he continued at last. "That was the only thing that I ever concerned myself with in Thelma's life–her work and her beauty."

"I often told her she should watch her hours. I know she drank very little the last few weeks. Her beauty was her career...."[2]

For the first week of the Todd death investigation, West sidestepped every direct question about his relationship with Thelma Todd. Not that this task was particularly difficult–as one newspaper noted, the authorities were "surprisingly delicate in shying away from the greatest motive of tragedy in the world–the love motive." Although, the journal conceded, "it was well that the love affairs of an international beauty be not exploited in public," too many of the unanswered questions surrounding Todd's death centered on the West/Todd relationship.[3] Despite West's equivocations and the gentle handling of investigators, insinuations persisted that it involved more than the café partnership. Louella Parsons wrote candidly of a romance between the two, implying West's wife, Jewel Carmen, wore blinders when it came to the romantic activities of her husband.[4] Todd's attorney, Ronald Button, told reporters Todd was "very fond" of West and "had not spoken to me in recent months of any other man in her life," while other unnamed sources reported "Mr. West was . . . very much in love with Miss Todd and . . . resented the attentions of other men to the famous beauty." Even Pat DiCicco, who some news reports matched with West as a rival for Todd's affections, identified West as "the last man in [Thelma's] life."[5]

Only Thelma's mother supported West's denials of a romantic relationship. "I knew Mr. West had the run of Thelma's apartment above the café, but he was her business partner and maintained living quarters there, so it never seemed to me that was unusual," she told the Grand Jury. West treated both Thelma and her "very nicely," she added.[6] Still, it was hard to understand why two people would live so closely without intimacy. A week later, after a report that the layout of Todd's apartment was altered prior to the Grand Jury's visit, Mrs. Todd refused to comment.[7]

Two letters received by investigators implied there was a reason for the investigators to take a closer look at the relationship between West and Todd, financial and otherwise. The LAPD received the first, handwritten and anonymous, a few days after the discovery Todd's body.

> This is to inform you that I was on my way to Frisco Sunday Dec. 8 the first party to offer me a ride was a lady only going a short distance. so I kept on going. it began to get dark when another lady came along & asked if she could give me a lift I told her where I was going & she said she was going up the road a short distance. she asked why was I going to Frisco. I told her to seek work. that I couldent find it in Hollywood.
>
> She said every one has their troubles havent they she said hers were different from mine but worse. said she was in partners with a man she had advanced money to & now he didn't want to return it & was trying to frighten her out of it. she said I guess I need what you have courage. she said he had tried to frighten her at times & that she felt funny about it. I laughed and told her he was bluffing. at the time I didn't know who this lady was until she stopped at Thelma Todd's cafe, she said if you don't find employment in Frisco stop in your way back as I expected to make some changes. perhaps I can do something for you.[8]

What the LAPD made of this tale is not recorded. However, at least one other report reached investigators that claimed Thelma was unsatisfied with her relationship with West, romantic or otherwise. Helen "Kewpie" Ainsworth[9], who one newspaper described as an "Amazonian couturier," told investigators of two intimate conversations she had with Todd during the week before her death. During the first, a private luncheon on Tuesday, December 10, Thelma exclaimed, "There's going to be a big change in my life this week. I'm pulling out of there, if you know what I mean .... I don't know why I'm living the way things are. There must be a change."[10]

The next day, Todd and ZaSu Pitts went Christmas shopping together, visiting dress designer Robert Galer in his salon at 8830 Sunset Boulevard, where Ainsworth worked, around 7:30 in the evening.[11] According to both Galer and Ainsworth, who stayed late to wait on her, Thelma seemed in a "terribly depressive mood."[12] "You know, Helen," Todd told her, "I've been going to a psycho-analyst in Hollywood[13] and he's psycho-analyzed me pretty thoroughly. He looked into my eyes and said that I've been under the stress of weird dreams and mysteries and worries. He told me that I hadn't, for the last year or so, made the right use of my brilliant brain and my youth and beauty. And, my dear, he hit the nail precisely on the head." Todd, famous for her hats, purchased a new one that day for delivery the following Tuesday.[14] "Miss Todd sat down to write a check for the hat and said 'You better get your money now because I may be broke by the first of the year,'" Ainsworth recalled. At the time, Ainsworth interpreted the statement as a droll allusion to Christmas shopping, but Todd's death caused her to reconsider its significance.[15]

Ainsworth also told investigators Todd complained the Sidewalk Café was losing money and "there had been a little trouble." Her financial condition was more doubtful because her contract with Roach studios would expire at the end of the year. "I really don't know that I have anything much to live for," Ainsworth quoted Todd, adding that she also remarked she had "never loved anyone and never wanted to live."[16]

The second letter reached the office of District Attorney Buron Fitts on December 26. This missive challenged the testimony of several key witnesses in the Todd case, asserting Miss Todd and "a man whose name has been mentioned prominently in the case" became involved in a violent argument at the Sidewalk Café shortly before her death. The man, an "admirer" according to one paper, "struck her with his fist, knocking her across a table" before a waiter intervened to stop him. It was not the only time Miss Todd was assaulted, according to the letter.[17]

Both Rudolph Schafer and West quickly denied the report. "I never heard of such a thing," West scoffed when told of the asserted beating. "No one could row with Thelma Todd, or strike her, and get away with it. I know I never did. We have argued, but never in anger. If I wanted her to do something, we argued. Maybe she did what I wanted her to, maybe she didn't."[18]

The identity of the secret witness who made this report was not made public when the story first broke in late December, but investigators were said to be seeking a former waiter as a witness. In fact, the letter writer turned out to be the former headwaiter at the café, a thirty-three-year-old man by the name of Gustav Berger, who was in jail in San Diego on bad check charges. On request of investigators Winn and Yarrow of the LA DA's office, Harry Baugh, chief investigator for the San Diego County District Attorney's office, questioned Berger.

Berger claimed he witnessed several violent quarrels between the unnamed man and Miss Todd while working at the café from May to August 1934. All the quarrels took place after Pat DiCicco visited Todd. According to Berger, despite statements by both West and DiCicco that they never met,[19] the two men knew each other well; DiCicco often visited the café after his divorce from Todd and invariably West treated him surly and afterward quarreled with Todd. One night, while Berger was off duty, Miss Todd was badly beaten up and thrown out of the building into the rain. Or so several waiters told him.[20]

Berger's story evidently failed to impress either Fitts or his investigators, who eventually dismissed it as "too remote to throw much light on the actress' death." Still, it added to suspicion about Roland West's role in the comedienne's death. And the former director was about to testify in what Grand Jury foreman Rochester predicted would be the starring role of the inquest.[21]

West was slated to testify on December 27, but Rochester delayed his testimony until after the appearance of other witnesses in the case.[22] Day after day, he stewed in the Grand Jury waiting room, sometimes raising his voice in indignation against sensations leaking out of the Grand Jury room or bruited by the reporters. Other times, as when, after posing for the camera, he observed, "A photograph, like a glimpse in a mirror, is just an illusion," it seemed that he spoke simply out of the habit of a man whose dramatic flair had been rewarded by a lifetime of success.[23]

Despite his protests of the sideshow atmosphere surrounding the case, especially the entrance of Blanchard, York, and Lansdowne, West himself critiqued the dramatic content before reporters on December 30th, observing, "This story has everything— blood, sex, and mystery," that exceeded anything he himself had brought to the cinema. "Thelma was a grand heroine. She was, of course, one of the most beautiful women in the world; she was famous, and she was wealthy. No better type could be found." West cautioned that he believed the death was accidental, but he was willing to see the potential of the mystery. "[N]o girl as lovely as Thelma was could be without admirers, and although I know of no jealousy among them, it is not, considering the 'plot' of this case, illogical to believe that jealousy might have entered the web somehow."[24]

Some newspapers were ready to play up this theme. West's own expertise in the mystery genre was a made-for-order angle.[25] The *Los Angeles Examiner* published extended scenarios of two of his films, *The Monster* and *Alibi*. "Now West finds himself involved in a real-life mystery drama, 'The Strange Death of Thelma Todd,'" the newspaper observed as it introduced *The Monster*. "Roland West Now Center of Drama as Gripping as Film He Made," it proclaimed in its subtitle of *Alibi*.[26] Although the article was careful to not imply too much, some wondered whether this master of mystery and crime figured, in the words of one person close to the case, "I've done this in the films and I can do it in real life."[27]

On December 30, West finally appeared before the Grand Jury. Rochester, who acknowledged West as "our most important witness," predicted that his testimony would take several hours.[28] In fact, it took much longer.

West previously endorsed the Grand Jury investigation, conceding that although it was "terrible . . . that all the private moments of [Todd's] life must be searched out" the inquiry had to be "exhaustive and thorough." At the same time, he complained about his own treatment by the investigators. "You know," he told reporters, "I always thought third degrees were conducted in a room. I never knew there was anything like this. It is pounding, pounding, rush and wait."[29]

West arrived to testify in the company of Rudolph Schafer and another man named Harry Holzman, who lived on and cared for West's yacht in Coronado.[30] West would admit several days later that Holzman was his bodyguard.

> I have received threat after threat and I have turned over the sinister notes sent to me . . . to the Department of Justice. It has been necessary for me to keep with me constantly a friend, Henry Holzman. Each time I venture into the open, I fear an attack from ambush, and I have not allowed myself to be seen about the Sidewalk Café because of the possibility that some deranged person might come here for the express purpose of killing me.[31]

One note, handwritten and described as literate, an unusual characteristic of such missives, threatened West with death if he revealed anything to the Grand Jury about the death of Miss Todd.[32] Another stated that the "Thelma Todd death would never be solved and the rest who were at the party had better keep their traps shut or something else will happen."[33] West was particularly worried he might be the target of the extortionists who harried Todd before her death.[34] Evidently, he was not convinced the man in prison in New York was the only guilty party.

On the first day of his testimony, West testified on subjects ranging from his personal and business relations with Thelma Todd, the identity of the mystery guest that Todd allegedly intended to take to Martha Ford's party and the details of his activities on the morning of Sunday, December 15. His testimony began at 2:25 in the afternoon, following earlier appearances by Alice Todd, Harvey Priester, and Schafer. Visibly nervous, West sat hunched in the witness chair as the Grand Jury members leaned forward to hear his answers to hundreds of questions put forward by Deputy DAs Blalock and Johnson and, occasionally, the jury members themselves.[35]

Much of West's Grand Jury testimony repeated statements he had made to investigators and the press in the previous weeks. He denied again that he ever struck Miss Todd or any other women. He hashed over details of the financial arrangements between himself and Todd, revealing that since December 1934 he handled all the dead actress' investments.[36] However, he explained, Todd handled her negotiations with the studios herself. "I was not even Miss Todd's business manager," he told reporters earlier in the day. "She fired her business agent and handled her own contracts.[37]

He also recounted that he met Todd five years earlier when she starred in his film, *Corsair*, shot on Santa Catalina Island, She had moved into the Sidewalk Café in August, taking an apartment on the same floor as his own.[38] As he had done in his coroner's testimony, he flatly denied the suggestions that the relationship between him and Todd was on the rocks. Earlier, he told reporters the same thing. "I read statements where someone said she was 'pulling out if you know what I mean.' If she was leaving the café, which we were running in partnership, she never discussed it with me. If she was soon to be through with her studio contracts, what did she have to worry about? I know an influential producer who told us that when Thelma finished her contract he wanted her for feature roles."[39]

West tried to clarify some of his perplexing testimony before the Coroner's Jury, particularly that relating to his apparent lack of concern for Todd's absence Sunday morning. He explained that he instructed Thelma to go to her mother's apartment in Hollywood if she intended to stay out late Saturday night. When he did not find her at home Sunday morning, he assumed that she had done so. At the same time, he also speculated that she may have come home after all and slept on a couch in the ladies' lounge—as she had once before when she found her apartment door locked—then departed early in the morning. West admitted that he was worried about Todd Sunday morning, but his hunch that she went to her mother's from the Trocadero apparently calmed his fears and obviated any search for her that day.[40]

West also returned to the issue of the single key Thelma carried in her small purse the night she left for the Trocadero. He explained that when he bolted the side door to her apartment he assumed Thelma carried a key to the main door on Roosevelt Highway. He told the jury he now believed the single key *was* a passkey to the building's other entrances. Intrigued by this new possibility, the jury lent him the key to test. After the day's session ended, he took it home with him and tried it on the various doors of the Sidewalk Café. The following day he reported that he was mistaken—the key opened only the side door to Miss Todd's apartment.[41]

As West emerged from the jury room, his face showed the strain of his questioning. To the reporters who crowded around him, he maintained, as did Thelma's mother, Alice Todd, and her close friend, Harvey Priester, both of whom testified earlier that day, that Thelma's death was accidental. He opined, however, that nothing he told the jurors would dispel the mystery of Todd's death. Certainly, the mystery was not dispelled for Grand Jury foreman Rochester, who observed, "The further we go, the deeper this thing gets."[42]

ELEVEN: MURDER, SUICIDE OR ACCIDENT?

> ... [The] crime [theory in Todd's death] had little or no evidence to support it–save that all the other stories were equally hard to believe.
> – *Evening Post Record*[1]

While Roland West did not tell the jury anything that proved or even strongly suggested Todd was murdered, speculation about the possibility of foul play, fed by rumors of new discoveries and cover-up, continued after he testified.

Some of the rumors began before West took the stand. On Christmas day, newspapers reported that somebody in the Coroner's Office observed swelling and lacerations inside Todd's throat during the autopsy, injuries not noted in the official report. The bruises could have been made by jamming a bottle neck or a pipe into the actress' mouth, one article explained. Deputy DA Johnson doubted such obvious injuries were overlooked during the autopsy, but, speculating Todd might have been rendered unconscious by such "brutal treatment" and then placed in the running car, he directed investigators Winn and Yarrow to interview morgue attendants and embalmers. Grand Jury Foreman Rochester also jumped into the act, announcing that West's physician, Dr. Phillip Sampson, the first medical man on the death scene, might be asked to testify about the condition of the actress' throat when he examined her body. While Sampson was never called, Autopsy Surgeon Wagner scoffed at the reports in his testimony before the Grand Jury. The autopsy surgeon continued to maintain that Todd's body showed no evidence of violence. The small amount of blood about her nose and mouth was the natural consequence of carbon monoxide poisoning, the surgeon declared.[2]

The Coroner's Office continued to test the actress' vital organs, removed prior to her cremation, for signs of a poison or sleep-inducing drug. Despite a rumor that the Grand Jury requested that private chemists conduct the test, the task stayed in the hands of the Coroner's Office under the supervision of Wagner and County Chemist R.J. Abernathy. As no specific substance had been identified as a possible agent in Todd's death, the chemists performed a broad range of tests designed to detect various known poisons. Although some their findings leaked beforehand, the full report would not be presented to the Grand Jury until January 16.

Assisting the coroner's office with the forensic investigation was LAPD chemist Ray Pinker. Pinker performed tests on the blotches of blood DA investigator Tom

Cavett found on the phaeton's running board on December 20. Although his tests were completed by Christmas day and leaked to the press immediately, they were not made public until Pinker testified on January 7. Putting to rest conflicting newspaper stories about the test results, Pinker testified the bloodstains did contain carbon monoxide. This finding supported the LAPD conclusion that Todd bled after her face struck the steering wheel as she passed out from the poisonous gas.

Still, the blood on the phaeton's running board required further explanation. While Cavett speculated that Todd tried to climb out of the car in a frantic attempt to save her life, but then slumped back onto the seat when the carbon monoxide overcame her, an unnamed investigator for the DA's office painted a more sinister picture when he wondered if she were struck in the face to prevent her from escaping the automobile.[3]

One forensic matter became a hot issue on the final day of 1935. Testifying before the Grand Jury as to the time of death, Wagner repeated his estimate, based on the "gross appearance of the body," that she died 12 to 30 hours before he began the autopsy Monday afternoon. Fragments of food in the actress' stomach, including slightly digested peas and string beans, indicated she died no later than ten hours after eating her last meal, presumably at the Trocadero. The evidence of the undigested food thus complemented the police estimate of death in the early a.m. Sunday.[4]

Except for one thing. According to several newspapers and foreman Rochester, peas and string beans were not served at the Trocadero Saturday night. This startling revelation prompted Rochester to speculate, "Either Miss Todd came back to the table at the last moment and ate peas and beans from some other plate, or she stopped on the way home and ate these vegetables, or the entire theory she died Sunday morning is wrong. If she did not have peas and beans at the Trocadero, then she was living and ate such a meal some time Sunday." Besides bringing into question a critical factor in Wagner's estimate, the issue also raised questions about the surgeon's methodology. A UPI correspondent noted, "Dr. Wagner originally told a Coroner's Jury Miss Todd's death had occurred about 18 hours before he performed his autopsy, which would have placed it about midnight Sunday. Later he changed the testimony to conform to the Homicide Squad's report on the death hour [before 6 a.m. Sunday]."[5]

Hot on the story, *Illustrated Daily News* reporters visited the Trocadero that evening to get headwaiter Alex Hounie to check the menu of the Lupino party. Hounie, working a busy New Year's Eve, replied understandably—and, one suspects, with some exasperation—that he and his waiters were too busy to go into it.[6] The issue, seemingly unresolved, died from the papers and the press conferences as the new year began. However, it would raise its head again in the years to come.

A few other reports of newly discovered evidence for murder emerged during the last week of 1935. One was a report that the night watchman of the Castellammare neighborhood told friends he noticed unusual activity around Castillo Del Mar's lower garage during the weekend of December 14-15. When contacted by reporters at his

Pacific Palisades home, however, Earl H. Carter declared he had nothing of importance to tell the Grand Jury. He was not hired to guard the West property, he explained, but he noticed the doors of the garage were closed when he passed it a few hours before the discovery of Miss Todd's body.[7] The Grand Jury called him, anyway. On December 30, he described his patrol of the Castellammare community between midnight and daybreak on the morning of Sunday, December 15. The howling wind, the pounding surf, and the dark night made observation difficult, he admitted. Still, he saw nothing to arouse his suspicion. "I passed the garage at 17531 Posetano Road... at least 15 times," the night watchman maintained, "I never saw the garage door open, never saw a light, never heard a sound that attracted my attention."[8]

A report of an indistinct and partial palm print on the back of the phaeton's dust-covered car seat arose on January 6. Douglas Howatt, an LAPD fingerprinting expert, suspected the actress herself made it, but he could not prove this, since police took only her fingerprints prior to the closing of her casket and cremation. The week before, police had taken chauffeur Ernie Peters' fingerprints, but neither his nor those of anybody else in police records matched those found on the phaeton or on the door to Miss Todd's apartment.[9]

While fingerprint specialist Howatt was puzzling over the partial handprint at the scene, another specialist had examined Todd's shoes. The issue of the condition of the shoes resurfaced after one jurywoman, Mrs. Gertrude Rose of Pasadena, noticed her shoes were badly scuffed by the climb from the café when the jurors visited the site on January 3. Her comments prompted Rochester to order a microscopic investigation of Todd's shoes, a task that befell criminologist Frank Gompert of the Sheriff's department, an expert in tire and shoe prints. Gompert reported he found traces of wax from the Trocadero's floor, but it was left to Ray Pinker of the LAPD to testify on the scuffing issue. On January 7, the police chemist told the jurors the shoes did show scuffing, although the wear could have been made by any hard surface, not necessarily the street pavement or concrete steps Todd allegedly followed from the café to the garage. It was questionable anyway how rough the climb really was on new shoes: Pinker himself donned a pair and made the climb to the garage, finding no more wear than would have resulted from walking a similar distance on ordinary pavement.[10]

Although the physical evidence for murder seemed weak, hints of offstage maneuvering by studio figures, with whom DA Buron Fitts was known to have close ties, kept alive suspicion that a cover-up was in progress. DA investigators complained of "sinister influences" thwarting their probe and jury members who suspected murder maintained the studios were trying to keep the names of "well-known figures whose lives touched Thelma Todd's in a manner not yet revealed" out of the investigation. Supposedly, these famous characters were involved in the gambling operations the café was planning to commence.[11]

It was not the first report of the involvement of gamblers with the café. On December 18, two days after Todd's body was found, the *New York Daily News* printed a story by Hollywood news stringer Sidney Skolsky under the heading "Todd Death Clue in Gambler's War". Skolsky told of rumors of high-stakes gambling on the second floor of the café, the players including "celebrities with whom West had become acquainted with as a movie producer and director." He speculated that Todd might have been murdered "either because she rejected the demands of blackmailers or because enemies of West chose to strike at him by killing her."[12]

> Six weeks ago, Robert Goldie, whose real name was Goldberg, was murdered in San Francisco purportedly in a war for control of the lush West Coast gambling racket. For the time being, roulette wheels are spinning in the interests of a local clan, but for several months large Eastern interests have evinced a determination to muscle in...

On the day following Skolsky's report, Grand Jury foreman Rochester announced he had "inside information" gambling interests threatened Todd after she refused to permit them to open the café to gambling.[13] District Attorney's Office detectives Jess Winn and Lloyd Yarrow followed up on the gambling rumors. Among the witnesses they interviewed was Todd's friend Catherine Hunter, who recalled that Todd told her a new business would open on the café building's third floor on New Year's Day. Hunter could not confirm rumors this new business would involve gambling, however.

After reading Winn and Yarrow's report to the Grand Jury on the gambling issue, which noted only "as yet unexplained activity" to take place on the third floor beginning January 1, Rochester told reporters that he doubted illegal gambling interests were involved in Todd's death and, consequently, that the investigation was not seriously interested in the gambling rumors.[14] The rumors continued, however. Comments by Todd's attorney, A. Ronald Button, brought the issue back into focus on the day before Christmas. "I had a luncheon with Miss Todd a few days before her death," Button reported, "and she seemed like her old self, happy and gay and optimistic. But the last few times she came into my office there seemed to be something on her mind ... something she wanted to tell me about ... something that cast a shadow over her sunny personality. Several times, I am now convinced, she was on the verge of telling me what it was that was worrying her. But somehow, she never reached the point of disclosing her secret." With Button, Todd had never been reticent before. "She usually spoke fully and freely of everything she was doing. She asked my advice on everything—from studio contracts to the care of a sick dog." However, when he returned from Europe in September he found she had grown unaccountably reserved, though, curiously, she visited him more often. "Always before when she came to my office it was for legal help and advice. But in recent weeks she just came to chat. I sensed she wanted to tell me something, but never quite got to the point."

Overall, Button observed, Thelma seemed happy and excited about her café, which she was planning to enlarge after the first of the year. "She told me they were going to open up a new place upstairs and charge plenty. She hoped that the café would make more money." The same prospect, however, might have caused Todd's anxiety. She told Button "some time ago" a "group of gamblers" wanted to run games in her café. "She told me that she was opposed to gambling and she would have nothing to do with it," Button recalled, "but whether the gamblers ever made a deal, I do not know." The attorney also told one newspaper he had heard many reports the café would host gambling after the first of the year—and he "understood" Thelma was going to "withdraw from the café enterprise."[15]

The grand jurors themselves had an opportunity to look for evidence of gambling when they visited the café on January 3. After Rochester reminded them their sole interest in the case revolved around the possibility of murder, they drove up the coast to the café in modest cars one reporter contrasted to the fancier vehicles of the usual patrons of the café. As they approached the restaurant, the sunshine glistening on the ocean inspired one woman juror to compare it to Thelma's "sequin-spangled gown." Greeting them at the café entrance was Roland West, casually elegant in a blue sports jacket and meticulously pressed gray flannel trousers, a tall drink in his hand.[16]

Although investigators from both the DA's office and the police had gathered at the café, Rochester insisted that the jurors tour the living quarters by themselves. With West as a guide, they filed past a heavy exterior door bearing an ornate sign, "Thelma Todd Announces the Opening January XX of the Finest Restaurant in California"— the exact date blacked out—and up the stairs to the second story. There, in the northwestern wing of the building, leading off a wide corridor, they found a series of small, private dining rooms, each superbly decorated with a distinct color scheme. A sign at the building's entrance proclaimed that on January 1 these rooms would be incorporated into the Joyas Inn; in fact, they were in operation already, providing an opulent venue for a few hundred of Los Angeles' luminaries—film stars, studio heads, socialites, civic leaders, and politicians—to entertain their peers and paramours. West presided over the service personally, selecting the rooms to match their color schemes with the dazzling gowns of the ladies, insuring every course and event of the evening unfolded flawlessly. The price for this service was high; but high prices were no barrier to the desired clientele and they kept out the common sort.[17]

One room had excited the press's interest already. Off a small bar on the main corridor, it was to open on New Year's Day along with the restaurant, but its pleasures were not culinary: there, according to West, a "10-cent chip game" similar to roulette, but at which a player's losses were restricted, would entertain the guests.

Although the grand opening on New Year's Day was cancelled shortly after Thelma's death, the preparations for the new restaurant on the second floor were evident. The jurors also noted benches and other furniture in the hexagonal tower room that formed a third floor of the building, prompting some to wonder whether this larger area was also intended for gambling.[18]

The living quarters of the building were in the southern wing of the building, nearest the highway. In Todd's apartment, the jurors searched for clues to Todd's personality in her belongings and paid particular attention to the apartment's exterior door, which the actress should have entered on the night of her death. Each tested the key to the door's lock against other exterior doors of the building as they strove to make sense of West's testimony. A few pounded its metal sheath with their fists; its loud reverberations convinced them Todd could easily have awakened West, asleep only a few feet away. On the walkway outside her apartment, one juror declared it would have been easy for somebody to conceal himself at the top of the flight of stairs and set upon the young actress as she reached the top of the stone steps.[19]

Afterward, West guided them to the ladies' boudoir on the same floor, where he thought Todd had slept when he awoke on Sunday to find she was not in her apartment.[20] Then, he led them into a private dining room of the Sidewalk Café for lunch, seating Rochester at the head of the table. West declined to eat with them, explaining that he was not hungry, but Rudolph Schafer hovered nearby solicitously.[21]

The luncheon, including time after the meal for coffee and cigars, lasted nearly two hours. Afterward, the jurors walked out into the bright sunshine to climb the steep steps and winding streets to the infamous garage, West once more leading the way. A throng of detectives and reporters, who had dined at a local hot dog stand, followed in tow.

As they hiked to the garage, the jurors monitored their own experiences in hopes of better understanding the mystery. They disagreed on the difficulty of the climb, some finding it so exhausting they could not believe Todd could have made the climb herself, others not finding it severe at all.[22]

At the garage, with Homicide Chief Hubert Wallis looking on, Detective Bruce Clark climbed into Todd's phaeton to demonstrate the police accident theory, acting the part of the actress and describing the posture of her body when he viewed it late in the morning of December 16.

Afterward, as autos full of tourists drove by, the jurors explored the garage, testing the sliding doors, which several of the women found difficult to open, and even discovered a "blood" smear on the wall, which they promptly brought to West's attention. Although the discovery caused a minor sensation in the papers for a day, police chemists concluded quickly the smear was only rust stains from the door hasp.[23]

After an hour, they headed back to the café. Beyond gaining vague impressions about the probabilities of the various theories in the case, it was unclear what their tour of the café and garage had accomplished. One reporter found Clark's demonstration of the police theory of Todd's death unpersuasive, leaving "some members of the jury entirely skeptical of the suicide theory and completely convinced that Miss Todd did not die accidentally." But the jury was already broken into various camps on the question of the cause of death, and it is likely those who were now "entirely skeptical" of the suicide theory were also skeptical of it before their visit.[24]

Indeed, the investigators and jurors had divided into three factions, each favoring one of the three main theories, murder, accident, and suicide, while eyeing the other factions with suspicion. According to George Rochester, some jurors—evidently, those partial to murder or accident theories—believed there was a "plot afoot" to prove Todd was a suicide. "It looks as if 'they' are trying to build up this case as a suicide; but in the actual evidence, I have found nothing to support this theory definitely," the Grand Jury foreman declared.

It was the true that in the second week of the Grand Jury investigation Deputy District Attorneys Blalock and Johnson made evidence supporting suicide the focus of the investigation. Johnson disclosed investigators were looking into the possibility a suicide note was found at the site. A few days later, he and Blalock blamed efforts to make Todd's death appear accidental for retarding a solution to the case, even charging two witnesses were withholding convincing testimony of Todd's suicidal inclinations.[25] They did not explain why anybody would want to divert the investigation from the suicide theory, but Todd's friends and family were unhappy with suggestions the actress killed herself. The interest of several jurors in determining whether Todd's life insurance policy carried a suicide exclusion suggested they suspected another, more mercenary, motive.[26]

For a week, the Grand Jury heard testimony that Todd was in a self-destructive frame of mind: Arthur Prince and Ernie Peters' observations of her despondent mood as she departed from the Trocadero, numerologist Patricia D' Este's account of the actress' precipitate declaration that she did not want to live anymore at attorney A. Ronald Button's party a few weeks before her death, and an odd report by Roland West (subsequently denied by Alice Todd) that he had discovered Thelma and her mother crying together Saturday afternoon.[27]

One person who may have shed light on Todd's mental condition was her psychiatrist—the man who allegedly told her she was not making the most of her brains and beauty. Despite speculation he would be brought forth to testify, he was neither called nor identified. Instead the inquiry into Todd's psychology centered on the decidedly unprofessional observations of on an odd assortment of persons who claimed they were the actresses' confidants.[28]

One of these, Robert Galer, the owner of the millinery shop where Helen "Kewpie" Ainsworth worked, described Todd's lack of gaiety when she visited his shop on December 10. "She was not the usual carefree, happy Thelma Todd we knew. We had never seen her that way before." Earlier that morning, Ida Lupino, who created a sensation a week before with her report of Todd's secret lover, the gentleman from San Francisco, told the jury of witnessing Thelma's "morbid streaks," while the comedienne lived with her family in London several years before.

"She said several times during her stay that she wished a tram car would run her over, that death would be welcome," the young actress recalled. "On numerous occasions she said 'I would be the happiest girl in the world if some catastrophe would befall me - if I would get killed in an automobile accident - get run over - or have the earth fall from under me.'"

Lupino also noted Todd seemed "tired and depressed" when she first arrived at the Trocadero on the evening of December 14. "She was talking to me in the cocktail room and I said something about being tired of this business and wishing I could go away somewhere and forget all about it. She said, 'I've been trying to do that all my life, but I guess there's only one way out.'" Then she suddenly brightened up and said, 'Oh, let's have a drink and forget about it.'"

Afterward, Lupino testified, Todd seemed gay for the rest of the evening, although an odd little event occurred as she left early the following morning. As Arthur Prince escorted her to her limousine, Todd touched her hand to her forehead and with a kind of salute appeared to be saying goodbye to the Trocadero. The gestured puzzled Prince, who mentioned it to the Lupinos and others still at the café.[29]

Some of Thelma's friends, however, disputed claims she was prone to melancholy. ZaSu Pitts contradicted Ainsworth's description of Todd's mood at the millinery shop. "I never saw Thelma happier in her life than that day. We went shopping and Thelma bought a lot of Christmas wrappings and seals, and I am sure she intended to be alive and observe Christmas."[30] Catherine Hunter noticed no hint of suicidal tendencies or fear of murder when she talked with Todd on the Friday before her death. Nor, as she told the Grand Jury on January 6, had she ever heard a "despondent word" from Miss Todd. According to Hunter, the actress had no worries serious enough to make her consider ending her life.

Marion Wilkerson, another close friend, told the jury essentially the same thing. Wilkerson claimed she talked confidentially with Todd shortly before her death and observed she was happy both in her romantic and professional lives. Todd's French tutor, Georges Jomier also discounted suicidal tendencies in the actress, producing as evidence a bright, cheerful letter she wrote in early December to suspend her lessons until after the holidays. Wanda Gruidl, a studio extra whose startling resemblance to

Todd had led to work as her double, said simply, "She would never do that."[31]

Although not called before the jury, Todd's current partner in comedy, Patsy Kelly, also disputed the suicide theory. Kelly told DA investigators on December 21 that she was positive Thelma had not killed herself. "Since the terrible tragedy I've racked my brain trying to think of some word of unhappiness or any slightly morbid or discouraged utterance from Thelma's lips," Kelly declared. "But I could think of none. She exuded happiness and a love of life." Hal Roach made the same comment on the day of her death, describing her as "always joyous and happy."[32]

Overall, Thelma's friends and relatives convinced the jurors to reject the suicide theory. One reporter observed the number of jurors supporting the suicide theory, which at one point equaled those leaning towards a murder theory, declined during the second week of testimony.[33] By the end of the week, the *Los Angeles Examiner* could declare, "many jurors have lost all credence [in the theory] that the actress ended her own life."[34]

However, only a few jurors endorsed the police view that Todd died accidentally.[35] From the beginning of its investigation, most jurors regarded the accident theory with skepticism. Evidently, they could not ignore some of the inconsistencies and irregularities in the accident theory. For instance, several questioned why Todd did not turn on the garage's interior light or climb into West's Hupmobile if, as police believed, she walked to the garage to get warm; the Hupmobile was a roofed sedan while the phaeton had only a convertible top and open windows.[36]

Todd's friends and relatives, however, supported the police accident theory with increasing vigor and blamed grandstanding politicians for the continuing investigation. DiCicco expressed those sentiments precisely when interviewed in New York City, and others involved in the case soon echoed his words.

As the new year began, criticism of the investigation became more strident both inside and outside the Grand Jury room. The *Los Angeles Evening Post Record*, a journal on its last legs that might have profited from a sensational coverage of the investigation, grew increasingly cynical as the inquiry progressed and "mystery" men and women came out of the woodwork with their new angles. More critical was the increasing disgruntlement of two of the key witnesses in the case. Roland West, continuing to evade queries about his relationship with Todd, released a blunt declaration on January 7 that he would refuse to answer questions reflecting on her character. Thelma's mother, speaking with reporters outside the jury room after her second appearance, was equally direct. "This whole situation is unbearable," she declared with obvious indignation. "This investigation, the way it is being conducted, is only for the purpose of a lot of cheap politicians trying to get jobs. I am absolutely and utterly convinced that my daughter's death was accidental. I cannot understand why, if I am satisfied, the Grand Jury shouldn't be after all of this tireless questioning and requestioning of witnesses."[37]

The strain of Thelma's death overcame her mother several times, both inside and outside the courtroom. She was reported in a "state of collapse" around Christmas. Undoubtedly, delivering Thelma's Christmas gifts aggravated her suffering.[38] So must have an extortion letter, postmarked in Los Angeles on the day after her daughter's body was found and sent to her at the Sidewalk Café:

> *We will give you one week to contact us in the Times in the personal column or you will go next.*
> *We got her because she doubled crossed us and we will get you too. call me Ace and give me your telephone number.*
> <u>*No funny work*</u>
> <u>*No Cops*</u>
> *"Ace"*[39]

The handwriting of the letter resembled that of the extortion notes Thelma received during the year, but then anybody could mimic their style, since one had been pictured in the newspapers. The original "Ace" was in custody by the time Thelma died, but was he? The FBI continued to watch Harry Schimanski, the first man they accused of writing the extortion notes, but nothing would ever come from their efforts.

On December 31, following a barrage of questions directed, as the *Evening Post Record* described, at uncovering "some 'secret sorrow'" of her lovely, laughing daughter, which would throw light on possible motives for her murder–or at least prove interesting," Alice broke down in front of the Grand Jury. When the investigation dragged into the end of its third week, she began to counterattack against speculation about her daughter's love life and emotional problems. After declaring she would defend her daughter's reputation since her daughter could not do it herself, she strode away from reporters outside the jury room on the arm of Harry Holzman, West's friend and bodyguard.[40]

Before the Grand Jury, Alice Todd denied reports that she initially declared her daughter had been murdered, maintaining from the first that she believed Thelma died accidentally. Several days after her daughter's body was discovered, she had echoed Roland West, musing, "The way it happened was typical of her. She was impetuous, careless in little things, knew nothing of the mechanics of a car. I think it most probable that she turned on the motor of her car to warm the garage." During the weeks of investigation, she varied from this theory only to speculate that Thelma's heart condition and fainting spells may have had something to do with her demise, a conjecture Autopsy Surgeon Wagner quickly rebutted with his testimony that no physical evidence of a heart condition or a tendency to fainting was found during the autopsy.[41]

Still, while one could sympathize with Alice Todd's indignation, the investigators could hardly refrain from scrutinizing some issues touching on Todd's character. Her inebriation at the time of death, for instance, required explanation, as the patrons of the Trocadero seemed unanimous in declaring her sobriety—as well as their own. Sid Grauman, a self-proclaimed "fellow who never takes a drink," told the Grand Jury Thelma had a single glass of champagne at his table Saturday night and, although talkative and happy, was not intoxicated. Chauffeur Ernie Peters described Todd as "cold sober" when she entered his limousine at the end of the night. And yet, Wagner had measured her blood alcohol level at .13% [42]

Alice Todd's criticism of the Grand Jury investigation and West's defiance might have led to a confrontation with the investigatory body had not internal dissension already begun to cripple the inquiry. Disagreement in the Grand Jury room over continuing the investigation became public in late December after one juror complained the investigation was a waste of taxpayers' money. In the first week of the new year pressure mounted on the jury to get on with its other business—including preparations for handing over its responsibilities to the incoming 1936 Grand Jury. On January 2, the jury adjourned after lunch due to a lack of a quorum. Although it was unclear whether the absent jurors, counted variously by the press at two and five, were trying to quash the investigation or simply had other business to attend, there was little doubt the situation was deteriorating. On January 7, reporters heard raised voices behind the closed jury doors. The following day, the papers reported absences had already disqualified several jurors; two others, seeing no possibility Todd was murdered and hence no legitimate interest in her death by the Grand Jury, threatened to boycott the hearings and thus deny the investigators a legal quorum.[43]

Foreman Rochester continued to press on for further investigations, however. Increasingly, his was a lone voice crying in the wilderness. Having raised the possibility Todd was a "monoxide murder victim" even before the investigation began, he now pursued new leads pointing toward murder even as the newspapers, the city, and the nation turned from the story to other sensations. Repeatedly, standing before reporters at the end of the day, he predicted a big breakthrough was coming soon, perhaps the next day. When it did not come, when testimony of the key witnesses proved disappointing or when the sensational developments failed to materialize, his faith in the possibility of murder remained unshaken. If only some of the witnesses would only come clean, he suggested, the jury would break the case open. "We are not satisfied with all of the evidence we have heard," he declared. "We are convinced that some of the witnesses are not telling all they know, nor all the truth about what they have discussed."

On January 7, while the other grand jurors journeyed to the state women's prison at Tehachapi, Rochester took what amounted to a last stand for continuing the investigation. He drove south to San Diego with a DA's office investigator to interview Gustave Berger, the former waiter who claimed to have observed violent quarrels between Todd and a key witness. However, after listening to Berger, Rochester decided, as the DA's men had before him, that his story contained "little of value for the jurors." Still, he promised the inquiry would continue, "Until we have exhausted every lead and every bit of available testimony." Meanwhile, two of the rebellious jurors declared they were adamant against continuing the investigation, and one proved it Thursday, January 9, by not showing up for the morning session. Despite Rochester's intention of calling several more witnesses as soon as the toxicologists report was in his hands, other business was pressing, including a sensational forged will/murder case involving a former local beauty queen.[44]

In the face of internal dissension and his other responsibilities, Rochester could not prevent the jury from ending its investigation of the Todd death even as he insisted that more disclosures were at hand. After receiving chemist Abernathy's long awaited report that his search for drugs or poisons in Todd's organs had discovered neither, the jury's investigation ended. Despite speculation that the jurors might issue a statement acknowledging their investigation had not developed substantial evidence of foul play, they dropped the matter without any formal declaration. From a legal standpoint, no statement was required, but its omission left the case without formal closure.[45]

Except for the probate of Todd's estate, which began with the admission of her will towards the end of the month, the death passed quietly from the legal system with the ending of the Grand Jury investigation. The newspapers dropped their coverage of the mystery as well. In the coming decades, only the occasional tangential link, often to other Hollywood deaths and scandals, recalled to the pages of newspapers the mysterious death of Thelma Todd.

Exterior of the garage of Roland West's Castillo Del Mar (*Herald-Examiner Collection/Los Angeles Public Library*)

Hubert Wallis at the death scene (*Herald-Examiner Collection/Los Angeles Public Library*)

Roland West sits on the passenger running board of Todd's Phaeton (Bettmann U329690ACME)

West's Castillo Del Mar. Behind the trees on the lower left of the photograph is the garage
(*Herald-Examiner Collection/Los Angeles Public Library*)

Thelma Todd's Café and the Roland West's Joyas room in 1935
(*Santa Monica History Museum, Bill Beebe Collection*)

Trocadero Restaurant in 1936 (*Bruce Torrence Hollywood Photograph Collection*)

Coroner Nance and Roland West (*Los Angeles Daily News/UCLA Special Collections*)

Lansdowne and York before Grand Jury Room (*Los Angeles Daily News/UCLA Special Collections*)

Rudolph Schafer, Roland West, Anderson, and Mae Whitehead outside Grand Jury Room (*Los Angeles Daily News/UCLA Special Collections*)

Jewel Carmen in 1935
(*Los Angeles Daily
News/UCLA Special
Collections*)

Alice Todd leaving Grand Jury Room with Henry Holtzman
(*Los Angeles Daily News/UCLA Special Collections*)

From left: Pat DiCicco, Jean Malin, Thelma Todd and Lois Wilson at Malin's New Yorker Club in Hollywood. Malin would die when he accidentally put his automobile in reverse and backed off the Santa Monica pier. His passenger and Todd's comedic partner, Patsy Kelly, survived the accident.

Thelma / Studio photo 1931

Thelma in a vamping pose (*University of Washington Special Collections JWS21949*)

TWELVE: THE REPORTERS

The great reporters of the era were the best fictionalizers . . .
— Arnold B. Larson

The whimpering end to the Grand Jury's investigation and newspaper coverage of Todd's death left many observers puzzled.[1] How could a story that prompted several official inquiries, involved investigators from four government agencies and captured headlines for weeks conclude with so little resolution? What happened to the numerous revelations that were promised? Why was there no final legal decision on the cause of the actress' death?

The Grand Jury's decision to not issue a final report contributed to this perplexity and nurtured suspicion about the powerful criminal and studio figures that seemed to lurk behind the scene as the proceedings developed. A fertile field had been planted from which, in ensuing years, a harvest of fakery, folklore, and myth would deepen the already profound mystery of Todd's death.

The field was seeded by the efforts and blunders of many persons: the obstreperous foreman of the Grand Jury, George Rochester, with his continual predictions of new evidence or breakthroughs; the defensive and recalcitrant LAPD investigators; the seemingly confused and self-contradicting coroner officials; the high profile witnesses, often indistinguishable from out-and-out publicity-seekers; and the overly talkative investigators and jurors. Other, larger forces also played a part. Todd was a screen star whose image had been carefully nurtured by an industry sensitive to public approval, but her death was an opportunity for a print media hungry for stories to sell newspapers. Behind this simple dichotomy were machinery and practices that had been developing for decades and came to a particular manifestation in Los Angeles in 1935. The Todd mystery originated within the context of these practices, but it would continue to develop through the coming decades within other contexts, each in its own way exploitative of the actress and her tragic death.

The efforts of later writers to solve the mystery would be based primarily on the written record of the case in the newspapers of the time, a record profoundly influenced by the push and pull of news reporting and movie industry interests. While radio had already taken on part of the role of providing the public with news, newspapers were still the major source of public information at the time of Todd's death. In Los Angeles alone, six major papers published at least one daily edition. A few of these also regularly printed morning, afternoon and evening editions[2] and released special editions when big news stories occurred. Although on any given day a paper's later editions varied little from its primary edition, the big stories, such as the Todd mystery, required new— or at least rewarmed—copy.

The throng of reporters and newspapers covering the Todd story undoubtedly contributed to the confused record that survived. Reporters repeatedly stepped over each other trying to break new ground or find new angles. Sometimes the results bordered on the absurd, such as the *Herald Examiner's* December 20th article about the revelations of a psychic who claimed Thelma Todd had been attacked by a "gorilla man," or reports her death fulfilled the 1934 predictions of another psychic, Mahion Norvell,. At other times, the result was confusion and contradiction. When police chemist Ray Pinker released the results of his test for carbon monoxide in the blood splotch found the phaeton's running board, the papers reported diametrically opposite results. The evening *Daily News* claimed no trace of carbon monoxide was found, renewing speculation she was attacked prior to entering the car. Yet, the *Times* and the *Herald* stated the opposite: the blood did contain carbon monoxide.[3] The inconsistent reports added to the confusion at the time and laid a trap for the unwary or careless chronicler of the future.

Other, larger factors contributed to the disarray. Newspaper reporting had changed since the end of the World War I, partially because of competition from tabloids. Usually half the size of an ordinary paper, the tabloids used photographs to illustrate current events, with just enough text to explain them.[4] Using an informal and punchier writing style, they focused on the lurid and sensational.

The small-sized newspaper had a long tradition in the American press; the availability of newsprint and press capacity made them more economical. The extensive use of illustrations, first engravings and then photographs, developed in the late 1800s and appealed to recent immigrants with limited English.[5] While these tabloid elements were well established in the United States, the sensationalistic nature that ultimately defined their style began in Great Britain,[6] where it fed the British public's predilection toward crime, sex and scandal. In the United States, two American cousins, Joseph Patterson and Robert McCormick, inspired by the English-tabloid king, Alfred Harmsworth, established the first American tabloid in 1919. Their timing proved perfect.[7] The excesses of the Roaring 20's, bootlegging, gangsters, and flappers, free love and burgeoning wealth, made perfect grist for the tabloid mill. Patterson and McCormick's successful New York *Illustrated Daily News* inspired competition in that city, especially from William Randolph Hearst, who soon established the *Daily Mirror*, and Benarr MacFadden who, having already entered the tabloid fray in 1919 with the successful *True Story Magazine*, followed with the *Daily Graphic*.[8]

Throughout the twenties, the newly sensationalized tabloids engaged in an all-out circulation war. As they competed for readership, the search for scandal accelerated. For those with a morbid bent, the editors offered murders and executions; those seeking titillation got tales of infidelity and sexual peccadillo.

Those long ago images and stories still reverberate if now only half understood or remembered. In 1926, when the war of "gutter journalism" seems to have peaked, the Hall-Mills murder case made tabloid headlines. Four years earlier, the bodies of a forgotten preacher and choir singer had been found under a crab-apple tree on a New Jersey farm. The case went nowhere until the press uncovered new evidence implicating the preacher's wife, her brothers and cousins. Two hundred reporters covered the trial which climaxed in the testimony of a star witness tagged "the pig woman" by the press. Suffering from cancer, she was carried into court on a hospital bed. Despite the tabloids' bias, the jury acquitted the hapless widow, who went on to win a sizable libel verdict.[9]

The success of the tabloids in New York stimulated publishers in other cities to try the same approach. In Los Angeles, Cornelius Vanderbilt Jr.'s *Illustrated Daily News* began as a tabloid. Although never as salacious as its New York cousins, it emulated their extensive use of photos and lively writing style.[10]

The story of the kidnapping of Aimee Semple McPherson proved a boon for the local tabloid press. In the late spring of 1926, the renowned evangelist disappeared from Venice Beach. Mourned enthusiastically by her flock for a month, she reappeared in Douglas, Arizona with a bizarre story of kidnapping, drugging and torture in Mexico. Her story had too many holes, however, and officials and the press began to investigate. Soon they alleged that, instead of being kidnapped, Aimee had taken a romantic holiday from religious fervor with Kenneth Ormiston, the radio operator for her Temple. Los Angeles County District Attorney Asa Keyes promptly charged her with obstruction of justice.

In her defense, McPherson charged she was a victim of an underworld conspiracy; the vice lords, she claimed, were getting back at her for redeeming prostitutes from lives of sin. During the ensuing criminal trial, reporters packed the courthouse galleries and filled their papers with details from the lips of hotel chambermaids, house detectives and desk clerks who claimed to have seen the couple during their illicit sojourn.[11]

The popularity of the tabloid style prompted the regular dailies to devote more space to photos, often using them to cover their second and third pages. Other tabloid techniques found their way to the mainstream press. One was the so-called "composograph." Developed by the *Daily News* but brought to full fruition by the *Evening Graphic*, this was a photo doctored to portray a scene alleged to have happened, but which no camera had photographed.[12] When Rudolf Valentino died in August 1928, readers saw him surrounded by medical personnel on the operating table, and then standing on the steps of heaven with Enrico Caruso.

Despite their success, the era of the tabloids was brief. Their excesses inspired attacks from churches and the educational establishment, which regular dailies, eager to remove competition, quickly joined. The bleak reality of the Great Depression also helped seal the tabloids' fate. Readers, concerned with the serious social and economic issues of the 1930s, turned to more serious coverage. While many of the tabloids had disappeared from Los Angeles and the nation as a whole by 1935, they had left their mark, prompting mainstream papers to adopt livelier writing styles, use more pictures, and serve the public's taste for scandal.

Even without them, there was still a great deal of newspaper competition in Los Angeles. As in much of the nation, the local newspapers tended to represent the interests of a single man or family who used the paper to reward friends and punish enemies. The major newspaper of the city, the *Los Angeles Times*, had been forged by Harrison Gray Otis and his Son-in-Law Harry Chandler. United in their belief in unbridled capitalism and the acquisition of property and power, virulently anti-labor, the two helped define and promote Los Angeles' transition from a dusty frontier outback to the third largest American city.

The two differed in style, but not in their driving ambitions. Otis favored bombast, vituperation and the unwavering frontal assault. Progressives and politicians learned to fear his wrath. Competing papers might find their revenues dry up when merchants, afraid of Otis' retaliation, would refuse to place advertisements with them. In times of labor strife, the paper assailed workers and labor unions in its editorials.

Otis' motto for his paper, "Stand Fast, Stand Firm, Stand Sure, Stand True," [13] adorned the Publisher's Suite of the Times Mirror Company for many years, expressing perfectly the self-righteous zeal he brought to his self-appointed role as a champion of laissez-faire and grand traditions.

After Otis' death in 1917, Harry Chandler took command of the *Times*. Though less flamboyant than his predecessor, Chandler had already affirmed his commitment to Otis' basic principles. As early as 1904, he stated, "There is one city in the United States where a strike has never been able to succeed; that city is Los Angeles. The reason . . . is because it has . . . the *Los Angeles Times*." [14]

Chandler was deeply conservative in both his demeanor and philosophy. Unlike Otis, he avoided personal publicity and concentrated his efforts on expanding his extensive real estate and business holdings.[15] Realizing the growth of his financial interests was tied to the growth of Los Angeles itself, he used his paper to set an unrivalled standard of boosterism for the city, extolling its climate and economic opportunities with hyperbole and florid prose.

He also engaged in a more direct influence over the city's politics.[a] [16] As writer

---

[a] Allegations that Chandler dictated city policy via a direct phone line with the mayor's office were made repeatedly over the years. Apparently, the arrangement

Stephen Longstreet noted:

> It is public record that Harry Chandler became a multimillionaire through land deals, stockholdings, corporations that grew and expanded. That Harry was a political power, used and backed candidates like a party boss, supported party machines, backed city hall groups that often in the end were not working for the public weal—all this may be true, but there is no clear-cut evidence any of this was illegal to the point of coming into a court of law for a conviction. It was an age that was heir to Jay Gould, Jim Fisk, Daniel Drew, and John D. [17]

In addition to the newspaper, Chandler inherited Otis' rivalry with William Randolph Hearst. Hearst controlled two local papers, the *Los Angeles Herald-Express* and the *Los Angeles Examiner*. Like Otis, Chandler disliked Hearst's flamboyance, his posturing as a friend of labor and his "progressive" politics. Hearst resented Chandler's hidebound conservatism and superior influence in Los Angeles.

Frequently, their personal animosity boiled over into the content of the two publishers' newspapers. They dueled over issues of water, populism and public ownership of utilities. Hearst's editors once even ran an announcement offering condolences to the bride in an impending marriage to a member of the *Times* hierarchy.

Editorial content and reporting style often closely paralleled the interests and predilections of the publisher. Hearst's papers, like their owner, were sensationalistic and informal, devoting more space to gossip and pictures. In this way, they reflected Hearst's foray into New York's tabloid competition. The *Times* reporting was drier, its conservatism manifested by archaic spellings and an archly factual approach. Not surprisingly, the rivalry between the publishers spread to the paper's news departments. Reporters promoted the interests of their publisher, sometimes assailing politicians who impeded his business deals; other times exposing similar transactions involving his competitor.[18]

Of course, newspapers were not the only economic interests in town. Movie studios, public officials and gangsters knew the benefit of good press and understood

---

continued even after Harry's son, Norman, took over the reins of the *Los Angeles Times* in 1944. Jack Halstead, a retired LAPD captain, saw it in use. During a meeting with Mayor Norris Poulson to discuss an increase in the police pension fund, Halstead was told that the mayor couldn't support it and that Norman Chandler opposed it as well. To prove his point, Poulson escorted Halstead down a set of steps below the mayor's office to a tiny room furnished with only a small desk and telephone. Picking up the phone, Poulson asked to speak with Chandler. A few moments later, the publisher came on the line, confirming the mayor's message: the paper was opposed to any increase in the pension fund that year. Halstead left the room knowing it was a dead issue.

that a little entertainment, special attention or payola could get certain reporters to play ball. If it worked once, it might work again. If you write this, I'll feed you something else. For some reporters, a rapport could be established which down the line might lead to a cushy job with a publicity department or a government information bureau. For others, the rewards were more immediate: the politicos were always interested in good press, and more than often they were willing to shell out to get it. Veteran reporter Arnold Larson revealed years after his retirement he took money from racketeer Charlie Crawford during the latter's trial for conspiracy for framing a city councilman. He even bragged he tricked the underworld kingpin out of $250 by representing that he got the Judge to dismiss the charges. Another reporter, Morris Lavine, was reputed to be on Aimee Semple McPherson's payroll; he rarely had a bad word to say about her.[19]

The economic realities facing reporters undoubtedly contributed to their lax ethics. Chronically underpaid, many resorted to chiseling to make ends meet. "We men reporters were all chiselers," Arnold Larson recalled, "we were figuring angles all the time–trying to make side dough by doing publicity, reporting for out-of-town newspapers, fixing traffic tickets, or, in my case arranging to have big trials transferred to a specified court where the court reporters [who charged journalists per page for copies of their work] would clean up on the trial transcripts."[20] Reporters were well equipped to chisel. Working for a newspaper, especially on the city beat, gave them an inside knowledge of Los Angeles–its courts, police and power elite. "[T]he paper ran the courts and much of the city," Larson recalled. "Reporters had a sense of power, of participating and finagling and manipulating."[21]

In the days before centralized telecommunications, minicams and mobile units, reporters spent much of their time hanging and snooping about the places news might develop. Most developed favorite techniques and contacts to make sure they got to the scene with the firstest and mostest. For example, Norman "Jake" Jacoby, a young City News Service reporter in the late 30s, had an ongoing arrangement with the deputy coroners at the city morgue. Regularly, he would drop by to inspect the night's crop of intake cards spread across an unattended desk.[22] A casual perusal could lead to pay dirt: so-and-so movie actor found dead in a Laurel Canyon mansion, Joe Somebody of the mayor's office killed in a car crash, a local gangster shot down in front of his garage. Similar arrangements worked at the admittance station at "the Queen" (Queen of Angels Hospital) or any number of police division booking desks.

Poker, alcohol, or a night on the town worked wonders with the police, city and county officials and denizens of the underworld. Reporters even became extra police hands at times. As the official police yearbook, *The Guardian* recalled, "in the days when the force was particularly short-handed during the night and early morning hours, the police reporters, armed and equipped as were the officers, would pile in the fast cars and work side by side with the members of the old Flying Squad on all kinds of investigations."[23] Sometimes all they got out of a night with the cops was a hangover and a busted wallet, but sometimes they hit pay dirt with a scoop.

Public figures often used the reporter's hunger for a story and the public's love of sensation to further their own agendas. When Vice Squad detectives, acting under orders from the vice lords they were supposed to oppose, concocted schemes to frame reformers by luring them into compromising positions with women, they made sure the press boys knew about it in advance. In 1938, when wounded allegedly by an unknown assailant near his home in Duarte, District Attorney Buron Fitts had enough of his wits about him to travel all the way to the Central Receiving Hospital, where he knew the eager reporters on the city beat would be ready to photograph him as he arrived at the emergency room. Nobody seemed to question, at least at first, why, presumably in pain, he had traveled so many miles from the site of the shooting.[24] Later, many believed the shooting itself was a publicity stunt arranged by Fitts to curry public sympathy amid the mounting charges of corruption being leveled against him. According to reformers, the bullet hole in the roof of Fitts' sedan indicated the shots were fired from inside the automobile.[25]

Such stunts were a time-honored Los Angeles tradition. Local figures often resorted to such ruses to gain publicity or sympathy, sometimes with the direct support of the newspaper reporter. In 1913, reporter Adela Rogers St. Johns, the daughter of lawyer/campaign manager Earl Rogers, helped stage a similar attack on mayoralty candidate and chief of police Charles Sebastian; the stunt worked and Sebastian won the election.[26]

Sometimes the motive for such hoaxes was simply to enhance or revive a flagging story. Some of these hoaxes still live on in histories of the era today.[27] Arnold Larson recalled one such incident during an interview after his retirement. In 1922, when popular film comedian Fatty Arbuckle was accused of a drunken and brutal sexual assault in the death of a young actress, Virginia Rappe, papers nationwide stimulated the actions of outraged community leaders who organized protests and boycotts of Arbuckle's films, forcing their withdrawal from local theaters. Seeing an opportunity, Larson, then a cub reporter in Colorado, concocted a story about a "purity squad of cowboys" who broke into a movie theater exhibiting an Arbuckle film, burned the offending reels of celluloid and shot the theater's screen full of holes. Although the hoax was later revealed when the owner of theater returned the film to the distributor intact, the story or similar versions have been cited repeatedly over the years to illustrate the public furor over the Arbuckle case.[28]

In some cases, the press crossed the line of journalistic chicanery and interfered with active police investigations. During Prohibition, one reporter with interests in several speakeasies regularly tipped off proprietors of impending raids he heard about on the police beat. Once he slipped up and was chagrined to find himself covering a raid on one of his own establishments.[29]

Another reporter, Jack Carberry, was a hero to the local press corps for his ability to juice up a story. At least once, he went so far as to manufacture evidence at a murder scene. Putting on a pair of women's high-heels he bought at a second-hand clothing store, he clomped around the scene of the crime. To make sure the new evidence was not missed by the authorities, he then hurried back to the Inglewood police chief and asked, "Are you sure you have really looked around there thoroughly?" In another exploit, Carberry sent mysterious post cards filled with cryptic remarks about a crime to the City Desk of his own newspaper, hoping, as Larson explained, to "inject an artificial, fictional dose of suspense and mystery into a moribund story. Carberry's talent for "fictionalizing" was augmented by personal skills necessary for success in the newspaper game: "As far as actual reporting went, the best reporters were types that could bluster their way along as they worked a story. They usually were the most hard-boiled–most like cops; and able to bulldoze their way ahead, run over people, intimidate them and engage in implied blackmail and the whole thing."[30]

Part of the game involved cribbing copy or filching sources from competitors, making sure the first paragraph of each re-write contained the word "today," no matter how contrived it sounded. The practice was often brazen, and sometimes it backfired. In early 1937, the *Times* and the *Herald* battled for days after the *Herald* filched a picture of a local mobster from its rival. In the original photo, the mobster had a cigarette in his hand, which the *Times* editors airbrushed out before printing. The next day the photo of the mobster, sans cigarette, appeared in the *Herald*, exactly as it had in the *Times*. Seeing their opportunity to embarrass the rival journal, the *Times* republished the photo of the mobster as it had been originally taken–with the cigarette–setting off a lengthy exchange of denunciations and rebuttals between the two papers.[31]

Despite the hunger of newspaper management for the scoop and the consequent spikes in circulation, the pressroom gangs found ways to ease the burden of their jobs. As with most fraternities, the group disapproved of hot-dogging and preferred to share news sources and content discreetly rewritten under numerous individual leads and bylines. This practice, referred to as "syndicating," made reporters' lives easier, allowing them to while away the day drinking or playing poker. At the LA County Board of Supervisors, one supervisor himself joined the game from time to time, while another card game went on without cessation for several years at the old red brick County Courthouse.

Adela Rogers St. Johns described the logic of this process and what could happen to the reporter that scooped his peers:

> No one could cover the whole beat, so a man from one paper took the Emergency Hospital, another the police courts, another any trial of magnitude going on, someone else covered the booking desk, a man stood by for the breaks and also on any running story. Everybody took turns at ambulance calls depending on who was in and not doing anything. When Scotty [a reporter for the *Herald*] broke the

faith [by scooping other reporters on a story about a beautiful woman pickpocket], Tex Talbot of the *Times*, later decorated as a marine in the Argonne, chased him through the Third Street Tunnel shooting at his feet–all police reporters carried guns, of course.[32]

The fierce competition between the papers of the time undoubtedly contributed to the confusion surrounding the Todd case. Many involved in the investigation, including the police, believed the press deliberately prolonged the investigation and turned an open and shut case into a media spectacle.[33] In their view, objective investigation and reporting the news took a back seat to selling papers and advancing the interest of the papers and their publishers.

Given the cacophony of voices, methods, and sources, it is little wonder the record of Todd's death is convoluted. Under any circumstances, accurate reporting of the case would have been difficult. The pandemonium of facts confronting reporters, some relevant, many extraneous, posed a challenge to which many were unequal. It was perhaps inevitable the record they left is full of garbling, contradictions, and inaccuracies. Later writers took much of what they read in the contemporary press at face value, not understanding the extent to which the reporters were players in the drama, not just spectators. They fell into some of the same traps the original chroniclers of the case had fallen into and some the reporters were setting themselves.

THIRTEEN: THE PUBLICISTS

> I don't care what they call me as long as they mention my name.
> — George M. Cohan

Opposing and perhaps frustrating the press' interest in juicing up the Todd mystery were men whose interest was to manage the news coming out of Hollywood—the studio chiefs or moguls. In a little over two decades, they had helped transform a region known for churches and oranges into an entertainment mecca. It all started around 1912 when the burgeoning motion picture industry began to locate its production facilities in the sleepy suburban towns surrounding downtown Los Angeles. At first, there was considerable conflict between the older residents and the young film crowd. Many of the established residents objected to what they perceived as the loose morals of entertainers. Nevertheless, the city's leaders quickly recognized the movie industry offered the town some things it needed: jobs, homebuyers, and a great deal of free publicity to attract more folk from the Midwest. For their part, the studio heads recognized the importance of creating a favorable climate for the growth and continued prosperity of their enterprises. Once the studios themselves got rolling, the owners invested in hotels, restaurants, and theaters and contributed generously to charity. Much of their money also went into the campaigns and pocketbooks of politicians.

The moguls were self-made men with the political bias of self-made men everywhere: they respected initiative and zeal and had little patience for the collectivist notions of organized labor. In Los Angeles, they found a political climate as favorable to their interests as the natural climate was to making movies. The city had long favored industry and business, often at the expense of the working man's interest. Indeed, until after World War II, it was said often there were two parties in Los Angeles, but both of them were Republican. Shortly after the turn of the century, a group of young Republican professionals had spearheaded a progressive movement in the town, but their idealism, while far to the left of the established powers like the *LA Times* and the Merchant and Manufacturers Association, was still solidly in the business fold. Pro-labor parties rarely threatened the Republican hold on the town.

It is doubtful any city in the United States at the time could have been more accommodating to the fledgling film industry. Movies became one of the area's major exports, a powerful promotional device that identified the region with beauty and youth. News from the region often focused on Hollywood, its stars and coming releases, its hoopla and fads. Dozens of writers made good livings as "stringers," feeding stories about Hollywood to East Coast papers and the wire services. Others, working as free-lancers, satisfied the seemingly insatiable movie fan's appetite for star tidbits by selling their wares to the scores of movie magazines. Their efforts bore fruit. In the imaginations of many who lived east of the desert, movie stars strolled up and down Hollywood and Sunset Boulevards, danced the night away in lavish clubs, and frolicked along miles of beaches crested by mountains bathed in continual sunshine, the air perfumed by the pervasive aroma of orange blossoms. While Easterners and Midwesterners fortunate enough to visit were often disappointed to find the area's reality didn't live up to their charmed expectations, they found much to enjoy in the warm climate and natural beauty of mountains and sea. Returning home, they carried memories of an easier environment that could be replenished by every visit to their local theaters, where the region played as a backdrop to celluloid fantasies.

Particularly useful to the studio heads was the cooperation of the local newspapers. While the peccadilloes of bit players were often fair game for the press, transgressions by stars and the studio powers were more often handled with discretion, if they were noted at all. The production of movies was one of the town's big industries, and the assets of that industry, human or property, required protection and care. For a newspaper to fuss over the antics of players in its major industry was to bite the hand that fed it. Thus, a conspiracy of self-interest among the press, the Hollywood establishment and the Los Angeles booster elite developed and thrived.

The nature of this relationship has fueled a great deal of speculation surrounding the film industry's crimes and mysteries, with a number of writers claiming the studio establishment repeatedly subverted Los Angeles' criminal justice to protect its own. In particular, accounts of the deaths of William Desmond Taylor, Thomas Ince, Paul Bern, and Marilyn Monroe are infused with conspiracy theories charging obstruction of justice, destroyed evidence, bribed officials and suppressed prosecutions, purportedly engineered by moguls fearful of scandal that would offend the public and lead to theater boycotts or government regulation. Certainly, there is some basis to the speculation. In 1922, reacting to a series of scandals, particularly the death the year before of actress Virginia Rappe during a wild weekend in Fatty Arbuckle's San Francisco hotel suite, Hollywood established the Hays board to regulate the content of movies and head off any governmental regulation. Many studios also employed a "morals clause" in artist's contracts designed to reign in excesses in behavior, at least in public, through the threat of termination. The standard language read:

> The artist agrees to conduct himself with due regard to public conventions and morals and agrees that he will not do or commit any act or thing [that] will tend to

degrade him in society or bring him into public hatred, contempt, scorn or ridicule, or that will tend to shock, insult or offend the community, or ridicule public morals or decency or prejudice the producer or the motion picture industry in general.[1]

How much these reforms actually affected behavior is not clear. The Hays Board proved something of a paper tiger. Despite puritanical grumbling throughout the United States, the studio bosses knew sex and violence meant bigger revenues. Not until the Hays Board itself was reformed in the early thirties amid threats of congressional and state action, prompted by pressure from religious groups, did Hollywood start cleaning up its act.[2]

The morals clauses also proved something of a chimera. While it is likely they restrained some sinning, at least in public, incidents of moral turpitude, adultery, brawls and lawbreaking continued. Few stars were terminated—even those who got into public scrapes with the law.

Still, the legend of the power and effect of the reforms endures. So does the assertion that Hollywood often resorted to extra-legal or extraordinary measures to hide scandal from the public eye. Many writers claim Hollywood cover-ups were common. As one advocate of this point of view, John Austin, puts it:

For many decades, dating back to the Arbuckle scandal of 1921-22 . . . , many members of the Hollywood press corps have engaged in critical battles with those who rule the movie industry. During the Twenties and Thirties, reporters covering the industry were often victims of vicious, well-calculated cover-ups. News was altered to suit the circumstance. Journalists were to believe what the Hollywood oligarchy told them, whether it was the truth or not.[3]

Austin claims Thelma Todd's death figured among the cover-ups. "A 'neat and tidy solution' was 'requested' by the oligarchy, the Hays Office and the L.A County sheriff. They wanted a verdict (of accidental death) and they wanted it fast."[4]

Austin is among a long line of writers who saw the hand of Hollywood moguls playing a shell game with information about Todd's death. Like many others, he relies on a dubious syllogism to demonstrate his case: since Hollywood had a motive and the means to cover-up unseemly incidents, it must have done so. Unfortunately, like other writers who claim the studios interceded to suppress evidence in Todd's death, he provides no testable evidence to support his claim, only rumor, hearsay, and the dubious logic that what is possible must have happened.

Still, one must consider what, if any role, Hollywood's nervousness with scandal may have played in the Todd case. While it may be impossible to detail the activities of publicists and the studio protectors in restraining or channeling the flow of information, one can assume some amount of news management took place. Charged with sex, rumors of violence, and the possible involvement of underworld figures, the

Todd death had an undeniable potential to damage the film industry in the public's eye.

Day-to-day Los Angeles before the war ran on principles of reciprocity. People who lived there at the time often remember it, as Jake Gittes says in *Chinatown*, as a "small town." Everyone seemed to know everyone else. It wasn't really that small but, before television, its geographical isolation from the rest of the country was more palpable, making it a world of its own, an overgrown town. It was known for the movie industry, big oil and great weather.

Yet, there was a grittier reality to the town that Hollywood ignored. The bulk of the inhabitants lived the lives and pursued the occupations of ordinary Americans everywhere: insurance salesmen, beauticians, real estate developers and gas station owners. If some of these folks knew the stars as customers, clients or friends, they were inclined to take these brushes with fame in stride. You couldn't ignore the studios because a good portion of the town's economy depended on them. But, after a while, the movie industry became like any other dominant industry in a city, like cars in Detroit or steel in Pittsburgh. The message wasn't just magic. It was also money.

Protecting all that money—and the town's dominant industry—meant keeping the media in line. By 1935, the motion picture establishment through great expense had perfected the art of media manipulation. Each of the major studios had full time publicity departments. Depending on seniority and experience, publicists were assigned actors or actresses, some already stars and some being groomed for stardom. The publicist's job was to get as much positive press as possible and head off any negative coverage.

Public appearances by the stars were carefully orchestrated to present just the right image and create just the right level of excitement. It was an easy job when you were handling a big name like Joan Crawford, Shirley Temple, or Jimmy Stewart. Unknowns took a little more work and the fast crowd, those addicted to the nightlife, gambling or sexual adventure, could cause you lots of headaches. Sometimes it was just a matter of maintenance: a call to a friendly reporter with, "How would you like an interview with Gable?" or "Gloria's going to be at the Derby on Tuesday for lunch, why don't you stop by her table and find out what's new?" The results were often less than spontaneous and sometimes as well rehearsed as the dialogue for the star's next picture. Nevertheless, if the name was big enough, it didn't matter much.

Things really got hectic when the studio was getting ready to release a new picture. The publicity department would hold daily meetings counting down to the premier. Nothing was left to chance. Actually, the process of planting seeds with the press began months before, after the casting of the picture was completed. As the release approached, each day and each major player was utilized to whip up a fever pitch of excitement. The media might be offered interviews, staged photo opportunities, estranged and that West and Todd were still very much involved at the time of Todd's death. Yet, it was the more benign set of facts the reigning queen of gossip chose to reveal and endorse. By trading a breaking scandal for one safely in the past, she had perhaps done her friends Roland and Jewel an invaluable service.

Not everyone in the fourth estate packed the punch of Louella. Many columnists or movie reviewers were more than willing to cooperate with studio publicists knowing that doing so might lead to years of good copy and expanded readership. Some took on the role of conduits, funneling to the public whatever "news" they received, hoping sooner or later they would get something worthwhile. Others simply settled for what they could get.

The studio establishment also had the Hollywood-controlled press at its disposal. Dozens of publications, among them *Variety* and *Photoplay*, thrived by packaging and printing whatever the industry publicists wanted to provide. One tabloid, *The Hollywood Reporter*, became the virtual official organ of the studio system. Billy Wilkerson, a successful Hollywood entrepreneur, ran the paper.[14] The *Reporter* was filled with puffery, self-serving announcements, casting calls and actors' ads. When it took on the news, it did so with a predictable slant.

During the 30s, Wilkerson also owned the Trocadero and The Vendome restaurants, both of which also catered to the movie industry. Publicists used Wilkerson's restaurants as sets to show off the talent; columnists haunted and hyped them; photographers snapped the stars entering or leaving, at their tables and on the dance floor.[15] When the Lupinos chose the Trocadero for the fateful dinner party to honor Thelma Todd, they also chose the best spot to announce the arrival of Stanley in Hollywood.

Manipulation of a willing media anxious to supply the public with the stuff of movie magic, made such boosterism possible. As one critic of Hollywood's golden age described it:

> If it weren't for the press, the Louis B. Mayers and the Harry Cohns wouldn't have been half of what they were. They simply wouldn't have been able to get away with it. The Hollywood press reflects the larger community press of Los Angeles. The unfree press of Los Angeles is the worst in the country.[16]

One might quarrel with the latter statement at least as far as the Thelma Todd mystery was concerned. As has been demonstrated, the Los Angeles mainline press, no matter how influenced by the moguls, had a field day with the death of the actress. In fact, it is arguable they kept the story alive long beyond what the evidence warranted.

To what extent movie industry media manipulation influenced the record of the Todd case is difficult to determine. Aside from being a popular actress and valuable property, Todd died under circumstances that were anathema to the image the industry spent millions to construct. Rumors did surface at the time that Hollywood figures were trying to quiet the investigation.[17] Certainly, the men around her—Joseph Schenck, Hal Roach and even Roland West—had the means of manipulation at their disposal. Both Schenck and West promoted the accident hypothesis, either because they believed it or because it was the most palatable explanation.[18] The Hollywood-controlled organs, the *Reporter*, *Variety* and *Photoplay* fell in line, almost entirely ignoring the sensational elements and sticking to elegies of the actress.[19]

Ironically, writers in the Hollywood-controlled media of today have taken the exact opposite tack of creating highly speculative and sensationalistic articles on the subject. This makes perfect sense. In the mid-30s, it served industry interests to downplay the story; today as grist for screenplays, soft news retrospectives, and book-movie tie-ins, it is in the interest of the entertainment industry to accentuate the mysterious and scandalous elements. This, after all, was and is the business of Hollywood—to create myths for a profit. In the quest for profits, truth and accuracy are often not important.

Still, the question remains: beyond using its resources to downplay the scandalous, and even the speculative elements of the Todd death in the mid-thirties, did Hollywood cover up anything at all? While many secondary writers have speculated about such a cover-up, none has offered any real proof. Indeed, their reliance on the assumption that an all-powerful, monolithic, and sometimes sinister, oligarchy ruled Hollywood, ready and able to pull the strings to fix anything, even murder, is questionable at best. As Leonard Leff, writing about censorship in Hollywood, wrote:

> Who controlled Hollywood? Joe Breen? the studios? the Manhattan company presidents? the distributors and exhibitors? the banks and investment houses? A collaborative art form, movies were made by countless hands.[20]

Given these realities and the total lack of proof of cover-up by the Hollywood establishment, a more sober conclusion is warranted. While it is likely the movie industry in 1935 may have tried to contain the story, its actions tended merely to obscure it, giving later generations even more grist for the speculative mill.

FOURTEEN: THE MAKING OF A LEGEND

> Events that do not change shape into power, or which take place outside the normal circuits in which power is exchanged, outside of the normal circuits of legitimacy, of the institutional distribution and control of social goods—such events, in certain ways, do not make history at all. They are resistant to history, because history does not know how to account for them; and history resists them, because it can get away with it .... But because such moments do not turn into history, they lose their shape, and turn into self-parodies, legends, nonsense—old stories, told by cranks.[1]
> – Greil Marcus

In 1976, *Los Angeles Magazine* published an article on the Todd mystery with the following revelation:

> Several months later [after the close of the Thelma Todd investigation], the LAPD received a telegram sent from Ogden, Utah, by a middle-aged woman who stated that she knew the identity of the man who murdered Thelma, and that he was staying in a hotel in Ogden. The LAPD did not reply to the telegram, and it was only when Ogden's police chief Rial Moore and the mayor, Harmon Peery, after conducting their own investigation, sent a similar message to Los Angeles, that the LAPD deigned to reply. Ogden was told that Thelma had committed suicide and that the case was closed.[2]

The author, Nicholas Horden, was not the first writer to discuss the events that occurred in Ogden, Utah in late March 1936, nor would he be the last. The tale has appeared in several retellings of the mystery before he wrote his article and has appeared in many since. Almost every secondary writer on the Todd case has dealt with the incident—beginning in 1940 with Anthony Abbot in *Liberty Magazine*, continuing through William Carr's *Hollywood Tragedy* (1962), Charles Neutzel's *Whodunit? Hollywood Style* (1965), Jay Robert Nash's *Murder Among the Mighty* and *Open Files* (1983), Jody Jacobson's *Hollywood Heartbreak* (1984), and culminating with Andy Edmonds' *Hot Toddy* (1989). Without exception, each writer cast the story in substantially the same light as did Horden—with implications of neglect and even cover-up by the Los Angeles Police Department.[3] How, one must wonder, could the Los

Angeles police have been so indifferent to possibly critical information in the case—information, which, according to the long line of these writers, might have pointed towards a murderer?

The various writers culled the Ogden story from several newspapers published in late March 1936. According to these accounts, a middle-aged woman, using a "public telephone pay station" in Ogden, sent the LAPD a telegram naming a suspect in Todd's death. Tipped off by an operator listening in on the conversation, the Ogden authorities conducted their own investigation. They learned that the man whom the woman claimed was Todd's alleged killer was a "magazine subscription solicitor" in Ogden who had somehow gotten himself mixed up with his accuser. Ogden authorities questioned both him and the woman, but instead of arresting him on suspicion of murder, they let him go and gave the woman 24 hours to leave town or face the threat of arrest as a "public nuisance."[4]

Such was the basis of the various manifestations of the Ogden, Utah tale in the telling and retellings of the Todd mystery. While the details are sparse, it is clear that, whatever happened in Ogden during those few days in early spring 1936, the story reported in the contemporary newspapers did not match the one told by Horden and other Todd mystery chroniclers. The LAPD may not have pursued the new lead—which is not surprising when one considers the numerous false reports of Todd sightings they received in the week after her death—but the Ogden authorities did, and subsequently decided there was nothing to it. They were not and had never been "certain" that the man was Todd's killer, as one secondary writer suggested. Once the contemporary newspapers are reviewed, the Ogden incident can be seen in a completely different light, a pathetic footnote to the Todd case that probably involved the kind of abject personalities the police encounter too often. One can easily imagine an embittered, perhaps delusional woman, a down-on-his-heels salesman, too much alcohol, a quarrel and a nasty, muddleheaded attempt to get even. Gone is the intimation of apathy on the part of the LAPD investigators, or the implication they let a murderer slip through their fingers.

While the Ogden tale is unimportant to the core mystery of Todd's death, it is emblematic of a process that extends beyond 1936 to the present day. Usually reserved for the end of a piece because it occurred towards the conclusion of the contemporary events, the Ogden tale furnishes a kind of epilogue to the mystery. With few exceptions, chroniclers of the mystery consistently embellished the incident to create dark and dramatic undercurrents to a case already replete with enigma. The full facts of the affair, which would defeat this purpose, are expediently omitted.

Carelessness and exaggeration are common in many of the sideshow stories in the Todd mystery, just as they were in 1935. Another tale that has become almost de rigueur with Todd mystery writers involves a stolen ring. Like the Ogden, Utah story, this anecdote is usually placed at the end of the article to heighten conjecture that

Thelma Todd was murdered. Horden was the first to mention it.

> An extraordinary postscript occurred just a few months ago, as told to this writer by Thelma's old co-star, Patsy Kelly. Kelly was touring in Warren, Ohio in the musical *Irene*. A man came backstage, asking to see her. He was tall, dark, and dressed in a conservative suit. He said he was from Florida. But he said he once was in California. He took out a ring.
>
> 'That was Miss Todd's,' he said, looking hard at her and without offering any explanation. He left quickly without speaking another word.[5]

Jody Jacobson repeated the story in 1984. In her version, the man not only shows Kelly the ring but leaves it with her.

> Forty years later, Patsy Kelly was touring in *Irene*. After a performance in Ohio, a tall dark man who said he was from Florida went backstage. He'd been to California once and had something to give her. He slipped a ring into Miss Kelly's hand, and as he walked away said, 'That was Miss Todd's.'[6]

More drama was soon to be added. *Hot Toddy*, by Andy Edmonds, provided an even more embellished version. Edmonds wrote:

> Perhaps one of the most bizarre stories of all centers on a black and gold sardonyx ring, given to Toddy by Pat DiCicco shortly after their marriage. Inside the band was an inscription, TO LAMBIE, a pet name DiCicco called Thelma. She wore the ring after her divorce from DiCicco. It reportedly disappeared the night Thelma was killed.
>
> While touring in Warren, Ohio, in 1979 with the musical *Irene*, Patsy Kelly claimed a mysterious man approached her backstage, opened his hand, and held out a sardonyx ring identical to Thelma's missing band. The man said he was from Florida and that he had been in California. Then he stated, "This was Miss Todd's," and left. Kelly repeated the story to several people before her death on September 24, 1981.[7]

Bizarre, indeed. The incident Horden wrote about in 1976 now takes place in 1979. The ring Horden described generally suddenly takes on specific characteristics— "black and gold sardonyx"—with a very specific history. The ring, a present to Todd from DiCicco, disappears the night Thelma dies. Presumably, from her dead finger.

Edmonds asserts the ring "reportedly disappeared." Where, one wonders, is the report? There is no mention of a missing ring in the original record of the case. Todd's jewelry was examined thoroughly by the police and the Coroner's Inquest to determine whether robbery could have been a motive in the actress' death. Three rings were found on Todd's hands when the coroner examined her body. While it is possible she was wearing another ring, Harvey Priester, Thelma's long-term friend and reputed former fiancé, confirmed in his Coroner's Inquest testimony that all the jewelry she wore that night was found on her body. Mae Whitehead, who dressed Thelma for the party and first found her in the garage, also did not report any jewelry missing.

In fact, DiCicco did not give the sardonyx ring to Thelma at all. It can be identified in photos of the actress taken long before she ever met him. In all probability, it became the property of her mother, who brought it back with her to Lawrence.

The literature of the Todd case is replete with such examples of carelessness and exaggeration. Another area where the facts of the case have been routinely embellished involves jewels found on Todd's body. Repeatedly, writers estimated the jewels worth at $20,000,[8] a figure apparently taken from early press accounts of the death that reported, "Officers found a wealth of jewels about the throat and wrists."[9] Without exception, they omitted to mention a much lower estimate offered at the Coroner's Inquest and likewise neglected to mention that the estate appraisal valued all Todd's jewelry, including over two dozen pieces which she was not wearing when she died, at only $1,850.[10]

The Ogden, Utah and purloined ring anecdotes became intertwined with other facts and speculation in the Todd case, often embellished or rootless. Each secondary writer, after filching from previous writers' inaccuracies in judgments and facts, leaves to posterity a new set of errors and misunderstandings. Over time, the whole has taken on the quality of a legend in the making. Spanning over eighty years of development, the subject of newspaper and magazine articles, book chapters, television "soft news" segments, one made-for-television movie, and, more recently, internet sites and blogs, the mystery has reflected each medium's biases and obsessions.

The process sometimes has a lighter, even frivolous side. One author, L. Allen Smith, concluded his 1973 article about the case by exclaiming:

> Thelma Todd who had the figure of a goddess and the face of an Angel was gone but her memory lingers on and when "The Sunshine of Your Smile" was written, its composer certainly must have had the radiant, golden Thelma in mind.[11]

Hyperbole aside, the allusion to the song "The Sunshine of Your Smile" is at most an expression of the author's enchantment with Todd. Nine years later, it became a little more compelling when another writer, Tony Scott, stated, "The Sunshine of Your Smile" was reportedly written for Miss Todd.[12] In 1980, writer Al Stump took it one further. In a Sunday supplement to the *Los Angeles Herald Examiner*, Stump proclaimed that not only had "Sunshine of Your Smile" been written for Miss Todd, but it was also "played at her Wee Kirk O' The Heather chapel funeral services."[13] In fact, the "Sunshine of Your Smile" had nothing to do with Todd or her funeral, and was originally published in 1915, when she was only nine years old and years away from fame.[14]

Other issues are more crucial and demonstrate how easily the tendency of writers to borrow errors from one another can lead to substantial distortions of the record. There is, for instance, the matter of the 270 steps. Numerous writers focused on one of the dramatic features of Castellammare, a long series of cement steps that ascend the terraced hillside, linking the coastal road (now called the Pacific Coast Highway but named the Roosevelt Highway in 1935) with several hillside streets: Castellammare, Posetano, and Revello. The steps became critical during the investigation because investigators suspected Todd might have taken them to get to the garage. As such, they entered into key speculations about her movements, her motivations, and her physical faculties. In her fatigued and inebriated state, would she have climbed the hill to the garage? Could she have made the climb at all? What was her most probable route? What effect would such a climb have on the bottom of her evening slippers? Could someone have carried her up the hill?

One of the earliest references to the steps and their part in the mystery can be found in the December 22, 1935 edition of the *Los Angeles Examiner*. Beneath a photo taken at the bottom of the steps rising between Castellammare and Posetano is a caption that reads "The 270 concrete steps leading from Miss Todd's seaside café to home where she was found dead in garage. These steps have been inspected minutely by investigators."

Secondary writers, whether prompted by this source or another, consistently referred to the 270 steps as they try to elucidate the mystery, though one writer gave the number as 271, another claimed 208, and a third stated the number was 280.[15] None seems to have noticed that, of the 268 actual steps on the hillside, only 150 connect the Pacific Coast Highway with Posetano, where the garage is located. The remaining 118 steps carry on above to Revello Drive, leading to the main entrance of West's estate, Castillo Del Mar, far removed from the garage on Posetano. As there would have been no reason for Todd to climb to Revello Drive if her goal was to reach the garage, then the number of steps she would have climbed was only 150.

Why none of the later writers on the mystery noticed this simple fact is difficult to understand. It is a simple matter for anybody who visits the site to count them. Furthermore, the arrangement of the stairs, at least the crucial middle set between Castellammare and Posetano, was disclosed in newspaper accounts of the time. On the day after Todd's body was discovered, the front-page of the *Los Angeles Times* featured a diagram of the café and its environs that suggested two possible routes Thelma may have taken to the garage (See page vi). The artist, Athol Ewing, noted in the drawing that "63 steps divided into three sections of 21 steps each," connected Castellammare Lane with Posetano Drive.[16] Despite his care, Ewing's diagram became part of the deliberate inflation of the story in Edmonds' *Hot Toddy*, where the sketch was crudely redrawn by another artist. In this new version, Ewing's careful notation of 63 steps was replaced by a fallacious one of "270 steps." Thus, a fairly accurate primary source was altered to comport with the erroneous legacy of a long line of secondary sources.

While it is hard to excuse later writers from mistaking the number of steps Todd would have taken, it is understandable reporters at the time may have confused the issue from the start. Their count focused on the number of steps from the road to the front entrance of Castillo Del Mar on Posetano, as the caption of the photo indicated when it specified that the steps led "from Miss Todd's seaside café to **home** (emphasis added) where she was found dead in garage." It is also possible that the original "steps" referred to paces, not stair steps; that is, the number of paces Thelma Todd might have taken to reach the garage from the café. There is some evidence to support this possibility. On December 19, 1935, the day of Thelma's funeral, detectives Taylor and Romero visited the café, and retraced Todd's possible path, "step by step." [17] It is not clear what route they chose as most probable. But it is possible they paced off some 270 steps—perhaps 155—straight up the hillside, assuming one pace per cement step and including the number necessary to cross Castellammare, and an additional 115 to reach the garage along Posetano. Because a large section of the road between the top of the steps and the garage has since been obliterated by a landslide, the number of paces along Posetano can no longer be determined, but 115 does not seem unreasonable.

In either case, the later confusion over the "270 steps" probably began quite simply as a misinterpretation of the reports in late December 1935. Later writers either failed to understand the basis of the original count or the fact the home is on an entirely different street from the garage.

Other reports of the time similarly led to a progression of errors in the secondary sources. For example, a number of writers claimed the sliding doors of the garage stood partly open on the morning of December 16, when Mae Whitehead arrived at the garage.[18] How they got this idea is easy to trace. In newspaper reports in the early days of the investigation, Whitehead was reported to have told investigators she found the garage doors ajar, with an opening of six inches.

This "fact" inevitably leads to some interesting questions. If the garage door was ajar, why didn't the opening provide an escape route for the deadly carbon monoxide gas, thus bringing into question whether Todd actually died in the garage? And why did nobody notice it before Whitehead arrived on Monday morning? Most critically, what, if anything, can be inferred about Todd's death from the fact she -- or somebody else -- left the door ajar?

Not surprisingly, secondary writers often assumed the garage door was left open by somebody else, not Todd, and went to great lengths to account for this "fact". Horden cites a source who suggested the murderer, "struck her and then closed the door almost to 8 inches in a rage."[19] Edmonds describes the garage door creeping open unassisted several hours after Todd is murdered, explaining that, "The doors never did close properly unless they were shut tight and locked."[20] Without question, both claims are preposterous. An enraged murderer might slam a door shut, but it would take a clever, calculating one to close it to "almost 8 inches." And wooden sliding doors—viewed by some in 1935 as too heavy for Miss Todd to have moved by herself— would hardly "creep" open by themselves.

The whole issue is a red herring. It arose from confusion surrounding Whitehead's statements to investigators about her observations when she found Todd's body Monday morning. The door that Whitehead found ajar was the garage's, not the Phaeton's, but somehow the two doors were confused in newspaper reports and by other witnesses. Roland West clarified the issue in his testimony before the Coroner's Jury, explaining that Alice Todd had told him Whitehead had found the garage door open, but, after hearing Whitehead's own testimony that day, he realized that she was actually referring to the Phaeton's door. Alice Todd evidently misunderstood Mae Whitehead, as did most of the press.[21]

Later chroniclers of the Todd mystery, overlooking West's clarification, invented logical but fatuous solutions to the open garage door problem. Despite Whitehead's clear testimony that she went to the garage first in the morning, one even claimed that Whitehead was searching for Todd and had observed the open garage door from the café. In fact, the garage cannot be seen from the café.

This example demonstrates a critical problem in the historical and contemporary understanding of the Todd case. With its blizzard of references to doors, locks, keys, lights, steps, and apartments, which make even more perplexing an already baffling puzzle, the mystery is full of traps for the careless. Unwary and uncritical chroniclers, especially those overly reliant on previous writers, are likely to confuse one reference with another and then amplify the mistake by incorporating the errors into their analysis and speculation.

The plenitude of contradictions in the Todd record makes some mistakes inevitable. An often-reported story surrounds Ernest O. Peters, Todd's chauffeur on the night of the Trocadero party. According to the tale, on the way home Thelma ordered him to drive fast, because she was "afraid of gangsters."[22] Secondary writers repeatedly used this assertion to support the theory that Miss Todd was the victim of a gang hit resulting from her opposition to gambling on the third floor of the café building.

The report of Todd's fear of gangsters or kidnapping, a common worry in Hollywood at the time, arose when newspapers recounted the police re-questioning of Peters on December 17, one day before his coroner's testimony. One paper quoted Peters as telling police: "Miss Todd was afraid that because she had been the target of extortion notes she might be slain or kidnapped by gangsters. She told me to drive at top speed and not to make boulevard stops. I drove between 65 and 70 miles an hour." [23] Another prefaced the last sentence, "On the way to her café."[24]

However, in his Coroner's Inquest testimony, Peters did not attribute his fast driving that morning to Todd's fear of gangsters. He explained simply "that at that time in the morning there wasn't much traffic and we drove fairly fast all the way home, which was her custom." When asked why Todd wanted to drive fast, Peters said only, "She liked to go fast and wanted everybody else to go fast."[25] Nowhere in his sworn testimony, in fact, did he allude to Todd's fear of gangsters. In fact, he testified Todd "Never spoke to me from the time she got in the car when she said, 'We will go home,' until she got out."[26]

Why the inconsistency? Perhaps, when first interviewed by police on Tuesday, Peters spoke generally about Todd's fear of gangsters and did not refer to anything she said or did Sunday morning. Reporters or the police may have linked a comment about Todd's fear with his description of his fast drive from the Trocadero to the café early Sunday morning. In any case, the best evidence–Peter's sworn testimony at the Coroner's Inquest–counsels against the assertion of many secondary writers that Todd urged Peters to drive fast that night because she feared gangsters.

To some extent, confusion over specific elements in the admittedly convoluted record of the Todd case is inevitable. The problem is many writers recklessly followed a few erroneous facts to ludicrous conclusions. As in the literature surrounding the Kennedy assassination of John Kennedy, the death of Marilyn Monroe or the Jack the Ripper killings, a premium has been placed on imagination at the expense of careful study and reasoning.

Wild speculation is not uncommon for writers in the Hollywood mystery and scandal genre. General assumptions about Hollywood are asserted, rumors fly, and innuendo abounds. The flawed context is then applied to a specific case with a nod and a wink to the reader who presumably is expected to discern the fire hidden in the smoke. Unbound by the strictures of historiography or forensics, or even good journalism, they play fast and loose with facts, embellish freely, and spin their yarns, often only to be outdone by the next writer who takes up the inquiry.

Obscured in this inflationary cycle of speculation are the legitimate facts and issues of the Todd case. While most of the fabrications and fables discussed so far are not critical to the case, other more crucial matters have been subjected to an equal amount of distortion.

FIFTEEN: THE PATINA OF MYSTERY

> The researches of many commentators have already thrown much darkness on this subject, and it is probable that, if they continue, we shall soon know nothing at all about it.
> — Mark Twain

 To the lovers of mystery and detective fiction, the death of Thelma Todd offers an almost perfect blend of colorful characters, intriguing settings, and an intricate and engrossing mystery. The case resonates with elements of the great mystery genre traditions—the hard-boiled, the Gothic, and the drawing room.

 Its cast might have stepped from the pages of a Raymond Chandler novel: beautiful blond victim; reclusive and eccentric movie director; his estranged wife, pallid and spiritual; suave, handsome ex-husband; opinionated, insistent socialite. The supporting players aren't bad either: firebrand Grand Jury foreman; vacillating coroner; shadowy political and studio bosses hovering in the background; a chorus of aspiring actresses, psychics, and publicity seekers. While the world-weary police detectives try to keep the lid on the case, eager reporters try to bust it wide open. As one paper put it at the time, "The Strange Death of Thelma Todd," featured "as notable a cast of characters as has been assembled for a real life drama."[1]

 The setting is also enthralling. Like a great manor on an English sea cliff visited by Holmes and Watson or a New England dark house in a Poe or Hawthorne tale, the buildings of Castellammare sit in splendid solitude. The thickly walled and forbidding estate, the luxurious and slightly wanton roadhouse, and a half-dozen decadent mansions appear stranded like whales on the hillside. Rows of post-top street lamps glimmer wanly in the fog, illuminating a bleak landscape of empty streets that twist aimlessly along the wind-swept hillside. Steep cement stairways climb past barren lots and a broad Italianate promenade stretches along the hillside, awaiting strollers who never come. Across the winding coastal road from this surreal landscape, waves pound the lonely beach.

 While its exotic denizens pursue their privileged lives, surrounded by a retinue of servants and retainers, the community hoards its secrets and affects a past it never had. Then one cold, windy night something terrible happens. A beautiful actress, who reigns over the isolated community like a countess, is found dead in her luxurious automobile in a tomb-like garage. Through the investigation of her death, the place and its people reveal, first reluctantly, then in a flood, the hidden rooms, the dark passions and their spider web of relationships. The plot turns and twists like an Agatha Christie or Ellery Queen story. The body betrays no sign of violence, leading the police to a rapid presumption of accidental death. Then, suddenly witnesses come forward, claiming to have seen or talked to the victim after she was supposed to be dead. Clues abound: mysterious sightings and telephone calls, drops of blood, scuffed slippers, a faded camellia, tales of quarrels and despondent words, locked doors and missing keys, phantom automobiles.

Now come gather in the library, the great Chan or Philo Vance or the Thin Man is about to reveal how he has unraveled the mystery. Assembled are the loyal maid, the taciturn chauffeur, the jealous boyfriend and his estranged actress wife, the bumbling police detective, the crooked DA, the Italian ex-husband, all the usual characters. A hush falls as the detective goes from person to person, suspect to suspect, weaving together seemingly unconnected facts and revealing what everyone else has missed. What will prove the murderer's downfall: the whining dog, the missing key, or a few gallons of gas left in the tank? Or will the killer's own words trap him?

Because of these elements—characters, setting and plot—the story of the death of Thelma Todd almost begs for dramatization. In fact, a number of writers have been seduced by the story, transforming some of these elements into fiction, most notably, Raymond Chandler in *The Lady in the Lake*. Unfortunately, the power of the fictive elements has also led other non-fiction writers to muddle the real mystery. This tendency, observable in the original reportage of the case, is even more pronounced in the work of secondary writers, where the fiction often overwhelms the facts of the mystery. Indeed, these later accounts read as if Thelma Todd's death were the creation of a dime novelist of the thirties, not a real event in a real context. It is partially because of this tendency that the mystery has become even more opaque over the years. With each retelling, the real complexities of the case have been buried beneath a superstructure of false claims and misunderstood or omitted facts.

In fact, several of the best-known issues of the case, when scrutinized carefully, turn out to be red herrings. An excellent example is perhaps the best-known "fact" of the case: the issue of the unscuffed slippers.

As the story goes, Miss Todd wore new dancing slippers to the Trocadero on the night before her disappearance. According to newspaper accounts of the time and a bevy of secondary writers since, their soles showed little or no signs of wear when the shoes were found on her feet Monday morning, suggesting the actress could not have climbed the hillside to the garage, as police theorized. Had she done so, her shoes would have shown more scuffing. If she didn't walk, someone must have carried or driven her to the garage.[2]

For many, the evidence of the unscuffed slippers argues strongly against the police theory that Todd's death was accidental. It also lends credence to the notion that Todd was alive on Sunday. If she didn't climb to the garage and die early Sunday morning, somebody took her there on Sunday night.

The story of the unscuffed slippers figured prominently in the 1935-36 news coverage of the Todd case. Four days after the discovery of the body, questions about the slippers were suddenly raised. They apparently stemmed from a demand by Grand Jury Foreman George Rochester to reenact the walk up the Castellammare hillside to see if a woman of Todd's general "height and poundage" and wearing similar clothes and shoes could have made the climb. It was reported the Grand Jury was particularly interested in the issue of the slipper scuffing.[3] At about the same time, the District Attorney's investigators, recently assigned to the case by District Attorney Fitts, who had promised the day before to "trace all possible avenues of investigation," conducted an experiment on the Castellammare hillside.[4] A "woman operative" of Todd's general build, dressed in a gown, furs, and dainty slippers climbed the steps to the garage. Afterward, the investigators examined her slippers, and reportedly concluded they were not as scuffed as Thelma Todd's.[5]

The issue came up again two weeks later when members of the Grand Jury visited the café and the garage. According to one report:

> There has been a definite suspicion in the minds of the grand jurors that the blond actress never did not [sic] make that climb. This they were to attempt to determine by the stair climbing test this morning, including a comparison of the condition of their shoes with the condition of Miss Todd's slippers when she was found dead.[6]

One juror reported her shoes showed considerable wear after climbing the "271 steps." Another woman, a bystander who followed the Grand Jury up the hill in high-heeled slippers, had to stop and take off her shoes before she reached the top. According to one report, "Foreman Rochester said the jurors were particularly interested in view of the fact that Miss Todd's dancing slippers were said to show but little wear."[7] Because of these findings, Rochester ordered Frank Gompert, a criminologist with the sheriff's department who specialized in shoe and shoeprint clues, to undertake "a thorough scientific examination of Miss Todd's shoes."[8] The "microscopic expert" was asked to look for bits of gravel or cement embedded in the soles of the shoes, which would indicate Miss Todd walked in the slippers to the garage.[9]

If left alone, this record might justify the reports and conclusions of the secondary writers who have found sinister implications in the issue of the unscuffed shoes. Indeed, the story offers just the right clue that could demonstrate murder and lead to a killer. Raymond Chandler used a similar device in *The Lady in the Lake*.[10] In this 1943 novel, Philip Marlowe, Chandler's detective, trips up a murderer when he discovers that "a green velvet dancing pump," worn by a supposed suicide victim who, like Todd, was found dead in a garage several hundred feet from her home, is not scuffed. While Chandler complicates the plot by involving two pairs of slippers and a blackmailer in addition to the murder, the discovery of the unscuffed slipper proves the victim did not walk to the garage to commit suicide but instead was murdered.[11]

Similarly inspired, secondary writers have played up the unscuffed slippers in their own accounts, sometimes changing the facts to further their speculations. For example, while contemporary press accounts suggested only that the shoes worn by the "woman operative" working for the police were similar to Todd's, several writers have described them as identical.[12] Another implied the test took place on the same day the body was found instead of several days later.[13] In one imaginative variation, a writer merged Gertrude Rose with the woman operative from the DA's office, claiming it was a "persistent grand juror [who] climbed the 270 steps to the Todd-West home in a pair of satin slippers similar to those worn by Thelma."[14]

Embellishments or muddling aside, most of the writers who have dealt with Todd case treat the allegation that the slippers were unscuffed as an established fact. This has led to some ingenious speculations. One declared it the "clincher" evidence proving Todd "was murdered, probably by a hit man who was ordered to make it look like an accident."[15] Another created a scenario as convoluted as Chandler's plot. In it, after she returns home from the Trocadero and changing into bedroom slippers, Todd gets into a violent argument with West and storms from her apartment. West pursues her to the garage and closes the garage door as she turns on the phaeton's ignition. After she dies, he returns to the apartment, where he notices her evening slippers. He then returns to the garage, where he exchanges the evening shoes for her bedroom slippers, which he hurls into the ocean to conceal the scuffing on their soles.[16]

It is clear from this example how the non-fictional and fictional treatments of the Todd case have cross-fertilized each other. A detective novelist borrows the unscuffed slipper element from the real case; writers on the Todd mystery return the compliment by constructing solutions that seem like tales from a mystery novelist's pen. The unscuffed slippers appeal to the same predilections in both the novelist and the Todd mystery writers. They are the subtle clue that allows the great detective—Vance, Chan, Marlowe, or the secondary writer—to expose the crime the plodding cops missed, the linchpin on which turns the engine of their respective fictions.

However appealing the slippers clue may be to writers, in the real case they were of no consequence. The simple fact was that the slippers actually showed a great deal of wear, more than that would have been acquired by a single walk to the garage. Repeatedly during the investigation, this point was made clear. Captain Bruce Clark, the first officer on the scene on the morning of the body's discovery, examined the soles of the slippers carefully and affirmed at the Coroner's Jury Inquest that the "bottom of her shoes ... had the appearance, or gave the indication that she had walked quite some distance on cement. The bottoms of her soles were scuffed up quite a little bit . . . ."[17]

Tests performed on the slippers by Frank Gompert of the LA County Sheriff's department supported Clark's conclusion. Not only did the slippers show sufficient scuffing, they even bore traces of wax from the dance floor of the Trocadero.[18]

Police chemist Ray Pinker also testified before the Grand Jury on the matter. While he was careful to point out the tests on the shoes did not prove the actress made the climb up the hill, he noted, "she had walked on a hard surface."[19] Pinker conducted his own test by wearing a pair of "new" shoes and retracing Miss Todd's steps to the garage. Discounting the notion that the terrain was particularly rough, he reported his shoes "showed no more wear than if they had been worn on regular pavement."[20]

The police chemist went on to note that the tests were essentially meaningless: the shoes were not new and had been worn before.[21] For some reason, this simple fact, first mentioned by Mae Whitehead when she told the Coroner's Jury Miss Todd "had had a pair of shoes dyed for wearing that evening," was overlooked by several of the investigators and grand jurors.[22] Clearly, she had the shoes for some time and wore them on prior occasions. In fact, photographs of the famous footwear published in the papers at the time reveal them not as dainty slippers but substantial high heel sandals with insoles discolored from use and perspiration and leather that was soft and pliable—not stiff as one would expect in new shoes.[23]

Neither Clark's observations nor Whitehead's statement ever found its way into newspaper accounts about the unscuffed slippers. However, Pinker's testimony resolved the issue at the time. After his report, there was no further mention of the unscuffed slippers in the press. However, the revelations did not prevent secondary writers from continuing to base their conclusions on this red herring.

Why did the news reporters of the time perpetuate the story in spite of such early rebutting evidence? And why do more modern writers continue to subscribe to it, failing to report the countervailing evidence, even claiming what was never claimed at the time (and which was certainly not true), that the slippers were new?[24] Most likely, both the reporters and the secondary writers somehow missed the key evidence that discounted the story of the unscuffed slippers. Veteran news reporter Aggie Underwood even referred to the unscuffed slippers as late as 1949. While the press published some of the Coroner's Inquest testimony verbatim, Whitehead's and Clark's comments about the slippers were not printed. The full Coroner's Inquest testimony was retained by the Coroner's office, which eventually transferred it to microfilm where it languished unread for many years. Pinker's analysis of the shoes, however, was well covered. The secondary writers simply overlooked or ignored it.

The DA investigators' midnight simulation of Todd's hill climb to test the slippers and the reported results are more difficult to explain. It was this incident and the news coverage it received that launched the story in the first place, kept it alive at the time and provided fodder for a host of secondary writers. There are a couple of clues to why the story gained such prominence.

On December 20, one day before the test, without noting a source, the *Santa Monica Evening Outlook* reported Thelma Todd's slippers "were being scrutinized."[25] The *Hollywood Citizen News* asked the question: Are they scuffed enough?[26] The next day several papers reported the midnight experiment and its findings, focusing on the supposed fact the slippers were more scuffed than Todd's.[27] But, when the *Los Angeles Examiner* referred to the test on the following day, it ascribed a purpose different from that of testing the amount of scuffing in the slippers. According to this paper, the test was designed to determine "the effects of the climb on a woman of Thelma Todd's height and build." No mention was made about scuffing on the slippers.[28] In fact, the newspapers never directly claimed the test was conducted to determine how scuffed the slippers should be, though the *Chicago Daily Tribune* reported George Rochester demanded such a test. Nor were any of the reports about the lack of scuffing on the slippers ever attributed to the D. A. investigators themselves.

This sequence and the lack of attribution suggest the DA investigators never intended to test the slippers. It is also possible they had no real doubts or issues concerning them. Only out-of-town newspapers, dependent on the AP wire service, a single source, reported the investigators had doubts about the slippers' condition. In Los Angeles, the *Examiner* stated only there had been prior speculation about a lack of scuffing on the shoes, not that the DA investigators questioned their condition.[29]

In short, the slipper-scuffing clue may well have been either concocted or misinterpreted by the media. Given journalistic standards of the time, one cannot preclude outright fabrication, but it is possible much of the unjustifiable attention to the slippers came through honest mistakes. Rewrite men may have been misled by ambiguous references to prior speculation about the shoes in the initial drafts, for instance. In any case, the story of the unscuffed slippers gave the mystery some extra legs. It has lasted, all but unchallenged, for over three-quarters of a century.

So has the matter of peas and beans . . . or rather the lack of them. According to this tale, when the contents of Thelma Todd's stomach were analyzed at the autopsy, the medical examiner discovered a quantity of partially digested peas and string beans. Yet, according to numerous sources, neither vegetable was served at the Trocadero on Saturday evening. What, then, of the police theory that Thelma Todd died accidentally early Sunday morning, which assumed the peas and beans found in her stomach were part of the Trocadero dinner?

This story leaves a big footprint on the trail of secondary writers. First reported in a *Liberty Magazine* article as "the official knockout" to the LAPD accident theory,[30] it was repeated in 1949 by Aggie Underwood, who covered the Todd case for the *Los Angeles Herald Examiner*.[31] Later writers picked up and embellished the tale.[32] Several incorporated an explanation of the controversial vegetables into their speculations about the solution to the Todd case. One hypothesized that Miss Todd might have shared a post-Trocadero snack of peas and beans at her café with a jealous suitor before he closed the garage doors and ended her life. Andy Edmonds, after transforming the peas and beans to "peas and carrots," claimed Thelma consumed them Sunday night at a Beverly Hills dinner with a notorious gangster who would soon order her execution.[33]

As with the story of the unscuffed slippers, the peas and beans tale grew out of the original record of the Todd case. On the last day of 1935, testifying before the Grand Jury, Autopsy Surgeon A.F. Wagner described finding in Todd's stomach "a quantity of green peas and string beans [that] had hardly been subjected to digestive action."[34] The fragments of food could not have been eaten more than eight to ten hours prior to her death, according to Wagner.[35] As Miss Todd ate her last known meal at the Trocadero Saturday night, the undigested food reinforced the police estimate of death in the early hours of Sunday morning. That is, eight to 10 hours after the party guests consumed their dinner between 10:30 and midnight, placing the time of death between 6:30 and 10:00, Sunday morning.

Wagner's testimony set off a flurry of newspaper copy. One UPI story picked up by a Hearst paper, the *San Francisco Chronicle*, claimed the specific finding of peas and beans had been previously "unrevealed." Even more dramatically, the same story declared "peas and beans" had never been "officially" served Saturday night at the Trocadero.[36]

Here was a grand opportunity to second-guess Wagner's time of death estimate. As was often the case, the foreman of the Grand Jury, George Rochester, was ready to fan the flames of controversy. "Either Miss Todd came back to the table at the last moment and ate peas and beans from some other plate, or she stopped on the way home and ate these vegetables, or the entire theory she died Sunday morning is wrong," he told the UPI reporter outside the jury room. "If she did not have peas and beans at the Trocadero, then she was living and ate such a meal some time Sunday."[37] The reporter added his own commentary to the foreman's statement. "Dr. Wagner originally told a Coroner's Jury Miss Todd's death had occurred about 18 hours before he performed his autopsy, which would have placed it about midnight Sunday. Later he changed the testimony to conform to the Homicide Squad's report on the death hour [before 6 a.m. Sunday]."[38]

The *Herald Express* and the *Examiner* also commented on the case's new vegetable angle, as did the *Daily News*. However, the *Los Angeles Times*, whose increasingly truncated coverage of the investigation suggests it was losing enthusiasm for the case, was silent on the issue.[39] Silent also was the *Hollywood Citizen News*. It reported only that Wagner's evidence "had touched upon the condition of Miss Todd's body and the results of the autopsy and chemical analysis of the vital organs."[40]

The *Citizen-News* had good reason to ignore speculation about peas and beans. It had already disclosed that John Linden and Peter Imfeld, the two waiters who served the Lupino/Todd party Saturday night, told the Grand Jury the menu included "peas, string beans, filet mignon, salad, turtle soup and olives." The paper also noted at the time the menu "tallied with the autopsy surgeon's analysis of the contents of the actress' stomach. It was on the basis of the quantity of food in her stomach that the time of Miss Todd's death was placed at some time Sunday morning."[41]

Why the Hearst papers and the *Daily News* failed to note this testimony—and how they had in fact gotten it completely wrong, concluding the waiters testified instead that peas and beans had not been served—is perplexing. Easier to understand are the claims by secondary writers that the vegetables were not included on Miss Todd's plate. Only one newspaper, the *Hollywood Citizen News*, a defunct journal whose microfilmed editions were not readily available to researchers, reported peas and beans were served. Even if the writer did stumble across this report, he or she might figure it could be safely ignored in the interest of puffing up the mystery.

The peas and beans issue dropped from newspaper coverage after the first of the year. One can only speculate why, since there is no record of any resolution to the issue, however false, in the papers. Perhaps somebody nudged Rochester after his dramatic press conference and showed him the transcript of Linden and Imfeld's testimony of December 23. With the fact of peas and beans established, speculation about discrepancies in Wagner's time of death estimates, based as they were on rates of digestion and "gross appearance of the body," simply became too ephemeral to be persuasive. Not even the secondary writers perpetuated them, either because they required a sophisticated understanding of the case or because they failed to provide the simple smoking gun the genre demands.

The persistence of the issues of the peas and beans and the unscuffed slippers arise in part from the carelessness of the newspaper reporters of the time and the flawed analysis of subsequent writers. They also survive because they serve the purpose of the writers who perpetuate them and an audience who craves the thrill and drama of fiction in real events. For some, the clues of the unscuffed slippers and the peas and beans serve as a rebuff to the smug police findings; for others, they hint at dark deeds ready to be exposed through the interplay of obscure facts and brilliant deduction. Nevertheless, when fairly evaluated, these issues turn out to be the stuff of mystery and legend, not fact and analysis. Subsequent writers perpetuated the stories and their implications to expand upon the mystery.

While one can criticize the approach for its lack of rigor and tendency to mislead, its faults are of the venal variety. Unfortunately, in dealing with other issues in the Todd mystery, some writers have gone much further, seriously misstating the original record and sometimes departing from it completely.

SIXTEEN: FRAUDS AND SLANDERS

> Scandal is what one half of the world takes pleasure inventing, and the other half in believing.
> – Paul Chatfield

Beyond the mistakes and hyperbole, the embellishments and huckstering that evolved with the telling and re-telling of the Thelma Todd mystery lay a more troubling phenomenon—the rebirth of tabloid journalism.

While the tabloid newspapers peaked in the mid-1920s and failed in the early 1930s, their traditions continued in ensuing decades, adapted to new forms and audiences. The Forties and Fifties saw the flourishing of true detective and crime magazines. In the following decades, tabloid weeklies, replete with grotesque births, reports of flying saucers, and the sexual escapades of film celebrities, appeared at newsstands and supermarket checkouts lines. By the 1980s, the tabloid legacy found expression in the television news magazine, the docudrama and the made-for-television movie. In so doing, it made inroads into the domain of the electronic news establishment, particularly the local 11:00 o'clock news half-hour, which itself came to focus increasingly on blood and sex stories. In the late 1990s, tabloidism found deep roots on the Internet leading to increased celebrity scandal coverage via websites, blogs, and tweets.

Like an opportunistic disease, the tabloid ethic also infected the realms of history and biography and insinuated itself into the book lists of major publishers. The profits realizable through tabloid-style coverage encouraged publishers to issue book-length exposés of the lives, loves and indiscretions of Hollywood's Golden Age stars and personalities. Blending elements of sensationalistic fiction and scorning research, these tattlers exaggerated and distorted historical events and personalities, emphasizing the salacious and scandalous, and often casting their fables against a backdrop of stealth and conspiracy to meet the public's paranoid faith in the intrigues of imaginary national and multinational cabals.

In recent years, reborn tabloid journalism has redefined the death of Thelma Todd. In fact, it is through its treatment in magazine articles and book chapters, as a staple of "unsolved murders" or "great Hollywood mysteries" retrospectives, and finally in a full-length book that spawned a television movie that the case is best known today. The tabloid genre has clearly left its mark on the public's awareness of the Todd mystery. Operating outside of a discipline of criticism or review and with little or no fear of action for libel, most of the case's principals having died long ago, this new tabloidism sensationalized many elements of the case beyond the imagination of the press of Todd's era.

The trend began in the 1960s with the publication of several book-length Hollywood exposés and was in full swing in 1975 with the American publication of *Hollywood Babylon*.[1] Written by former child actor and enfant terrible director Kenneth Anger and illustrated by photos drawn from his personal collection, it proved something of a watershed in the coverage of Hollywood scandal. Filled with murders, suicides, and allegations of rape and orgy, it purported to lay bare the dark underside of the entertainment industry in its halcyon days. Throughout, the reader is treated to a freak show of grotesque photographs that reveal its subjects in various stages of undress, decline, disgrace, and death.

The death of Thelma Todd was given a prominent place in this book although the mystery behind that death was grievously short-changed. Anger's description of Todd's corpse short-circuits the conundrum of accident, suicide, or murder; Todd's body had been found "after a struggle . . . her mouth, evening gown, and mink coat spotted with blood," with her clothing in "state of rumpled disarray."[2] For Anger, there was no question of the primary cause of death here. It was murder pure and simple although the how and why and who of it would remain "one of Hollywood's most vexing enigmas."[3] Who killed her? Anger suggested several suspects. Roland West, he claimed, admitted to a violent quarrel with Todd when she returned to the café from the Trocadero; after West shoved Todd outside, neighbors heard her pounding on the apartment door trying to get back in. Still, according to Anger, West's confession and "the scream and kick routine on West's doorstep" may have simply been a decoy. At the time, he claims, there was speculation that, while West and a girl friend staged a fight, West "knocked Thelma out, placed her in the car, turned on the ignition and closed the door of the garage." As for motive, Anger suggested that West wanted to end his relationship with the actress and decided that killing her would not only accomplish this goal but also allow him to commit a perfect crime, ". . . as in his film *Alibi*."

Anger's piece was filled with errors, some trivial, some profound. On the trivial side were his claim that Thelma owned a "Packard convertible," not a Lincoln phaeton, as well as his misidentification of the West/Todd restaurant as the "Roadside Rest" instead of Thelma Todd's Sidewalk Café. He also blurred the legal procedures of the case, attributing the verdict of "Death due to carbon monoxide poisoning" to the Grand Jury instead of the Coroner's Jury. Other secondary writers would pick up these errors, making them part of the mystery's tradition of misinformation.

Other mistakes were more serious. Anger claimed, for instance, that the inquest established that Thelma's ex-comedy partner, ZaSu Pitts, had lent her thousands of dollars that were "swallowed up" in financing the café. In fact, neither the Coroner's Inquest nor the Grand Jury established that Thelma was indebted to ZaSu Pitts or anyone else; nor did Miss Pitts or any other person make a substantial claim against Todd's estate.[4]

Equally unfounded were claims that neighbors reported a row between West and Todd in the "wee hours" that Sunday morning and that kick marks were later found on the apartment door.[5] No contemporary report indicates that the neighbors–who were few and far between in Castellammare in 1935–noticed anything. If they had reported any activity, it would certainly have made headlines. Similarly, the door, which Anger described as "hacienda-style" apparently confusing it with some other door, perhaps the garage doors or the door to Castillo Del Mar, was examined by grand jurors when they visited the café. They found it covered with heavy metal sheeting, which was not likely to show the kick marks of a diminutive actress wearing opened-toe evening shoes.[6]

Nor did West admit that he had a fight with Thelma early Sunday morning. In fact, West consistently claimed he never saw Todd alive after she left for the Trocadero.

Perhaps Anger had some other source for this claim, outside of the recorded testimony and newspaper accounts.[7] In all likelihood, his report of the quarrel was pieced together from thirty years of gossip and speculation among movie folk, arising originally from West and Todd's "quarrel" that took place *before* she left for the Trocadero.

While unreliable as a source for any serious appraisal of the Todd case, Anger's piece serves as something of a benchmark in the literature of the mystery. While passing blithely over the complex issues of the Todd case, it introduced–or first documented–some of the recurring themes of a developing legend surrounding her death. The book became a cult classic, inspiring dozens of copycat publications, many with chapters on the Todd case that repeated *Hollywood Babylon's* factual errors and groundless speculations. As time passed, the claims and suppositions have become progressively unfounded and salacious, amounting in some cases to outright fraud and character assassination. Predictably, the purveyors of the new tabloidism most often exacerbated or manufactured the elements the genre thrives upon–violence, sex and drugs–a process which reached its zenith 15 years after Anger's book, with the publication of Edmond's *Hot Toddy*.

From its beginning paragraphs, Edmond's account of Todd's death is filled with factual errors and contradictions of sworn testimony. Mae Whitehead's arrival time is moved back a half hour, Todd's apartment is relocated from above the café to its rear, and it is the garage door, not the car door, that Whitehead finds open by six inches. Most significantly, while Edmonds' narrative utilizes Whitehead's repeated statements that she didn't notice any injuries and believed Todd was merely asleep behind the wheel, she describes Todd's corpse as "bloodied and battered," ignoring testimony of a half dozen eyewitness that only minor spots of blood were found.

The author goes on to itemize evidence of the battering, including "lacerations and contusions around Thelma's neck," two cracked ribs, a broken nose and a chipped front tooth,[8] astonishing details that appeared neither in the coroner's transcript nor in the press accounts of the Grand Jury and police investigations. One can only guess from where these details came since the book does not acknowledge its sources. There seem only three possible explanations. Either the author discovered evidence that the authorities missed or covered up, she embellished the original reports and those of subsequent writers, or she simply made the injuries up.

As to the first explanation, it is hard to believe the authorities of the time could have missed a broken nose, two cracked ribs and the injuries to the neck. A full autopsy was conducted and dozens of people saw the body. It is also difficult to believe such visible and obvious injuries could have been covered up with so many people and agencies involved in the investigation. Those attempting to do so would have had to stifle much of institutional Los Angeles, including, the press, the police, the coroner's office, two independent juries, and the district attorney's office. Edmonds does not explain how this amazing feat was accomplished other than to suggest that the man who she claims killed Todd, arch-villain Lucky Luciano, could have done so.

The second hypothesis is more plausible. Some details in Edmonds' description can be linked to original accounts. An anonymous report of the time, supposedly from an attendant at the Todd and Leslie mortuary, held that Miss Todd's throat showed signs of swelling and lacerations. Although it was vehemently denied by Autopsy Surgeon Wagner, the rumor persisted in later accounts of the death, perhaps until Edmonds transformed it from swelling and lacerations in her throat to the more visible "lacerations and contusions around Thelma's neck." Similarly, Edmonds' cracked tooth may have come from the fact that Todd's temporary tooth was found loose in her mouth, apparently having been dislodged when her mouth struck the steering wheel.

The exaggerations and misstatements in *Hot Toddy* culminate a trend that has been evolving since the end of the reportage on the Todd case. For example, author Jay Robert Nash reported in his 1983 book *Murder Among the Mighty* that

> ...the actress' face had blood on it and there was blood splattered on the seat and running board. Yet Thelma's body revealed no open wounds, only a few bruises. The bruises were later explained away by investigators as having been received when Thelma apparently fell forward on the steering wheel of the car. (An autopsy later disclosed that the <u>inside</u> of the actress' throat 'was bruised' with the kind of marks a bottle might make if jammed down her throat.)[9]

According to Nash, "If the coroner's jury had been correct, there was still no explanation for the blood covering the actress or her car. Her clothes were in a rumpled disarray when the body was found, and this suggested some sort of a struggle."[10]

While Nash correctly reports that no wounds were discovered on Todd's body, his description of blood "splattered" on the seat and running board and "covering the actress" as well as bruises on the body is exaggerated. Miss Todd's mouth suffered only slight bruising, consistent with injuries caused by her face hitting the steering wheel. In addition, investigating officers reported no rumpling of the actress' clothing and no sign of struggle. This did not prevent later writers from expanding on these themes, claiming there were "throat lacerations," and "unexplained bruises on her body."[11] To some extent, Edmonds' account is only the last—one would hope—event in this evolution.

Even with these antecedents, it is difficult to account for the level of mayhem in Edmonds' description, in particular, the broken nose and ribs. None of the secondary writers, with all their exaggerations, even hinted at these injuries. Edmonds herself denies she used the secondary sources for her accounts of the extensive injuries, claiming they were "part of the record" and "well known at the time."[12] Yet, she cites no extant documentation to support her claims.

To some extent, Edmonds' inaccuracies may be the logical result of her conclusions. While other murder theorists can get by with slighter evidence of murder, relying on a more cunning killer, her theory requires that the actress suffer a terrible beating, be rendered helpless, and then placed in the garage to die of carbon monoxide poisoning. Hence, she is compelled to exaggerate the physical evidence of violence at every opportunity. Ironically, these fabrications undercut some of the most compelling aspects of the Todd case that other murder theorists have tried, however unsuccessfully, to address. If Miss Todd were murdered, how did the culprit accomplish the crime without leaving any but minor injuries to the body?

Attempts to exaggerate or manufacture the injuries are natural to the tabloid approach. When the facts are there, they can be exaggerated; when they are not, they can be made up. Anything can be stated to assure a pat and dramatic conclusion or to titillate an audience. The minor controversies over the condition of Todd's corpse are so inflated in some of the later secondary accounts that readers must be mystified why there was any issue about the cause of death in the first place. Clearly, with so much blood and so many bruises, it would appear that Todd must have been murdered.

Tabloid biases have led many writers to discover in the Todd mystery the themes they had already planted themselves. The character and habits of Miss Todd gave an even greater opportunity for sensation. Reports that she used drugs and considerable evidence she used alcohol, sometimes to excess, have fueled this process. According to Lina Basquette, an actress of some note in the 20s and 30s and a friend of Todd's and others who knew her, Todd drank heavily at times—a claim supported by the post-mortem blood-alcohol findings.[13] Rudy Schafer, son of café manager Rudolph

Schafer, recalls his father telling him Thelma was "hell on wheels" when she drank too much and that her standard drink was three fingers of rye—a dose not for the faint of heart.[14] The evidence of Todd's drug use, however, is somewhat equivocal. Basquette acknowledged that Thelma, like many other actresses, would pop "pickup pills" in the morning. Similarly, Fred Guiles in his 1980 biography of Stan Laurel also claimed to have come across reports of Todd's drug use:

> Today, Roach survivors speak of Thelma Todd's 'killing'. Some, Ruth Laurel (Stan Laurel's third wife) among them, go further and say they think she was murdered. 'Why', Ruth asked, 'would she come home in a limousine, climb all those steps up the cliffside to the garage to her convertible to kill herself? She was known to have had lots of pills and some other drugs that were not available at the pharmacy, and she could have taken an overdose.' [15]

Yet, Richard Bann, film historian and Hal Roach's longtime confidante and biographer, denied Todd used drugs. Well acquainted with many of the so-called "Roach survivors," Bann claims Hal Roach himself did not believe Todd used drugs, and that rumors of her drug use were not prevalent among those who knew her.

In the literature of the Todd mystery, however, her drug use is accepted with scarcely any question. Edmonds claimed Todd became addicted to amphetamines in the form of diet pills after first taking them to stay thin for the camera. She also claimed the mob then turned her onto "pure speed" and supplied her with the drug to keep her under its thrall. In part, Edmonds blames Hal Roach and Thelma's studio contract for Miss Todd's plight, asserting that a so-called "potato clause" had been inserted in the agreement to assure she would not exceed a certain weight.

Other writers have gone even further. Jay Robert Nash stated, "It was also rumored that she was addicted to drugs, especially heroin, but this was never proven." Nash failed to provide a source for the rumors, although, despite his disclaimer, he has no problem passing them along, anyway.

The speculations of one writer, Charles Neutzel, while not specifying the drug of Todd's addiction, provide an insight into the workings of the tabloid-oriented writer's mind. In his 1965 piece, he states:

> The fringe element which bordered the gangster was around the Hollywood social circle. It was not difficult, therefore, for a woman of Thelma Todd's beauty and charm to capture the interest of the top figures in these dubious fringe groups. The repeated rumor that she was a dope addict certainly suggests that she had some sort of 'working arrangement' with those underworld figures who could obtain for her the illegal drugs. And although no facts or specific names are available, it can be assumed that Thelma might well have socialized with one who, at the very least, had strong connections with the underworld and who perhaps deliberately got her

started on dope in order to bring her under the influence.[16]

The "repeated rumor" serves as a linchpin for this concoction of flawed logic and circular reasoning, all based on a fatuous understanding of pushers and addicts. Thelma was beautiful; gangsters like beautiful women; gangsters have drugs that they use to hook beautiful women. Therefore, the drug rumors around Todd, whatever their merit, connect her to gangsters who come to control her. All that's missing are the "facts and specific names" that would provide some basis for this series of speculations, assumptions, and generalizations. Neutzel's speculations foreshadow those advanced by Edmond's in her book published some 15 years later; just insert a "specific name" (offered by Anger), a specific drug, and no matter how fanciful, you have the thesis of *Hot Toddy*.

The allegations of drug use in the Todd case demonstrate how writers can get maximum use out of a minor or equivocal matter. Through embellishment, a generality can be made quite specific. Bootstrapping a specific rumor, however unsubstantiated, can be used to imply much more.

Nowhere is this tendency demonstrated more perniciously than in characterizations of the actress' moral character and love life. In this area, the tabloid approach to the story has not only ignored the record, but has resorted to baseless and cruel character assassination. As is often the case, Andy Edmonds' *Hot Toddy*, its TV movie version, *White Hot: The Mysterious Murder of Thelma Todd*, and the attendant publicity for both, are by far the worst offenders. Portraying Thelma Todd as a willing *sexual* victim of powerful men who control, abuse and eventually destroy her, Edmonds draws a pat, amateurish and unconvincing psychological portrait of the actress based on ideas that appear to spring from the worst manifestations of the 1980s pop self-awareness movements. What emerges are cartoonish versions of an over-the-top dysfunctional family: a cold and corrupt power-brokering father (John Todd), an unbelievably pushy and self-serving, archetypal stage mother (Alice Todd) and Thelma, a girl trying to break free from the stifling strictures of her mother and compelled to seek approval through sex from powerful men in order to compensate for her father's rejection.

Predictably, the men in Edmonds' account of Thelma's life are just as one-dimensional: Pat DiCicco, a social climbing Lothario who uses her to advance his own career and then passes her along to a powerful gangster to whom he is indebted; Roland West, who exploits her for financial reasons, then abandons her; and the powerful mobster himself, portrayed as the devil incarnate, who seeks to control Thelma for his grand scheme of taking over Hollywood and then destroys her when she resists. All the while, Thelma indulges in an orgy of self-destructive behavior, including promiscuity, an eating disorder, alcoholism, pill popping, and the use of dangerous drugs.

Although the book and movie share many elements, Todd's character in the book was slightly modified in the movie, possibly in order to create a stronger image for Loni Anderson who portrayed Thelma. Still far removed from the historical Thelma Todd, the Thelma of *White Hot* is more assertive and gutsy in dealing with her diabolical antagonist, the famous underworld boss. The makers of the movie also chose a stock blond-goddess characterization to comport with the leading lady's more statuesque build. While the effect is more of a "Stiff" than a "Hot Toddy," there are still plenty of allusions to the scandalous themes of the book.

As in the book, the characters in the movie seem like cardboard cutouts fashioned by a stereotypical and middling soap opera vision of Hollywood in the golden age. Roland West is cast as an effete has-been, a kind of drawing room priss who minces around the primly decorated café. Pat DiCicco is the archetypal, if polished, toady, unctuously trading on his Neapolitan charm to gain advantage, willing to commit any betrayal. Mrs. Todd is the stage mother from hell, thwarting Thelma at every turn, undercutting her friends, and seeking to benefit from her daughter's fame. True to its genre, the movie does not surprise the viewer with real characters.

Statements by the movie's makers help illuminate the attitudes that shaped the production as well as the choices made in bringing the book to the screen. In a review entitled, "Murder of 30s starlet Thelma Todd no longer a mystery," one reviewer quotes Paul Wendkos, the director, who described Thelma Todd as "the Madonna of her day, a hot mama, a peroxide blond, wisecracking, very sexy with an outrageous sense of humor." The movie's executive producer, Frank Von Zerneck added another element of their film's vision: "There was a Marilyn Monroe feel to her, a tragic character. All she really wanted was somebody to respect and care about her. Someone powerful. If she hadn't died, one hopes she would have eventually found the right man, but I kind of doubt it." A source involved in the production, who did want to be identified, stated, "Thelma was far worse than we were allowed to portray. She did a lot of drugs, alcohol, men. We didn't show her as bad as she actually was because then you'd lose sympathy for her. Basically, she was a tramp."[17]

It is harder to imagine a clearer demonstration of how the cynical cycle of tabloidism and mutual promotion operates in modern media. An inaccurate and preposterous book is written and published on a historical event, without footnotes or other mechanics of scholarship that normally serve to keep writers honest. A movie is produced based upon the book and further distorts the subject. A publicity blitz is launched to promote the project. A television reviewer, who makes a living catering to the industry, perpetuates and even inflates the falsehoods.[18]

The temerity of those involved is complemented by the superficiality of their opinions. Clearly the movie makers did no checking of the material contained in the book, as they repeated its errors quite faithfully, and even added a few of their own. Clearly, the reviewer had no knowledge of the subject, but merely gave the movie a promotional forum and constructed his article to emphasize the sleaze.

The review, however, does shed additional light on the tabloid mindset. The various attempts of some of the film's principals to peg Thelma Todd's style and personality to modern pop icons such as Madonna and Monroe are particularly revealing. In fact, except for her platinum hair, Todd had little in common with either of the later figures. Unlike Madonna, she was guarded about her private life, shutting the press out almost entirely. Nor did she exhibit anything like Monroe's shifting and vulnerable emotional states. With Todd, there were no tear-choked press conferences, no missed work, no record of raw and hysterical phone calls, and no shared sense on the part of intimates and associates that anything was wrong at all. Indeed, the main reason many of her friends rejected the notion she committed suicide was that they viewed her as so well balanced.

Despite these essential differences, the filmmakers thought of the later "bombshells" when they created Todd's character in the film, resorting to a kind of sound bite, popular psychology to dramatize her. Lacking any historical perspective or knowledge, they overrode the past with current trends, preoccupations, fashions and fixations.[19]

The issue of drugs is a case in point. As has been noted, the claims that drugs were a significant factor in Thelma Todd's life have no basis in the original record. Instead, they can be traced mainly to the works of secondary writers in the decades of the 60s, 70s and 80s. It seems likely the increased focus on the use of drugs, first couched as a rumor, then boldly asserted, owed more to the evolution of public awareness and attitudes about the subject of drugs during those later decades than to any real facts about the Todd case.

What then of the real character and relationships of Thelma Todd? As might be anticipated, the historical record discloses a portrait much different from that presented by the tabloid writers.

Todd was reported to have had romantic attachments with a number of men, and several were said to have proposed marriage. In Hollywood, besides Pat DiCicco, whom she married, she was linked to insurance broker Harvey Priester, band leader Abe Lyman, actors James Ford, Ronald Coleman, Robert Andrews and Dennis King, New York millionaire James Bush, writers Charles Furthmann and Austen Parker, Lazar Kauffman, a "prominent doctor," and Roland West. Back in Lawrence, the young Miss Todd also attracted men, including wealthy suitors, among them Ivan Lebedeff and Lew Eidam. None of this is surprising. As a "town beauty" in Lawrence, and as a vivacious movie star in Hollywood, it is not surprising that Thelma was sought after. In addition, considering the time frame of some eleven years between the time Thelma completed high school and met her death, the number of her reported relationships does not seem unusual.

One also must consider the sources of speculation about her relationships. The tabloid-oriented press in 1935, as today, took an inordinate interest in the romantic intrigues of Hollywood, often speculating and gossiping about who was involved with whom. Merely showing up at a party or nightclub with a member of the opposite sex could start tongues wagging and typewriters pounding. There also could be an incentive for being linked to an actress like Thelma. Lina Basquette described it this way, "If you escorted Thelma Todd somewhere you got your name in the columns, your picture in the papers, maybe a job."[20]

It was well known that Thelma herself was quite independent, often choosing an escort to an event at the last moment with no particular romantic interest in the fellow at all. Given these tendencies, it is quite possible that many of her romantic entanglements were much more casual than reported. On several occasions, she denied them. For example in 1928 columnists claimed she was about to marry James Bush, a New York millionaire, a story Todd quickly denied, calling it a "press agent's dream." Later, she also denied rumors she was to wed actor James Ford.

Besides the number of her reported male attachments is the question of their nature. Thelma herself had a reputation for keeping her own counsel on such matters and avoided gossip whenever possible. One *Photoplay* writer described Todd's aversion to rumor and approach to avoiding it:

> Thelma found too, that Hollywood gossiped viciously. No person was safe from the 'pack.' It was smart for women or men to launder an absentee's linen and to strip the victim of his or her reputation. It was smart to be familiar or to assume familiarity with private lives. Thelma was appalled at the cheapness with which Hollywood treated its own.
>
> Thelma shrank from this drawing-room destruction. She chose her course, and the course was that advocated by railroad crossing signs in an effort to decrease mortality: Stop, Look, Listen. Thelma added another word: Silence. She would not gossip, neither would she mingle too freely. She would make few friends and she would not countenance large social gatherings. To this day, she abides by this rule. ZaSu Pitts is practically her only girl friend, and her men friends are seldom known to any but a few intimates until Thelma is ready to be seen with them.[21]

Beyond her distaste for gossip, Thelma Todd also had an aversion to forward men and easy women. In a 1929 interview, she spoke out on the issue:

> Men have a more familiar manner toward actresses. I noticed that as soon as I left Lawrence for New York where I entered the Paramount school. It isn't the actors who are at fault. I've found them to be clever, amusing, a lot of fun. They may try to get you to play around but they'll drop you if you don't encourage them. But the business, the outsiders, who smirk suggestively when they learn that your work is acting. A movie actress. Well. Not so long ago I had an appointment with

a well-known photographer. After the sitting, he invited me to stay for tea and of all things he chose to talk about—degeneracy. Do you think he would have dared if I had come to him as a school ma'am instead of an actress? Yet you can't be openly offended; you need the good will of everybody in this game.

Of course, girls out here have cheapened themselves by permitting too much familiarity. Girls who can't get anywhere by their own merits, who'll be nice to anybody if it will advantage them the slightest bit. I guess men get cynical and hardboiled. Maybe they shouldn't be blamed for holding us in such poor esteem.

I'm too thoroughly New England to get away from the fundamentals of life. I like to play, to make eyes at the boy-friends. Youth has the right to play. But things are so extreme here. I can't quite get Hollywood. People here have no sense of value. They don't know how to live. Everything is done for effect. There is no sincerity, no balance. Twenty-four-year-old girls with the experience of forty.[22]

Thelma apparently practiced what she preached. According to an article in *Photoplay*, soon after her arrival in Hollywood, she had been asked to return to the studio unexpectedly one day. Believing the request meant re-takes, she went to the set, but was ushered instead into an executive office. There she recognized familiar executive faces and a number of young girls making merry. Thelma tried to leave, but was cajoled to stay. After a violent argument, Thelma left, much shaken by the experience.[23]

According to the article, Thelma was blacklisted for her obstinacy and became a relative rarity in the Hollywood contract system—a free-lancer. She persisted and continued to work getting roles, often minor, from a variety of studios until she finally landed her first Roach contract.[24] While it is difficult to estimate what effect this episode had on Todd's overall career, it is remarkable nonetheless. Few actors or actresses bucked the studio system at the time and fewer still went public when they did.

Modern tabloid writers who have sought to cast Thelma Todd as a weak, sexual pawn, victim or tramp have fallen prey to their own inventions. Quite to the contrary, based on the standards of her own time, she was relatively conservative in her romantic and sexual life. She seems to have been a woman of some courage, grounded in her own principles, and quite willing to buck the expectations of powerful males.

What then is the legacy of the secondary writers who have addressed the strange death of Thelma Todd? As has been noted, some merely confused the case by garbling the original record through carelessness, ignorance or overreaching embellishment. Others, carried away by the mystery, emphasized and perpetuated a variety of major and minor red herrings—peas and beans, scuffed slippers, the Ogden, Utah story, 271 steps, etc. The worst of the lot completely distorted history through a combination of sleaze, baseless speculation and outright literary fraud.

Other factors contributed to the distortions. The journalists of the time, eager to hype every angle and sustain the story, left a babble of contradictions and loose ends. Some of the official investigators themselves contributed, fueling many fires, but rarely putting them out. Hollywood too, its army of publicists, self-serving personalities and paranoid concern about its image, cast a shadow over the case prompting speculation and doubt. In short, the faulty record created in late 1935 and early 1936 laid a perfect foundation for the reckless legend makers of the future.

Los Angeles, the setting for the mystery, the land of half-truths and hoopla, and until recently often ignored by scholars and serious writers, provided the perfect atmosphere for myth making. Furthermore, the subject matter, most likely perceived as only fitting for the Hollywood scandal or True Crime genre, almost assured there would be no corrective inquiry into the case and its context. To a large extent then, secondary writers were free to make as much hay from the story as they could.

Interestingly, a few did not do so, and instead provide generally accurate facts and sober reportage. It will come as no great surprise that those closer to the events, unaffected by the speculative inflation of later writers, did the best job of sorting through the original record and defining the mystery of the death of Thelma Todd correctly, albeit briefly.

Bob Thomas, a newspaperman of some note for many years, is a case in point. Writing in 1949, on or about the fourteenth anniversary of Todd's death, Thomas provided a short retrospect of the case that admirably captured its essence. As he stated, the "mystery never has been penetrated, and today no one can say whether [the] actress was murdered, was a suicide, or died accidentally."[25]

In spite of all the material published on the Todd case over the years, Thomas' statement is as true today as it was then.

SEVENTEEN: KEEPING THE LID ON

> It is not the underworld that is to be dreaded. It is the underworld, supported and defended by the police department.
> – Robert Shuler[1]

Most of those who write about Thelma Todd's death as a murder agree the culprit got away through the machinations of the rich and powerful. While Kenneth Anger did not suggest a cover-up, those following in his grisly wake, although misconstruing the public record and the dynamics of 1935 Los Angeles and Hollywood, presumed only men with powerful positions in the region's political and legal structure could have fixed the murder of a popular actress. It is hard to quarrel with such a presumption if one believes Todd's death was a murder. The spotlight shone on the case was too bright for any but the cleverest illusionist in the art of public deception.

Not surprisingly, the more the writer exaggerates the physical evidence of murder in the case, the broader is the conspiracy to cover up the crime. The reason is simple: if murder were the obvious cause of Todd's death, the collusion necessary to fool the press and public into thinking it was an accident or a suicide had to be broad-based. With Andy Edmonds, the trophy winner in the game of bloodying up Todd's corpse, the cover-up reaches its widest expanse. "Luciano was the only man capable of pulling off such a murder and such an elaborate cover-up," she argues. "Only Luciano could have ordered the fraudulent medical reports, the destruction of evidence, the disarray of witnesses."[2] However deficient Edmonds' understanding of the real history and power of her villain may be, her assessment of the requirements for such a cover-up is not far from the mark. To her list could be added a few additional ones: the complicity of the city's reporters, police, and prosecutorial agencies.

Certainly, during the investigation rumors abounded that a conspiracy was afoot. Reports of behind-the-scenes maneuvering by powerful film industry figures plagued the case. DA investigators complained of "sinister influences" hindering their probe. Jury members who favored the murder theory protested that the studios were shielding the names of "well-known figures." Supposedly, these famous characters were involved in the gambling operations supposed to begin at the café on New Year's Day.[3] Although the powers maneuvering to impede the investigation were never identified, the allegations fueled speculation–then and afterward–of a cover-up.[4]

While most writers take it for granted that the machinery for such a wide-ranging conspiracy existed in 1935 Los Angeles, charges that corruption in the department compromised the investigation were not made publicly until the seventies, when the case became a staple of Hollywood Mystery anthologies. By that time, the widespread corruption of the pre-War era had taken on proverbial dimensions, mainly due to the era's detective fiction. Raymond Chandler's novels and film noir, which continues to the present day with movies such as *Chinatown, Bugsy, LA Confidential* and *Gangster Squad,* have provided the public with a rough backdrop of the once specific foreground. The real-life operators of 1935 Los Angeles, however, are largely forgotten. With a few notable exceptions, secondary writers rely on the rough backdrop, omitting the details of how a cover-up of Thelma Todd's murder would have worked and why anybody other than the murderer would have wanted it to happen. The town was corrupt, they seem to suggest, the studio bosses held sway; expecting their readers to share their naive cynicism, they go no further than a wink and a nod. As with many other issues in the Todd death, however, when it comes to the issue of a Big Fix, too much has been misunderstood and taken for granted.

Despite the press' reticence about the LAPD's motives, there were rumors at the time that the police were scotching the investigation. Undoubtedly, widespread distrust of the LAPD was behind the rumors. Scandals involving corrupt police officers had rocked the department and city with dispiriting regularity for decades. It seemed that at least some cops viewed their job as an opportunity to make illicit money. While some assignments, such as the auto detail, were not as lucrative as others, a clever and dishonest cop could figure ways to make the job pay much more than his salary. Policemen extorted "license fees" from pickpockets and bunco operators who fleeced tourists, accepted kick-backs from lawyers and bail bondsmen for steering arrestees their way, and even took bribes from defendants to reduce felony charges to misdemeanors. Some profited from assignments as "policeman-in-residence" at disreputable hotels. Here they would work with young girls to lure unsuspecting johns into violations of the rooming house law, a puritanical bit of local legislation that made it illegal for two unmarried people of the opposite sex to occupy a room furnished with a bed. Others extorted money from unprotected bootleggers and gamblers or citizens caught in traffic violations. A few entered the bootlegging trade themselves by posing as prohibition agents in order to hijack the wares of rumrunners. One enterprising group of police detectives even opened funeral parlors, paying commissions to officers who sent cadavers to their establishments.[5]

If much of the police crime was entrepreneurial, there was also an organized system of corruption stemming from the most lucrative moneymaker—vice. In Los Angeles, as elsewhere in the country, prostitution, drugs, gambling, and illegal alcohol were the mainstays of organized crime and police corruption. A loose affiliation of business, political and criminal interests known by insiders as the Combination had controlled the city since the early 'teens, maintaining a thriving trade in gambling, prostitution, and alcohol.[6] Using bribery and blackmail as its carrot and stick, the Combination persuaded the venal and indiscreet among the city's officials to do its bidding.

The mechanisms of corruption were often well defined. In the earlier days, madams and gamblers gave set operating fees to "bag" men, sometimes beat cops, who took cuts of the payoff money before passing the rest on to their lieutenants. They, in turn, passed the money along to their superiors after taking their cut, and so on, until it reached the highest echelon of the racket, the political boss or mayor. Later, agents outside the police department replaced the beat cops in the role of bagmen, passing the payola directly to the head of the rackets. Depending on who controlled the police chief and his key subordinates at the time, this might be a political boss, mayor, or a vice concessionaire who had purchased the right to franchise vice establishments from a political boss. The "cuts" were then taken from the top down, sometimes all the way to the precinct captains, but rarely as far as the beat cops. The latter were ordered not to interfere with vice activities on their own initiative, but to report them to the vice squad.

On one level, such a policy seemed legitimate. "They're gonna handle it. Because they're experienced on it and you're not," as one veteran recalled years later. But the real situation soon became apparent to the cop on the beat. "They're not gonna do anything. So, just learn to keep your mouth shut. If you don't, why, you'll get in trouble." Cops who refused to go along with the system found themselves reassigned "to the sticks"–the San Fernando Valley or other outlying districts. The winners in this game were the racketeers, who could operate freely while only having to pay off the upper tier of the police force and the vice squad.[7]

Other procedures for passing protection money were not as clearly illegal or organized. One method was to hold a card game and invite cooperating politicians and police officers. Despite the fact that the hosts were often professional gamblers, the guests invariably won. When the recipient of the bribe was a financial or legal professional, a lawyer or banker, the money could be passed in the form of retainer or fee. The professional took his cut, using the remainder to purchase the neglect of the appropriate officials.[8]

Bribes were not the only methods of persuasion. Blackmail could be equally effective under the right circumstances. Often, the Combination used the community's intolerance of vice to compromise the very leaders who tried to challenge the trade. Councilmen who spoke out too loudly against prostitution or gambling often became victims of "set-ups" with prostitutes who catered to their private cravings while vice squad members watched or listened. Usually, merely the threat of public exposure was enough. From time to time, however, the criminal bosses decided to "cool" a public figure by unmasking his sins in *flagrante delicto* before supporters. This happened to City Prosecutor Guy Eddy, author of the "rooming house" or "resorting" law, mentioned earlier. Members of the LAPD, purportedly acting on behalf of underworld figures whose business was hurt by Eddy's ordinance, put up a young girl to seduce the prosecutor, a leading reform candidate for District Attorney. After peering through the holes they drilled in his office door during the previous night, the cops burst into Eddy's office and arrested him. Although it was never established beyond doubt whether Eddy's pants were on or off, the young lady, alleged by the prosecution to be sixteen but proven by the defense to be a married twenty-one-year-old, described her seduction with painstaking detail, titillating the courtroom audience and testing the skill of reporters to substitute less graphic accounts in their squeamish newspapers. Eventually she confessed that the whole job had been put up.[9]

At times, the vice leaders and crooked cops didn't have to orchestrate the exposure of their all too human enemies. A little bungling in the view of the intolerant public would do the trick by itself. In 1916, Mayor Charles Sebastian had to resign when his wife presented a newspaper publisher with his love letters to his mistress. A former Chinatown vice raider implicated in 1909 as a bagman in the Harper-Kern scandal, Sebastian helped suppress organized vice while chief of police from 1911 to 1915. His replacement, Frederick Woodman, also left office in a vice scandal after the *LA Record* revealed his scheme to join with Horace Karr, a *Los Angeles Times* city hall reporter, and two black vice operators, George Brown and George Henderson, to open Central Avenue, the main commercial and cultural thoroughfare of the black community, to gambling, prostitution and booze.[10]

The architect of the Combination was Charles Crawford. Crawford hailed from Seattle, where he got his start by booking dance-hall entertainers for performances in the boomtowns of the Yukon gold rush. Later he expanded into club ownership, opening an elaborate gambling establishment named the Northern Club on Seattle's Yesler Way. After local authorities launched a graft investigation to find out how the club could operate in open violation of the city's gambling laws, Crawford turned states' evidence against Chief of Police Charles Wappenstein to save his own neck. While Wappenstein went to the penitentiary in Walla Walla, Crawford beat a path south, arriving in LA in 1913.[11]

Over the next decade, Crawford used his social and political skills to advance himself to leadership of Los Angeles' vice scene. After organizing opposition to prohibition ordinances, he purchased the Maple Bar at Fifth and Maple. Soon the establishment was a watering hole for prominent politicians, cops and confidence men. Along Fifth, Wall and Maple streets, Crawford expanded his enterprise to include other bordellos and gambling joints. In the latter venture, he was assisted by Guy McAfee, a former vice squad cop who the LAPD fired in 1919 for running a crap game in the department's squad room.

While McAfee and another longtime LA gambler, "Farmer" Paige ran gambling throughout the city, Crawford brought an old associate from Seattle named Albert Marco to run prostitution. Crawford himself concentrated on expanding his real estate investments downtown and providing protection for the gamblers and bordellos. Working with Kent Kane Parrot, the leading political fixer of the twenties, he kept the wheels of vice running smoothly in the city. The era was the Combination's heyday. The spoils were reserved for those who won the favor of paying off Crawford and Parrot; those who didn't were shut down, imprisoned, or run out of town by the DA and the LAPD. Only bootlegging remained a contested criminal activity. Profits from alcohol were so great that unprotected criminals were willing to risk a pinch.

Still, the party could not last forever; there was too much going on and too many other players wanted to get in on the action or stop it altogether. Stock swindles, bribery, payoffs, extortion rackets, battles over spoils and pestering reformers pushed the Combination off balance in the late twenties. Feeling the heat, Crawford went abroad, leaving McAfee in charge, but when he returned McAfee was unwilling to return control to him. In response, Crawford launched an anti-vice campaign against McAfee, enlisting the support of Presbyterian minister Gustav Brieglieb and newspaperman Herbert Spencer. It ended badly. Along with Spencer, Crawford was gunned down in his office by a former deputy District Attorney who was running for Municipal Court Judge.

By the mid-30s, the gambling and vice business in Los Angeles was under assault from reformers, some of whom were legitimate and others just out to extort from the vice leaders, and other groups wanting part of the spoils. In particular, Joe Shaw, Los Angeles Mayor Frank Shaw's younger brother, was making a move. A former lieutenant in the US Navy, Joe Shaw retired to join his brother's administration. Forty-three years of age, he had come up through the ranks of the Navy, serving as an executive officer on several ships, and working with the service's intelligence bureau. He was a tough, stern man, disregardful of courtesy, accustomed to giving brusque orders and seeing them obeyed, and impatient of red tape and bureaucracy. After his brother appointed him as his personal secretary, he moved quickly to take charge of promotions and appointments in the police and fire departments. Jobs had a price, and the price had to be paid to the Shaws. Dissatisfied with the trickle of loot that flowed from the Combination's system, he sought direct control over the payoff rackets within the police department, attempting to divert the enormous take from commercialized vice straight to the mayor's office. Soon, Joe was known by the allusive sobriquet, "the corner pocket," which referred both to the location of his office in City Hall and his key position within the city. It was commonly said that if you wanted anything done, whether it was a favor, a contract, or permission to open an illegal gambling joint, you went to see the "corner pocket."[12]

Joe allied himself with a group of Italian mobsters who for years had pecked away at the crumbs the Combination let drop on the edges of the city's operations, including Johnny Roselli, a close associate of Columbia Pictures head Harry Cohn, and Jack Dragna, a mafia associate who had been around LA for years without much success.

Roselli and Dragna had teamed up before, launching several ill-fated adventures, including a short-lived dog track in Hollywood. Shaw also brought into his camp former vice squad policeman Rusty Williams and veteran racketeer Andy Foley.[13]

Joe also reached into the LAPD for allies, acquiring the services of the Police Intelligence Squad, headed by Earl E. Kynette, who effectively reported directly to him. Kynette had been a Fifth Street druggist who worked for whorehouse owner Albert Marco in the early twenties until he joined the police department. In 1925, Sgt. Sidney Sweetnam of the Vice Squad arrested him after Kynette shook down a streetwalker who was competing with Marco's girls. Booked on bribery, Kynette was sprung the next day on orders from Chief Davis. Although a police trial board found him guilty of extorting money from prostitutes, the Police Commission overrode the decision and restored him to full service in 1927.[14]

Ultimately, the partnership of the Shaws and Kynette would prove fatal to the Combination, its competitors, and the corrupt cops within the LAPD. Kynette and other members of the Intelligence Squad tried to "cool" Harry Raymond, a longtime figure in local law enforcement with a spotty reputation, by planting a bomb in his automobile in 1937. The resulting scandal would lead to the recall of Frank Shaw and the election of Fletcher Bowron as mayor, the dismissal of the ring of corrupt cops in the upper echelon of the LAPD, and ultimately the abandonment of illegal gambling in Los Angeles as vice figures retired or retreated to operations in Las Vegas. What was left of organized vice in Los Angeles fell to Tony Cornero whose offshore gambling ship operations continued until California Attorney General Earl Warren intervened. Ben Siegel, who had been buying into the beachfront rackets, bought a share of Cornero's Rex and fumbled about for several years, until he realized the real action was now in Las Vegas. A score of lesser lights such as James Utley, who had worked with the reformers to bring down the house and now hoped to profit from the disorder, stuck around hoping for something to fall their way.[15]

EIGHTEEN: THE BIG FIX

> Among the members of the fixing profession, scientific advances of the last ten years have caused the old adage, "You can fix anything but murder," to be amended to read: "You can fix anything—but murder costs a little more."
> — Charles "Brick" Garrigues[1]

In the atmosphere of deceit and corruption of 1935 Los Angeles, it was small wonder many would question the diligence of the investigation into Todd's death. Rumors of corruption or unseemly associations with suspected grafters tainted the reputations of many of the principals in the investigation. Allegedly, Vice Squad detective Dick Lucas and private detective Harry Raymond, investigators of the infamous kidnapping/murder of 12-year-old Marion Parker in 1927, had blackmailed Autopsy Surgeon A. F. Wagner; Lucas and Raymond supposedly possessed evidence linking Wagner's son to the crime, for which William Hickman was hanged in 1928. William Clark, an investigator in the Todd case and the brother of detective Bruce Clark, the first police officer at the scene of Todd's death, quit the LAPD in the late thirties and took up with ex-city Councilman William G. Bonelli. In the early forties, Bonelli was prosecuted for corruption.[2]

Two other key figures in the Todd case were caught up in a purge of LAPD top brass in 1938, when reform mayor Fletcher Bowron tried to clean house on a police force riddled with corruption. Joe Taylor, head the Detective Bureau at the time of Todd's death and a key figure in the investigation, was forced to retire, while Hubert Wallis, the Homicide Captain, was sent to the sticks—the Venice Detective Bureau—and resigned shortly afterward.[3] Wallis came under criticism for the Homicide Department's failure to solve the gangland style murder of gambler Les Bruneman, a figure with a long history in the LA underworld. Several months before assailants shot Bruneman, an associate of casino owner Eddie Nealis, while he was walking with his girlfriend on the beachfront walk in Redondo Beach. He survived that attack only to be gunned down a few months later in a Hollywood restaurant. His killing was widely regarded as a mob hit—years later, the hit man would be identified as Frank "the bump" Bompensario, though an ex-con named Pete Pianezza served time for the murder.[4]

Wallis was a longtime target of reform groups. The ambivalent ethics characteristic of many police officers of the time marked his career. Born in the

Wiltshire town of Marden on April 24, 1880, he served as a London bobby for six years. In 1907, he arrived in Los Angeles, where he worked as a bricklayer until 1914, when he joined the LAPD. By 1925, he made detective after winning distinction in mail fraud and robbery cases.[5]

Wallis first ran afoul of civic reformers in 1927 during his tenure as Captain of the Vice Squad, when he figured prominently in the infamous frame-up of city Councilman Carl Jacobson. Jacobson had been appointed to one of the council seats vacated when several members of political boss Kent Parrot's clique were convicted of accepting bribes. Jacobson's denunciations of Los Angeles' open vice on the floor of the City Council raised the ire of the local crime leaders, who turned to the Vice Squad for help.

One of the Vice Squad members, Frank Cox, had a sister-in-law who had met Jacobson in Indio, California a few years before. The woman, Callie Grimes, met Jacobson again when she attended a meeting of property owners in his district. In late July 1928, Grimes asked Jacobson for a private conference to discuss assessments in the district. The Councilman agreed to meet her the following week.[6]

Grimes invited Jacobson to an apartment on the west side, but he declined because of his busy schedule. However, he agreed to see her that night at her home at 4372 Beagle Street in Lincoln Heights. A half hour after he arrived, a squad of senior officers, including Captain Wallis, burst into the house after "observing" an open bottle on the kitchen sink and Jacobson and Grimes embracing on the living room sofa. The Councilman was caught with his pants down–literally; or at least that is the way the cops told it. According to Jacobson, he was merely sitting in the front room discussing taxes with Mrs. Grimes, whom he knew as Hazel Ferguson, when the cops crashed through the door. Moments later, the Councilman testified, the cops hoisted him upside down and relieved him of his pants. They then photographed along with Mrs. Grimes, who had removed her dress.

According to his own account, the police offered the Councilman a deal. Sign a typewritten statement confessing to the crime of "resorting" (apparently it had been prepared at the police station before the raid began), return to his job on the city council, and keep his mouth shut about the vice conditions; or face prosecution. When Jacobson indignantly refused to sign the confession, the surprised cops marched him off to the home of a police commissioner, who also tried unsuccessfully to persuade him to agree to the deal.[7]

The case immediately became a *cause celebre* in the city. After obtaining bail, Jacobson charged he had been framed. Religious leader Robert Shuler held meetings at the Trinity Methodist Church to protest his arrest, as did local citizens within the Councilman's district. Although authorities moved to quash the charges against him, Jacobson insisted on a trial. The City Prosecutor obliged him and sent a note to the Grand Jury asking it to investigate Jacobson's allegations. The Grand Jury dutifully issued an indictment.

The details of the frame-up became clear during Jacobson's trial. Three high-ranking police officers, an auto theft squad detective and two of the city's premier vice peddlers were eventually indicted on conspiracy charges.[8] They were a remarkable set of defendants. Besides Wallis and Grimes, to some extent the dupe in the affair, there was Dick Lucas. In 1926, Lucas had gunned down bootlegger and hijacker "Mile Away" Thomas (so named because he once claimed he was a "mile away" from the scene of a crime he allegedly committed). The previous month, accompanied by "Rough-house" Brown, a notorious police thug, Lucas had beaten up two innocent citizens he suspected of bootlegging. Then there was Rusty Williams, eventual ally of Joseph Shaw in the latter's attempt to control the city's vice rackets. Harry Raymond, years away from being blasted into prominence and civic grace by a bomb placed in his car by the LAPD's Special Intelligence Squad, was also indicted. And, certainly not last nor least, were vice leaders Charlie Crawford and Albert Marco.

Their defense team was no less remarkable; it included Jerry Geisler, the preeminent criminal defense attorney of the city and Grant Cooper, who would become a major figure in the DA's office during the reform administration of Fletcher Bowron. With such a cast, the addition of *Los Angeles Times* reporter Al Nathan, publisher Harry Chandler's staff *fixer*, as a key witness seemed almost superfluous, but it did underline the loose alliance between the town's business, police and criminal enterprises, which shared a common interest in preserving the status quo.[9]

The case was tried in court in the same way it had been tried in the papers, with a focus on whether Jacobson allowed himself to be seduced by Grimes. As both Robert Shuler and the trial judge pointed out, for somewhat different reasons, this was not the issue. "Los Angeles is divided as to the actual guilt or innocence of Jacobson but there is no division within this city as to the fact that he was 'framed,'" wrote Shuler two months after the arrest of Jacobson, echoing an editorial in the *Hollywood Daily Citizen*.

It was hard to dispute Shuler on this point. Wallis' claim that he assembled a squad of three of the highest ranking officers within the department and a private detective working with the Auto Theft Squad and afterward invited along a police reporter, all on the strength of an anonymous tip about wild parties (which was never recorded in the Vice Squad's log), was patently ridiculous.. In addition, his admission that, on finding no evidence of unlawful activity when they first arrived at the Beagle Street address, the police staked out the house for two hours before Jacobson arrived must have left many citizens wondering whether the police officers had too much time on their hands. Whether or not Jacobson voluntarily removed his pants, it was clear that ranking members of the police force went out of their way to arrest him. As Judge Woods declared during Grant Cooper's closing argument on behalf of Captain Wallis, the arrest of Jacobson was fundamentally improper, since the crime of "resorting" applied only to public places, such as hotel rooms, and not to private homes.[10]

In the end, the trial resolved nothing. The indictments of Crawford and Marco, which arose from evidence of a phone call one of the arresting officers placed from a gas station near Grime's house to a downtown hotel where Crawford was staying, were dismissed by the court soon after the prosecutors presented their case.[11] The jury deadlocked on the charges against the remaining defendants. A second trial also resulted in a hung jury.

After a certain amount of legal and administrative wrangling, all the cops accused in the Jacobson frame got their jobs back. Although Wallis took a lot of heat because of his involvement–and probably did not make any friends among his co-defendants when rumors arose that he planned to turn state witness against them in exchange for an acquittal–his career was not entirely off track. His name was blackened among the city's reformers–especially Shuler, whom he allegedly threatened "to get" if it took the rest of his life after the latter charged that Wallis owned a brothel. Nevertheless, among those who really mattered he was still jake. All that was needed was a change in the city's political lineup and a new chief. Frank Shaw's election in 1932 and the subsequent reappointment of ex-Vice Squad officer Jim Davis as chief, laid the groundwork for Wallis' complete rehabilitation. In 1934, after several years in precinct detective work, he was back on top as head of Homicide.[12]

It was not just the motives of cops that were suspect, however. The reporters were untrustworthy as well, and not just for the careless journalistic practices detailed in earlier chapters. Many made money promoting and serving the rackets. Horace Karr, a *Los Angeles Times* city hall reporter, was a central figure in a vice scandal of the 'teens. His successor, Al Nathan, was known as the newspaper's fixer during the twenties and thirties and, according to information gathered by the FBI, had interests in several illegal gambling clubs.[13] Others used their writing talents to shake down the racketeers and celebrities of the era. Jack Carberry, admired by other reporters for his skill in manufacturing stories, allegedly wrote under the name of Don Mealy for *Inside Detective Secrets*, a "blackmail tabloid" published by Harry Raymond. The idea was to attack organized crime figures until they paid off. Crawford was a target of one Carberry/Raymond extortion plot, but the Lone Grey Wolf outsmarted them by plying Carberry with prohibition alcohol, causing the star reporter to lose his bearings so totally he failed to get out a crucial election eve edition loaded with prepaid political advertisements. As a result, Raymond had to repay the ad money, and the paper bellied up. Reportedly, Raymond afterward chased Carberry out of town, threatening his life should he return.[14]

With so many players and factions allegedly involved in the city's racketeering games, it is impossible to sort out who if anybody was telling the truth. What can be said with some degree of certainty is that the strife over gambling spoils between the Combination stalwarts, the Shaws, upstart local hoodlums, and "Eastern interests" provided a fertile soil for gambling rumors swirling around the Todd case. The tainted reputations of many of those involved in the investigation undoubtedly contributed to doubts about the way the case was handled, which became more frank as secondary writers explored the mystery. Unfortunately, the perspective time and further developments afforded was largely squandered by later writers. The real history of the city's criminal organizations slackened into fable and myth. Secondary figures like Cornero and Siegel, whose methods and deaths appealed to the public's imagination, supplanted the real principals of LA gambling in popular history, while Lucky Luciano, a man with no proven connection to either LA or Thelma Todd, became a prime suspect in her death.

Todd's involvement with gambling figures was real, however. Roland West may have been a minor player, but he associated with others who were significant, in particular, Joseph Schenck. Schenck, an inveterate crapshooter, was in thick with gamblers, particularly the Wertheimers and Orsattis. In the summer of 1935, in fact, while he was in Europe, the Wertheimers, operators of the Clover Club on Sunset Boulevard, where Schenck had dropped a fortune at the tables, rented his home in the Hollywood as a gambling den, knocking out a wall to accommodate a roulette table. Reformers often linked Schenck with gambling Czar Guy MacAfee.[15]

Kent Kane Parrot's entry into the mystery in the last days of the investigation revealed another link between Todd and the gambling establishment. Reports Todd turned to him when she received new extortion notes in late fall of 1935 and claims that the two were seen together in nightclubs in recent months must have triggered a great deal of speculation about their relationship in 1935 among reporters following the story. It is curious, in fact, that news stories about Parrot's relationship with Todd were so restrained. Despite his well-known links to organized crime, none of the reports discussing his involvement in the Todd mystery went beyond calling him a "longtime political power," a euphemism often used to denote the city's fixers. After the reports of a gambling connection in the Todd death, one would expect the introduction of the name of a central figure in the city's rackets to prompt at least one newspaper to a circumspect observation of the coincidence.[16]

Parrot, known as "the man behind the throne" during the administration of Mayor George Cryer in the twenties, had a career characterized by opportunism and a scrupulous avoidance of notoriety. A native of Kennebunkport, Maine, he grew up in Boston, one of four brothers who repeatedly scraped with the law. In 1907, when he was twenty-four years old, he moved to Southern California with his young wife, the future author Mary O'Hare, who had married him despite her father's objections, to enroll in USC's Law School. After graduating in 1909, he joined a law firm that included several members of his graduating class as well as the dean of the College of Law.[17]

Throughout his career, Parrot skillfully avoided publicity. Still, he was recognized as the city "Boss" by both the *Los Angeles Record* and the *Los Angeles Times* after the latter split with the Cryer administration over the issue of public versus private control of water and power utilities. He engineered Police Chief James Davis' first appointment in the mid-twenties and controlled several of the city councilmen of the era.

In the late twenties, however, his loose-knit organization began to break apart. Key allies were indicted for bribery and sent to prison, among them DA Asa Keyes. The general stench of corruption throughout the civic government, together with backroom infighting in the Parrot organization, led to the electoral defeat in the 1927 city council elections of most of his candidates. In 1929, Parrot's candidate for mayor also lost.[18]

After these setbacks, Parrot concentrated on the brokerage of power in the vice arena.[19] From his suite on the southeastern corner of the seventh floor of the Biltmore Hotel, he provided the link between the worlds of politics and organized crime. His involvement with gambling figures began after his ascension to power behind Mayor Cryer. As Cryer entered office, leadership of the vice business in Los Angeles was split among several figures, but control of the Los Angeles Police Department, and in particular the Vice Squad, rested with banker Marco Hellman. In 1922, however, after Police Chief Oakes resigned following the exposure of his involvement with a prostitute, Hellman's influence with the LAPD waned quickly. At this point, Parrot made his move. Consulting with Judge Gavin Craig, he allied himself with Charlie Crawford, the liaison between the vice leaders and crooked cops inside the Vice Squad. This relationship continued until Crawford's European holiday, when MacAfee and several specialized and lesser figures, including "Farmer" Page, Bob Gans, who ran the slot machine racket, and Les Bruneman, who specialized in dog tracks, took over.

Throughout the thirties, Parrot continued to serve as a liaison to local government and an overall dealmaker and fixer. Although many writers and reformers would attribute to him overall control of LA vice during the era, it is doubtful he or any man exercised such wide authority. However, he was undoubtedly a key player in keeping the local rackets profitable.

The press was fascinated with him no doubt in part because of his studied inaccessibility and aura of power. A. Brigham Rose, attorney for the reform interests, once remarked one "cannot receive an audience with him except through other members of the [criminal] syndicate."[20] Years before, a reporter described Parrot "[shooting] a thrill into the courtroom when . . . he was called as a final witness for former Mayor Cryer" during the latter's libel suit against preacher/reformer Robert Shuler.

> There was a certain easy confidence about this 'boss' as he sank into the witness chair that held the jury and spectators in tense expectation. The Parrot right hand went casually up to the judge's desk and the Parrot left arm over the back of his

chair. The Parrot smile, a disarming weapon, a boyish good-natured grin in sharp contrast to the normally stubborn jaw and combative eyes, was directed at the jury. Several women jurors resolutely refused to meet it.[21]

Part of Parrot's allure was his sophistication, unusual among those who ran the criminal enterprises of LA in the 1930s. Even Grant Cooper, another principal of the legal arm of the reformers, remembered him as a "gentleman." But this gentleman had a rough edge one ignored at his own peril; as Rose remarked, "Parrot's decisions are final, and his judgments are terrible; they have no restraint. It is reliably reported that he is deemed accountable for more than one one-way ride hereabouts."[22]

Among Parrot's many associates was West's close friend, Joe Schenck. Press documentation of their relationship spans from 1928, when the political boss attended a benefit in Schenck's honor at the Hotel Roosevelt, to an intriguing notice in the *Los Angeles Examiner* a week after Todd's death. According to the notice, Parrot placed an admission of a $31,625 debt to Schenck on the county records.[23] Parrot himself had been in trouble with the IRS for years, so it is possible the purpose of this formal legal admission was to deflect some of his own problems; on the other hand, Schenck may have wanted legal proof of an uncollected debt to offset his income. Indeed, it is possible Parrot, like Roland West, was part of Schenck's ruses to avoid income taxes.

The links between West and Schenck, Schenck and Parrot, and Parrot and Todd form a cobweb of associations with strands stretching past the principals to other infamous characters: Guy MacAfee, Victor Orsatti, Lew Wertheimer, "Farmer" Page, and dozens of lesser players. This sinister network may explain the repeated allegations of a cover-up.

Without question, there was gambling at the Sidewalk Café. There is also clear evidence Roland West, either with or without Todd's full agreement or approval, had plans to expand this operation. Most likely, the gambling plans involved somebody close to Schenck, perhaps Vic Orsatti, also a close associate of Louis B. Mayer, who had a beach house nearby where gambling and girls were available to the studio crowd.

The short shrift reporters gave to the story, their lack of follow-up and probing, was in keeping with the big lie the city had told of itself for so many years. The White Spot ideal and the protection of the homegrown vice industry made money for lots of local power brokers, including reporters, studio moguls and newspaper owners. Like a dozen episodes in the long, dishonorable history of the city, the death of a popular actress held the potential of exposing the city's vice, blowing the lid off, in the vernacular of the times, as would happen several years later when Harry Raymond, the shabby ex-cop working a shakedown racket and feeding information to a religious reformer, turned on the ignition of his car and blew his garage to bits.

Seen from this perspective, one can argue there was a Fix in the Todd case, even if it had nothing to do with murder. The Combination, its stooges in the LAPD, the DA's office, the newspapers, the studios, and even the county Grand Jury, whose vocal leader steered clear of the gambling angle from the outset, successfully deflected the investigation from the gambling rumors, possibly to save the reputations of some prime acting properties and certainly to prevent any scrutiny of local operations. Possibly, some of the curious twists in the case, the pairings of assertions and disavowals that torment the public record, emanated from the furtive activities of Combination bosses as they tried to keep the lid on the gambling angle of the case.

While secondary writers interpreted the rumors of hush-up in the contemporary journals as evidence a murder was being concealed, there is no significant evidence to support their argument. Had a **murder** cover-up occurred rumors of the subterfuge would certainly have survived in the memories of those connected with the public institutions of the time. Yet, none of the ex-police officers interviewed for this book remembered anything of the sort with the Todd case. Although William Clark could no longer recall details of the Todd investigation when interviewed in 1985, his wife remembered he remarked years before that the case was "just what it appeared to be, only they just kept prying and prying." Jake Jacoby, who for over 50 years worked in the City News Service, which coordinated news released from the LAPD to the media, never heard of any rumors of impropriety with the investigation. Even Grant Cooper, a member of the DA's staff in 1934 who became a major force in the reform movement of the late thirties and eventually returned to the DA's office as an assistant DA after Fitts' departure, could not recollect anything amiss with the Todd investigation. Very possibly, despite the corruption rife in the law enforcement agencies of the time, the investigation of Todd's death was proper and thorough.

Even when the whole town is on the take, not every death is a murder.

NINETEEN: THE CASE AGAINST ROLAND WEST

> There is no worse lie than a truth misunderstood by those who hear it.
> —William James

Of the characters in the Todd drama, Roland West has drawn the most scrutiny from murder theorists. Even those who have only a casual knowledge of the Todd mystery, garnered from dinner table discussions or sweeps weeks segments on the mystery, tend to focus on him. In many ways, West is the logical suspect; he alone appears to have had the means and opportunity to kill Todd. But another factor exists in some of these suspicions, one less rational and more intuitive. Despite an interval of eighty years, West's appearance, statements and actions—and undoubtedly his wealth and power—still inspire antipathy and distrust; especially it seems, among women. Something about the man almost cries out his guilt.

At the time of the original investigation, West's relationship with Todd was scrutinized during both the Coroner's and Grand Jury's investigations. While the investigators made no direct accusations, they grilled West about his financial and romantic relationships with the actress and the nature of their argument as she left for the Trocadero. They also asked why he had locked her apartment late Saturday night and failed to search for her the following day. In addition, they pondered the claims of Gustav Berger, the former headwaiter of the café, who charged that, following a visit to the café by Pat DiCicco, an unnamed man who could only have been Roland West, had beaten Miss Todd in the presence of the restaurant staff.

Despite their suspicion, authorities treated West from the beginning as a trusted and insightful witness rather than a suspect, quickly endorsing his theories about Miss Todd's death. The grand jurors even entrusted West with the key found in Todd's purse, a significant piece of evidence, to try on the various doors of the café building to determine which entrances it would unlock. While they suspected his exchange with Todd over the hour she would return home Saturday night was more than innocent banter, they treated West's and Todd's relationship and living arrangements with remarkable discretion, eventually abandoning the gentle probing entirely when West balked at their questions.

Not that the investigation was always easy on West. He was interrogated repeatedly by the police, testified for a lengthy period before the Coroner's Inquest, and spent more time by far on the stand of the Grand Jury than did any other witness. At one point, he bristled at the intense questioning he was under, comparing his treatment to the "third degree," though he was quick to assure listening reporters that he would cooperate with the investigation. In the end, however, he faced no formal charges; indeed, none was even hinted. Whatever happened that dark December night when Thelma Todd approached the locked door of her apartment, there was no tangible evidence she was murdered, let alone that she died at the hands of her "best friend" Roland West.

Still, Todd's death left a cloud over West. As the years passed, more writers, drawing on suspicion, rumor, and innuendo, questioned his innocence. Finally, in 1987, a fully developed accusation was directed against him. In December of that year, Kathleen Mader and Marvin Wolfe published a piece in *Los Angeles* magazine entitled "Thelma Todd's Murder Solved!" In it, they charged Roland West with Todd's death.

Actually, the solution they proposed—that Todd died at the hands of Roland West—was not altogether new. It had been around for a long time, minus the details and window dressing. Like many of the sensationalistic elements of the case, its first published manifestation was in Kenneth Anger's *Hollywood Babylon*. According to Anger,

> It was also suspected, but never proven, that some sort of staged event had taken place, arranged by West, aided by a girl friend who was made to pass for Thelma. The stand-in is said to have gone through the scream and kick routine on West's doorstep, while behind the door West knocked Thelma out, placed her in the car, turned on the ignition and closed the door of the garage.[1]

Soon afterward, another version of the tale, attributed to Pat DiCicco, appeared in an article by Nicholas Horden. According to Horden, DiCicco also believed West killed Todd, though "the killing was unintentional."

> West...waited for her to come back from the Trocadero on the following evening, and that she got into the car to go to another rendezvous (and who would know better if the rendezvous had been with DiCicco himself?), had started the motor, had a "spat" with West, who didn't want her to leave. He struck her, and then closed the door almost to 8 inches in a rage. He wanted to teach her a lesson, that's all, opined DiCicco.[2]

A similar story appeared in 1985 in Scott MacQueen's film essay on the career of Roland West.

> Thelma . . . was partying very heavily, and as she announced her departure for the Trocadero she and West exchanged angry words. He locked her out that night.

The fight was resumed when she returned so she stormed to the garage after announcing that she'd go to any party she felt like, such as Mrs. Wallace Ford's. 'You've just been to one party, you're not going to any more!' announced West. Thelma was now in the Lincoln, ready to drive off. To make good his threat and teach her a lesson, West closed and locked the garage. Stubborn Thelma sat, the engine on, waiting for Roland to open the doors. She didn't consider, in her anger, the odorless carbon monoxide filling the garage. Neither did Roland.[3]

While MacQueen's account of Todd's death exonerated West of a specific intent to kill Todd, it essentially followed the same pattern as the Horden/DiCicco story: West and Todd argued, West shut the garage door out of spite and Todd died from carbon monoxide poisoning. It also added a new detail to explain how the anonymous source presumably found out about Todd and West's last encounter:

> West made a complete confession to the police, who believed him when he claimed her death was not premeditated. No charges were filed, and the Coroner's verdict was fudged. West's penance would be to live out his days with his own conscience.[4]

MacQueen characterized his source for this account as "someone intimately involved with the personalities and events of the time, and who prefers anonymity." In private, he revealed the source was Hal Roach. Mader and Wolf also based their solution to the case on an interview they conducted with Roach, including details similar to those in MacQueen:

> On December 17, 1935, the day after Todd's body was found, three Los Angeles County sheriff's detectives came to Roach's studio office. The deputies told Roach that Roland West, under intense questioning, had confessed to killing Thelma Todd.
>
> 'West was very possessive, very controlling,' said Roach, the last survivor of the affair. 'He told Thelma she was to be back by 2 a.m. She said she'd come and go as she pleased. They had a little argument about it, and then Thelma left for the party. When Grauman called West, about 2:30, to tell him Thelma was leaving, West went to her apartment and locked her out. He was going to teach her a lesson.'
>
> 'Apparently when Todd returned at almost 4 a.m., she declined her chauffeur's offer to walk her upstairs because she knew there would be a scene with West. When she found the door locked, she shouted at him, and they had another argument through the door. West told her he didn't want her going to so many parties. Todd, still a bit drunk, screamed that she'd go to any party she pleased. She was invited to one later that day, at Mrs. Wallace Ford's, and she said she'd just go to that party now.
>
> According to Roach, she climbed the steps to the garage. West followed.

When he arrived she was already in her car. She started the engine and he locked the garage door.

After daylight West returned to the garage to find Todd's body. 'He didn't know what to do,' says Roach. 'So he did nothing. He closed the door–but didn't lock it–and went back to the café. All that day, when people called for Thelma, he didn't know where she was. If he really <u>hadn't</u> known where she was, he would have been calling all over trying to find her. That's the kind of man he was.' [5]

Mader and Wolf claimed Roach told them that the sheriff's deputies asked him what they should do about West's confession. Roach told them to forget about it, believing: "He wouldn't have gone to jail anyway, because he'd have the best lawyers, he'd deny everything in court, and there were no witnesses. So why cause him all that trouble."[6]

Mader and Wolf supported their theory with two other sources. First, they cited Don Gallery, the adopted son of ZaSu Pitts, Todd's first comedy partner at Roach, who recalled his mother "had once confided an almost identical version of Todd's death."[7] Additionally, they claimed Chester Morris, star of several of West's dramas in the late twenties and early thirties, told director Alex Gordon that he (Morris) heard West's deathbed confession that he had killed Todd in 1952.[8]

As has been demonstrated, the story Roach told Mader and Wolf had been around a long time. Some of it, such as the "argument through the door," resonates with elements of the Anger tale. It also resembles closely the DiCicco tale told by Horden, adding West's confession while omitting any claims that he struck Todd. In addition, it is an almost verbatim, if greatly embellished, account of the MacQueen version of the story as well, although the latter does not mention that the sheriff deputies told Roach of West's confession.[9] Not surprisingly, it also echoes ZaSu Pitts' story, as recounted by her son. Having been closely associated with Roach and the Roach lot, she likely would hear the same scenario, perhaps from its main source, if not originator, Hal Roach.

Without question, Roach, who employed Todd for much of her career, deserves respect as a commentator on her life and death. Yet, logical problems inherent in the West-as-killer theory, clearly promulgated by Roach, need to be addressed. A reader pointed out one such problem in a letter to the editor of *Los Angeles* magazine in the issue following the publication of Mader and Wolf's article.[10] It offers a simple, but powerful observation. If West locked the garage door on Todd, why didn't she simply turn the automobile's ignition off, thus stopping the production of carbon monoxide gas? The scenario described in the story asks us to believe that the couple had been arguing quite heatedly, that West closed the door and–presumably–that Todd tried to get out of the garage, but could not because West had locked the door. Why would she then return to the car and sit passively in the garage while the garage filled with the deadly fumes?

Second, according to the Roach version of the story, Todd went to the garage after threatening to go to the Wallace Ford's party. That party would not begin until the next afternoon. Why would Todd, even if intoxicated, threaten to leave immediately for a party more than twelve hours in the future, and why would West, cold sober, try to stop her?

And what of the statements of Charles Smith, who was in the apartment above the garage when these events supposedly took place? While the investigation established that he would not necessarily have heard the start of the phaeton's engine, the commotion implied by the story is another matter. Would he not have heard the loud words and angry voices? Was he simply lying when he told investigators that he heard nothing that night?

Finally, there are the three sheriffs who allegedly visited Roach. Where did they come from, and how did they know about West's confession? Castellammare was clearly under the LAPD's jurisdiction. All official records and newspaper accounts of the time specify that LAPD detectives questioned West, not those of the sheriff's department. With the major exception of Frank Gompert, the sheriff's department tire and shoe print expert, there is little reference in the press to any deputies in the case.

Such involvement would have been unusual. Even the District Attorney's office, a County agency, used its own investigators, not those of the Sheriff. While Mader and Wolf sidestep this problem, acknowledging, "Though it's rare, the sheriff's department can intervene in the investigations of crimes committed within its boundaries," they offer no evidence they did so in the Todd case beyond Roach's purported allusion to the three deputies.

Indeed, there is compelling evidence that the events described in the accounts of Mader and Wolf and their predecessors could not even have occurred. To understand why this is so, we must first winnow the West-as-killer tale down to its essential elements as told and undoubtedly embellished over the years by Roach.

Much of the earliest published version of the story, which originated with Kenneth Anger, can be safely discarded. Like many writers on the Todd mystery, Anger tried to account for evidence that never existed. Kick marks were not found on the apartment door and neighbors did not report hearing a screaming fight. It is impossible that they could have. The apartment door was well recessed into the café and the pounding surf and heavy wind would have smothered any sound not deadened by its walls. The closest neighbors in 1935 were far away, up the hill or down the coast.

Anger likely heard a version of the Roach tale, in which Todd and West argue through the closed *garage* door, and simply created his own narrative to incorporate it, combining details such as the kick marks and the neighbor reports from other dubious sources.

Similarly, the DiCicco version, as related by Horden, must also be dismissed. Had

West struck Todd hard enough to knock her out, the coroner's autopsy would certainly have noted the injury. But for the slight contusion under the actress' lip and the displaced temporary tooth, Wagner and his associates found no evidence of trauma on Todd's body. Had they done so, the death would have been a murder case from the start.

Although the MacQueen version came from a second-hand source, presumably without an ax to grind and lacking the detail of the Mader/Wolf version, it probably best represents Roach's original tale. To it, we can add elements from our own research.

On the publication of the Wolf/Mader article, we tried to contact Roach to verify the story. Through his "representative," he declined an interview, claiming he had been ill served by the article and had been misquoted. The "representative" would only say that the law enforcement officers had not told Roach everything Mader and Wolf reported.[11] Eventually, we discovered that Roach's representative was film historian Richard Bann, a longtime associate of the aged mogul. Bann told us that Roach was furious over the Mader/Wolf article, which implied strongly his complicity in a cover-up of Todd's death. He also explained how Roach's speaking habits made it easy to misconstrue him. According to Bann, Roach frequently introduced ideas and left them hanging for the listener to interpret; he "starts a sentence and you finish it." He was known during his studio heyday for calling writers with an idea then aborting the conversation with a quick, "you know what I mean." Bann, who was present during Mader and Wolf's interview of Roach, suspected Roach's speaking style confused the writers. According to their own description of the meeting, they were in awe of the man. They may not have pressed him enough for clarification.[12]

Bann confirmed that Roach had been telling the story reported by Mader and Wolf for many years.[13] After we discussed some of the key points of that story, Bann volunteered to question Roach for us. Through him, we learned Roach claimed he had been contacted by three law enforcement officials (not necessarily sheriff's department detectives), who told him West admitted to having locked Todd inside the garage doors during an argument. He said the law enforcement personnel visited him on the Monday of Todd's death at 10:00 a.m. Mae Whitehead accompanied them to the lot at the time although she was not present when they interviewed him. The officials told him they decided to turn to him because Alice Todd was "back east" and could not be reached. While Roach was perplexed as to the reason for their visit, when told that there was no way to convict West, he opined, "There was no use ruining the fellow's career."[14]

Despite his close association with Todd, Roach's account was puzzling. Clearly, it was necessary to examine his recollection critically. He was reporting events that happened over five decades earlier in which his involvement had been only tangential: in the original investigation, he did not testify at any of the hearings and was cited in the newspapers only for his expressions of sorrow at Todd's death.

We soon discovered how little Roach really knew about the case. After Bann passed on to him a copy of the long-lost Coroner's inquest report, Roach admitted that many of the facts of the case surprised him. Evidently, he based the story he repeated over the years about West's responsibility for Todd's death on facts gleaned from verbal reports and the newspapers of the time.

On some details, Roach's memory clearly failed him. His claim that the detectives visited him at ten o'clock Monday morning, before Mae Whitehead found Todd's body, did not make sense. (Wolf and Mader reported the day of the investigators' visit as Tuesday, but, according to Bann, Roach insisted that the visit occurred on Monday.) His statement that detectives told him that Mrs. Alice Todd was out of town or "back east," when they visited him was also unlikely, as Mrs. Todd remained in Los Angeles throughout the investigation, leaving only in mid-February for Lawrence after Todd's affairs were arranged. Yet he insisted Alice Todd was not in town when the visit occurred–a fact of significance to him, since it led him to speculate that the police turned to him in her absence for guidance as to what should be done about West's "confession."

Clearly, Roach was either wrong about the date of the detective visit or mistaken about many of its details. If the former, the meeting probably took place much later than the Monday or Tuesday of the week Todd's body was found, perhaps on some Monday at ten o'clock after Mrs. Todd returned east. This would place it sometime after mid-February, long after the investigation ended. Why the police would have approached Roach with evidence of West's culpability at that time is hard to fathom.

Still, however much Roach may have misremembered or misconstrued the ancillary details of the visit, one had to ask whether the essence of his story–that Roland West confessed that, after arguing with Todd, he followed her to the garage and locked the garage doors after she started the car, thus causing her death–made any sense. All other details aside, this is the central thrust of the Roach tale. Is there any evidence extant today to either verify or refute this account?

Testimony of various witnesses sheds some light on this issue. Several observed that the conditions around the garage seemed quite normal when they viewed them. For instance, Charles Smith, the septuagenarian café manager who lived in the apartment above the garage, claimed he neither saw nor heard anything unusual around the garage after he returned to his apartment around 2:30 a.m. Sunday morning. As he passed by the garage doors on his way back to the café the following morning, he noticed they were closed.

Another witness, Robert Anderson, testified he closed but did not lock the garage doors after parking Miss Todd's car early Sunday morning. In fact, he testified they were "never locked."[15] Mae Whitehead, who retrieved Todd's car from the garage scores of times during the time Todd lived at the café, supported Anderson's observations about the garage doors when she testified that, to her knowledge, the garage door was "never locked" and that she "always found them unlocked" when she went to the garage.[16] Evidently, security at the garage was not an issue. Not only were the doors not locked, the car keys were left inside the vehicle. Apparently, the greater concern was convenience: shuffling keys among all who might need access, Todd, West, Whitehead and Anderson, was just too difficult.

Finally, E. H. Carter, who was employed as a night watchman by various residents in the Castellammare area, though not by Roland West, testified he did not notice any suspicious or unusual activity around the garage as he passed by it approximately fifteen times Sunday morning. Assuming he was regular in his rounds, we can posit that between four and six a.m., Carter passed the garage about every twenty-five minutes.[17] Obviously, he not only missed Todd entering the garage but any confrontation between West and her in front of it as well.[18]

The latches on the doors themselves provide crucial evidence of the viability of Roach's story. Except for the fact that the metal, shiny and relatively new in 1935, is now painted black, these mechanisms have not changed. Today, as when they were installed, each of the double sliding doors, about nine feet across, is equipped with a metal 90 degree bar hasp which fits over a thick staple on the door frame. To lock either door, it is necessary to slide the door against the frame and insert the shackle of a padlock or some other rod through the staple after the hasp has closed over it. If nothing is inserted through the staple, the door slides open easily either from outside or inside the garage. Both garage doors, which enclose a single, undivided space, must be secured with padlocks in order to trap somebody inside. Thus, one could not simply "run around and lock the garage door," as Mader and Wolf have it in their version of the tale. If only one of the parallel, sliding doors is locked, the person trapped inside can easily go to the other door, slide it open, and escape.

How then, could Roland West lock Thelma Todd in the garage on that night? If there were normally no padlocks on the door, as seems certain from the testimony of the witnesses, he would have had to bring two along with him—a bit of preparation that would hardly have been in keeping with the impulsive behavior attributed to him in the Roach tale. The only other way he could have locked the garage door would have involved quick thinking and action in finding something—pins, or bolts, or sticks—that he could slip through the staples of both doors. In either case, it is likely that, at least once during his rounds between 3:45 a.m. and dawn, Carter, trained to observe such things, would have noticed that both the garage doors were suddenly "locked" with either padlocks or some improvised shafts. In fact, he stated he noted the garage was not locked—in other words, there was nothing in the locking mechanism to prevent the doors from being opened.

Between the contradictions and logical problems in Roach's recollection, the incongruities between the locking mechanisms and his murder scenario, the story told by Hal Roach and purveyed by secondary writers fails by its own weight. There is too much evidence against it and virtually none in its support.

What then do we make of the story Hal Roach told? In all probability, it grew out of a simple misunderstanding of a complex set of facts. Reporters and investigators at the time often were confused by the various sites, events, objects and time sequences in the mystery. As they tried to follow Todd's journeys from the café to the Trocadero, from the Trocadero back to the café and the apartment, and finally to the garage and the phaeton, a jumble of allusions to keys, locks, doors, apartments, and automobiles befuddled them. Not helping the matter was that their main tour guide through this bewildering landscape was Roland West, a man whose best efforts at description achieved only a limited degree of coherence. Which door did Todd usually use? The side door, the café door, the apartment door? Why and how were they locked? Which keys did she normally carry and which did she have with her? Was the key in the phaeton? Why was its door opened? Were the doors to the garage opened or closed? Were they locked?

The confusion of keys and doors and locks led to a muddled journalistic record that would mislead secondary writers in the years that followed. Incorporating the errors of the earlier writers into their speculations, they in turn passed them on to other writers waiting in the wings, few of whom visited the Castellammare complex to sort it all out, or researched the case in any real depth.

If these problems bedeviled the reporters of the time, who followed the case for weeks, and the secondary writers, who at least had the accounts of their predecessors to rely on, what effect did they have on Hal Roach? In our discussions with Richard Bann, we discovered Roach had only a rudimentary knowledge of the case. Given the passage of time, his age, his other interests and his tangential role in the investigation, this is quite understandable. It also helps explain the probable origin of the Roach scenario.

At some point, law enforcement officers, probably the LAPD, visited Roach. It would be natural for investigators to contact Thelma Todd's employer to check on her financial condition or to ascertain the actress' state of mind near the time of her death. In the course of the interview, they told Roach what they thought to be the truth of the matter. Based upon what we know of the police beliefs about the case, they probably told Roach something like the following: "During our questioning, Roland West, admitted to us that he had a quarrel with Thelma because she was 'stepping' on him and he didn't want her to go to the party. They argued. To teach her a lesson, West locked the door on her. He didn't mean to hurt her, but she died in the garage of carbon monoxide. West is taking the whole thing pretty hard and feels responsible for her death. With all the negative publicity, Roland West is ruined. What do you think we should do about it?"

The visit may also have had political overtones. The police, eager to close the case, but goaded by the press and members of other investigatory bodies who wanted to keep it open, might have been trying to feel out Roach's view of their findings and conclusion. He was, after all, a powerful studio mogul closely linked to the deceased. If they could get his endorsement or, at least, his acquiescence to their resolution of the case, the critics would have less fuel for the fire. This might explain why they told him Mrs. Todd had left town, or was not available, leaving the implication that his decision was a crucial factor in closing the case or pursuing it.

It seems clear Roach misconstrued what the police told him and the real reason for their visit. Following the case generally in the papers or listening to others talk about it, he could have easily misunderstood much of what the officers told him. He may have mistaken the reference to the argument between West and Todd, thinking it occurred when Todd returned to the café from the Trocadero, not when she left for the Lupino party. He may have misunderstood the reference to the locking of the door, thinking the police meant the garage door, when they really meant the apartment door. Finally, he may have misconstrued the nature of West's admission, thinking West confessed to "killing" Todd when actually he only acknowledged responsibility for her *accidental* death.

Out of Roach's confusion, the legend of West's covered-up criminality developed, first as a chestnut told, embellished and polished by Roach and later repeated by others until it was picked up by various writers, reaching its fullest fruition in Mader and Wolf's murder solution, with a conspiracy theory as a backdrop.

Roland West's "deathbed" confession, purportedly made to his old colleague Chester Morris, likely has a similar origin. Cited by MacQueen and Mader and Wolf, it was originally reported by director Alex Gordon. The authors contacted Mr. Gordon, who graciously provided clarification.[19]

Gordon, who was somewhat amused at the notoriety his story had gotten over the years, explained the whole interchange with Morris about the Todd case lasted only for a few moments on a break during the filming of *The She Creature* in 1954. As Gordon recalled, Morris asked him what he knew about the Thelma Todd case. The men talked briefly, and at one point Morris disclosed that, shortly before he died, West told him that he, West, had killed Todd. Gordon said Morris did not give him any details about the murder but he did say something about West having "locked the door." Gordon only later took this statement as a reference to the door of the garage. It was a natural assumption for anyone who knew Todd died in a garage but did not understand the critical controversy during the 1935 investigation that surrounded West's locking of the apartment door.

When asked directly whether Morris suggested West murdered Todd, Gordon replied Morris said, "West had told him he was responsible for her death." While secondary writers, Mader and Wolf in particular, have termed West's statement a confession, it was probably nothing more than an expression of remorse for having locked her out of her apartment, an action that at least contributed to her death.

Like many other mysterious and oft reported elements in the Todd case—the scuffed slippers, the peas and beans, the condition of the body—the Roach scenario and Roland West's deathbed confession do not hold up to close scrutiny. Still, while the case against West as the murderer of Thelma Todd can be laid to rest, the issue of his culpability in her tragic death is still open. After all, if West had not locked the door of the apartment in either an act of spite or one of domination and control, she would not have died. This was the fact he had to live with for the rest of his life.

TWENTY: THE MYSTERY OF ROLAND WEST

Man's character is his fate
— Heraclitus

What, then, can be said about Roland West's real role in the mysterious death of Thelma Todd?

One thing is certain. Based on the historical record and the research of the authors, West's account of the events and actions surrounding Todd's death is inconsistent and, at points, contradictory. While the record does not support claims he murdered Todd, questions remain about the role he might have played in her death.

The most extensive remaining record of West's explanation of the Todd death, his testimony before the Coroner's Inquest, is far from clear. As with all transcripts of live testimony, some of this confusion surely derives from the absence of facial expressions, gestures and inflections that may have clarified his meaning. Still, one suspects that even with these visual and audile aids West's testimony must have been bewildering at times. Words fail him frequently; other times they tumble out chaotically. Often, returning to emphasize a key point, he contradicts himself. In several instances, when the internal logic of an assertion drops away, he blithely leaps the chasm as if nothing happened and beckons his listeners to follow. While nothing he says amounts to a smoking gun, it is clear he is sometimes evasive. The question is: just what was he trying to hide?

West's testimony is most baffling when he answers questions about the living arrangements at the café. His description of Todd's apartment, his so-called sleeping quarters behind the "heavy wooden doors" and the adjacent areas of the second floor of the café building, are impossible to reconcile with contemporary floor plans of the building. As the Coroner's Jury and interrogators did not have the plans before them, his obfuscations went largely unnoticed.

West had been involved with the building for several years. Originally built in the mid-twenties to serve as a community center for the Castellammare residential development, under his control the three-story Mediterranean-style building was transformed into an elegant restaurant and bar to suit the posh tastes of his clientele. Its two wings centered on an imposing arched entrance, adorned with bas-relief colonettes and vaulted by recesses of painted tiles. The two-story northwest wing, a tall glazed arcade of seven arches beneath a second story lined with rectangular windows and a low, red-tile roof, stretched a hundred feet along the highway terminating in a square tower with a false balcony. The southeast wing, a stubby version of the northwest, with only three arches but featuring the same rectangular windows and roof, angled obtusely towards a pedestrian bridge spanning the Roosevelt Highway. Above the gabled roof of the entranceway rose a third story, a hexagonal tower with seven casement windows on each side and a pyramidal roof.

Prior to West's ownership, the building was held jointly by the residents of the Castellammare development. Constructed in 1927 as the flagship edifice of the hillside community,[1] it was conceived as a beach club and retail business center for the upscale residents of the hillside.[2] The first floor of the community center housed various retail and service shops, including a drug store, the development's realty office and a small restaurant catering to the beach crowd. The second floor was not as fully utilized. The northwest wing consisted of a large club area replete with a fireplace lounge, which was converted in the late twenties into a grocery store and meat market.[3] The southeast wing's second story contained restrooms and showers for bathers and an undeveloped space for shops.[4] The third floor turret, a hexagon, nearly sixty feet across, was designed to serve as a community meeting and social area. It is rumored that, during Prohibition, it was used as a speakeasy.[5] A thick metal door with a seven by ten inch peephole still blocks the front stairwell entrance to the turret, while another steep stairwell descends to the building's northwest wing, perhaps once providing a route for patrons escaping from police raids. If the allegations were true that West planned to set up gambling in this room, these features might have been put to good use again.

The building may well have continued as a community center were it not for the slump in the fortunes of those who could afford to develop villas on the Castellammare hillside. Unfortunately for the original speculators who conceived the hillside community (Frank Meline, Inc., Mesa Unit Trust, Mesa Unit Castellammare and the Los Angeles Mountain Park Company) the development went from success to failure within a matter of a few years.[6] By the early 30s, the building had become a bit of a white elephant with little or no community to serve. But West, who owned three lots farther west along the Roosevelt Highway in the Castle Rock area where the Los Angeles Athletic Club hoped to build a yacht harbor[7] and whose estate, Castillo del Mar, was used as a model to attract other homebuilders, saw another potential for the building. Acquiring it in 1932,[8] he set about turning it into a restaurant, slowly at first, and then with gusto.

West's first task was to get the city to abandon its right-of-way to the public walk running through the community center. The walkway was an extension of Malibu Walk, an eight-foot-wide promenade originating at Sunset Boulevard a half-mile to the southeast and paralleling the highway along the base of the Castellammare bluffs. It coursed along the second floor of the building, at the time an open terrace, on its way to Porto Marino, the street immediately to the northwest of the building.[9] In the twenties, one could pass through the building to a rear courtyard and climb a set of stairs connecting to those ascending the terraced hillside.

The city agreed to abandon its right-of-way after making plans for a replacement set of hillside steps immediately to the south of the building's property line.[10] West proceeded to enclose the second-floor balconies and the corresponding arched walkways on the first floor, cutting off public access from Malibu walk and enlarging the space of the building.[11] Café operations then began on the first floor, the northwest wing serving as a café during the day and a cabaret at night. The first floor of the southeast wing, once allocated to small shops, became a cozy cocktail lounge for the café.[12] In addition, West constructed a state-of-the-art barbecue in an interior area at the back of the building nestled into the hillside.[13]

In this, West had an ultimate vision. He had a long-term interest in cooking through a friendship with Henri Carpentia, a noted Long Island restaurateur.[14] With Thelma Todd as a lure for the Hollywood set, he planned to establish a first-class restaurant on the beach, serving the finest food and drink, and catering to a very exclusive clientele. When others scoffed at the notion that rich film folk and other wealthy diners would travel so far and pay so much, West had a ready answer. He would offer services they could not resist, including private dining areas where producers and casting directors could bring their compliant ingénues and secretaries for an uninterrupted dining experience featuring the best champagne and gourmet food, served by discreet waiters.[15] For this purpose, the former walkway on the second-floor northwest wing was enclosed to create seven exclusive and private dining rooms with ocean views. West also invested heavily in decor, embellishing the original architectural features of the structure with a whimsical and colorful movie palace motif. The old interior arches were given decorative facades and corbels. Ornate doors were added and restaurant and lobby furniture was constructed in a similar, eclectic fashion.[16]

On the southeast side, West turned the second story into an apartment of five contiguous areas. The promenade became a small kitchenette and an exterior area overlooking the ocean. The building's old arches joined newly constructed interior walls to define an outer area of 17 by 19 feet and an inner chamber of 15 by 15 feet, with an adjacent bathroom tiled in cobalt blue. A set of sliding wooden doors divided the inner chamber from the outer area.[17]

West moved down from Castillo del Mar and began staying in these accommodations after he separated from Jewel in the early spring of 1934, perhaps to be close to the café, where operations were moving into full swing. Thelma Todd moved into the rooms in August 1935.[18] She had been renting a house up the hill at 17925 Tramonto Drive, where she moved after her divorce from Pat DiCicco a year before.[19] What prompted her to move into the café building is not clear. Certainly, it was convenient to the restaurant, which now bore her name. Fear also may have played a part in her decision. She was still receiving extortion notes and her house had been burglarized that summer.[20] Perhaps she sought the support and protection of the employees of the café. On the other hand, perhaps she simply wanted to live with West.

Despite West's obfuscations during the inquiry, anyone who examines this apartment quickly realizes he and Todd shared the rooms. The inner chamber served as a bedroom, where West slept on the night of Todd's disappearance. Next to the bedroom was the small bathroom. The outer area became a sitting or living room adjoining the kitchenette. West's assertion Todd regularly stayed only in the outer room, with no bed or bathroom and no privacy from the occupant of the inner chamber, who would have to cross it every time he left the apartment, is impossible to believe. Undoubtedly, he didn't fool any of the detectives and reporters who visited this apartment after Todd's death. In fact, Mae Whitehead, who had complete knowledge of the place, admitted during the Coroner's Inquest testimony that the entire apartment was the domain of her mistress, though she equivocated when it came to the question of other occupants

> Q: How much of the apartment did Miss Todd have there where she lived?
> A: Two rooms.
> Q: And that consisted of her sleeping room and living room, or what were they?
> A: Yes.
> Q: And a bathroom, I suppose?
> A: Yes.
> Q: And did anyone live in the apartment with her?
> A: Not that I know of.
> Q: Did she have any guest occupying the apartment at any time recently that you know of?
> A: No.

While Whitehead was careful to neither confirm nor deny that anyone else was living in the apartment, there was no ambiguity in her answers when it came to affirming Todd herself occupied the entire apartment, and not just part of it.[21] When asked to describe the same apartment, however, West's response was less clear:

> Q: Now, what are the apartments at the café, the living arrangements, how are they arranged?
> A: Well, there is this one main room and the outside one is always Miss Todd's and that is as large as this court room and it is divided off with pillars and whenever I sleep at the café I went into the back room and there are folding doors which are locked between and outside the lobby is all private and couches out there and places to sleep.

Q: How many entrances to those apartments?
A: The main entrance is through a room which has never been opened and occupied as a ladies' boudoir and going from there is the main room to the main apartment.[22]

Later, when asked to account for his actions on Sunday morning, he provided another description:

A: I went out to see, opened the door, rapped, went out ...
Q: You mean out where?
A: Out into the big room, like this court room, I saw she wasn't there, and then I went into the lady's, opened with my pass key and examined the huge couch in there because she had slept on that couch and there was what I considered an impression on that couch, thought she had slept there because nobody else could have done that. Then I figured she had gotten up and went to her mother's.[23]

Within this pair of descriptions dwelt one of the major problems in West's testimony. In the first statement, to make sense, the "lobby" reference must signify the area outside the apartment, at the back of the stairwell leading from the first floor and under the huge arched window overlooking the Pacific. However, when describing the layout from the opposite direction, West claimed the main entrance to the apartment was "through a room that has never been opened and occupied as a ladies' boudoir." While the two descriptions sound as if they refer to the same area, it is impossible to believe he meant that a boudoir would be in such an exposed area. In the first description, he referred to the room "outside" the sliding doors as "always Miss Todd's." This area, as has been noted, was used as a sitting room. Separated from the bathroom by the inner bedroom—West's sleeping room—it could hardly serve as a separate apartment for Miss Todd.

Throughout his testimony, West employed a dizzying array of terms to describe various areas of the apartment complex, including "main", "ladies", "other ladie's", "bedroom", "backroom", "lobby", "inside door", "main door", and "main entrance". The references undoubtedly had a specific meaning for him, but they are almost incomprehensible to anyone familiar with the layout of the café, let alone to those with no knowledge. Relying on West's testimony alone, without the benefit of visual aids or an on-site visit, the inquest jurors could not possibly obtain an accurate picture of the environs of the café or its living arrangements.[24]

West's evasions may have arisen simply from a desire to protect his own reputation and that of the late actress. On the other hand, he may have worried the intimacy between him and Todd would make him the logical suspect should the evidence point towards foul play.

In any case, his misleading testimony about living arrangements complicated and perhaps even lengthened the investigation. Had he been forthright about their relationship, much of the apparent problems in his testimony might have fallen away. As it was, the Grand Jury only got a clear, if perhaps somewhat altered, picture of the café premises when its members visited the site in the first week of January. Jurors noted the outside door to the apartment was very close to the bed chamber, making it likely West would have heard Miss Todd had she tried to get in.[25] They must have puzzled over his earlier descriptions of the apartment, which seemed to conjure up a much larger and more complex dwelling.

It is easy to understand why West, who stuck firmly to his belief that Todd's death was accidental, would consider their relationship their own business and try to conceal it, especially after he came to believe the investigation had become unwarranted, sensationalistic, and perhaps politically-motivated. Under the circumstances, he may have felt justified in stonewalling.[26]

Whatever significance can be drawn from West's description of the living arrangements at the café, his testimony concerning the events immediately surrounding Todd's death raised additional questions that dogged the investigation from beginning to end. His account of the events of early Sunday morning presented a variety of twists and turns, including at least two time-related shifts in perspective, and a number of puzzling assumptions. Behind all this appeared to be a simple goal: to absolve himself of any responsibility, even indirect, for Todd's death, and for his failure to search for her the following day when she was found missing.

Inevitably, the investigators focused much of their attention on West's deadbolting of the door, the act that, assuming Todd's death was accidental, appeared to set off a tragic chain of events. During the coroner's investigation, Nance moved quickly to this issue as he questioned West about his conversation with Todd as she left for the Trocadero; newspaper accounts of the ongoing mystery returned repeatedly to this issue as well. Indeed, the character of that conversation might also feed either a suicide or a murder hypothesis. If West and Todd had quarreled, it might have indicated an ongoing problem in their relationship and contributed to Todd's depression, thus lending credence to a suicide hypothesis. A quarrel also might cut another way, provoking West to a crime of passion or jealousy when Todd returned late after a night on the town.

West offered two versions of the conversation when he testified at the Coroner's Inquest. Both made it seem lighthearted and playful. In the first, he reported he and Todd bantered over the hour she should return home, West suggesting two o'clock, Todd playfully arguing for five minutes past two, West insisting on two, Todd still holding out for five past. In the second version, given after a lunch recess, he added he told Todd that, if she stayed out past two, she should go to her mother's to sleep because she needed to maintain her beauty.

Was the exchange really as good-humored as West claimed, did it have an edge, or was it actually a spat? There is no way to tell from the record. None of the other witnesses present, Mrs. Todd, Ernie Peters, or Mae Whitehead, was questioned on the point. Nevertheless, the police, after talking with West on Monday, concluded the couple argued. "It's my opinion," stated Capt. Burt Wallis, "she and West had a tiff Saturday night when she was leaving for the party she attended."[27] Wallis went on to claim West told him the actress had been "stepping" on him and that his admonition that he would lock the door at 2:00 arose from his hurt pride.[28]

In his Coroner's Jury testimony, however, West tried to downplay any hint of conflict in his warning to Todd about locking the door.

> Q: Did you say, "If you are not home at two o'clock, I will lock you out?"
> A: No, I said, "After two o'clock the outside door is locked."

West's use of the passive voice suggested he was reminding Todd of a practice which necessity, not his own desire or anger, required. When the coroner asked what he meant by his statement, he replied simply "Well, we have heard people around there and I had bars put up at the window." In other words, what he meant by the statement was not that he wanted to lock her out, but that the security of the building required the apartment door be locked.[29]

West sounded the same theme when he claimed that on Saturday nights Todd would never enter her apartment through the apartment door. What was special about Saturday nights or why the prowlers he and Schafer feared were so much more a threat on Saturday nights than on others, he never explained. Still, according to West, Todd "never came in that door on Saturday nights, because it was always bolted when the maid left on Saturday night."[30] The implication seemed to be that the practice of deadbolting the door was known and accepted by Todd, justifying West's assumption that she would not attempt to enter the apartment through that door, but through the main entrance downstairs.

Despite West's care in pressing this point with the coroner, the statements of other witnesses cast doubt on his contention that Todd knew the apartment door would be locked. Ernie Peters testified he dropped Miss Todd off five times in the last year and always escorted her to the apartment's side door.[31] Mae Whitehead declared she deliberately selected a key to the side entrance to place in Todd's evening bag.[32] Moreover, West's warning to Todd as she left for the Trocadero that "after two o'clock the outside door is locked" demonstrated even he realized Todd was likely to come in by that door—why else mention the door would be locked? His anecdote about Todd coming to the side door on a previous Saturday night and breaking a window to wake him also proved she did not recognize a customary practice of deadbolting the door.[33] Although he claimed it was the only time she ever used that door on a Saturday night, it was also, as he himself admitted, "An experience to let her know that she could get in that door."[34]

When first interviewed by police and reporters at the garage, he suggested Todd attempted to enter through the apartment door on the fateful night:

> About 3:30 I was awakened by the whining of my dog and I knew it was Miss Todd at the door, because if it had been anyone else, the dog would have growled. But she didn't make any noise or attempt to awaken me. Instead, she must have walked to the garage, in which she kept her car, and becoming cold, started the motor.[35]

At another point, he observed that, having awakened the dog, Todd "made no sound and apparently went away, for the dog stopped whining."[36]

The following day, West admitted to Bert Wallis the same hurt pride precluded him from searching for Todd on Sunday also kept him from investigating the dog's whining to see if Todd was at the door.[37] On the Coroner's witness stand, however, he testified somewhat differently about the inferences he drew from the episode, claiming the whining dog persuaded him at the time that Todd had arrived safely at home and was then in the building:

> I was awakened about three thirty by the dog whining and he never whines—he has a habit of whining when he gets uncovered, and I looked over to see, to cover him up and he was all covered, and I looked at the clock and it was exactly three thirty. Whether that clock was right or not I don't know, it was a table clock, and I called out to see if Miss Todd was home and received no answer, but I heard the water running in the building and figured that there was nobody up, figured she had come in from the outside the regular way and gone to bed, and the dog was quiet and I went to sleep.[38]

Later, West altered his interpretation of the incident, downplaying the implication the animal whimpered because Todd had come to the side door. Although he had just told the jury the dog was covered by the blanket, now he suggested it was uncovered:

> I went to sleep—first, I got up and examined the dog to see if he was uncovered, he always whines when he is uncovered, and I covered him up and lay there a few minutes and heard the water running in the other lady's and figured it was Miss Todd.[39]

Perhaps, he tried to suggest, the dog whined because it was uncovered and not necessarily because it recognized Miss Todd.

West also testified the sound of running water persuaded him Todd was safely in the café building. This testimony carried its own set of problems. After having consulted with Schafer, the café's manager, during a break in the Coroner's Inquest, West speculated the source of the sound might have been the "carbonator," a pump in the restaurant bar for carbonating water and soft drinks that came on automatically at intervals.[40] While it is impossible to determine now whether this could have accounted for the sound, it seems curious West was unfamiliar with it. Having slept in the building many nights after the staff left, he should have heard the carbonator start previously. Yet apparently on those occasions, he did not assume someone was up and running water as he did on this particular night. Perhaps he never really paid attention to the carbonator before, but this night, because he was lying awake listening, trying to determine whether Todd had entered the building through the main door on Roosevelt Highway, he heard it for the first time.

West's handling of these matters—covering/not covering the dog, not checking the window, and the running water—could be interpreted in different ways. One gets the impression West was an imprecise speaker by nature and perhaps that is all there is to some of his apparent contradictions. Nevertheless, it is also possible he was playing two ends against the middle as he tried to rationalize his actions and failures to act that night. Indeed, it is hard to avoid the impression that West's story changed as he grasped it was playing badly in the minds of the investigators. He had already revealed too clearly to police that his anger with Todd precluded him from searching for her when he found she was not at the café on Sunday. They might easily surmise the same anger or hurt pride motivated him Sunday morning when he failed to respond to Todd at the apartment door. By changing the story to emphasize the dog's whining was merely a part of his impressions that night and important only in that it awakened him to hear the sound of running water, West refocused the incident to bolster his reasons for assuming Todd had arrived home safely.

At times West also seemed to argue that, even if he did lock Todd out, no serious consequences should have arisen. Todd, he suggested several times, was not one put off by a locked door. "She could get in better than you and I if she wanted to get in, and nobody could make her do anything she didn't want to do. You could advise her and talk to her and she would judge what is right."[41] He struck a similarly laudatory theme when asked if he ever reprimanded Todd about her late hours:

> Not reprimand; I would talk to her. You could not reprimand Miss Todd; Miss Todd had everything a man has, she had money and plenty of everything; you could not reprimand Miss Todd; she was an individual with the strength of any man in this room.[42]

While on one level this statement served as a tribute to the dead actress, on another it was a sly attempt at self-exoneration. The stronger and more willful he could make Todd seem, the more responsible she became for her own death. If Todd previously had "an experience to let her know that she could get in that door," then she could have done so that night, even if it meant breaking another windowpane. That she did not do so meant she must not have wanted to get in at all, perhaps out of consideration for West's rest. Taking this tack, all questions about the evening argument in front of the café and the locking of the door became less relevant, as Todd had it in her power to overcome any of his acts.

West relied heavily on the meager evidence that Todd slept in the building to explain the second key issue of his potential culpability in Todd's death: his failure to investigate Todd's absence on Sunday.[43] He stressed throughout his testimony how his belief that Todd had been in the building motivated him, reinforcing the point by describing an interaction he had with employee Robert Anderson on Sunday:

> Q: All the time up until you went downstairs, about one [o'clock], you heard nothing whatsoever regarding Miss Todd?
> A: No, I thought she had gone to her mother's.
> Q: And you didn't make any inquiry about her?
> A: Not until I got downstairs.
> Q: And then what happened?
> A: Well, I asked the boy that takes care of Miss Todd's car which car she had used.[44]

Questioned again on this point later by one of the jurors, West emphasized the precise phrasing of his question to Anderson.

> Q: Mr. West, you made a statement to the effect that you asked this man Bob [Anderson] whose car—
> A: Which car.
> Q: Which car she took?
> A: No, which car Miss Todd used that afternoon.
> Q: Which car Miss Todd used that afternoon?
> A: That is correct.[45]

As in the case of his comment to Todd that "After two o'clock, the outside door is locked," West's insistence on the exact language of the exchange with Anderson betrayed his sensitivity about the issue at hand. He had a point to make, an obscure one perhaps, but one that he did not want the coroner or jury to miss. In his mind, the specific way in which he asked the question objectively demonstrated his assumption that Todd entered the café building that night and then departed in one of the two automobiles in the garage. At the same time, his convoluted language may have been chosen to stress another message, since any question about the absent actress that did not imply West knew **when** she left and **where** she was could have raised the eyebrows of the young waiter and others at the café. What he really wanted to know from Anderson was whether a car was missing from the garage, but he could not ask that question without revealing he did not know where Todd was. So instead, he asked a question that implied he knew she had departed by car, only he did not know "which car." He must have hoped the young man checked the garage that morning, and, if not, that an inquiry from West would induce him to do so.

Certainly, the most obvious motive for asking "which car" she used would be that West was himself contemplating a drive that day. However, West later admitted he rarely drove either car and had not driven the Hupmobile for a month. He did not attempt to drive the automobile that day, and, as far as we can know, never even visited the garage. His real interest was not in knowing which car Todd had taken, since he had no plans to use either automobile, but whether she took any car at all. Bob Anderson could give him that information, if he would just go to the garage and look.[46]

His insistence on the precise utterance reinforced his point that he assumed Todd went to her mother's, a point the juror grasped a minute later:

> Q: Well, but if you asked the question, "Which car was used?
> A: Yes sir.
> Q: Wouldn't you naturally assume there was one or the other cars to use outside there?
> A: She could use both; they were both in the garage. She could use either one she wanted to. I wanted to know which car she used.
> Q: I get the point. You presumed she went to her mother's?
> A: I presume she went to her mother's.[47]

As long as he could argue that he assumed Todd was safe at her mother's, one could hardly blame him for not worrying about her.

Overall, if one tries to believe West's testimony about the living arrangements and his happy relationship with his good friend Todd, it is difficult to understand the assumptions he made. By his testimony, it is clear that, when the dog whined and he heard the water running, he assumed Todd was inside the building and preparing for bed. He claimed the impression in the couch he observed the next morning reinforced this assumption. Why, then, did he suppose that, once she was safe at home, she arose at daylight and went to her mother's? For this, he offered no explanation. Certainly, she did not do so because he told her if she came home after two, the doors would be locked, and she should go to her mother's, nor because of his advice that, by doing so, she could save an extra half hour for her beauty rest. Neither reason would apply once, as West presumed, Todd was home and inside. Rising at daylight to visit her mother after she had been out past 3:30 would be unlikely in any case.

In short, West's major underlying assumption—that Todd got into the building, slept a few hours and then went to her mother's—made little sense. While he pointed out his assumptions varied with the information he possessed at the time, on Sunday or after Todd's body was found on Monday,[48] his inference that she entered the building Sunday morning should have precluded his other inference that she went to her mother's.

Even if one supposes there was another reason for West's failure to explain why a happy, untroubled Todd would rise in the early morning after only a few hours' sleep and leave for her mother's apartment, one wonders why he thought she would do so dressed in the evening gown and fur she had worn to the Trocadero. He testified that on Sunday evening he believed Todd would soon return to the café because "I knew she went out with an evening dress, I couldn't see any other way she could have any other clothes if she went to her mother's."[49] How he knew this is hard to figure, given his prior testimony. Previously, when asked whether at any point he checked her clothing to determine whether she had changed from her evening gown, he replied, "No, because she had so many clothes that I could not tell, I don't think that anyone could tell."[50] Most likely, he was telling the truth when he stated he knew she was still in her evening gown and prevaricating when he said he could not know what she was wearing because of the extent of her wardrobe. He did not need to check her closet to know she had not changed from her evening gown—all he had to know is that she could not have changed her clothes because she never entered their apartment. By this telling *faux pas*, West let slip that he never believed Todd entered the building Saturday night. Curiously, West himself never seemed to realize what he had revealed and continued to stick to his story throughout the investigation.

Nothing on Sunday confirmed West's assumption Todd had gone to her mother's. At 6:00 p.m., after George Baker's call from the Ford's residence, he knew Todd had not arrived at the cocktail party, which he claimed he knew she was going to attend. After seven o'clock, he knew she had failed to meet Skourases at the café for dinner. Yet all that day and evening West made no effort to determine where Todd was beyond his careful question to Anderson as to "which car Miss Todd had used." He dismissed the suggestion of investigators that he might have called Mrs. Todd to see if Todd was there. "I've never called up Miss Todd's mother in my life," he declared. "I was not going to call up her mother and admit I didn't know where she was."[51] According to one newspaper, he admitted his hurt pride precluded his acknowledging to anybody—the employees at the café or Mrs. Todd—the fact he did not know where Todd was and was worried.

By midnight, Todd had still not shown up, nor had there been any word from her. In spite of this, West went to bed. He claimed to have trouble sleeping that night, though he did not attribute any anxiety to the fact he had not heard from Todd for nearly 30 hours.

There remains one more difficulty with West's actions and testimony. To expose it, we must return to the garage on the morning her body was found. While West went into considerable detail concerning his observations at the time, we know he failed to tell the coroner's or Grand Jury at least one thing.

According to Capt. Bruce Clark, when he arrived at the scene around noon Monday, the body of Miss Todd was "lying on the front seat of the car."[52] He then identified a photograph he took showing the actress with her head against the left door.[53] Yet, Mae Whitehead, who discovered the body somewhere around 10:30 a.m. that morning, testified Miss Todd was sitting behind the steering wheel of the phaeton, listing slightly to the left, her arms in her lap, her head slumped down on her chest.[54] Obviously, between the time Whitehead found the body and the arrival of the police, the body had been moved. Equally obvious is the fact Roland West moved it, most likely when he was alone with the corpse after sending Whitehead up to the house to get the Schafers. Strangely, although both the coroner and the examining district attorney queried Whitehead and Clark diligently on the position of the body, they never asked West if he moved it. Nor did West ever make any public statement about the matter.

Why West moved the body might never be known. He may have done it to shield his paramour from the eyes of strangers or the cameras he knew would soon arrive. Perhaps he felt compelled to exchange the awkward and unnatural pose of death with one more evocative of sleep. Maybe he feared the body might tumble out of the automobile onto the garage floor. Yet it is also possible he was trying to modify the position of the body to throw off the police investigation—either to make an accident or murder look like a suicide, or a suicide look like an accident or even a murder. While it is impossible to determine why he moved the body, we can be assured he did so.

What then are we to make of Roland West's account of the events surrounding the death of Thelma Todd and what conclusions can be drawn concerning his culpability? It is clear he tried to obscure the nature of their living arrangements and, with it, the nature of their relationship. He may have been trying to protect her reputation or his own, or trying to distance himself from the implication of too much passion, thus blunting conjecture about a crime motivated by jealously and rage with him as the likely suspect. It is also clear that West intended to lock Todd out of her apartment. Perhaps, as he claimed, he was unaware she didn't have the key for the main entrance below; maybe he was merely trying to inconvenience her out of spite for her failure to return at the appointed hour. Alternatively, perhaps he expected she would knock on the door, allowing him an opportunity to confront her about her tardiness. Whatever his motives, his actions contributed to her death. Had he not deadbolted the door, or had he sought her out when the dog whined, before she started her climb up the hill, Thelma Todd would have lived.

It also seems likely West was not certain early Sunday morning that Todd got into the café building; nor was he convinced later that morning that she went to her mother's. Perhaps, he suspected she had gone somewhere else: to a friend's, perhaps, or to meet another man. His failure to search for her in spite of a good deal of evidence there was something amiss, his comments about being "hurt and proud," and his guarded inquiry to Anderson about "which car" Todd used, suggest a jealous, controlling personality which, not getting its way, responded in a truculent and peevish manner. That he maintained the fiction of his belief that Todd had gone to her mother's throughout the investigation did little to shore up his credibility.

Indeed, there is evidence, albeit hearsay, that in his own mind, West bore responsibility for the tragedy. Chester Morris' comment to Alex Gordon that West felt guilt over having "killed" Todd–discussed in the previous chapter–is one item. Another comes from Robert Hanlon, who married West's widow, actress Lola Lane. According to Hanlon, Lane claimed West never completely recovered from the trauma brought on by Todd's death.[55] Certainly, her demise marked a turning point in his life. Before it, he had been a successful vaudeville actor, playwright, film director and producer, and restauranteur. After it, his life was filled with difficulties and discord. He underwent a bitter divorce and property squabble with his first wife, Jewel Carmen. He tried with meager success to carry on restaurant operations in the café building, first continuing under the name of Thelma Todd's Sidewalk Café, then as Chez Roland. By the mid-forties, however, the restaurant only opened for special clients. Shelly Winters claimed Howard Hughes took her there one time on a date, and she got the distinct impression that the restaurant was open to serve just them. Apparently, West continued in his vision of catering to wealthy patrons by mixing a unique dining experience with a place of assignation. Louella Parsons also told of dining at Chez Roland once with her husband, Dr. Harry Martin, Joseph Schenck, and heiress Evalyn Walsh McLean. "During the course of dinner [McLean] said to Roland, 'Now come on, did you or did you not murder Thelma Todd? Everybody says you did!' West made no comment, merely turned on his heel and walked away." The following week, Parsons went on to recount, McLean dined at Chez Roland's again in a party of six, and West presented her with a bill for $890–well over $10,000 in 2016 dollars.[56]

West's film career was also over, but most likely, it had ended with *Corsair*. As early as 1930, apparently tired of production work, he talked about retirement. Between the making of *Corsair* in 1931 and Todd's death, he made no efforts at movie making. He had little financial incentive to do so, having already amassed considerable wealth.[57] Instead, he devoted himself to a range of interests: yachting, the restaurant, real estate and investments, and the management of his still extensive intellectual property. While some secondary writers like to attribute the end of his film career to Todd's death and insinuations about his part in it, the truth was he had moved on and so had Hollywood.

Ultimately, the question of West's personality and character and how it bears upon the mystery surrounding Thelma Todd's death is almost as intriguing as the mystery itself.

By most accounts, West was a remote, reserved, even diffident man who seemed uneasy in social and professional situations alike. Regis Toomey, an actor who worked with him described him as "a difficult man to get to know. He was rather shy, very reticent, a very retiring man. He had very little to say."[58] Others who worked with him, such as Hal Kern and Una Merkel, made similar observations.[59]

Don Gallery, the adopted son of ZaSu Pitts, often accompanied his mother for lunch at Thelma Todd's Sidewalk Café. While Todd would be bubbly and warm, he noted West always hung in the background attending to business and seemed very distant and "managerial."[60] Another frequent visitor to Castellammare, café manager Rudolph Schafer's son Rudy instructed to call West "Uncle Roland," did not like West and was convinced West did not like him or other children. The only time West paid any real attention to him, Rudy later remembered, was when he accidentally closed the car door on Rudy's finger.[61] Others took away an even less charitable impression. Florian "Jack" Sauer lived up the street from the café and owned a garage in Pacific Palisades that tended to West's and Todd's cars. Based on many interactions with West while visiting at the café, he found West "cold and hard." As far as Sauer knew, "he never had a friend in his life"; his one interest was making as much money as possible. For Sauer, one image captured him more than any other: West with his hands folded behind the small of his back, silent and unsmiling, watching everything.[62]

All this would seem to make West and Todd a very odd couple. Her friendly and outgoing manner must have contrasted dramatically with West's reticent and closed nature. She loved nightlife, parties and fast cars; he preferred to nest at the café, rarely ventured into town, and owned and only occasionally drove a seven-year-old Hupmobile, hardly a sleek roadster. His apparent need to control and fuss over her career and beauty provoked her to stay out late and attend even more functions, with or without an escort. Her self-deprecating, and sometimes broad sense of humor seems out of step with West, a man given to witticism and epigram who could not resist the opportunity to display a sense of irony, even if he sometimes came off as somewhat pompous or inappropriate. Once, while posing for a photograph with a kind of detached graciousness during the Grand Jury hearings, he felt compelled to quip: "A photograph, like a glimpse in a mirror, is just an illusion." The *Daily News* reporter, Vincent Mahoney, described another West "witticism", his comment during the Coroner's Inquest that he was not in the "café business" but soon would as "startling", since it implied that Todd's death had effected the change.[63]

Todd actually fit a strong pattern in West's relationships. He had a penchant for young, beautiful actresses early in their careers. In 1918, he married Jewel Carmen, a rising star with a number of motion pictures to her credits, whom one reviewer called "one of the prettiest and most capable actresses in motion pictures."[64] In 1934, according to Carmen, Jewel and West separated, in part because of West's interest in Thelma Todd.[65] Finally, several years after Todd's death West began a long-term relationship with another attractive young actress, Lola Lane, whom he wed near the end of his life.

All three were considerably younger than West. All three were attractive. All three were ambitiously pursuing acting careers. West, older, wiser and well established in the industry, took on a mentor role with the actresses. We certainly see this in his relationships with Jewel Carmen and Thelma Todd, whom he featured in various films, and whom he coached and clucked over in various aspects of their careers, even attempting to change Todd's screen name to Alison Loyd. Not surprisingly, in two of the three cases, contrary to the conventions of the times, West held himself aloof, avoiding marriage and exercising a good deal of caginess in his financial dealings with his paramours.

In 1939, when Jewel sued West for divorce and a share of their property, some of which West had registered in her name over the years, West not only contested the financial claim but also denied a marriage ever took place.[66] Though the couple reached a separate maintenance arrangement and settlement, West continued to deny the marriage. As Jewel could easily disprove his claim by producing a marriage certificate, one suspects his denials were truthful.

It is not clear whether West and Todd ever contemplated marriage, but questions arose about their financial arrangement concerning the café. In spite of speculation that she owned a share of the restaurant enterprise, Todd had no interest in the café.[67] As West disclosed during the investigation, Todd and he had an agreement that she would gain a one-half interest only if he died before she did.[68] Strangely, this agreement does not seem to have been in writing.

West and Lane married in 1945 and remained together until West died in 1952.[69] Lane inherited an estate, including the café property, valued at approximately $50,000.[70] Even in this, there is controversy. A neighbor of the West claimed that, shortly before West's death, Lane confided her concern to him about West's failing health and the fact that she had only a verbal promise that he would leave the café to her. Fearing Lane was naive and too trusting, the neighbor persuaded her to put pressure on West to formalize the arrangement.[71] It turned out to be a good move. Soon after West's death, a former restaurant employee, "Queenie" Eileen Shannon, came forward with a claim against West's estate. Shannon asserted she was hired as a featured act at the café a few weeks after Thelma Todd's death, had stayed on to manage the restaurant until

1946, and departed only after West married Lola Lane. She maintained that before her departure West acknowledged she was due a share in the restaurant enterprise and promised to take care of her in his will. However, the will, written only two weeks before West's death, contained only the following bequest: "I do not leave more than $1 to Miss Shannon for the reason she has squandered or wasted all previous sums given by me to her." Shannon retained an attorney to contest the will but in the end got only the dollar.[72]

West was often reluctant to commit financial obligations to writing, especially with those close to him. Queenie Shannon suffered as a result; Lola Lane ultimately had her bequest put in writing, but only at her insistence. Jewel Carmen prevailed, but only by resorting to the services of one of the best attorneys of the era, Jerry Geisler. As Sauer declared, West's primary passion in life was money; relationships came second.

All this contributes to the sense that West had a worldly, venal streak quite in keeping with his self-made attributes, the era and avocation in which he rose, and his associations. Indeed, there is much to suggest an amoral strain in West's character. It finds expression in his vision of the café as a place of easy assignation for movie executives; men whom he knew would appreciate and respond to a secluded and accommodating spot to practice the art of the casting couch. It resonates in his desire to bring illegal gambling to the café. It also finds expression in his dealings with his lifelong friend, and founding Hollywood mogul, Joseph Schenck.

Joseph M. Schenck, like Roland West, was self-made and came up the hard way. He immigrated to the United States in 1892 from Russia with his younger brother and parents. As teenagers, with little formal schooling, he and his brother Nick became clerks and delivery boys at a drugstore near the Bowery in New York City. Later, they owned two pharmacies of their own. Always enterprising, the boys moved into the amusement business, first establishing the downscale Paradise Park at Fort George in Upper Manhattan, and later purchasing the more lavish facility, Palisades Park, across the Hudson in New Jersey.[73]

As nickelodeons were standard fare at such places, the Schencks soon became involved in the infant motion picture industry, first as exhibitors, then distributors. They associated with Marcus Loew and became the principal figures in his theatrical enterprises. By the late teens, Joe Schenck branched into producing, with Roland West in the director's chair. Their friendship would last until West's death in 1952.[74]

Though largely overlooked today, Schenck was a formative figure in the early motion picture industry. As an independent producer, he was instrumental in the careers of Roscoe Arbuckle, Norma and Constance Talmadge, Buster Keaton, Gloria Swanson, Corrine Griffith and John Barrymore. In 1924, he became Chairman of United Artists, which had been formed in 1919 by Mary Pickford, Charlie Chaplin, Douglas Fairbanks and D.W. Griffith, and helped expand it into a major Hollywood studio. He later established 20th Century and engineered its merger with Fox Studios.[75]

He had the reputation of a shrewd, but forthright and generous man. Many of his deals were consummated with a handshake. He was known for being good to his word, win or lose. Other moguls sought his advice in their own dealings, earning him the sobriquet "the Buddha of Hollywood." He learned that working quietly behind the scenes could bear impressive results and that long-term positive relationships paid off in the end. Few others contributed as much to charity or gave more time for a good cause.[76]

However, there was another side to Schenck. Always more flamboyant than his brother, Joe loved the fast life. An inveterate gambler, he played hard at both the track and in the gaming room. [77] A playboy, he maintained mistresses until near the end of his life. An entrepreneur, he won and lost several fortunes, investing in gambling resorts in both California and across the border in Mexico.[78] It should come as no surprise that all these activities brought him into close association with those who crossed the boundaries of law and traditional morality.

It was to Joe Schenck that the industry turned in the mid-thirties when it was being shaken down by labor extortionists who had gained control of IATSE, the International Alliance of Theatrical and Stage Employees. He served as a go-between, delivering payoffs from the producers to the mobsters. Unfortunately for Schenck, in 1940 one of the payoffs, approximating $100,000, showed up as a discrepancy when the Internal Revenue Service audited his tax return. Schenck's explanation that the sum constituted a loan led to an indictment charging him with perjury and tax evasion.[79]

The subsequent audits and trial ensnared his old friend Roland West when a questionable deal between them, consummated in 1935, came to light. Schenck had sold West shares in the Agua Caliente resort near Tijuana. On his income tax return, Schenck claimed a significant loss on the transaction. He asserted he was forced to sell at a discount because the Mexican government under President Cardenas had outlawed gambling.[80]

The federal government saw the deal in quite a different light. Prosecutors noted Schenck not only transferred the stock but also advanced West the purchase price as a loan, and that West never repaid the loan. Furthermore, they noted that Schenck retained voting rights in the stock by proxy to one of his associates. The prosecution charged Schenck concocted the deal to engineer a fraudulent write off, while at the same time, maintaining control of Agua Caliente in the reasonable belief that the Mexican government would be persuaded through bribery to restore gambling.[81]

While West was never charged, the transaction once more raised the specter of the death of Thelma Todd. West's accountant, Erwin Luttermoser, called by the government in its case against Schenck, claimed that, when the loan became due in 1936, West did not pay because Miss Todd had a twenty percent interest in the value of the café upon which her mother, as her heir, may have had a claim. This eventuality could have required an adjustment to his business, making the loan repayment problematic.[82] This was the same Erwin Luttermoser who testified before the Grand Jury six years earlier, verifying West's claim that Todd had no interest in the café because she had never put money into it and had only received proceeds from its operation for the use of her name.[83]

Interestingly, the press never commented on the apparent contradiction. One could argue from a strictly legal basis that both contentions were tenable. That is, even though Todd had no valid claim on a share of the café, her estate or mother might have made a claim anyway, exposing West to a potential financial liability that he had every right to prepare for by holding cash in reserve. Still, the about face on the issue is troubling and Luttermoser may have been working in a very gray area.

Strict legality aside, the deal between Schenck and West was likely just what the prosecutors suspected. Schenck was trying to evade taxes and approached his old friend West with a sweetheart deal that would profit both. While West was never charged with a crime in the transaction, the prosecution did prevail against Joe Schenck. He was convicted of tax evasion and sentenced to seven years in the federal penitentiary. Ultimately, he served only four and one-half months and was pardoned by President Truman in 1945.[84]

West's dealings with Schenck in this episode provide another example of West's tendency to play both sides against the middle when confronted with an implication of impropriety. It reiterates his lack of scruples when making deals, especially when his own interest was at stake. It also demonstrates his capacity to play the legal system when required. This latter factor may even shed additional light on his performance on the witness stand during the Todd inquiries.

There is one more bit of evidence, albeit of a different kind, which may bear on West's character and personality, or more accurately, worldview. That is, the body of his work as a writer and director. One must be careful, of course, in the literal interpretation of an artist's work. Bram Stoker, after all, was not a vampire. It is just as dangerous to ascribe direct psychological meaning. Yet, West's play and screen writing may say something about his attitudes and interests, especially given its consistency. As Scott MacQueen writes:

> The stories of West's pictures are seemingly interchangeable. People parade about in dual or concealed identities, indulging in murder, vice, theft and racketeering. The Police and the Social Order are either ineffectual or as unscrupulous as the underworld they would restrain. Solutions are reached via an internal moral code which often verges on vigilantism. The disturbing sameness of incident in his scripts is more properly a single recurring theme. In an era of growth and rampant opportunism marked by robber barons operating within the fringes of the law, and equally capitalistic gangsters at work just beyond its perimeter, West's films don a guise of melodrama to meet this contradiction.[85]

West's work certainly reflects a certain aspect of the world in which he lived. In the urbane milieu where he thrived, it was an age of graft, personal and political power and advantage for those with the right connections. Many who projected respectability and success had an inside track and more than a few skeletons in the closet. While they were not strictly above the law, they knew how to manipulate the law to their own advantage and, as a result, developed a level of contempt for it.

It also may reflect something of West himself. As numerous episodes in Roland West's life demonstrate, he was a man of his age, not as colorful or complete as the characters he drew for his melodramas, but in his own small ways, a player nonetheless. Though successful at his own craft, one gets the feeling he wanted to be more, or at least different: a would-be gambling impresario, a proprietor of a swank and notorious roadhouse, a manipulator of beautiful women, a sharp dealer, a player with the big boys, and the detective, who from the witness stand, solved the mystery in which he was the logical suspect. Always the actor, he sometimes chose his roles badly.

None of this makes him a murderer. As has been demonstrated, the stories and theories naming him one are baseless. Nevertheless, his character and actions may have contributed over time to the impression that he was guilty. The reporters of his era may have zeroed in on West as the logical suspect because he fit a favorite profile—a rich, powerful man with lots to hide and who acted the part. Friends and associates of Thelma Todd may have focused on him because they knew what he was like, did not like what they knew, and made the same assumptions as the reporters. Subsequent writers, wanting a ready solution, simply followed the scent, replacing facts with speculation, and arrived at West's doorstep.

In all this, there is a sad irony. More than the reporters, or the friends and associates, or the secondary writers, the person most responsible for West's sordid reputation today is West himself. It is likely that, but for his dabbling in the demimonde, his posturing, and his performance in the investigation and on the witness stand, he would be remembered for something else today.

Film historians have rediscovered his work and give him high marks for his technical innovation and cinematography. In one critique, reviewers ranked him "alongside Chaplin and von Stroheim as an individualistic and eccentric actor-producer-writer-director…." [86] But they concluded their piece with the truism: "Unfortunately, he is remembered more as a principal figure in the unsolved mystery surrounding the death of Miss Todd in 1935 than for his screen contributions."[87]

And more than likely, so will he remain.

Kent Kane Parrot about to testify before 1935 Grand Jury probe into LA County gambling. (*Los Angeles Daily News/UCLA Special Collections*)

Thelma reinvented as Alison Loyd 1932 (*Herald-Examiner Collection/Los Angeles Public Library*)

Jewel Carmen in 1923 (*University of Washington Special Collections JWS30755*)

Roland West in his vaudeville days, 1908 (*University of Washington Special Collections JWS21135*)

Lola Lane
 (*University of Washington Special Collections JWS20872*)

Castellammare Community Center in the early 1930s (*Prelinger Archives Home Movies*)

Second story of the Castellammare Community Center in the early 1930s
(*Prelinger Archives Home Movies*)

View from second story dining area
(*Prelinger Archives Home Movies*)

Castillo Del Mar Under Construction
(*University of Southern California Libraries/California Historical Society*)

TWENTY-ONE: THE PRINCE OF DARKNESS

The more gross the fraud, the more glibly it will go down.
— Charles Caleb Colton[1]

The mystery of Thelma Todd's death has been solved more than once. Just as in life Roland West competed with rivals for the affection of the beautiful actress, in death he contends with another for the ignominy of her murder. And his opponent here is a formidable personage, a man clearly capable of homicide. Though long dead, he would make any "Who's Who List" of American villains and any history of organized crime. He is the all-time capo di tutti di capa, archfiend, and crown prince of evil: Charles "Lucky" Luciano.

As with many of the ersatz elements in the Todd case, Luciano's name was first uttered by Kenneth Anger in *Hollywood Babylon*. While Anger's contribution to the Luciano legend was meager, it was the springboard for much more to come:

> Thelma's lawyer demanded a second inquest which he said would bolster his theory: she had been murdered by hit-men working for Lucky Luciano. Luciano was then making inroads into illicit California gambling establishments. He had approached Thelma with an offer to take over the upper story of her café for the installation of a secret and crooked casino which she was supposed to populate with fashionable customers from among her famous friends. The lawyer was convinced that in turning down Luciano's offer, Thelma had signed her death warrant. Producer Hal Roach turned grey at the mere mention of Luciano's name. He prevailed upon the attorney to the let the matter drop.[2]

This single paragraph inspired twenty years of speculation about Luciano's involvement in the actress' death. Nicholas Horden repeated Anger's story in *Los Angeles Magazine* in 1976,[3] while Al Stump recapitulated the tale in the *California Living* magazine four years later, adding, "Luciano was in the Trocadero during the Saturday champagne fete held for Todd."[4] Both writers claimed Luciano resembled the "foreign-looking" man Jewel Carmen saw in Todd's phaeton Sunday evening after Todd disappeared.

The story popped up again, much embellished, in a 1987 book by Michael Munn, *The Hollywood Murder Casebook*.[5] While echoing key elements of the story first told by Anger ("Thelma's lawyer" fingered Luciano, but Hal Roach–turning "white" as opposed to Anger's "grey" when Luciano's name is mentioned–inhibited the investigation out of his fear of the gangster),[6] Munn also provided additional details about Luciano's motive for the killing, details he credited to "Thelma's lawyer":

> His belief was that when Thelma Todd had turned down Luciano's deal, she had, in effect, signed her own death warrant. Lucky Luciano was not the kind of man to reveal his illicit plans unless he felt sure that whoever knew them would remain silent. If he couldn't buy them off, he would bump them off. It seemed perfectly logical to this lawyer that Luciano had no intention of taking any risks as far as Thelma Todd was concerned.[7]

Munn explained Todd was killed not just because she refused Luciano's gambling offer, but because she knew too much about his plans to take over California and Hollywood gambling. Her death was also a warning to others who might oppose him. According to Munn, the message was understood:

> It was certainly enough to ensure that the stars and moguls of Hollywood learned to treat Mr. Luciano and his colleagues with respect and caution. They figured they knew what could happen to them if they didn't.[8]

The introduction of Luciano's name into the mystery decades after Todd's death is curious, especially when one notes the chain of speculation from Anger to Horden to Stump to Munn had no basis in contemporary sources. Neither the investigators nor the press mentioned Luciano during the original investigation. While "Thelma's lawyer," A. Ronald Button, suggested somewhat offhandedly to reporters that an attempt by gamblers to set up operations in her café might have troubled Todd, he did not name any specific crime figures or charge that hit men working for gamblers killed her. As for the allegation that he had been stricken white or grey with fear when Luciano's name was mentioned, Hal Roach claimed years later he never heard of the gangster until long after Todd's death. There was no reason he should have: Luciano's name did not become public currency until several months after Todd's death, when he was indicted in New York on vice charges.[9]

The advent of Luciano in the Todd case is stranger still when one considers that, before Anger, secondary writers failed for forty years to produce him or any other mob figure as a murder suspect. During that time, Luciano and the Mafia had become major interests on the part of the public, partially because of hearings in the fifties by the US Senate's Kefauver Committee and evidence that linked Luciano to the international heroin trade. The nation came to see organized crime as a powerful, sinister force in American life. As the decades progressed, this perception was reinforced and enlarged by a spate of fictional efforts, including the *Godfather* films and their progeny in the early seventies. Tabloid historians seized on the growing mystique of the Mafia, laying a number of deaths and murders at its feet, including those of John F. Kennedy and Marilyn Monroe. It seems natural now that the mob should also get the blame for the Todd death.[10]

The Luciano tale reached its full fruition in 1989 when Andy Edmonds published *Hot Toddy*. Edmonds not only named Lucky Luciano as the man who ordered the killing of Thelma Todd, but also detailed a love affair between the murderer and his victim as well as the events that led to her demise.[11] According to Edmonds, Pat DiCicco introduced Todd and Luciano in 1932 when Luciano was in town to do battle with the Capone gang of Chicago for control of Los Angeles' gambling and filmland labor extortion rackets. Over the next two years, according to Edmonds, between the gangster's frequent trips back to New York, Luciano and Todd engaged in a passionate affair. While Todd's beauty and feisty personality captivated the crime boss, she also provided an entree to the Hollywood elite and its money. To exploit this connection, Luciano schemed to establish gambling operations at her café. Plying Todd with powerful diet pills and encouraging her drinking, he tried to gain control of both the actress and her café, sabotaging the finances of the latter. Just in time, Todd realized what he was up to and decided to stop him. When she refused to let him open a high-stakes carpet joint on the second floor of her café to fleece the Hollywood crowd and contacted the DA's office to expose his other rackets, Luciano had her killed by an underworld goon.

The tenor of *Hot Toddy* is inductive and imaginative, rarely deductive and critical. Edmonds appropriates the novelist's arts to tell her story, inventing dialogue nobody but Luciano and Todd could have heard and providing details about Todd's psychological and sexual makeup that even her most intimate friends could not have known. The author claims the dialogue "is based upon these stories or gleaned from letters saved or conversations remembered by friends of the actress," but its detail goes beyond anything that would be recorded in a letter, let alone remembered and retold. She also claims "interviews and...personal letters and memorabilia of Thelma Todd's" formed the basis of her research, yet fails to document any sources and offers only a sketchy bibliography of general works unrelated to the Todd case.[12]

Nevertheless, within the text and in interviews after the publication of her book, she declared the details of Todd's killing came from certain anonymous "men who live on the other side of the law, who had inside knowledge of the killing or the workings of Luciano, Al Capone and Frank Nitti."[13] These figures include a "powerful and prominent" associate of Luciano who, on the condition of anonymity, gave her "the details of the meeting with Luciano and Todd in his Beverly Hills home" on the night Todd died. Edmonds dubs this figure "Trust me."[14] Implicitly, the reader is asked to trust both him and Edmonds.

Unfortunately, the book is so rife with errors of fact, logic and consistency, some trivial, some profound, it is difficult to accord much faith to anything in it. The author's handling of Todd's earlier life is a case in point. To provide a foundation for her psychological portrait of Todd as self-destructively attracted to criminals, her father is cast as "one of the most important men in the East" and an associate of criminals to boot. In truth, John Todd was a small town functionary, a minor footnote to Massachusetts's history. His most significant public offices were within the municipality of Lawrence, Massachusetts. He was Commissioner of Public Health and Charities, Alderman, and, from 1915 to 1925, Assistant Superintendent of Streets. (As part of her exaggeration of his importance, Edmonds promotes him to the **State** Commissioner of Public Health and Charities.) Nothing in the historical record or the living memory of witnesses links him to crime or criminals. While Edmonds places him on the city's police force, the closest job he ever came to police work was as night watchman at an athletic field.[15]

Similarly, Edmonds fixes on the death of Todd's younger brother, William, as the start of both the disintegration of Todd's parent's marriage and Mrs. Todd's domineering attention towards Thelma. Actually, the Todd's son, William, was Thelma's **older** brother, and he died in an accident when Thelma was only five years old, some fifteen years earlier than Edmonds would have us believe. Even in her narrative, the boy's age shifts four years in seven pages; he is described as five years younger than Thelma (who was born on in 1906) at one point, but when he dies, in 1925, Edmonds tells us he is ten. Besides having his age wrong by fifteen years, Edmonds' fictionalization of his death includes details that completely contradict the actual record. These details include the remarkable claim that, after his tragic death, the boy's body was never found, an assertion vehemently disputed by surviving family members and contradicted by newspaper accounts of the boy's death.[16]

Such egregious mishandling of simple facts is characteristic of the book. Hollywood history changes to meet the demands of the narrative, with Todd fighting with Hal Roach over permission to star in *Hell's Angels* in 1931. (The film was in fact released in 1930. Todd was involved in the aborted silent version in 1929.) As the book gets closer to the center of the Todd mystery itself, inaccurate facts and overreaching conclusions abound. The author misconstrues the living arrangements at the café and the intimate relationship between Todd and West, making Todd's normal route of entrance and exit through the back of the building to Castellammare Drive, rather than through the side entrance to the Roosevelt Highway below. She ignores numerous reports in contemporary newspapers that West and Todd had planned and worked for many months to open the Joyas Room restaurant on the second floor of the building in time for New Year's Eve 1936. Instead, she develops the improbable scenario that Todd tried to subvert Luciano's demands for a gambling den by planning, constructing, and outfitting a new steakhouse to occupy the second floor in just two weeks' time. She confuses proceedings and testimony before the Coroner's Inquest with those of the Grand Jury and quotes Grand Jury transcripts that not only were never released but also were never transcribed.

Almost all the errors, distortions and embellishments of the secondary writers who preceded Edmonds find their way into her story, inspiring her to a great deal of Procrustean cutting and rearranging. In the process, she develops clever solutions to several non-existent problems. She echoes the decades-old confusion about the eight-inch opening in the garage door (as noted before, the car door, not the garage door, was open) and then explains the garage doors "never did close properly unless they were shut tight and locked." To account for the spurious clue of the unscuffed slippers, she has Luciano drop the actress next to the garage instead of at the café. The false problem of Todd's final meal of peas and beans is supposedly solved by the Beverly Hills dinner Todd enjoys with Luciano, but oddly, in Edmonds' version, the offending vegetables change from peas and beans to peas and carrots. The Patsy Kelly missing ring story leads to the claim that Pat DiCicco gave Todd a "black and gold sardonyx" ring before their marriage and that her murderer removed the ring from her finger. In fact, the ring identified by Edmonds can be traced in photographs as belonging to Todd in the late 1920s, years before she met DiCicco. All the jewelry Todd wore that fateful night was accounted for by Mae Whitehead and the investigators.

Hollywood even shifts from the east to the west of Beverly Hills in order to explain Jewel Carmen's sighting of Todd and a "foreign-looking man" after the supposed final "peas and carrots" meal ("They traveled the route from Beverly Hills to Hollywood to Santa Monica down Wilshire Boulevard"). The author zealously incorporates every reported Sunday sighting into her account of Todd's ride with Luciano to the café and garage. Even the second brown phaeton, supposedly identical to Todd's, seen around Los Angeles on Sunday and posited by investigators as the explanation for some of the sightings until they discovered it had not been driven that day, finds its way into the narrative. This leads the author to the bizarre assertion that Luciano had purchased an identical phaeton for his own use.

Why Edmonds felt compelled to recapitulate all this nonsense and incorporate it into her book is a puzzle since her assertion that Luciano murdered Todd does not require that every red herring and every dubious claim be made to fit. Nor was it necessary Todd's corpse be bloodied and broken to prove that she was murdered. Still, Edmonds insists on the mayhem, asserting Todd was "brutally disfigured" and suffered a broken nose and teeth and several fractured ribs when the hit man savagely beat her and jammed her limp body into the front seat of the phaeton. This despite the fact that both those who saw the body of the dead actress in her automobile (including Mae Whitehead, Roland West, Dr. Sampson, the mortuary attendants and the police) and those who examined her afterward during the autopsy, consistently maintained that Thelma Todd's only injury was a slight contusion to the mouth. As a result, *Hot Toddy* never confronts the real mystery of the Todd death, which arose directly from the body's undamaged condition. Instead, we are told the obvious injuries were simply covered-up, and "Only Luciano could have ordered the fraudulent medical reports, the destruction of evidence and the disarray of witnesses." How, might one ask, did Luciano also silence the numerous functionaries and witnesses who saw the body and the dozens of news reporters who covered the story?

Like other proponents of Luciano as Todd's killer, Edmonds seems ignorant of a great deal of fact about him. Nowhere in her book does she mention, for instance, that two months before Todd's death, Luciano engineered perhaps the most famous mob killing in American history, the murder of Dutch Schultz, or that he landed in Dannemora prison the year following Todd's death, sentenced to up to 50 years (though he served much less) for vice convictions. Perhaps the absence in her bibliography of any standard sources on Luciano, organized crime or Los Angeles history in the 1930s account for these omissions.

What she does tell the reader about Luciano and mob history is marred by the same carelessness about the facts that characterizes her biography of Todd. For example, she claims that Al Capone was born in Italy near Naples; in fact, he was born in Brooklyn.[17] To lay a basis for a rivalry between Luciano and Capone, she concocts a fanciful myth that they were members of the same teenaged gang on the streets of the Lower East Side.[18]

More fanciful still is Edmonds' treatment of the supposed connection of Lucky Luciano to Los Angeles. She claims that Luciano first came to Hollywood in 1929 intending to take over the illegal drug trade and found the town wide open and ready to control.[19] He met, according to Edmonds, with immediate success. She explains it this way:

> Though Luciano shunned the limelight, he was already notorious. Few pictures were ever taken of the gang lord, but when they were, they were circulated from coast to coast. Whether he liked it or not, his face was his Hollywood calling card. His name never needed to be announced twice. When anyone heard 'Lucky Luciano,' they opened doors in awe; especially stars who already fantasized about such men, who already knew Capone and the lore of gangsters.[20]

Edmonds is correct that Luciano eschewed public notice and that few pictures of him before 1936 were published. How these few were circulated from coast to coast is a worthy question, but more important is her assertion that Luciano had a presence in Los Angeles after 1929.

The record is overwhelmingly clear that he did not. Outside of the secondary writers on the Todd case there is not one source, historical or contemporary, that mentions Luciano in connection with Los Angeles. The vigorous and vocal reformers of the time, who were not loath to name names, never mentioned Luciano's. In self-published magazines, Grand Jury reports and radio broadcasts, they kept a running tally of prominent and not-so-prominent racketeers who operated in and around Los Angeles decrying their presence in America's "white spot." Luciano's name never shows up in their material or in newspaper coverage of the time, as do those of the local talent and invading racketeers from the east and mid-west, such as "Bugs" Moran, John Roselli, and Benjamin Siegel. (The appearance of Siegel's name in the papers is especially noteworthy; if his presence is so often noted, why not that of his longtime associate in the New York mob, Lucky Luciano?)

More mysterious, given Edmond's claim that Luciano was well known to the Hollywood community, is the lack of any reference to him in any star biographies or industry histories. Other out-of-town gangsters–Longy Zwillman, Micky Cohen, and Benjamin Siegel–are mentioned, but not Luciano. Is it credible to think that all the writers who reported on every nook and cranny of Hollywood in its golden age missed such a key personage?

The writers of the history of America's underworld are similarly silent on Luciano's connection to Los Angeles.[21] In the period Edmonds claims Luciano was making inroads into Los Angeles, he was in fact building his operations in New York City, first as an independent, then as an underboss, and finally as the first among equals in the Italian dominated rackets. But unlike Capone in Chicago, Luciano kept a much lower profile. As Robert Lacey, a biographer of Meyer Lansky, put it, "Little known previously outside of his own, shadowy circle, Charlie was made famous by his downfall."[22] Lacey's insight is corroborated by *The New York Times* front-page story that chronicled his arrest in 1936–three and a half months after Todd's death–on charges he controlled prostitution rackets. The paper misspells his name, calling him Luciana instead of Lucania (his birth name) or Luciano.[23]

As for Luciano's biographers prior to Edmonds' book, they make no mention of either Thelma Todd or of his alleged activities in Los Angeles. For that matter, they never place him in LA for even a day.[24] Luciano himself noted his travels were limited primarily to the vicinity of New York City and other East Coast spots where he held gambling interests. "Sure, I knew Chicago and Miami, and Hot Springs and Saratoga and all the towns in between, but I didn't know much else. Before I went to work in Dannemora library, if you asked me where the hell Des Moines was, I couldn't have told you."[25] We can confirm that he traveled west as far as Chicago, where he was photographed by the police, and Hot Springs, Arkansas, where he was arrested in 1936 on an indictment brought by New York authorities. However, there is no record, or claim–outside of the secondary writers mentioned above–that he ever traveled any further west, let alone to Los Angeles.

Given the silence of the historical record on any relationship between Luciano and Los Angeles, Edmonds' premise that he was actively involved in trying to take over the local drug racket or establish a gambling empire in Southern California is simply not credible. At the least, when trying to re-write history, one must be required to provide compelling sources supporting the revision. Yet, in this case all we have are Edmonds' assertions, based on vague sources she fails to reveal. These factors alone are adequate to consign Edmonds' theory to the realm of tabloid fantasy, yet there are even more compelling reasons to do so. In fact, had Charles "Lucky" Luciano ever been charged with Todd's murder, he could have produced an almost airtight alibi.

According to Edmonds, Luciano visited Los Angeles at least three times during the period of October through mid-December 1935, once in October, when he took a drive with Todd, again sometime around Thanksgiving, when they had dinner at the Brown Derby, and finally on December 13, when he returned to set up Todd's murder. In addition, Edmonds has him "moving freely around Hollywood" since September.[26]

Actually, during this time, Luciano was occupied with his East Coast enterprises, which had come under the scrutiny of New York's racket-busting special prosecutor, Thomas E. Dewey, whose forces were primed to end the gangster's criminal career in the United States.[27] After the murder of "Dutch" Schultz on October 23, Dewey directed his efforts to nailing Luciano in his quest to break the power of the New York mobs. Luciano, a logical suspect in the Schultz murder, soon skipped town and headed for Miami to wait for things to settle down in Gotham.

That Luciano was not busying himself with his purported Los Angeles operations is evident from evidence produced during Luciano's criminal trial in spring of 1936. In September 1935, when Edmonds has Luciano traveling to Chicago to confront its mob bosses and then to Los Angeles for an October dinner with Todd, he was actually in New York conducting business as usual, as proven by phone calls he made to his co-conspirators at Celano's Gardens in New York City. The calls originated in Saratoga, New York, a favorite haunt of Luciano's, and in his Manhattan suite in the Waldorf Towers on September 10, 16, 21, and the 30th.[28] Naturally, Luciano disputed he personally made these calls. Had he been in Chicago and Los Angeles at the time, as Edmonds claims, his defense attorney certainly would have introduced his travel records as evidence on his behalf.

As one looks closer at Luciano's activities around the time of Todd's death, it becomes clear the mob boss simply could not have been where Edmonds places him. Phone records demonstrate that following Dutch Schultz' murder on October 23, Luciano stayed in New York until October 29. He then flew to Miami, where he registered as a convicted felon with the Miami Police Department. Though the Miami police offered to extradite him, the New York authorities had no grounds yet for his detention.[29] The mobster stayed in Miami on and off until December according to newspaper reports of the time.[30] "Cokey" Flo, one of the prostitutes who testified against him at his trial, claimed Luciano returned to New York briefly in the late fall, where she saw him at Celano's Gardens between Thanksgiving and Christmas.[31] He then traveled to Hot Springs, Arkansas and then back to Miami shortly before Christmas. In early 1936, he returned to Hot Springs, where he was arrested several months later.[32]

Luciano's own words corroborate the newspaper and court accounts of his movements. Claiming the warrant issued in October was stale because the authorities had ample opportunity to serve it before his arrest on April 1, he stated:

> [I] left New York the later part of last year and I went to Miami and conferred with the chief of police in that city telling him who I was and telling him that I would be in Miami. The New York authorities knew that. They knew also that I had come to Hot Springs and was here before Christmas, that I went back to Miami and later returned to Hot Springs. They knew where I was at all times.[33]

Luciano's account of his whereabouts between late October and his arrest in April comports almost exactly with newspaper reports and evidence produced at his trial. It also lends credence to reports the New York authorities had him on a short tether throughout the period. Not only are all of these sources consistent, the story they tell makes perfect sense. Concerned with his legal status, Luciano sought refuge in places he knew and where he could count on sympathetic local authorities when, and if, the indictment came about.

The implications of these facts, of which the proponents of the Luciano theory seem blissfully ignorant, are quite clear. Prior to and after the killing of Dutch Schultz on October 23, 1935, it would have been all but impossible for Luciano to be in Los Angeles trying to establish a gambling room at a seaside café, cavorting with Todd and masterminding her death.

Given the overwhelming evidence in the historical record that Luciano was never involved with either Todd or Los Angeles, one wonders how the Luciano/Todd fable ever came into being. Undoubtedly, the rumors about gambling at the café and threats against Todd's life prompted secondary writers to go looking for a suspect among the underworld. Luciano's name may have come up accidentally or by result of simple misunderstanding and ignorance. By 1970, the organized crime figures who controlled Los Angeles through the twenties and thirties had long been forgotten by the press and ignored by the movies and other purveyors of popular history, while those connected with the eastern Mafia, such as Mickey Cohen, Benjamin "Bugsy" Siegel, and even Jack Dragna, had become legendary. Perhaps the long association between Luciano and Siegel and the prominence of both their names in the public mind led to confusion between the two. Perhaps writers figured since Siegel had been in Los Angeles, Luciano must have been as well. From such slender threads the whole fabric of the Luciano/Todd tale may have been woven.

Whatever the origins of the Luciano myth, the notion that Thelma Todd was the victim of a mob hit makes little sense. Though her café served a tony clientele, there were plenty of such places for gamblers to set up shop in 1930s' Los Angeles without having to resort to murder. Even if Todd opposed some group trying to set up gaming, why would it risk killing a prominent and well-connected public figure? If discovered as a mob action, such a heinous act would have created a public furor. Why would any gangster take such risks for so little gain?

Few mob murderers employ subtle methods such as carbon monoxide poisoning, a point perhaps realized by proponents of the Luciano theory and the explanation for why they so consistently exaggerate the injuries found on Todd's body. The goal of a mob hit is not to hide the method, but to choose one that will terrorize others into compliance. Even if Thelma Todd were murdered, the mob-hit scenario fails as a reasonable explanation. It was the wrong method for the wrong victim for the wrong reason.

Still, beyond Anger's garish sensationalism and the indiscriminate borrowings of the writers who followed him, one senses the Luciano fable came into being because it supplies a fittingly dramatic solution to the Todd mystery in a manner the Roland West scenario could not. By accusing West, we have a tale of murder stemming from jealousy and a thwarted spirit of dominance, which is afterward buttressed by a cover-up arising from the self-interest and callousness of the movie industry. With Luciano, the story broadens into one of mythic proportions, with Todd combating corruption and wickedness on a grand scale. Edmonds' claim that Luciano was known as Charley Lucifer among his contemporaries—a fact somehow missed by the chroniclers of organized crime in this century—suggests the full flowering of this fable, with Todd as martyr, opposing the devil Luciano's schemes to enslave the Hollywood community in gambling and sin. Had this story come about in a less cynical age, it is easy to imagine how Todd, unburdened with unsubstantiated rumors of drug use and sexual promiscuity, might have emerged as a saintly figure. Perhaps if the Todd story develops for another century along the lines it has so far, with each retelling trimming off more and more of the antithetical details, it might still.

TWENTY-TWO: LET THE EVIDENCE SHOW

> Get your facts first, and then you can distort 'em as much as you please.[1]
>
> — Mark Twain

Over eighty years have passed since Thelma Todd died. During that time, her world has changed utterly. Not only are most of those who knew and loved her now dead, but many of the places she frequented no longer exist. The Café Trocadero has been torn down, The Ambassador Hotel is now a school, and a modern industrial park sits on the site of the Hal Roach Studios, whose founder lived long enough to witness the defamation of the young woman he admired. Much of the landscape Todd viewed every day as she rode in her big phaeton from her apartment to the Roach studios is now buried beneath the stucco and sprawl of modern Los Angeles. Yet those places most important to an understanding of Todd's death—the café and the apartment she shared with Roland West, his ocean view home, Castillo Del Mar, and the garage where she died—remain. From them one can still tease some of the secrets, the mysteries within mysteries, surrounding her death.

Although threatened, like most of the homes in Castellammare, by land movement and autumn brushfires, the café building still nestles into the hillside beside the coastal highway. After Todd's death, it continued as an occasional restaurant and the residence of Roland West until just before his death in 1952, when it passed to his second wife Lola Lane, who made it her home until she moved to Santa Barbara in the early 1970s. A devout woman, she transferred the property to the Paulist Fathers for the use of their media wing, whose major activity is the production of religious films. It has continued in that capacity ever since.[2]

In spite of the passage of years and a number of internal and cosmetic changes, the structure is a virtual time capsule of Todd's era. On approaching it today, one is struck by how little the exterior of the old building has changed from the gleaming newness that reveals itself in black and white glossy photos of the mid-thirties. The signage is gone: the neon block letters designating "Thelma Todd's Inn," the scripted word "Cocktails" punctuated by an arrow pointing to the lounge, and the proprietor's boast of "Steaks Unequaled." Gone also are the immaculate planter boxes with their shrubs pruned in the French style into perfect spheres of green.

As one passes beneath the ornately tiled arch of the main entrance, one senses the essence of the grand old place, even though many of its accoutrements disappeared long ago. To the right is the door of the once cozy cocktail lounge of the café; now it opens onto a production room. On the left, another door opens onto the old first floor kitchen, still partially tiled with the small hexagons popular in the 1920s. The cold storage units that once held the rich meats for West's elegant fare are there, but now they are used to file cans of film. Behind the kitchen, the old first floor dining and cabaret area stretches along the highway.

On the first landing is a set of wooden and glass doors. The word "Joyas," the name West bestowed on the restaurant that was to open January 1, 1936, two weeks after Thelma Todd died, is etched into one pane. Beyond the doors, a wide, straight staircase leads to a second-floor gallery, where a large arch enclosed with a central French door and surrounding windows looks out into a courtyard girdled by cement stairs that ascend to Castellammare Drive. In 1935, the courtyard was open, but now high walls protect it from the street above.

Turning back toward the front of the building, one may round the balustrade stairwell to the right or the left. To the right, elaborate double doors, studded and covered with leather and featuring small diamond-shaped windows sporting the signs of the zodiac open into the old second-floor main dining room and kitchen area. The rooms are all but empty now although several of the old café chandeliers still hang from the ceiling. On the gallery's left are another series of doors. Behind the first, a stairway leads first to a residential addition built by Lola Lane and then to the third floor hexagonal turret room, which served as Lane and West's bedchamber. The next door opens on a restroom that served as the ladies lounge when the café was in its heyday.

Nearby is the door to the men's lounge and shower room, now gutted and used as a projection room. At the opposite end of the gallery, a spacious lobby area fronts a huge arched window overlooking the Pacific, through which the dinner guests gazed at lingering sunsets as they waited for their tables on the fancy, overstuffed couches. To the right, stretching down a long hallway of the café's northwest wing, are a series of small rooms with ocean front views. Now offices, these were private party dining rooms under West's personal supervision, where the wealthiest and most discriminating guests were served.

To the left of the lobby, stands a door leading to the secret heart of the place. Through it, one enters the personal rooms of Thelma Todd, where the actress lived the last three months of her life, dressed for her last gay outing, and spatted with West over the hour of her return from the party at the Trocadero. Here also West slept that fateful night.

Time did not stop on Todd's death for these rooms either. After West died, Lola Lane lent them to girlfriends down on their luck. Visitors of that era claim some of her books were still on the shelves.[3] Later, the apartment became the offices of Mike Rhodes, a producer and director of Paulist Productions.

Today, the apartment is much as it was when Todd lived there, save for many subsequent coats of paint and the absence of her furnishings and belongings. All the features that played a key role in the 1935-36 investigation are still there: the solid side entrance door that blocked her entrance to the apartment, the barred windows West referred to in his testimony, the sliding wooden doors he passed through in his cursory search for Todd Sunday morning. Even one of the lobby couches West described as a suitable place for sleeping remains, ready to offer comfort to a long ago guest or the weary actress returning from a night on the town.

A few hundred yards from the café building is the lonely, tomb-like garage where Todd's body was found. It is a somber spot, especially when the night wind blows from the shore, rustling the eucalyptus and cypress trees and carrying the relentless crash of the breakers from the beach below. So much the more it must have seemed in 1935 when it stood in almost total isolation, flanked, then as now, by a cyclopean retaining wall and a hillside covered in thick chaparral. While the vacant lots that separated it then are now filled with a dense and eclectic mix of large homes, the garage, the apartment above it, the entry door and stairway climbing to Castillo Del Mar remain substantially unchanged from Todd's time.

The garage building is constructed of reinforced concrete walls twelve inches thick. As such, it serves as a solid anchor for the massive retaining walls that hold back the steep hillside rising above. Built on two levels, the bottom houses an open rectangular garage space approximately 24' by 20' with an 8-foot ceiling; the top consists of an open-plan apartment with a living area, a bedroom alcove, a small bathroom and a kitchen nook. An open-beam domed ceiling and a carved loft nestled under the central turret enlivens its interior. In 1935, this was the apartment of Charles Smith, the café accountant, and his wife.

Above the garage, several hundred feet up the steep, terraced hillside, is Roland West's dream house, Castillo Del Mar. The estate occupies three levels of the hillside. The top level is made up of a master bedroom suite and kitchen, the middle level contains a cathedral living room and formal dining area, and the bottom level consists of two guest suites. At the time of Todd's death, the house was occupied by Rudolf Schafer, the café manager, and his wife, Jewel Carmen's sister. To reach the garage from the house, one can take a car from Revello Drive to Posetano or walk down the cement steps from terrace to terrace until they transact with a path immediately behind the upper floor of the garage that connects with the stairway leading to the entry door on the right side of the garage. This was the path taken by the Schafers on December 16, 1935 when Mae Whitehead, at Roland West's orders, summoned them to the garage.

Today, the interior of the garage serves as a storage place for the current owners of the estate. Crammed from corner to corner with a numbing variety of odds and ends, it still differs little from the night when Thelma Todd breathed her last breath. The interior wood slats of the garage doors appear to have been stained only once since that time; the simple 1" by 1" interior wooden door handles clearly show the worn-through original color, a turquoise blue. Portions of the original electrical system also remain, including an old fuse box filled with cardboard backed, glass fuses that look as they might have been placed there by the hand of Roland West himself.

The garage ceiling, removed in places to counter deterioration caused by water leakage nearly eighty years ago, has never been replaced. It is easy to imagine Roland West gazing up at the damage after a rainstorm, then hiring workers to cut out the damage, never suspecting a day would come when police would ponder whether the resulting holes could or should have served as an escape route for the carbon monoxide gas that killed his lover. One can also imagine the activity there in the hours and days and years following Mae Whitehead's grim discovery of Todd's body. West's examination of the garage, the stunned observance of Todd's friends, the anguish of her mother, the police and the reporters and the other investigators peeking and peering from every angle, taking photographs, jotting notes and shaking heads. Legions of passersby, gawkers and sensation seekers, who, barred entrance from the garage itself, stood outside its doors, pointing and puzzling about the dark events that may have taken place inside. As the months passed, new drama and scandals and faded memories robbed the garage of popular interest. Eventually only those who stumbled upon the tale of Todd's death in magazines or True Crime books took the trouble to visit the spot and speculate about the secrets suspended within its cold, concrete interior.

A great amount of evidence, some gruesome, some mundane and some poignant, was gathered from the garage during the 1935 investigation. As we have seen, the efforts of later writers have done as much to obfuscate as to clarify the findings of the original investigation. Misunderstood facts have led to sometimes bizarre and groundless conclusions that have, in turn, formed the basis of even more unfounded speculation. While not all issues surrounding the Todd death can be definitively resolved, it is possible to put to rest some of the errors that have grown up around the mystery, perhaps even to form a solid factual base upon which the true story of the Todd death might eventually be constructed. In the following pages, we will try to inventory the solutions to some of the more salient controversies, the mysteries within the mystery, and to determine as best as can be done what we really know about that terrible Monday so long ago.

The Discovery of the Body

Mae Whitehead discovered Todd's body shortly before 10:30 a.m. on Monday, December 16, 1935. There is considerable confusion in the primary sources about the time Whitehead arrived at the garage. The press reported the time of Whitehead's arrival variously between 10:00 and 10:30. Together with West's conflicting estimates of the time of his notification of Todd's death, this can cause some confusion. Testifying at the Coroner's inquest, however, Whitehead clearly stated she arrived in Castellammare at 10:30.

> Q. When did you plan to see her the next time?
> A. Monday morning.
> Q. What time?
> A. Ten thirty.
> Q. Were you there at that time?
> A. Ten thirty o'clock.
> Q. Didn't find her there?
> A. I didn't go to the apartment.

It is arguable, in the context of this exchange, that the pronoun "there" refers specifically to the café and that Whitehead responds to the questions as such. Even so, her activities at the garage and the drive down to the café could not have normally taken more than 5-10 minutes. As such, leaving out the possibility her sense of time or watch was off, she probably did not arrive at the garage before 10:15.[4]

Whitehead had come to the garage to switch her car for Todd's, her normal practice each morning. While at least one secondary source would claim Whitehead came to the garage in search of Todd, there is no evidence to support this claim.

Whitehead found the sliding doors of the garage closed. There was confusion about this point at the time of the investigation and since as Whitehead's remarks regarding the open automobile door were transposed to the garage door; however, her testimony before the Coroner's Jury makes the point quite clear: the garage door was completely closed.

Whitehead did not notice anything unusual about the garage. The lights were out[5] and there was no particular warmth or odor.[6] West's Hupmobile, a roofed sedan, rested in its normal space behind the left garage door; Todd's 1932 dual cowl Lincoln phaeton sports coupe was backed into the space behind the right door.[7] The motor of the phaeton was not running.[8]

The driver's door of the phaeton was partially opened. Again, a great deal of confusion exists here because Whitehead's statements about the door were transposed by several witnesses to the garage door itself. The confusion was cleared up at the time of the investigation, but that did not prevent a number of secondary writers from claiming the garage door was open a few inches.

Todd appeared to be sleeping behind the steering wheel. When Whitehead first saw Todd, the actress was seated, slouched and bent, on the driver's side of the phaeton's bench front seat, behind the steering wheel. Her head slumped toward the left and rested on her chest, almost as low as the bottom of the steering wheel. Her feet were planted on the floorboard, not on the pedals. Both of her arms were in her lap. Whitehead at first thought the actress was asleep.[9]

Todd was dressed in the same clothes and jewelry she wore to the Trocadero on Saturday night. While Whitehead did not notice every detail, including the jewelry and the faded camellia that would become for the investigators a key piece of evidence, she testified that "nothing at all" had changed from the time she had last seen Todd.[10] True, in the gloom of the garage, the silver weave of her blue "ultra-modern" gown no longer glittered, but the luxuriant, thick fur of a full-length mink coat still enveloped the dead actress' shoulders.[11] On Todd's fingers were three platinum rings, encircling her wrist was a jeweled, platinum wristwatch.[12] Holding back her curls, investigators found two jeweled clasps snapped to the collar of her dress. A slim circle of platinum was tied at the side in a delicate bow and scattered with tiny sapphires and diamonds. Pinned below the left shoulder, this brooch affixed the little browned and wilted camellia Ernest Peters, the chauffeur, purchased for her on the way to the Trocadero party.[13] While the ultimate value of this small trove in no way approached the exuberant estimates of $20,000 originally made by the press, its value, and the fact that every item was accounted for, ruled out robbery as a cause of Todd's death.

Once the body was removed to the morgue, an accounting was also made of Todd's undergarments, "dainty underthings" as the press called them.[14] They amounted to one pair of panties, a girdle, and two pairs of light-colored stockings, the second pair perhaps for warmth against the chill of a December evening.[15]

Next to the body on the passenger side of the front seat was Todd's white, satin evening purse, right side up and open, the top of the thin bag pointing toward the front of the car. Inside Detective Clark found "about four handkerchiefs of hers and a cigarette case and lipstick and white coin purse, containing nothing but a key, a Yale key."[16] The 35 cents Whitehead placed in her mistress' purse on Saturday night had disappeared, but everything else was the same.

There was no sign of struggle or disturbance in the garage. Todd's clothes were perfectly arranged, the body showed no indications of violence, and no weapons or objects of violence were discovered.[17] A thick layer of dust covered the seat to the right of the body and the top of the backrest.[18] But for a single, smeared palm print on the back of the seat outlined in the dust, investigators noted no fingerprints or disturbance in the accumulation.[19]

The Condition of the Body

Todd's body showed no bruises or damage other than a displaced temporary tooth. Attendants at Todd & Leslie Mortuary in Santa Monica, where the body was taken prior to its trip to the downtown morgue, found a displaced tooth—the upper left lateral incisor—in Todd's mouth.[20] The artificial tooth was part of a bridge that had been fitted by Todd's dentist, Ralph J. Arnold, who may well have adjusted it on the Saturday afternoon prior to her death, when Todd interrupted her Christmas shopping to visit her dentist.[21] Coroner Nance confirmed the dislodged tooth while discussing autopsy results with the press on December 18.[22]

Staff members of the county morgue were rumored to have made a more sinister discovery. On Christmas Day, a story spread that during the autopsy someone noticed lacerations or swelling on or inside Todd's throat.[23] One journalist speculated they might have been made by jamming a bottle or pipe down the actress' throat. Such "unverified reports" had already reached the Grand Jury.[24] "I am not inclined to discount anything in this case," observed Deputy DA Johnson, "But if she were dead the number of hours she was supposed to be, I can easily see how the throat might be affected."[25] He promised he would question the morgue attendants and autopsy surgeon. Dr. Wagner beat him to the punch. Contacted by an eager press, he flatly declared his examination uncovered no such swelling.[26] He also repeated his denial before the Grand Jury.

Given the anonymous nature of the claim, its prompt repudiation, and the fact the matter was dropped in all subsequent news accounts, it is safe to discount this supposed injury. As previously mentioned, various secondary writers have cited this incident, but the "bottle or pipe" scenario has the earmarks of journalistic manufacture, similar to the rape by champagne bottle rumor leveled, but never proved, in the sexual assault trial of Fatty Arbuckle of some 13 years earlier. It might even be derivative from that previous scandal.

There was a small amount of blood on and about the body. When Whitehead found Todd's body, she observed blood "around her nose."[27] After rushing to the garage, West stated, "I put my hand onto her face and there was blood and I wiped it off on my handkerchief." He characterized the blood as "drops."[28] Rudolf Schafer, the third person on the scene, stated, "There was some blood over her mouth and run down on the seat right where head was." Jack Sauer, a friend of West and Todd's, who arrived with Dr. Sampson, recalled a little blood on the mouth. Clark reported a "small amount of blood at the nostrils and at her mouth; "Just a speck," he later added.[29]

Two days after the inquest, the district attorney's office sent its own detectives to examine the car and the garage. It was then that investigator Tom Cavett discovered dried blood in three different places.[30] First, there was a blotch beneath the steering wheel, about eight inches inside the door. Schafer mentioned this blotch at the inquest but it raised few concerns, as Todd's mouth was resting on the car seat at this spot.

Cavett also found two drops of blood on the metal strip at the bottom of the car door. A third blotch, about three inches in diameter was on the running board of the Phaeton, several feet from the body and well beyond where Todd's head had hung.[31] Since the actress, in her original position of death had not been near the door, these stains required an explanation. Cavett speculated that the actress, at some point, might have tried to get out of the car.[32] This notion had some grounding in the fact the driver's side door was open when Whitehead found the body. It was also supported by the detection of carbon monoxide in the blotches by police chemist Ray Pinker, which indicated that Todd was injured after she started the car's engine, since the poison does not bond with blood in the open air but only enters it through the lungs. At some point, it seemed, the actress became aware of the danger and made an effort to save herself.[33]

The small quantity of blood around Todd's face also presented a problem. At autopsy, Dr. Wagner reported the blood on the nose and mouth was the "only hemorrhage that I saw."[34] He also stated, "There were no marks of violence anywhere upon or within the body. A superficial contusion on the lower lip did not penetrate beneath the skin."[35] None of the other witnesses noticed any wounds either. Whitehead testified she saw no sign of injury; neither did officers Wallis and Clark, observers with considerable training and experience. Even Dr. Sampson told police he briefly examined the body for signs of beating, but found nothing.[36]

With no appreciable wounds, where did the blood on her face come from? The medical men in the case offered a variety of explanations. Dr. Sampson, the first on the scene, looked briefly at the body and speculated the blood might have resulted from a heart attack, but Wagner found no evidence that her heart malfunctioned.[37] Wagner himself offered a couple of different opinions. Originally, he seemed agree with Coroner Nance that the blood came from a nosebleed. "When she slumped over on the wheel of her car in the death attack, she struck her nose and it bled."[38] However, two days later, he told the coroner jurors the blood was not necessarily "due to any bruise or any fall or any violence at all."[39] Rather, it was the result of "frothing." As he explained:

> Most cases, especially after they have been dead any length of time . . . the mucus membrane congests and they bubble up a little froth that is blood stained, and these [carbon monoxide] cases do the same thing, but when these cases do it, that froth is usually fairly red. . . . The blood that was seen around this case had no significance other than just the poisoning of the gas.[40]

While it is important to note this explanation came before the discovery of the blood samples on the door and floorboard of the automobile, the fact remains that frothing is a common post-mortem phenomenon, caused when a person continues to breathe after blood enters the air passages. A thick froth forms, which, in extreme cases, if the face is turned upright, can emerge from the mouth and nostrils, appearing very much like swollen cotton wadding.[41]

It seemed likely the blood around Todd's nose or mouth resulted from blood froth. It was also possible she suffered a nosebleed as a result of striking the steering wheel or some other part of the car. The loss of the temporary tooth might also have caused her gums to bleed. The actress had been undergoing treatment for pyorrhea, a gum disease that causes tooth loss in advanced cases and tenderness and bleeding in even minor cases.[42] These latter factors could have accounted for the small amounts of blood on the door and on the running board. In addition, as Wagner indicated, "blood coagulates less rapidly in carbon monoxide poisoning than it does in other conditions," a factor which may have caused the blood to flow more freely from even small wounds.

Unfortunately, the authorities never reached a definitive conclusion on the source of the blood and admitted as much.[43] The body had been cremated, leaving no opportunity to go back and ascertain the specific source, a point publicly regretted by several of the grand jurors.[44]

In spite of these anomalies, the Todd case forensic experts could be definitive on a matter of greater import, at least as far as they were concerned: the direct cause of death.

TWENTY-THREE: THE CAUSE OF DEATH

> If we begin with certainties, we shall end in doubts; but if we begin with doubts, and are patient in them, we shall end in certainties.
> — Francis Bacon

As in most deaths, the main evidence in Thelma Todd's was the corpse itself. While the position and condition of the body in the garage on Posetano were important evidence, it was the testimony concerning the internal body, as developed through the lengthy autopsy and subsequent tests, which spoke most definitively about the cause of Todd's death.

The Setting of the Autopsy

The autopsy was held at the county coroner's facility and morgue in the basement of the Hall of Justice in downtown Los Angeles. The body arrived at the morgue at 3:45 p.m. Monday afternoon.[1] Autopsy Surgeon Wagner began the examination between 4:30 and 5:00 and continued the next day with a variety of tests on the blood, brain, liver and stomach.[2] More tests were ordered on Wednesday before the Coroner's Inquest got underway.[3]

Findings

The body showed distinct reddening indicative of carbon monoxide poisoning. In his examination, Wagner began with a cursory examination of the body and noted a "red discoloration." He then opened the skull and examined the brain finding the blood in the tissues showed a "scarlet red color." Finally, on opening the body, he found all the vital organs were normal and free from organic disease, but again they showed a vivid red coloring. The bright red infusing the blood and tissues was a likely indicator of carbon monoxide poisoning.[4]

The blood revealed a high level of carbon monoxide. Two tests, one by an associate and one by Wagner himself, confirmed Todd's blood contained lethal levels of carbon monoxide—75 to 80 percent saturation.[5]

The blood also demonstrated Todd was intoxicated at the time of her death. Todd had consumed considerable alcohol. Her blood alcohol level was .13 percent–

"only a few drinks," according to Wagner; "enough to have stupefied the woman," opined Coroner Nance.[6]

There was no sign of other pathology in the internal organs of the body. Wagner examined the actress' internal organs and concluded they all seemed to be in working order. "The heart especially was free from any chronic ailment," announced Coroner Nance, though Wagner added the alcohol had probably taxed it.[7] The liver was also in good condition, showing no sign of intemperance despite Todd's reputation as a heavy drinker. [8]

There was no evidence heart failure played a role in Todd's death. Wagner pointed out the blood on the seat and in spots on the car's doorjamb and running board demonstrated the actress' heart continued to beat long after she turned on the engine and began to inhale carbon monoxide.[9] The high level of carbon monoxide in her blood could also imply Todd's heart kept beating for some time. Her lungs must have kept working for some time, and so too her heart.

There were no signs of trauma sufficient to indicate any violence involved in the death. With the body exposed, Wagner was able to examine it for signs of bruising. He did not discover any injuries to indicate Todd was the victim of an assault.

Based on physiological evidence only, the time of death was from 12 to 30 hours before the Monday evening autopsy. The best estimate was that Todd died 18 hours before (around 10:30 Sunday night).[10] While movies and books often portray investigators using physiological factors to pinpoint the time of death to within hours, if not minutes, in the real world observable changes in the body after death offer only approximate gauges for determining the time of death. Four of the broad indicators of time of death are body temperature, the advance of rigor mortis, livor mortis or lividity, and the state of digestion.

Decline in Body Temperature (Algor Mortis)

When a person dies, the metabolic processes cease and the body no longer generates heat. Because it is a relatively poor conductor of heat, the body will begin to cool slowly during the first one to three hours after death. After a few hours, the rate of cooling will become proportionate to the current temperature of the body and the current ambient temperature; the greater the difference between the body's temperature and the temperature of the air, the faster the body will cool. Eventually, its temperature will approximate the temperature of the air surrounding it.[11]

While various factors make the process uncertain, including external temperature changes and the victim's age, clothing and body mass, rough estimates of the time of death can still be calculated if careful measurements are made of the body's temperature and its rate of cooling.[12] Unfortunately, Dr. Wagner did not report taking the body temperature of Todd's corpse. As the autopsy began over five hours after Whitehead found the body, during which time the ambient temperature probably increased steadily through the afternoon, the corpse's temperature would have had doubtful value in determining time of death, anyway. However, the first detective on the scene, Bruce Clark, reported the body was already cold to his touch when he examined it four hours earlier. It was reasonable to conclude, as Wagner did, that by late morning Monday, the actress had been dead for more than a few hours. Using one of the rougher rules of thumb in calculating temperature loss, the Simpson formula, ("under average conditions the clothed body will cool in air at the rate of about . . . [2.7 degrees F.] an hour for the first 6 hours and average a loss of some . . . [1.8 degrees F.] for the first 12"), it is likely she had been dead for at least twelve hours when Clark examined her at 11:30 a.m. Monday.[13]

Rigor Mortis

The degree of rigor mortis of a corpse is often used to estimate time of death. After death, muscles throughout the body begin to contract and stiffen as adenosine triphosphate (ATP) depletes and the myofibrillar proteins, actin and myosin, lose their extendibility, causing the muscles to stiffen. While rigor affects the muscles uniformly, it is first noticeable in the tiny muscles of the face and hands, then in the larger muscles in the jaw and neck, and finally the massive muscles of the limbs and torso. At its height, rigor can be quite dramatic, stiffening the corpse overall. Rigor departs the body in the same order, releasing the small muscles first and then the larger ones as the muscle fibers decay. It can also be "broken" by bending a muscle of a joint and thus tearing the muscles; in such a case, assuming it was fully developed, the rigor will not return.[14]

By noting the state of rigor at the time the body is found, rough estimates can be made as to how long the person has been dead.[15] It is generally agreed that rigor affects the jaws and neck within two or three hours after death, the torso and legs within four to eight hours, and the rest of the body within eight to twelve hours. The body can remain in rigor for twelve to eighteen hours. It can take another twelve to eighteen hours to resolve or pass off. The entire cycle lasts between thirty and fifty-four hours.

Many factors affect the onset and duration of rigor. Heat quickens the process while cold retards it. Physical exertion before death exhausts the body's supply of ATP, lessening the degree of rigor and accelerating its onset and resolution. Muscular persons have more ATP and thus experience a higher and lengthier rigor than persons with less muscle.[16]

Carbon monoxide poisoning affects rigor mortis in several ways. As Wagner pointed out at the inquest, it tends to slow its onset.[17] Additionally, the poison causes the body to appear hunched with the hands curled inward in what has been called the "pugilistic attitude."[18] Examination of photos of Miss Todd taken in the garage as she lay on the phaeton's front seat seem to show this condition, even when one takes into account that the position in the photos is not that in which she was originally found. It is easy to imagine her position when Whitehead first discovered her, sitting more upright with hands curled awkwardly in her lap, a posture maintained when the body was moved, left shoulder down, onto the driver's seat.

Unfortunately, the authorities in 1935 were not specific as to the state of rigor as observed in the body of Thelma Todd. Detective Clark reported when he first examined the body "rigor mortis had set in; she was cold, and apparently had been dead for some time."[19] Wagner took Clark's description as one basis for his estimate of the time of death, but he did not describe the state of the body's rigor when he examined it some four and one-half hours later. While it is possible the rigor had been "broken" forcibly by the attendants who moved it to put it on the gurney, the state of rigor at the time of the autopsy would have been instructive, especially if it were departing the body at that time.

The many factors that might have influenced the onset and departure of rigor, when combined with the sparse observational record in the Todd case, make it difficult to draw any firm conclusions. Even so, the rigor Clark noticed earlier would imply a time of death at least twelve hours before he examined the body shortly before noon on Monday—in other words, a death that occurred before Sunday at 11:30 p.m. and possibly earlier. The opinion of one modern expert is of note here. While warning the use of rigor is "extremely unsafe" to use in time of death estimates, Bernard Knight states, "the only possible use is in the period around the second day, when body temperature may have dropped to environmental but putrefaction has not yet occurred. If full rigor is present, then one might assume that this is about the second day following death, depending upon the environmental conditions." While the autopsy record does not mention putrefaction, Knight's observation implies the combination of rigor, assuming it was full, and low body temperature, at least to the touch, may have indicated Todd's body was found on the second day following her death.[20]

Lividity or Livor Mortis

Another method for determining time of death is by post-mortem lividity, or hypostasis. When the heart ceases to function, blood circulation ceases and blood in the various tissues gravitates to the lowest point, staining the surface areas of the skin. Thus, a body in a reclining position on the floor facing up will develop lividity on its back. However, skin in direct contact with the floor or other surface—on the shoulders, buttocks, and calves—will not take on the stain because the pressure of contact retards the flow of blood into these areas. The condition can develop sufficiently within one-half hour of death to be detectable by a trained investigator. Within eight to twelve hours, it is unmistakable even to an untrained eye. Up to about three hours after death, the discolored or livid flesh will blanch when pressed, but soon the blood will congeal and the lividity will become fixed.[21]

While the phenomenon is of limited use as a measure of time of death, it is an excellent indicator of whether a body has been moved. If the state of lividity is already advanced before the position of the body is changed, new stains will not develop, or will do so only to a lesser extent.

None of the authorities in the Todd case remarked directly on the state of lividity. However, it may have contributed to the early suspicion of carbon monoxide poisoning, which tinges the blood a cherry-red color; lividity staining accentuates this color at the surface of the skin. In addition, it is possible that lividity alerted the authorities to the fact the body had been moved, prompting their questioning of Mae Whitehead on this point at the Coroner's Inquest. The patterns of lividity would have been distinctly different between a sitting, slumping corpse and one lying on its side.[22]

State of Digestion

The state of digestion in the stomach of a corpse is another rough guide as to the time of death. Under normal conditions, the human stomach digests food and empties itself within six to seven hours after a meal. As Todd's stomach still contained some of the same food (the peas and beans she ate at the Trocadero dinner) it was reasonable to conclude she died within three hours after eating.[23] However, as many know through experience, various factors can retard this process, including indigestion, stress and alcohol.[24] Todd's intoxication, combined perhaps with distress over her love life, may have caused her stomach to require a full nine hours or more to empty after her last meal.[25] While she may have continued to snack at the Trocadero into the wee hours of Sunday morning, the partially digested food observed in her stomach suggests a death between six and nine o'clock Sunday morning.

Aside from the purely physiological evidence developed during the autopsy, the coroner determined from circumstantial evidence that it was likely Todd died early Sunday morning. Circumstantial determinations are made by linking the time of death to observable phenomena or logical inference. For example, the time of death of a bludgeoning victim might be determined from the fact his wristwatch was smashed in the attack, while a gunshot victim's moment of death could be inferred from a witness' report of gunfire.[26] In the Todd case, there were two circumstantial items of evidence to pinpoint the time of death. First, the actress was wearing the same clothing she wore to the party. While it is conceivable that she could have continued to wear the dress on Sunday, especially if she did not have access to her wardrobe, this fact was a powerful argument that she entered the garage directly after returning from the Trocadero. A second an even more powerful argument was derived from the faded camellia found pinned to her dress. This poignant souvenir of Saturday night's gaiety would have started to wither by late Sunday morning; even if Todd were still dressed in her Saturday night gown, it was hard to believe she would not have removed the withered flower and discarded it.

Taking the physical evidence and the circumstantial evidence together, the coroner concluded Todd died in the early hours of Sunday morning, probably between six and eight a.m. The physical factors alone placed the time of death just outside this period although they were made more variable by the cold of the garage. The history tended to indicate an earlier point of death within the time frame, rather than a later one. Besides the fact she was wearing the same clothes and the faded camellia, her state of digestion suggested she did not survive too many hours after her presumed last meal at the Trocadero. That her stomach was still half-full suggested to Wagner that alcohol and stress delayed the digestive process somewhat, but that she must have died within six to seven hours after she stopped eating. In drawing his conclusion, Wagner relied on the "history" of Todd's death as supplied by the police based on the reports of patrons of the Trocadero, Ernest Peters, and Roland West, together with the clothing on the corpse—all of which pointed towards a death early Sunday morning.

Wagner also recognized the significance of the peas and string beans in Todd's stomach. Ironically, despite the controversy about these two vegetables raised by the press at the time and repeated by subsequent writers, the vegetables strongly support an early Sunday morning death. That they *were* served at the Trocadero and found only partially digested in her system is strong evidence Wagner got the time of death right. How likely would it be that Thelma Todd consumed another such meal containing string beans and peas on Sunday?[27]

Unfortunately for the police theory, Wagner's physiologically based calculations of the time of death could not definitively rule out Todd being alive throughout much of Sunday. This fact opened the door to many of the claims she was seen or talked to after the time the coroner estimated she had died, including those of W.F. Persson and others at the downtown cigar store, Martha Ford, Jewel Carmen, and Sara Kane Carter. If Todd were alive to be heard or seen by any of these claimants, the accidental death theory would have been all but eliminated as an explanation for the tragedy.

No evidence of drugs or poisons was found in Todd's body. To determine whether Todd may have been drugged or poisoned and placed in the car, Rochester ordered tests be conducted on Todd's vital organs. Todd's body was returned from the morgue and the vital organs were removed for testing.[28] J. Abernathy, a chemist for the coroner, was assigned the task of running the tests.[29]

A great number of substances could have caused Todd to be incapacitated. To determine which one might have been present in the tissues of the dead actress required each be tested with a separate re-agent.[30] In 1935, each required a different test tube procedure. For example, consider a standard test for the poison cyanide:

> Acidify a quantity of minced organ with a solution of tartaric acid in a conical flask. Cork the flask and hang from the cork a strip of filter paper

impregnated with 10 per cent solution of guaiacum resin which has been moistened with a 0.1 per cent solution of copper sulphate just prior to use. Warm the flask and allow it to stand. In the presence of cyanides the paper will assume a blue color. The flask may be required to be left overnight if the quantity is very small.[31]

Even today, with advanced techniques such as computer-assisted mass spectrum analysis, a criminalist who is not able to search for a specific substance is at a severe disadvantage. So it was in the Todd case, as Coroner Nance explained when he noted, "We don't know what to look for."[32] There is no foolproof testing procedure to follow if the symptoms or clues gathered in the investigation do not indicate a specific type of poison.[33] In 1935, the task was considerably more daunting.

The standard minimum tests for poison in 1935 probably included a search for arsenic, cyanide and barbiturates.[34] Cyanide was a likely candidate; like carbon monoxide, it can tint the skin with a reddish hue.[35] However, cyanide is a relatively fast acting poison that would have killed Todd before she could have breathed in the amount of carbon monoxide found in her blood.

While Nance at first estimated the tests would take a few days, their results were not released for nearly a month.[36] When the official report was finally submitted to the Grand Jury, it read as follows:

> L.A. County Health Department Sample 4156
> Form Lab 1. Bureau of Laboratories/Chemical Division
>
> Date Submitted: December 19, 1935
> Material Tested: Stomach, liver, kidneys (embalmed)
> Tests Desired: Poison
> Test Results: No Poison Found
>
> Executed by J. Abernathy Chemist Grade III
> Dated and Signed January 16, 1935 [37]

By any standard, the report was bereft of detail, certainly when compared with today's procedures that would require an item-by-item listing of the specific tests performed. In 1935, however, such a report was common when noting merely negative results.[38] Its brevity and conclusion must have seemed a numbing anti-climax to the reporters who had heralded its coming for several weeks and for the murder enthusiasts, such as Rochester, who hoped it would breathe new life into the investigation. In fact, the report marked the effective end of the Todd case and news coverage about it.

The evidence gathered and analyzed in the Thelma Todd investigation failed to provide a definitive conclusion to the mystery of the actress' death. The car, garage and body provided several tantalizing clues, but no solid evidence of foul play nor definitive proof of accident or suicide.

As for accident, many questioned why Todd would go to the garage to keep warm, why she would start the engine and why she would not extricate herself once the acrid fumes from the exhaust reached her nostrils. Besides, what could be said about the half score or so of those who claimed to have seen or heard from Todd after the supposed accident stole her life? Beyond the logical reservations lay emotional ones. How could one so glamorous, so accomplished, die in such an unpredictable and trivial a manner?

The suicide hypothesis suffered from similar problems. First, her mother and West and other intimates had come forward claiming Todd had everything to live for, was generally happy, and as far as anyone knew, incapable of taking her own life. Here too, emotions probably played a part. Why would anyone so beautiful, intelligent, and successful end her own life?

Yet, finding any evidence of murder proved just as elusive. The quest for a motive for murder ran into dead end after dead end. Nor did authorities uncover any physical evidence that supported the theory. Suspects were also scarce. DiCicco, the ex-husband, produced an airtight alibi. The gentleman from San Francisco never turned up. The gamblers supposedly angered by Todd's refusal to install games of chance at the café and the gangsters playing out another extortion scheme remained elusive. The second-hand rumors that someone close to the actress, presumably West, assaulted her during a quarrel at the café were not proven. With two major witnesses, Alice Todd and Roland West, refusing to cooperate any further, with the Grand Jury in open rebellion, Foreman Rochester became the lone voice for a murder theory, predicting startling breakthroughs that never came. Eventually, even the press stopped listening.

Despite the claims of numerous secondary writers, the 1935 investigation was no rush to judgment. Nor were the resources expended unsubstantial. Given the technology of the time, the authorities were both diligent and thorough. The police, though concluding early on that Todd's death was accidental, spent numerous hours following up leads to the contrary. In addition, investigators from the district attorney's office shadowed the police efforts. Although they found evidence missed by the police, they uncovered nothing to challenge seriously the police conclusions.

Even Wagner's much castigated time of death estimates stand up to modern scrutiny. The triangulation of carbon monoxide, alcohol, and stomach contents (particularly the notorious string beans and peas) do support their finding that Todd died early Sunday morning; the circumstances of the death only add support to the fact.

Still, questions remained. In particular, how does one account for the numerous Sunday sightings of the actress?

TWENTY-FOUR: THE SIGHTINGS

> It is said that a wonder-rabbi of Chelm once saw, in a vision, the destruction by fire of the study house in Lublin, fifty miles away. This remarkable event greatly enhanced his fame as a wonderworker. Several days later, a traveler from Lublin, arriving in Chelm, was greeted with expressions of sorrow and concern, not unmixed with a certain pride, by the disciples of the wonder-rabbi. "What are you talking about?" asked the traveler. "I left Lublin three days ago and the study house was standing as it always has. What kind of wonder-rabbi is that?" " Well, well," one of the rabbi's disciples answered, "burned or not burned, it's only a detail. The wonder is that he could see so far."[1]
> – Richard Lewontin

Were it not for Martha Ford's alleged telephone conversation with the supposedly dead actress, there might never have been any serious controversy or mystery surrounding Todd's death. While Ford was not the only person who declared Todd was alive on Sunday, her tale was by far the most compelling. Without it, the simple accident theory the investigators adapted from Roland West might have gone unchallenged.

Despite the fact that investigators rejected her claims about the phone call, Ford stood firm, refusing to the end to recant or admit self-doubts and confronting suggestions she may have mistaken another friend, Velma, for Thelma by confirming Velma did not call her that afternoon. Her claim Todd alluded to a mystery guest who would surprise her and her party guests became a major focus of the investigation. There was a touch of the absurd in this process: the claims of Lansdowne and York; West's avowal and subsequent retraction the following day that he would name the mystery guest; much of the conjecture about the gentleman from San Francisco and DiCicco/Todd reconciliation. All over a conversation that none of the investigators believed took place.

From the distance of over eighty years, it is difficult to assess Ford's credibility or to reckon how the investigators evaluated her. Born Martha Haworth, she met her husband actor Wallace Ford in 1922 when they acted together in the Broadway hit, *Abie's Irish Rose*, she in a supporting role and he in the male lead. They married soon afterward; her Christmas party was also a celebration of their thirteenth anniversary.

The couple remained together for forty-two years and died within months of each other. Wallace was profuse and public in his affection for her.[2]

While she had achieved some notice as a magazine writer during the twenties and thirties, writing a theater gossip column for a magazine called *Broadway*, and was known as clever and humorous,[3] journalists during the Todd investigation concentrated more on her physical appearance than on her character. "Mrs. Wallace Ford, beautiful, blue-eyed blonde, attired in a stunning black dress" wrote one, while another exalted "there was no more smartly dressed woman among the witnesses than Martha Ford...." The *Illustrated Daily News*, which, among the local papers, was generally the most faultfinding of the early investigation, described her as the "striking ash-blond wife of Wallace Ford." The paper's report that she was a "self-possessed, highly intelligent woman" was a vote for her credibility.

Still, even intelligent people are sometimes the victims of deceit and self-delusion. While they did not comment publicly on her character, there were hints investigators saw Ford as a bit credulous, even gullible. Chief of Detectives Joe Taylor suggested early on that she might have been the victim of a prank. Another guest at the party may have used an extension in another room and pretended to be Miss Todd, Taylor argued. The Coroner picked up this idea and used it in his interrogation before the Coroner's Jury, quizzing Ford on the number of extensions in her home phone service. Even after one acknowledged pranks were *de rigueur* with the theatrical set—according to a local columnist, another group of Ford guests planned to astonish their hosts and fellow film artists by arriving in a hearse, but were unable to obtain the vehicle—this counter theory seemed a bit of a stretch.[4] Indeed, Ford's claim that she answered the phone herself, as her servants were busy, rebuffed the argument since she would have had to hear the phone ringing to know to answer it, and a phone would not ring if the caller were on another extension of the same line.[5]

While police investigators kept a politic silence on the subject, the coroner jury transcript and contemporary newspapers offered clues to the credibility of Ford and other Todd sighters. A careful analysis of those sources may clarify just why the investigation ultimately ignored their claims.

Ford claimed Todd called her sometime between 4:00 and 4:30 p.m. Sunday afternoon, when her party was in "full swing." She answered the phone herself. The details of the conversation varied somewhat as she retold it to the various investigators and newspaper reporters, but it consisted of four main elements:

The caller identified herself as "Thelma."

During her Coroner's testimony, Ford claimed this was the "first thing she said." At first, Ford thought the caller identified herself as "Velma," another of her girlfriends who was coming to the party. "When are you kids coming out?" Ford asked, and the caller, apparently noticing her confusion, asked in response "Who do you think this is?" When Ford answered "Velma," the caller said, "No, it is 'Hot Toddy.'" "That was a joke between Thelma and myself," Ford explained to the Coroner.[6]

Ford told much the same thing to reporters and investigators, with some minor variations. According to the *Los Angeles Examiner*, she recalled the caller's correction of her mistake as spirited. "No, No, this is Thelma, Thelma Todd. You know, Toddy, your hot Toddy. Get a hold of yourself, Toots." When she testified before the Grand Jury, the same paper repeated substantially the same story, as did the *Los Angeles Times*.[7]

The caller was concerned about her dress.

When the story first broke, several newspapers reported Ford said Todd had explained she was wearing an evening gown and asked whether she could wear it to Ford's party.[8] Before reporters, Ford claimed Todd also alluded to a party the previous night to explain the evening gown. However, before the Coroner, Ford did not testify that Todd referred to the Saturday night party. She said only that Todd asked, "What are you wearing at the party?" and then remarked she had on an evening gown.[9]

The caller asked if she could bring a guest.

Mrs. Ford told an Associated Press reporter Monday evening that Todd said, "Darling, do you mind if I bring a guest?" When Ford asked who it was, Todd answered, "You'd never guess and you'll be surprised when you see." Another newspaper reported a more animated conversation: "'the only hitch is—can I bring a guest?' I said, 'Certainly.' She said, 'When you see who I am bringing, you are going to drop dead.'" Whether Ford claimed Todd identified the sex of her guest varied from one newspaper account to the next. One said Ford asked whether the guest was Patsy Kelly; Todd answered "No!" and was "particular" not to reveal whether it was a male or female she was bringing. Another reported Todd called the guest "a new escort" and told her Ford would "drop dead" when she saw him. Ford told reporters she was "dying of curiosity, but [Thelma] would not tell me anything more."[10]

Before the coroner, Ford testified Todd *informed* her "she was bringing someone with her"—not *asked* for permission to do so. Ford asked if it were a girl friend. Todd replied no, but when Ford asked who the man was, she refused to tell, explaining, "I want to have the fun of seeing your face when I come in the door."

Testifying before the Grand Jury, Ford again recalled Todd's use of the phrase "just one hitch." She also repeated the phrase "drop dead"—which she omitted on the witness stand of the Coroner's Inquest—and said she told Todd it was "a dirty trick" not to tell her who her guest was.[11]

The caller asked for directions to Ford's home.

When she first reported the mystery phone call, Ford told reporters Todd asked for directions to Ford's home. At one point, Ford related, the actress referred to a slip of paper containing Ford's address.

Evidently, when Ford called Todd's apartment to invite her to the party the previous week, Mae Whitehead took down the wrong address. Ford gave Todd the correct address over the phone, but could not help when the actress asked about a shortcut via Ventura Boulevard. Todd predicted she would arrive within 30 minutes. Believing she was calling from Santa Monica, Ford remarked, "That's fast traveling from Santa Monica to Laurel Canyon, Toddy."[12]

Before the Coroner's Jury, Ford seemed to recall different, and fewer, details:

> And she mentioned something about going through a short cut or something like that and I said I didn't know much about that part of the country and I said if you know about it, all right, there is such a place, and she said, 'I will take a chance,' and she spoke of the address being wrong, and she said, 'I will be there in half an hour,' and I said, 'All the lights will be on and you can't miss the house because there will be plenty of cars there.' and she said, 'O.K.'[13]

If she testified on this aspect of the phone conversation before the Grand Jury, she did not mention it to reporters or they did not report on it.

Support for Ford's testimony came from three directions. First, Ford offered the corroboration of several guests at the party who observed her speaking on the phone and heard her remark that she had just talked with Todd. Second, she claimed the authority of her friendship with Todd and her familiarity with the actress' voice over the phone. Finally, elements of the purported conversation were largely self-corroborating, as they fused with or at least did not contradict known facts of the case.

Corroboration by Guests.

Ford claimed several of the party guests could confirm she received the phone call at 4:10 p.m. Sunday. After speaking to the woman she believed to be Todd, Ford said she announced to several guests, including Peter Hancock and Eddie Gargan, who had just walked in the front door, "The party can go on now, Toddy is on her way over." Soon afterward, according to another party guest, Warren Stokes, Ford declared, "Thelma Todd is coming over with 'someone who would surprise us all.'" Still later, Ford told George Baker, an assistant director at the Hal Roach Studios, that Todd was due to arrive shortly.

When Todd did not arrive, Baker—rumored to be one of Todd's many suitors—began to worry. Sometime between 6:30 and 7:00, he telephoned the café and spoke with a man, later identified as Roland West, who told him Todd had not been at the café all day but was expected there in a little while.[14]

Ford's Familiarity with Todd.

The second proof Ford offered of the call was her familiarity with Todd and her voice. During her Coroner's Inquest testimony, she testified she spoke often with the actress over the phone and was familiar with her voice. While she admitted she had not spoken with Todd for a month, having last seen her in Hollywood three or four weeks before, she claimed she had talked with her over the phone "twice or three times" during the last few months.[15]

Corroboration Within the Call.

Certain elements of the alleged phone call conformed to known facts of the case. Foremost among these elements was the caller's allusion to an evening dress. Arguably, this was the strongest evidence Ford could offer that Thelma Todd herself called Sunday afternoon. As the world learned Monday, alive or dead, on Sunday afternoon Todd was still wearing the evening dress she wore to the Trocadero the night before. However, few could have known this fact Sunday afternoon— only Todd herself, assuming she were alive, perhaps Roland West, a Sunday afternoon companion, or a murderer who left her dead in the garage that morning and was scheming to throw off the investigation with a bogus telephone call.

The evidence Ford advanced to support her claim was not without problems, however. While the four guests Ford named as corroborators did support her statements, it is not clear just how far their support went. Only Baker testified before the Grand Jury and none testified before the Coroner's Inquest. Gargan, Hancock and Stokes did support Ford's testimony in statements to the press and presumably told the same thing to investigators when questioned on Tuesday, December 18. Precisely what they may have corroborated is open to speculation, however.

Neither the guests nor Ford claimed any of her guests actually overheard her half of the conversation. With approximately seven other persons in the room, the guests likely were too occupied with the chatter in the living room to focus on Ford's phone conversation.[16] They probably did not realize Ford's comments about Todd's arrival related to a phone call that had just occurred. Unless they saw her speaking on the phone (which we have no evidence one way or the other, since she did not specify the location of the phone she used), they may not have inferred from her comments that she had *just then* talked with Todd but assumed instead the hostess' comments referred to a prior conversation. Key to this issue is how attentive the guests were to Ford's remark that "The party can go on now" which implied an event just occurred to allow the party to develop. If Ford did not use these words (she was the only one who quoted them) or her guests did not pay close attention to them, Hancock, Gargan and Stokes may have inferred Todd told Ford earlier (perhaps when invited days before) that she was coming and bringing a mystery guest.[17]

Of the guests, Baker was the strongest corroborator of the mysterious phone call. According to Ford, he began to worry over Todd's failure to appear forty-five minutes after the phone call, which would have been around 5:00 p.m. Yet, although Ford implied his worrying began in the context of the mysterious phone call, Baker never stated this was the case. When he called the café and spoke to Roland West, he did not mention the alleged phone conversation. It would have seemed natural for him to do so, to say something along the lines "Thelma had said she'd be over in a half hour, and that was two hours ago!" Perhaps he did not do so because he wanted to avoid causing unnecessary alarm, or perhaps he sensed Todd might not want this fact to be known to the man on the other side of the line. Alternatively, perhaps his call was not directly related to Ford's alleged call from Todd, but was inspired only by the knowledge that Todd was supposed to attend the party and had not yet arrived.[18]

We must not lose sight of the fact that none of the guests corroborated that Ford spoke with Todd only that she **said** she had done so. Their testimony was only as good as her certainty of the identity of the caller. Despite her emphatic assertions that she knew Todd's voice, Ford testified she did not recognize her voice at first, confusing Thelma with Velma, another of her girlfriends coming to the party. That she could be familiar with Todd's voice over the phone and yet confuse it with another friend's is not necessarily a contradiction. We have all had the experience of misidentifying a familiar voice coming unexpectedly over a phone line, especially when we have been tippling and are anxious about a developing social event. The more so when the voice seems filtered by distance or a poor connection, as Ford's impression the phone call came from Santa Monica would suggest. One must wonder, however, whether the police theory that Ford may have been the victim of a prank involving a phone impersonator rested on the implications of Ford's Velma/Thelma confusion and her comments about the origin of the call. Perhaps, they assumed Ford did not recognize Todd's voice because it wasn't her voice. Perhaps an impersonator persuaded her she was Todd with her assertion it was her "Hot Toddy" and let Ford attribute any doubts she may have had to a poor phone connection.

As evidence that Todd was the late afternoon caller, Ford's testimony that Todd identified herself as "Hot Toddy" was also somewhat problematic. Ford told the Coroner's Inquest she "perhaps" first dubbed Todd "Hot Toddy," but claimed Todd's other friends also used the nickname. However, Mae Whitehead told the Grand Jury Todd did not like the nickname and objected strenuously once when one of her friends used it. The deputy District Attorneys pursued this issue with other personal friends of Todd, all of whom supported Whitehead's testimony. Although neither the DA nor the jury members commented publicly on this controversy, it did not bolster Ford's credibility. On the one hand, it suggested Ford might have been overstating her intimacy with Todd; on the other, it raised the possibility she had been duped by a prankster posing as Miss Todd, one who was also not aware of the actress' real antipathy for the nickname.

The third support for Ford's call—that it meshed with other known facts of the case—is a powerful one, but it also has its problems. Indeed, Ford's own testimony before the Coroner's Jury called it into question. Asked by Nance when Todd responded to her invitation, Ford testified

The next I heard was about 4:30 or 5:00 on Saturday, and my maid told me Miss Todd had called—of course she does not know Miss Todd—and had told her she was bringing a guest, and asked the maid, I guess, what I was wearing, because she said I was wearing hostess pajamas—I think I may be a little confused or mixed up on what the maid said.[19]

This quotation merits close scrutiny. First, Ford recounted she learned from her own maid "about 4:30 or 5:00 p.m. on Saturday"—a time almost exactly twenty-four hours prior to the mysterious Sunday afternoon call—that Thelma Todd was coming to her party. According to Ford, her maid identified the caller as Miss Todd. Although Ford later learned Mae Whitehead placed the call, not Todd herself, she learned this only after Todd's body was found on Monday. On Sunday afternoon, in other words, she believed Thelma Todd herself called her maid the day before to accept her invitation to the party.

Before she interrupted her testimony at the end of this passage, claiming she "may be a little confused or mixed up on what the maid said," she already had added two critical elements to the information her maid gave her on Saturday. First, her **maid** told her Todd was bringing a guest, and, second, her **maid** told her Todd wanted to know what Ford would be wearing. As Mae Whitehead testified that she mentioned Todd's guest when she called for her on Saturday, it is possible both critical elements of the Sunday afternoon phone call—the guest and the question about what Ford would be wearing—actually took place during the Saturday afternoon maid-to-maid conversation (during which both maids assumed they were speaking with the other maid's mistress).[20] The detectives may have inferred from this jumble of phone calls that Ford somehow confused the Saturday call with the Sunday afternoon call. Coroner Nance appeared to be exploring this possibility when he asked Mae Whitehead if she was certain she talked with Mrs. Ford Saturday and did she identify herself at the time as Miss Todd?[21]

With Christmas party guests numbering over four hundred, all invited by telephone between Wednesday and Friday of the previous week, it is not surprising the hostess may have become confused about the phone calls. Assuming one phone call would result in two guests attending and not all the invitees were able to accept the invitation, one must figure that Mrs. Ford must have personally made at least two hundred phone calls over the three days. Some of these, naturally, would have resulted in return calls. Although Ford's maid handled the return call from Todd's maid, Mrs. Ford likely would have personally handled some of the others. Additionally, some calls likely were made to the Ford residence on Sunday, before or after the mystery call. Many of the Sunday calls may have been from guests who were lost on the way to the party, or wondered, as Todd allegedly did, what the best route was to get there. Taken altogether, one must calculate Ford personally placed or received three hundred calls between Wednesday and Sunday, not including diverse caterers and other purveyors necessary to the success of her party.

During these conversations, Ford must have heard some questions repeatedly. Indeed, most of the elements involved in the Todd call can be reduced to three common questions guests ask of any host:

> What should I wear?
> How do I get there?
> Can I bring a guest?

Ford must have heard these questions, or variations on them, repeatedly during the past few days. Many guests, one would expect, would have also inquired about the wearing of eveningwear to a party scheduled to begin in the late afternoon—a dinner after the party, perhaps at a restaurant that required formal dress, would have been natural. The location of Ford's home, somewhat off the beaten track in 1935 Los Angeles, would also have elicited many questions from potential guests, and it is hard not to believe a few would have inquired about alternative routes via Ventura Boulevard, as Todd allegedly did. Given these possibilities, one suspects Ford unwittingly confused some of the details of other calls with the alleged Todd call. Her confusion over Todd's question about her own dress—whether she heard it from Whitehead or heard it Sunday afternoon from Todd herself—may well have arisen from the glut of phone calls to and from her home that week.

Still, even if one argues Ford was simply mistaken about the phone call Sunday afternoon and innocently transposed the message from her maid on Saturday to a message from Todd on Sunday, it is still difficult to account for some of the specific details she attributes to the call—for example, Todd's allusion to a party the night before. But here again one might suspect Ford's memory may have embraced facts outside of the alleged call—radio reports of Todd's death may have mentioned Todd was found in the dress she wore to the party the night before—and unwittingly appended them to her own recollection. Perhaps it was a suspicion that Ford's memory was inaccurate, rather than their earlier speculation that she may have been the victim of a prank, that led authorities to downplay her testimony. No doubt, their doubts may have been fed by the social context of Martha Ford's claim—a large party where there was lots of drinking attended mainly by the Hollywood set, a group notorious for seeking press coverage on and off the movie lot. Certainly, in the face of compelling contradictory evidence—particularly the physical evidence of the body and the death scene—Ford's claims may simply have seemed unpersuasive.

Other claims that Todd was alive Sunday also failed to turn the case. Sara Kane Carter, a movie fan who lived in Laurel Canyon, proclaimed she saw Todd make a phone call in a booth at the Laurel Drug Store. This was around 4:00 Sunday afternoon, about the time of the Ford phone call. As the police investigators noted, Todd's alleged question about a "short cut" via Ventura Boulevard to Ford's Laurel Canyon home made some sense if she called from the drugstore, since from that point a driver might want to know whether to take Laurel Canyon Boulevard or the Cahuenga pass and Ventura Boulevard.[22]

Carter supported her claim much as Ford had. She said Todd was wearing an evening dress and claimed she, Carter, commented at the time on the oddity of a woman so dressed on a Sunday afternoon to two store employees, Hamilton Wimscott and Irving Hamilton. She also claimed familiarity with Todd, whom she saw in the drugstore and elsewhere on several occasions.

The tardiness of her allegations worked against Carter's credibility, however, especially since some of the more striking details of the case—such as the fact the actress was found in the same evening dress she had worn on the previous evening—were published before she came forward with her story. Additionally, phone records of the pay phone at Laurel Drugstore—kept on an automatic tape attached to the phone itself—revealed no record of a call to the Ford home that afternoon. Other pay phones in the vicinity, which the police checked in case Todd had not completed her call from the drug store and stopped again to use another phone, also had not been used to call the Ford home Sunday. The hard evidence that might have proven Carter's claim was simply not there.[23]

W. F. Persson's claim that Todd was the shaky, haggard-looking woman who used his store phone to make a call came earlier in the investigation. According to the cigar store owner, the woman was wearing a blue sequined evening gown and blue high-heeled shoes like the ones Todd wore to the Trocadero. Two of his customers successfully selected Todd's evening gown instead of another dress Grand Jury foreman Rochester displayed in the Grand Jury room (of course, they had a 50% chance of being right only by guessing).

One detail of Persson's testimony about Todd's clothes did not mesh with the known facts of the case, however. He claimed Todd's dress was covered with dust and her shoes were also dirty, but neither her dress nor her shoes were soiled when her body was found Monday morning. While it is conceivable Todd may have somehow changed her shoes before she died, (Fisher believed she was wearing other shoes when she entered the cigar store, though he admitted he did not look at them carefully), it seems unlikely she had her dress cleaned as well.[24]

The storeowner also admitted he had never seen Todd before and knew her only from movie fan magazines at his store. His description of the woman as between 5'6" and 5'8" tall did not match with the actress' actual height 5'3". Although several of his customers corroborated his story, only one, Robert Fisher, identified the woman as Miss Todd. Other pedestrians in the neighborhood—possibly churchgoers—reported seeing the woman and her heavy-set companion sitting on the steps of a nearby church, but none claimed she was Miss Todd. Platinum curls were the rage among young women in Hollywood and its environs in 1935, so it is possible some other young woman wearing an evening dress from the night before and perhaps unsteady from a night of partying walked into Persson's cigar store that Sunday morning.

Another alleged Todd sighting occurred early Monday morning at a Christmas tree lot in Santa Monica. Like the Carter story, this one suffered from tardiness in its report: the two alleged sighters, Cummings and San Juan, did not contact the police until Friday, December 20, days after the Todd story first became headlines in the local press. Like the Persson tale, this sighting placed Todd in the company of a man—described as about 26 years old, of dark complexion, with heavy dark eyebrows and dark hair, though not necessarily heavy-set. Several days later, the same two men returned to the Santa Monica Police Station to report both were warned separately to keep out of the Todd case. While it was arguable nobody would bother to threaten them unless they had seen Todd and knew something, neither man could prove either the initial sighting or the warning. Neither the District Attorney nor the Grand Jury foreman bothered to interview them.

The report of a dark-haired companion to Miss Todd resonated through a host of other sightings. While newspapers alluded to many such reports, they detailed only one, that of Jewel Carmen. Her description of Todd's companion as "tall and dark" and "foreign-looking" seemed to complement that of San Juan and Cummings, and perhaps even encouraged them to come forth with their own, for one reason or the other.

For credibility, Carmen relied on much the same kind of support Ford and other Sunday sighters of Todd had used. First, she cited her acquaintance both with Todd, claiming they were friendly, even intimate, and Todd's automobile, in which she claimed to have ridden. Then, she referred to a witness to her sighting experience. In this case, it was an after-the-fact witness, but one who could counter suspicions arising from her tardy report of her sighting. Sonia Ardell, a friend, confirmed Carmen exclaiming, "Why I saw her just before midnight last night!" when Mrs. Ardell called her Monday around 3 p.m. to tell her of the discovery of Todd's body.[25]

Still, the timing of her report, which came on Wednesday evening just as the investigatory heat was turned up on her former husband Roland West and the striking, if not implausible, coincidence that she, of all people, would see Todd that evening did not help her credibility. As the investigation continued, she seemed less certain Todd was the passenger in the automobile and eventually admitted to the grand jurors that she was not sure at all. Perhaps, she had never been positive. Despite her exclamation to Ardell Monday afternoon and statements to reporters she was sure in her identification, she told other reporters she could not "positively identify Miss Todd."[26]

Piecing together Carmen's account from the various journals, it is difficult to see how she could have been certain. She claimed she first recognized Todd's chocolate brown phaeton with its white sidewall tires in front of her own vehicle as she drove on Hollywood Boulevard around 11:00 p.m. Sunday. Although she did not follow Todd's car but just "unconsciously drifted along" towards her home behind the phaeton, she did admit she "stepped on the gas and drew as close as possible" to the phaeton.[27] Both the phaeton and Carmen turned south onto Vine Street. At Santa Monica Boulevard, Carmen moved into the left lane and drew abreast the phaeton as it then turned right, heading west, while she continued south on Vine towards her home.[28] As it turned, she caught a "fleeting glimpse" of the man driving the car, but not a "full-face" view of him or Miss Todd. All she could say of the former was that she had never seen him before and could not hope to identify him in the future. As for her identification of Todd as a passenger in the car, it seemed to rest on her "golden curls" and the "smart" or "pert" hat the woman was wearing.[29]

For several reasons, then, Carmen's value as a witness seemed doubtful. She never got a close look at the occupants of the car and could identify the automobile only by color and general body style. The one detail she named, the hat Todd was wearing, was not supported by the known facts of Todd's dress either Saturday night or Monday morning. (In response to doubts about the hat, Carmen backpedaled, admitting she had only an "impression" Todd was wearing a hat.) Despite her avowal that she was certain the passenger in the car was Todd, she expressed doubts about her own story. Perhaps most significantly in the mind of the investigators, her motives and honesty seemed suspect. Her failure to disclose her sighting when first interviewed, coupled with an air of disingenuousness about the experience—as if the sight of her estranged husband's mistress with another man would only provoke a faint curiosity on her part—may have persuaded the investigators there were simply too many problems with her account.[30]

To a great extent, what was most persuasive about the sighting reports overall was simply their number. They tended to buttress each other, the more so when they meshed in time or detail, as in the repeated references to a dark-haired, foreign-looking man. However problematic each may seem when viewed independently, there were simply too many to dismiss outright.

Yet experience teaches us that sometimes the quantity of such claims does not count for much. There were plenty of young attractive blonde women in Los Angeles at the time who could have been mistaken for Thelma Todd. Even today, it is sometimes difficult when watching films of the era to tell one platinum blonde actress from another. Undoubtedly, some of the reports of sightings came from confused personalities, the kind that seem to pop up in every mystery involving a popular figure, and there were plenty of those individuals to go around, even in 1935. While the investigators did not publicly question any of the sighters' grasp of reality, stating only when pressed that so-and-so's story "just doesn't make sense" or "doesn't add up," one can imagine some of the reports they received came from the kind of people they had learned through experience to distrust. A movie fan, a washed up actress with a live-in personal psychic, an overwrought hostess—one can see why the investigators chose to disregard them.

Faced with the prosaic realities of an investigation with its inevitable limits on time and resources, the detectives of the LAPD and DA's office could not act simply on tenuous reports, no matter how numerous. Unless there was tangible evidence to back up a sighting, such as the actress identifying herself to any of the various persons who claim she stood before them, or some ancillary corroboration, such as Ford's number in the pay telephone tapes, there was little argument for continuing the investigation in the face of the forensic evidence that Todd died accidentally Sunday morning. To some extent, the quantity of the sightings even worked against their credibility. One would expect that in at least one case some persuasive, undeniable fact would have emerged to bolster the claim. Such a fact would have been something upon which the detectives could have gone forward, something that would have argued persuasively to the coroner that the "history" surrounding Todd's death needed to be revised along with his estimate of the time of her death. And yet no such fact emerged.

TWENTY-FIVE: SUICIDE?

The hell where youth and laughter go
— Siegried Sassoon[1]

Most writers on the Todd mystery have discounted the possibility she committed suicide.[2] There are some simple reasons for this. To some extent, the lack of interest in a suicide theory may reflect superficial research. During the early part of the investigation, the time frame most likely to be thoroughly researched by secondary writers, suicide received scant attention from investigators and reporters. Only towards the end of the Grand Jury investigation was the possibility she took her own life explored in any depth and then only as interest in the case waned and coverage began to retreat from front-page headlines. This shift in the contemporary investigation toward suicide as an explanation of Todd's death is easy to miss, especially if one is already persuaded by other explanations.

The lack of interest by reporters and secondary writers in the suicide theory is also attributable to the practical dramatics of their narrative. Suicide simply does not make as good a story as murder: the best most writers can do with such a scenario is to cast the comedienne as a victim of her industry and associates. Murder, on the other hand, opens up a whole world of grievance and injustice, especially when one charges it with the ostensibly omnipotent power of Mafia bosses.

While witnesses were found to testify in support of a suicide theory during the Grand Jury investigation, those closest to Todd uniformly rejected suggestions she was suicidal. Harvey Priester knew of no reason she would take her life.[3] Mae Whitehead agreed, adding she was always, "happy and cheerful."[4] Roland West declared, "Miss Todd was never unhappy; she had everything to be happy about, everything."[5] Pat DiCicco and Todd's mother also saw no reason she would take her own life, while Todd's friends and comedy-short co-stars, ZaSu Pitts and Patsy Kelly strongly rejected the suicide theory. Pitts maintained until the end of her life that Todd did not kill herself,[6] while Kelly told investigators at the time that Todd had "every reason to live."

Still, some witnesses did come forward to describe another side of the actress. Ida Lupino's account of her cocktail room conversation with Todd at the Trocadero and Todd's morose comments in London suggested, at the least, the famous outward gaiety of the actress might have masked a troubled interior. Rumors of a secretive and darker side of the actress reached the press. As one paper reported:

> It was recalled by those who knew her best, she frequently became subject to moods of melancholy . . . She was wont to drive her powerful, 12-cylinder phaeton . . . on solitary trips to none knows where . . . Waiters and bartenders have told District Attorney's investigators that Miss Todd . . . often had sat alone, for many hours, in other establishments, apparently deep in thought.[7]

While the comments attributed to Todd by Ida Lupino and Helen Ainsworth may have been nothing more than flippant world-weariness, the possibility Todd killed herself demands serious consideration, if only because of the circumstances of her death. Carbon monoxide poisoning has been used many times by suicides. Moreover, some of the difficulties in ascribing the actress' death to accident melt away if we introduce intentional self-destruction into the equation.

As a primary matter, it is important to distinguish between a legal or forensic determination of suicide and a psychological one. Making a legal determination of suicide requires a higher order of proof than is required by a psychological or lay conclusion. In the past, when suicide was considered a crime,[8] to prove suicide the state had to demonstrate that the deceased specifically intended to kill himself. Today, to avoid payment on a life insurance claim, the carrier must prove the same intention. In some cases, metal capacity becomes a key issue: if the deceased was under severe mental stress or delusion, or impaired by alcohol or drugs, a court might find he or she lacked the capacity to form the requisite intent. As one authority puts it, "Generally, coroners list suicide as a cause of death only where circumstances unequivocally justify such a determination—suicide note, history or tendencies, previous attempts, or when no other explanation is possible."[9]

These legal criteria shed light on the Todd investigation. From the beginning, the police and the district attorney investigators failed to turn up any direct evidence of suicide. In many cases, such indications are manifest—a gunshot wound to the temple, a pistol in the hand, an open, empty bottle of sleeping pills nearby, a body hanging from a rope in a locked room. Even in carbon monoxide deaths, evidence of preparation is often apparent. Indeed, around the time of Todd's death, newspapers reported three apparent suicides by carbon monoxide. In two of the cases, the deceased connected a hose from the tail pipe to the closed interior of an automobile. In the third, the victim inhaled the carbon monoxide directly from the tail pipe, presumably in a closed garage.[10] In each of these cases, there was direct evidence of an intentional act and no evidence the intention was that of another person, a murderer; all were ruled suicides.

In the Todd case, however, there was no evidence of preparation or device. Therefore, some other proof of intent was required, such as a note testifying to the intent or a compelling motive. Despite rumors a note had been found and concealed by one of the principals in the case, however, none was ever produced. The failure to find a suicide note was not proof Todd had not committed suicide—in only a third of suicides do the victims leave notes—but the lack of a note or other physical evidence of a self-destructive intention weakened the case for suicide.[11]

Still, one might question whether Todd had a psychological basis for committing suicide—in other words, whether the actresses' behavior indicated a predisposition towards suicide. In such a pursuit, advances in the study of suicide since Todd's death may aid us. Still a cautionary note is necessary. Such advances may offer new insights, but care must be used in when we apply modern understandings to past events. Changes in demographics alter statistical analysis, while environmental factors that might lead to psychological stress and ultimately to suicide are difficult to correlate over a gap of over seventy-five years. In addition, when data surrounding a specific case is incomplete and contradictory, as it is in Todd's death, it is easy to be misled by generalizations. Still, modern insights into the nature and causes of suicide offer some tentative insights as to whether Todd took her own life.

One development in the study of suicide since 1935 is the use of "psychological autopsies." Developed by psychologists Edwin Schneiderman and Norman Faberow, this technique is designed to "reconstruct the final days and weeks of life by bringing together the available observations, fact and opinion about a recently deceased person in an effort to understand the psychological component of death."[12] Team members carefully consider the person's routine in the days and hours before death and try to reconstruct a sense of the person's character, personality and state of mind. An approximation of this approach might shed light on the question of whether Todd committed suicide.

Suicidologists are generally united in identifying the factors most commonly associated with self-destructive behavior. They include illness, a family history of suicide, alcohol and drug abuse, a serious loss, despair, depression, and schizophrenia.[13] In Todd's case, there is no evidence of schizophrenia or a family history of suicide and, despite early reports of fainting spells and a weak heart, no evidence that she was seriously ill. There is strong evidence, however, that Todd could be a heavy drinker. It is clear she was intoxicated at the time of her death. Whether her drinking was long-term and signified alcoholism is an open question. Nevertheless, intemperate drinking is often an indicator of underlying depression and feelings of hopelessness. In addition, alcohol can seriously undermine a person's judgment and thought processes. A person who is both despondent and impaired by alcohol may be prone to attempt suicide. Not surprisingly, alcoholics have high rates of suicide when compared to the general population.[14]

Loss is another key reason people kill themselves. The loss can be that of a relationship, a job, or something as intangible as a sense of security.[15] Arguably, in the period leading to her death, Todd suffered several major losses. The failure of her marriage to Pat DiCicco two years earlier struck a heavy blow; friends testified she had been heartbroken. The fear generated by the ongoing extortion attempts may have undermined her sense of security. She also may also have been distressed over her relationship with West and the possible loss of her association with the café. Finally, while Todd was still working in film, her career was not thriving. Only three more shorts remained on her contract with Roach, who would all but abandon the genre by April 1936, and she only did two features in all of 1935.[16]

Depression is the affective condition most often associated with suicide. In fact, an estimated 50 percent of suicide victims suffer from some form of serious depression.[17] Depression itself can be triggered by a significant loss. Among the symptoms of a suicidal depression are preoccupation with themes of death, changes in appetite or weight, apathy, withdrawal, and feelings of worthlessness, self-reproach and guilt.[18] The excessive use of drugs and alcohol can also be associated with depression as the victim seeks to block emotional distress.

There is circumstantial evidence Todd was clinically depressed in the period leading to her death. She had suffered a series of significant losses. As photos of her at the time show, she was subject to radical weight gains and losses. She drank heavily. She was reported to have made a number of morbid statements. Perhaps depression led her to seek therapeutic help.

Even if Todd were depressed, there is no proof she committed suicide. Few depressed people take their own lives. According to researchers in the field, what is needed to turn a depressed person into a suicide is an overwhelming and inescapable hopelessness.[19] Several of Todd's reported statements indicate she might have experienced such feelings of hopelessness, but again the record is contradictory.

In addition to hopelessness, suicidologists have identified several other warning signs that point to a greater likelihood a person, particularly one who is depressed, might commit suicide. They include a previous suicide attempt, talking about suicide, the making of final arrangements, and sudden shifts from an energetic personality to lethargy or apathy.[20] In Todd's case, except for the ambivalent evidence of suicide talk offered by several witnesses, none seems to apply. Even though family members and close friends may have not been forthright in providing evidence of such talk, those who knew her best, with the possible exception of Ainsworth, reported no such communication. Even Lupino's examples harkened back several years.[21] There is no indication Todd ever tried before to kill herself, no indication of her making final arrangements (unless one exaggerates the Ainsworth debt payment out of all proportion), and no evidence of radical behavioral change. In fact, it appears Todd was enormously energetic in her last days and was planning for the future. Her Christmas plans and work on the new restaurant indicate a clear intention to live. She had even bought a piece of property near the café and was in the process of engaging an engineering firm to grade it for the construction of a garage, presumably so she could park her car nearby without having to climb the hill to West's garage. This is certainly a terrible bit of irony that speaks not only to her intention to continue living, but to continue living with West.[22]

Another development in suicidology since 1935 that may shed light on Todd's death is in the concepts of "acute" and "chronic" suicides. The former describes suicide that is triggered by a specific factor, while the latter refers to suicides arising from longer-term conditions.[23]

Under the acute model, one might argue Todd had been depressed, possibly for some time. The depression, spurred by the break-up of her marriage to DiCicco, the extortion notes she received, and perhaps a rocky relationship with Roland West, led to excessive drinking. Symptoms of her acute depression included rapid changes in body weight and a sometimes morbid temperament. All that was needed to propel Todd to the suicidal act, what suicidologist Edwin Schneiderman has described as the "final straw," was a situation that, to the actress in her depressed state, seemed hopeless.[24] The quarrel with West as she left for the Trocadero and the cruel snubbing by DiCicco, which may have dashed her hopes for a reconciliation, perhaps provided this, triggering a dangerous mood swing that was amplified when she found herself locked out of her apartment.

This is the model, stripped of modern theory and research, which the original investigators of the case seemed to pursue. However plausible, it has problems. First, it requires a level of impulsiveness in Todd's decision to kill herself. We know, however, that she made plans for Sunday, including attending Martha Ford's party and hosting a dinner for the Skouras brothers at the café. While she was gloomy towards the end of the Trocadero party, reports from those who attended her party at the Trocadero do not indicate a consistently morbid mood. If she did kill herself, she must have decided to do so on the way home to the café—or perhaps after she found her apartment door locked. Such impulsiveness in the decision to commit suicide, according to experts, is rare.

The method of death in Todd's case also works against the acute model. While the use of gas is not uncommon in suicides, ranking behind firearms, poison and hanging/strangulation, the advantage this method may have over others in its relative painlessness and non-violence may not have been borne out in the Todd death.[25] The phaeton's huge 12-cylinder engine produced plenty of carbon monoxide, but it also produced clouds of noxious fumes. According to the detectives who tested the automobile in the closed garage, within a minute and a half of starting its engine the phaeton produced enough fumes to make the air unbreathable, producing coughing fits and stinging eyes. It is difficult to imagine Todd willfully sticking it out long enough under these conditions to inhale sufficient amounts of carbon monoxide to kill herself.

None of these factors absolutely precludes the possibility of an "acute" suicide, but they raise the stakes for demonstrating it. On balance, there is more evidence against this kind of suicide than for it.

If Todd's death resulted from a depressed state, a more likely explanation for her demise rests with the "chronic" model of suicide. According to famed suicidologist Karl Menninger, chronic suicides are those who exhibit ongoing, self-destructive behavior that is as likely to end in accidental death as it is in any intentionally suicidal act.[26] Researchers have demonstrated that many accidents, especially those involving motor vehicles, drowning and drug overdoses, can be interpreted as resulting from unconscious self-destructive drives.[27]

Thus, Todd's death may have been partly suicidal.

TWENTY-SIX: AN ACCIDENTAL CONCLUSION

> When the impossible is eliminated, whatever
> remains is the truth.
> — Conan Doyle

Of the three overarching explanations for Thelma Todd's death, the accident theory has received the least support over the years. Even during the initial investigations, many participants doubted that Todd's death was accidental, except, of course, the police, who advanced it immediately. Subsequent writers are also united in their contempt for the accident theory, recounting it mainly to expose its feebleness.

Initially, the authors of this book were also skeptical of the accident theory. The LAPD's rapid conclusion Todd died accidentally seemed a classic rush to judgment. In addition, the main proponent of the theory was Roland West, who was neither an expert nor an objective observer. Finally, the idea of accident under the circumstances, at least as described in the newspapers, seemed improbable on its face. Why would Thelma Todd, a headstrong and prominent personality, on finding herself locked out of her own apartment by a man she knew she could awake, go meekly to the garage to await the opening of the café? Why would she fail to extricate herself from danger once the fumes of the exhaust alerted her to the peril? How would her blood get on the running board of the phaeton if she died in the auto?

The best argument for the accident theory, however, arises from the weaknesses of the murder and suicide theories. Much of the supposedly contradictory evidence that points towards murder, the unscuffed slippers, the mysterious sightings, peas and beans in the stomach, and blood on her corpse, weaken under scrutiny. In addition, despite some evidence of morbidity and depression, Todd was not a likely suicide. If nobody else killed her and she did not kill herself, one must consider again whether her death was an accident.

To begin such an inquiry, it is important to recall the basic outlines of the accident theory. Originally proposed by Roland West on the day Todd's body was found, it maintained that the actress walked to the garage of West's estate after she found herself locked out of her apartment.[1] As West speculated in his Coroner's Inquest testimony,

> Perhaps she had tried that door, didn't want to waken anybody, may have thought she would go to the car, stay there and wait until the porters come in the morning,

which is six o'clock, and say she went there at three thirty or four, she may have got chilled, and started the car and may have thought she would drive down to her mother's, starting the car and warmed it up and then open the doors—she would never think of little details.... [2]

Because the police could find no evidence of foul play and because the postmortem exam demonstrated the cause of death was carbon monoxide, they endorsed accident as the cause of death just six hours after the body was found. Throughout the twists and turns of the investigation, with few exceptions, they stuck to this view.

There were problems with the accident theory although they were fewer than supposed at the time or afterward. Broadly, the problems fell into two groups: those of physical fact and those arising from the testimony of witnesses. Most of the former had to do with the conditions inside the garage that cold December morning and the condition of Todd herself. The latter challenged the police presumption she died Sunday morning with claims she was still alive later that day. To understand how the police might have been correct in their initial determination of accident, one must take a close look at these sets of problems.

A key component of the first set was the automobile in which Todd's body was found. A limited-production automobile, chocolate brown in color, Todd's Lincoln phaeton was a 1932 model, bearing California license plate 4R 80. It featured a cloth top, wide running boards and a powerful 448 cubic inch V 12-cylinder engine.[3] The exhaust system, primitive by today's standards, included a pipe that ran in front of and below the engine block.[4] With a wheelbase of 145 inches, the car crowded its narrow garage stall, a large splayed tailpipe tight against the rear soot-stained concrete wall, chrome-plated headlights only a few inches from the sliding garage door.

To determine whether the phaeton could have killed Todd, the authorities had to answer several critical questions. First, there was the problem of the gas remaining in the tank. If the actress died accidentally, why had the automobile's engine stopped when it still had gas? If it stalled, how long had it run before doing so? Would it produce enough carbon monoxide in that time to kill the actress? Why wouldn't the air circulating in the drafty garage have dissipated the deadly fumes?

From the start, the police discounted the possibility someone else turned off the automobile engine after Todd was dead and sought more innocent explanations. Early in the investigation, they speculated that carbon monoxide and other gases displaced the oxygen in the garage, thus retarding the engine's combustive capacity.[5] On his final day of testimony before the Grand Jury, police chemist Ray Pinker claimed the tests proved this theory. Others, including Dr. Wagner, noted that, since the garage was not airtight, it was likely enough oxygen would remain for the engine to function.[6]

Other experts pointed to mechanical causes for the engine to stall. According to mechanics consulted by the *Daily News*, the phaeton's brake booster, which maintained a steady pressure on the wheel drums by conveying air from the carburetor's intake, might have played a role. As the emergency brake would have been set while the engine idled, this mechanism might have reduced the ratio of air to gas to the point where the fuel mixture was too heavy for combustion.[7]

Robert Cooper, an automobile salesman familiar with Todd's car, provided another explanation. Because the cylinders of Todd's automobile were "out of round," the oil was forced out of the engine block by the piston's compression, a process called a "blow-by." The oil might have fouled the spark plugs and stalled the engine, especially when the car was idling.[8]

With several plausible explanations for why the motor might have died on its own, the investigators turned their attention to the timing of the stall. On December 22, they conducted several tests to determine how long the car's engine would run in the garage, carefully airing out the garage between each test to supply fresh air. The results varied. When started cold with the garage doors closed, the engine ran for two minutes and 40 seconds. When slightly warmer, it ran for four minutes and 55 seconds. Thoroughly warmed, its throttle slightly advanced, it ran for 46 minutes and 40 seconds.[9]

Unfortunately, the tests were of questionable value. Too many key factors varied between early Sunday morning, when Todd supposedly entered the garage, and the following Friday afternoon, when the police ran their tests. The cold air Sunday morning would have made the engine more likely to stall than the warmer air of Friday afternoon, for instance, but when Todd turned on the ignition Sunday morning, the engine may still have been warm from Robert Anderson's drive from the café two hours before. She may also have pumped the gas pedal slightly to keep the motor running.

Still, the police tests did prove the car could run for a prolonged period in the enclosed space when sufficiently warmed or tended by an advanced throttle. As Detective Whitehead told the Grand Jury, it would not require much time, just two minutes and 40 seconds, for the Lincoln to generate enough monoxide to endanger human life.[10] The investigators learned this fact from another series of tests. The first involved exposing a pair of lovebirds to the exhaust in the closed garage.[11] In another, Whitehead himself stayed inside the garage holding a stopwatch and started the engine, while Pinker closed the garage door. A minute and a half later, Whitehead was pounding on the door. While he coughed and patted his watering eyes with a handkerchief, Pinker sniffed at the interior of the garage and announced, "It would just about do it now." "I was nearly fainting," Whitehead explained to reporters after he recovered. "The engine was running at only idling speed but gasses filled the garage almost instantly."[12]

These tests left a lot to desire. The physiognomy of lovebirds and human subjects are hardly comparable; lovebirds are used for early warning in coal mines because they will succumb to carbon monoxide **before** humans do. Even an experienced and clever investigator like Pinker could not determine lethal levels of odorless carbon monoxide by smelling the air. One suspects the authorities knew this, but wanted a visual and dramatic staging for the benefit of the press to confirm what seemed obvious to them: that the Lincoln could produce fumes and therefore carbon monoxide quickly. If this was their real motive in conducting the tests, they were successful. Almost immediately, newspapers across the country trumpeted the findings as proving the phaeton could kill in just two minutes.[13]

However, in trying to make their point, the police unwittingly may have raised a possible objection to their theory of Todd's accidental demise. If Detective Whitehead "nearly" fainted from the fumes produced by the Lincoln's engine, it was clear the atmosphere inside the garage became oppressive before it became deadly. His irritated eyes and throat and the coughing sensation were not symptoms of monoxide poison. Clearly, he was responding to the exhaust fumes themselves, which he found intolerable after only two minutes. How then could Todd fail to realize her plight within minutes after she started the engine and long before the deadly monoxide overcame her?

A week after the tests, Capt. Burt Wallis, Chief of Homicide, acknowledged his puzzlement on the issue. Even if Todd knew nothing of the effects of carbon monoxide, he reasoned, she could not have failed to notice the car fumes and their odor. He guessed she might have been unconscious.[14]

The police also tried to gauge the degree of air ventilation in the garage, a crucial factor since carbon monoxide is deadly only at significant concentrations. Bruce Clark noted there was a slight gap of about two inches at the top of the garage doors and a gap of about one inch at their bottom.[15] Robert Anderson confirmed the gap in his testimony at the Coroner's Inquest, but believed it to be about one inch top and bottom on the left door only.[16] This condition would permit only minimal ventilation in either case, but a police test showed that some air did circulate even when the doors were closed: the flame of a match held at their bottom blew inward while one at the top blew outward.[17]

A second source for ventilation, the holes in the ceiling of the garage reported by Jewel Carmen, proved illusory. While plaster had been removed because of leakage and resulting dampness, the hole did not go through the ceiling to the apartment above. Police monitoring the test in the apartment detected no fumes, effectively corroborating the testimony of Charles Smith, the occupant of the apartment, who claimed he never smelled exhaust in the apartment.[18]

A final source of ventilation, also reported by Carmen, was never definitively investigated. Carmen revealed the garage featured an aeration system consisting of "extra ventilating pipes" which to her mind "would have kept the place clear of gas— even with an auto motor running and the doors closed."[19] The police were also aware of the pipes and cited them to support their contention that the fumes did not reach Smith's apartment because the "garage air vent" opened to the outside.[20] A ventilation pipe is still extant above the roof on the north side of the garage building, but it is impossible to know whether it was functioning in 1935 or how effective it might have been. Perhaps the police, armed with incontrovertible evidence that Todd died of carbon monoxide poisoning in an environment likely to foster it, felt no need to run tests on the ventilation pipes. For them, the fact the actress succumbed to the gas proved the ventilation system had not been sufficient.

In spite of the results of the police tests and their confidence in them, during the final days of 1935 rumors arose that the Grand Jury was on the verge of abandoning the accident theory. On January 1, word came from reporters that the majority of jurors had done just that. Three reasons were given for their conclusions that Todd had not died accidentally. First, the light in the garage was not on when Todd was found; if she went there to keep warm and wait to get into the café, they reasoned, she would have turned on the light. Second, Todd was found in the phaeton, an open car. If she were trying to keep warm, why didn't she get in the closed Hupmobile parked right next to the phaeton? Third, there was no reason for her to go to the garage in the first place. If she had been locked out, why didn't she just break a window to get into the apartment, as she had done previously?[21]

It is doubtful these were the only factors influencing the jurors' minds. Despite the efforts of the police detectives, the jurors may also have wondered how the automobile, with its tendency to stall, could have produced sufficient carbon monoxide to kill Todd unless someone kept priming the accelerator. There was also the question of Todd's level of intoxication. Patrons of the Trocadero recalled that Todd had only a few drinks, certainly not enough to account for .13 percent blood alcohol level found in her body at autopsy. To the jurors, this might have indicated an entirely different scenario, one in which Todd lived through Sunday imbibing more liquor to account for the higher levels. In making the shift, jurors were also undoubtedly influenced by their foreman, George Rochester, who continued seeking evidence of foul play, and the district attorney personnel assigned to guide their investigation, who had begun to discount accident and focus on suicide.

Still, in spite of official misgivings in 1935 and subsequent doubts of secondary writers, a strong case can be made that the accident scenario was not only possible, but also probable. Two factors are compelling: the extreme lethality of carbon monoxide gas and Thelma Todd's blood alcohol level.

Carbon monoxide gas is the product of the incomplete combustion of carbonaceous materials. It is naturally present in smoke and in many fuels. It is colorless, odorless, tasteless and highly poisonous.[22] Its danger to life arises from the fact that, when inhaled, it bonds with the blood's hemoglobin and displaces the oxygen the blood carries from the lungs to the rest of the tissues in the body.[23] This produces, as Medical Examiner Wagner described it, "internal or blood asphyxiation."[24]

While carbon monoxide will eventually affect all organs, its most insidious effect is on the brain. At 20 to 40 percent saturation, deprived of the oxygen vital for its processes, the brain reacts in a way that victims often mistake for mild indisposition: headache, drowsiness, faintness, malaise and a flickering before the eyes.[25] As a result, they often make the potentially fatal mistake of lying down to wait for the feelings to pass, all the while continuing to inhale the deadly gas. At 40 to 50 percent saturation, confusion and numbness of the limbs set in abruptly. By the time they realize the danger, the victims often lose the capacity to act, the body having grown too weak to respond and the mind too clouded to determine an escape. One authority has observed, "In a strikingly large number of cases of carbon monoxide poisoning the victim is found close to a door he was not able to open, or by a window which he was not able to or did not think to break the glass." Soon thereafter, a complete loss of motor control occurs, followed by convulsion, respiratory arrest or heart attack, and death.[26]

While the victim's health and age are factors, a potentially fatal process is set in motion every time a person inhales air with carbon monoxide in it. The extent of ill effect depends upon the amount of monoxide in the air and the length of time the victim is exposed to it. For example, if carbon monoxide makes up 0.15-0.2 percent of the air by volume, an hour's exposure to it is quite dangerous; 0.4 percent can be fatal in less than an hour and 0.5 percent can be fatal quickly, leading to a blood saturation level of 73-76 percent in two to fifteen minutes.[27]

When considered along with the physical characteristics of the garage and Todd's phaeton, these facts, derived from research done mainly in the years following Todd's death, allow us to calculate the lethality of running the automobile in that setting.

Measuring approximately 20' x 24' x 8', with at least 20 percent of its space displaced by solid objects, including two cars and a variety of storage items, Roland West's garage had a gaseous volume of approximately 3,072 cubic feet.[28] 15.3 cubic feet of carbon monoxide, or .5 percent of this volume, would have been required to knock out Todd in a few minutes, but to kill her in less than an hour 12.3 cubic feet would have sufficed. With prolonged exposure, even 4.6 cubic feet could have been fatal.[29]

By any standard, the phaeton's 12-cylinder engine produced significant quantities of exhaust. Using conservative estimates, it could produce at least one cubic foot per second. In 1955, when the composition of exhaust was first being studied due to the burgeoning smog problem, auto exhaust averaged between three and six percent carbon monoxide, climbing at times to ten percent.[30] We can assume that in 1935 the levels were at least that high. While exact calculations of the carbon monoxide concentration in the garage are not possible, the amount emitted by the phaeton can be approximated using the engine's displacement (448 cubic inches), and a standard idle speed of 600 rpm. On this basis, the carbon monoxide emission rate would have ranged between 4.7 cubic feet per minute (assuming three percent carbon monoxide) and 15.6 cubic feet per minute (assuming ten percent carbon monoxide). While some of the carbon monoxide would have leaked out of the garage, even at the lower emission rates the gas would have reached a lethal level in a matter of a few minutes. The length of time required for only 40 percent saturation and its attendant mental and physical incapacity would have been even shorter.

Another factor in the possibility of accidental death was Todd's state of inebriation as reflected in her blood alcohol level. Measured at .13 percent during the autopsy, it must have been at least .14, as .01 percent can be expected to dissipate after a body dies and the metabolic processes cease.[31] Additionally, at least one hour, perhaps several, had elapsed since she departed the Trocadero—and presumably stopped drinking—and when she died. Since the body will excrete between .015 percent and .020 percent alcohol per hour, her blood alcohol level would have been considerably higher when she left the Trocadero, at least .155 percent, possibly .17 percent or more.[32] In short, she must have been quite intoxicated when she climbed into the phaeton. This could have been a significant contributor to her death.

To reach a blood alcohol of .17 percent, a woman of Todd's weight, assuming she had eaten a full meal, would have to consume between five to six drinks in the six hours of the Trocadero party.[33] Witnesses at the Trocadero, however, claimed Todd drank only moderately at the restaurant, while chauffeur Ernie Peters observed she appeared quite sober when he drove her home. These assertions must be considered in light of what we know about the situation at the restaurant that night as well as Todd's well-known proclivity for alcohol in an industry sensitive to the public's antipathy for excessive drinking.

As any host knows, it is difficult to determine the amount of alcohol any one guest has consumed over the length of a party, especially one lasting as long as that at the Trocadero. For nearly six hours, Todd moved from one table to another, quite possibly sipping drinks as she went. Perhaps she also had a few drinks in her apartment as she got ready for the evening. No one at the party claimed to have followed her every move, and therefore none were in a position to know how much she actually drank.

The film industry's proscriptions against public alcohol consumption may have induced some of the Trocadero witnesses to minimize the amount of liquor consumed at the party. During the investigation, several celebrities, notably both Sid Grauman and Roland West, went out of their way to mention how little they themselves drank. Those at the party may have taken a similar tack when asked about their own drinking. More importantly, they may have downplayed Todd's drinking that night.

The same sense of propriety may well have influenced Ernie Peters, who made a living out of catering to the Hollywood elite from his limousine station, just a stone's throw from the Paramount lot. Even if Peters had no such motive, he could have simply misread Todd's demeanor that morning. An experienced drinker like Todd—

one who, according to Pat DiCicco, knew how to hold her liquor—might well be quiet and distant rather than effusive and talkative, where the slip or slur of the tongue can betray intoxication. Moreover, a depressant like alcohol can bring on a variety of mood shifts. By all accounts, Todd was extremely gay and animated early in the evening, but became notably melancholy towards the end of the night. Considering the unpleasantness with her ex-husband and the lateness of the hour, this shift was natural and may well have been exacerbated by significant, if not heavy, drinking. The tally of her drinks by Trocadero bartenders, partygoers Harry Priester, Ida and Stanley Lupino, and Sid Grauman indicate Todd drank quite a bit that night.

Waiting for the guests to arrive at the restaurant's downstairs bar, talking to Ida Lupino about boyfriends and the film industry, Todd had at least one cocktail, according to both the Lupinos and Priester. If she had no other drinks, by the time the party had moved upstairs to the dining room, around 10:30, her blood alcohol level was a mere .014 percent. By midnight, however, having consumed two glasses of champagne and a brandy along with her dinner of a seafood cocktail, salad, turtle soup, filet mignon, green peas, string beans, and olives, it must have reached .11 percent or higher. Dancing and enjoying herself—except when quarreling with Pat DiCicco—wandering among the guests and, according to hatcheck girls, repeating a catch-phrase of the day, 'I resent it,' Todd, as usual the life of the party, dissipated a little more alcohol from her system by her activity, but not so much as really mattered. Another champagne at Grauman's table while she talked about the old days in New York with her former producer, William Rowland, must have brought her alcohol blood level back up to .14 percent by one a.m. In the next two hours, if she drank no more than one and a half additional glasses of champagne at Grauman and Rowland's table, it hovered around .15 percent by the time she was ready to leave the Trocadero. Despite her sober demeanor, she was quite intoxicated when she stepped into Ernie Peter's limousine.[34]

Certainly, she was no stranger to alcohol. Many of her acquaintances interviewed for this book noted she drank more than she should have. Lina Basquette recalled Todd always had a flask with her whenever she would come to visit in the late twenties; on many occasions, Basquette had seen her drunk, even once at the Trocadero shortly before her death.[35] Jack Sauer, another interviewee, stated flatly that she drank too much, often while playing a horse race gambling game that she had rigged to win with a wire while West looked on disapprovingly. West himself implied her experience with liquor indirectly when he remarked during the investigation that she "drank very little in the last few weeks." (Of course, if one is to believe Basquette's anecdote about seeing her shortly before her death, she may have been drinking more than he thought.) Autopsy Surgeon Wagner's report that he found no physical evidence of habitual intemperance while examining her liver may have supported West's comment; perhaps, whatever problems she had with alcohol in the past were over. If so, she suffered a relapse that night at the Trocadero.[36]

Given the lethal nature of carbon monoxide and the strong evidence Todd was thoroughly intoxicated, accident seems a likely cause of her death. Of course, any accident theory must confront the evidence found at the scene of death that tends to suggest a different, more sinister explanation. It must also deal with the objections raised to the theory at the time and since.

First, why Todd didn't become alarmed when the noxious fumes filled the garage? There are several possible explanations why she did not realize her danger and escape. She might have either passed out or fallen into an alcohol-induced sleep shortly after turning on the engine, oblivious to the fumes until it was too late. The fumes themselves may even have contributed to her intoxication and incumbent disorientation. Auto exhaust and other petroleum-based products such as glue can produce a feeling of euphoria. While Todd did not intentionally ingest the fumes, they may have intensified her intoxication, making it more difficult for her to behave in a rational and life-saving manner.[37]

Second, how does an accident theory account for the blotch of blood deposited on the running board? Three inches in diameter, the blotch was "several feet" from her body, "well beyond the spot where Miss Todd's head was hanging." As the blotch revealed a high content of carbon monoxide, Todd evidently had been out of the car after the engine had started. Why then was she found back in the car?[38]

The blotch is consistent with what criminologists call a low-velocity impact, such as a punch to the nose, which causes blood to drip straight down to the floor and tends to deposit large spots of blood. If, as the police suggested, Todd hit her nose and mouth on the steering wheel and bled, the shock of the concussion may have temporarily alerted her to her danger. She may have tried to pull herself out of the car and bled on the running board before falling back into her monoxide-induced confusion. Such a scenario is not unusual in carbon monoxide poisonings, the victim often faltering in an attempt to save herself. Cavett, the investigator who found the blood, suggested just such an explanation to the skeptical reporters, who were probably unfamiliar with carbon monoxide poisonings.[39]

It is also likely reporters misconstrued the position of Todd's body and exaggerated the distance between her head and the blood blotch. In any case, the distance between her head and the blotch is not determinative, since it was likely, as noted in an earlier chapter, that West moved her body before the police or reporters arrived. Photos of the phaeton's running board reveal the place where the blood blotch was found could easily comport with Cavett's explanation.

Several grand jurors brought up a third objection to the accident theory. Why, they asked, would Todd have chosen to wait in the open phaeton when the closed, and therefore much warmer, Hupmobile was only a few feet away? And why wouldn't she have turned on the overhead light? If one assumes Todd was seeking shelter in the garage, these are valid objections to the accident theory. However, if one assumes Todd did not intend to wait until morning, but only as long as it took to become sober or rested enough to drive to her mother's apartment in Hollywood, or to a friend's house, the problems disappear. In such a scenario, it is natural for her to choose to drive her own car.

As for the electrical light, when one considers it was located in the other stall of the garage, where the Hupmobile was parked, and that Todd would have had to open the other garage door to turn it on, it is not surprising she did not do so. In fact, it is possible she did not know where the light was, since she rarely drove the car from the garage herself, but relied on employees of the restaurant to fetch it for her.

The grand juror's objection that Todd would not have gone to the garage in the first place because she could have broken a window to get into the café is also shaky. Again, the jury seems to have been heavily influenced by West's testimony, specifically, by his anecdote of a similar incident in which the actress did break a window to rouse him. Nevertheless, on the night of her death, Todd had good grounds for not repeating her window-breaking escapade. She had quarreled with West earlier, she may well have been upset by her experience with DiCicco at the party, and she was drunk and tired– all good reasons for avoiding a potential confrontation. Besides, if she had wanted to rouse West, she could have done so by merely pounding on the apartment door, located just a few feet outside the windows of the chamber in which he was sleeping. That she did not demonstrated she had decided against sleeping in the apartment that night. Several jurors noted the proximity of the door on their field trip to the café, but by that time, they had already abandoned the accident theory.

In spite of the Grand Jury rejection, the skepticism of reporters and the hostility of secondary writers for over three-quarters of a century, accident is by far the most plausible explanation for Todd's death. While the details of her last moments can never be known, we can offer a reasonable re-construction of her final hours based on the evidence of the time and modern research.

At approximately 3:45 a.m. Sunday morning, Ernie Peters deposits an inebriated Thelma Todd at the sidewalk in front of her café. She has been quiet on the ride back to the beach, perhaps because of fatigue and depression brought on by the events at the Trocadero. Realizing an ugly scene with West is likely because of her failure to arrive home at his appointed hour, she declines Peter's offer to accompany her to the apartment door and, as the chauffeur turns his car around on Roosevelt Highway, climbs the concrete steps towards her apartment.

At the top of the stairs, Todd notices that the lights in the windows adjacent to her apartment door are off. West is already asleep. Pausing and trying to be quiet, she takes the apartment key from her white evening bag and tries the lock. It turns, but as she leans into the door, it refuses to budge. Immediately, she realizes the deadbolt is engaged. Gazing at the single key which Mae Whitehead put on her key ring, she also comprehends she cannot enter the front entrance to the café.

Sighing, she removes the key. Tired, drunk and depressed, she weighs her limited options. Banging on the door would lead to a confrontation with West, who had warned her about the doors being locked. The prospect of another quarrel only makes her more unhappy. Suddenly, she has a plan: she will get her car and drive back to Hollywood, perhaps to her mother's, perhaps to a friend's.

Slowly, somewhat unsteadily, she starts the long climb up the cement steps to the garage. At the top of the first flight, she turns right on Castellammare to avoid the second set of punishing stairs. While the route is a little longer, it is more gradual. Clutching her mink cape closely, she makes her way along the dark street. The cold wind buffets her, carrying with it a bit of the spray from the pounding surf below. Passing one, then two, then three darkened houses, she finally reaches the pool of dim light cast on the rough pavement by the post-top street lamp at the base of Stretto Way. Here she pauses to catch a breath. Then she turns left and begins the steep climb up the short winding road to Posetano towards Castillo del Mar.

By the time, she reaches the garage she realizes she is too tired or too drunk to drive yet. Tugging open the right sliding door, she slips inside, quickly closing the door behind her against the wind and cold. She pauses again to catch her breath and then begins feeling her way in the dark along the phaeton's fender and running board to the driver's door. She opens it and slides onto the seat.

It is now almost 4:00 a.m. Out of the wind, safe in her car, Todd takes stock. Perhaps she smokes a cigarette and mulls over the events of the evening. At some point, she opens her white evening purse and removes the handkerchiefs inside. Perhaps she flips on the car's headlights and uses the handkerchiefs to freshen her make-up in the light reflecting off the turquoise interior of the garage door.

A little later, dulled by drink and fatigue, Todd drops off to sleep. She dozes for perhaps an hour, maybe for only a few minutes. On awakening, she feels better. She figures she can drive. She flips the ignition switch and advances the throttle. She will warm up the engine and then go.

Pumping the accelerator a couple times, she presses the starter button. The 12 cylinders of the phaeton's engine quietly hum to life. Todd settles back to wait for the few minutes it will take for the engine to warm up, feathering the accelerator with her foot to keep up the idle. She closes her eyes.

Minutes pass. Two, three, four, five. The fumes from the phaeton fill the garage, a bitter, stinging smoke in which the odorless, noxious carbon monoxide lurks like a poisonous snake. Suddenly she awakes. She begins to cough fitfully. She pivots upward on the seat, but immediately feels the numbing effect of the poison already gliding through her arteries. Weak and dizzy, she topples face forward into the steering wheel. The glancing blow to the mouth and nose starts a flow of blood. She lunges toward the car door and fumbles with the latch. It opens and she grasps at its top edge to pull herself out, but her arms and legs fail as she tries to rise. Floundering, she hangs her head over the edge of the seat. Blood from her nose splatters the forward part of the running board. With what little is left of her strength, she manages to sit up again for a second before falling backwards into a position behind the steering wheel.

Inexorably, her strength and will seep from her oxygen-starved brain. Her struggle for life becomes perfunctory; her gasps for air only bear more carbon monoxide into her lungs and brain.

The phaeton's engine runs on. When it dies suddenly minutes later, it no longer matters. Carbon monoxide permeates the air in the garage. As long as she continues to live, the unconscious actress must breathe it. With every breath, her blood absorbs more carbon monoxide, eventually reaching .75 percent absorption. Death is only a matter of time.

In the apartment above, Charles Smith slumbers, unaware of the tragic drama taking place below. Outside, the blustery December night slowly gives way to a dawn Thelma Todd will never see.

Many of details of this reconstruction are arbitrary, but they comport with the known effects of carbon monoxide poisoning, the contemporary accounts of the situation surrounding Todd's last party, and the evidence collected at the scene and during autopsy. Of course, several accidental death scenarios are possible. The actress may have fallen asleep after starting the engine, which may have cut off after only a few minutes; in such a case, with a lower concentration of carbon monoxide in the air, she might have lived for several hours. Then again, she may have fallen asleep after turning on the car lights when she first seated herself in the phaeton. Awakening with a start a few minutes later, she may have worried over the automobile's chronically weak battery and fired up the engine to make sure the car would still start, and then continued to run it for a few minutes to re-charge the battery. It is even possible, given the disorienting effects of the poison, that the injured actress actually did get out of the car, stood bleeding and insensible over the running board for a few seconds, then got back in.

An incident recalled by Florian "Jack" Sauer, West's and Todd's neighbor in Castellammare and a Pacific Palisades garage owner who serviced the phaeton might say more about how Thelma Todd died than all the speculation of the past eighty years. It took place some months before Todd's death when she was living in a rented house in the hills above the café. One night after some heavy drinking, Todd got into her head to drive somewhere. She entered her garage, opening the door only wide enough for her to pass, and got into her car. Then she started the engine, put the car in gear, and drove straight through the garage door, causing extensive damage. Perhaps on her final night she made a similar mistake, albeit without crashing into the garage door, and lost her life because of it.[40]

As with all tragic accidents, it is tempting to wonder what might have happened if things had been a little different on that fateful night. If Todd had not drunk quite so much, if Whitehead had included all the keys on the key ring, if the actress had opened the garage door and driven straight off, if West had second thoughts about drawing the deadbolt, if DiCicco had not been so callous, if it hadn't been so cold, if she had fallen asleep straight through to morning. If, if, if. Instead of dying that night and planting the seeds of legend, Todd might have awakened the next morning with a bad hangover and passed away quietly fifty or even sixty years later in the Motion Picture Home, a nearly forgotten figure of a by-gone age.

On the other hand, even if she had survived that cold December night another tragic mishap might have claimed her a week, a month or a year later. While she may not have met all the criteria of Menninger's "chronic suicide," the record suggests something had gone wrong in Todd's life, prompting a number of self-destructive drives leading to a fatal accident. The symptoms were there—heavy drinking, rapid weight loss and gain, mood shifts, morbid talk. One can speculate about the causes—a deep sense of loss and depression fueled by failed relationships, disappointment about her career, both in Hollywood and in partnership with West in the café, the threats from extortionists. While the evidence does not suggest Todd killed herself, her behavior may imply a chronic carelessness that was implicitly self-destructive.

Ultimately, this observation too must be qualified, especially in terms of Todd's mental state at the time of her death. The record is both incomplete and contradictory. While some acquainted with Todd testified of a darker side to her personality, others claimed she maintained a positive and happy state of mind. It is impossible to know at this date who was right and it was probably impossible to know the real Thelma Todd, even in 1935. It is likely Todd imparted different messages to different people at different times and kept more than a few secrets to herself.

The accident theory rests on firmer ground. Many years of tabloid opinion to the contrary, there is simply no compelling evidence against it and much evidence to support it. While their reputation for dishonesty surely prompted much of the murder theorizing since her death, it appears the officers of the LAPD had the cause of her death right all along.

BIBLIOGRAPHY

Ames, Richard Sheridan & Todd, Thelma. "Twice I Tried to Trap the Hollywood Extortionist." Unidentified published manuscript in the Thelma Todd folder of the Dorothy Herrick Library, Academy of Motion Pictures Arts and Sciences. Date unknown, but probably Fall of 1935. Print.

Bergreen, Leonard. *Capone, The Man and the Era*. Simon & Schuster. New York. 1994. Print.

Bonelli, William G. *Billion Dollar BlackJack*. Civic Research Press. 1954. Print.

Briggs, Arthur E. *Southern California Renaissance Man*. UCLA Oral History. Print.

Carrol, Llewellyn. "What Hollywood Did to a New England Schoolmarm." *Photoplay*, Feb. 1932. Print.

Chamberlain. "FITTS: Protector of Womanhood", manuscript draft in Clinton Collection. UCLA.

Cohn, Alfred & Chisholm, Joe. *"Take The Witness!"* The New Home Library. New York. 1934. Print.

Creditor's Claim No. 144,304, In the Matter of the Estate of Thelma Alice Todd DiCicco. April 2, 1936.

Daniels, Bebe and Ben Lyon. *Life with the Lyons: the Autobiography of Bebe Daniels and Ben Lyon* London. Odhams Press Ltd., 1953. Print.

Day, Sandra. "For a New Outlook on Life—Get a Hat." *Milwaukee Journal*. Nov 11, 1935. Print.

Delahanty, Lou. "The Real Wallace Ford," *Shadowplay*. June, 1934. Print.

Dewey, Thomas. *Twenty Against the Underworld*. Doubleday and Company, Garden City. 1974. Print.

Dieckmann, Edward A. *Practical Homicide Investigation*. Charles C. Thomas.1961. Print.

Donati, William. *Ida Lupino*, A Biography. University Press of Kentucky, Lexington. 1996. Print.

Dreisbach Robert H. & Robertson, William O. *Handbook of Poisoning*. 1987. Print.

Edwin Emery. *The Press and America*. Allyn and Bacon, Boston, 1997. Print.

Evans, Glen, and Faberow, Norman L. *The Encyclopedia of Suicide*. Facts on File. 1988. Print.

Fascinating Youth. Screen Scrapbook. Circa 1925. Print.

Finch, Christopher and Rosenkrantz, Linda. *Gone Hollywood: The Movie Colony During the Golden Age.* Doubleday. New York. 1979. Print.

Finney, Guy. *Angel City in Turmoil.* Amer Press. Los Angeles. 1940. Print.

Finney, Guy. *The Great Los Angeles Bubble.* Forbes. 1929. Print.

David Fisher, *Hard Evidence*, Dell Publishing. New York. 1996. Print.

Fox, Stephen. *Blood and Power, Organized Crime in Twentieth-Century America.* William Morrow and Company, New York. 1989. Print.

Stephan A. Flanders, *Suicide.* Library in a Book. New York, 1991. Print.

Garrigues, Charles H. *You're Paying for It! A Guide to Graft.* Funk & Wagnalls. New York. 1936. Print.

Giroux, Robert. *A Deed of Death.* Farrar and Giroux. New York. 1990. Print.

Goodman, Ezra. *The Fifty Year Decline and Fall of Hollywood.* A Macfadden Book. circa 1961. Print.

Gosch, Martin, A. & Hammer, Richard. *The Last Testament of Lucky Luciano.* Little Brown. New York. 1975. Print.

Gottlieb, Robert & Wolf, Irene. *Thinking Big: The Story of the Los Angeles Times, Its Publishers and Their Influence on Southern California.* G. P. Putnam & Sons. New York. 1977. Print.

Guiles, Fred Lawrence. *Stan, The Life of Stan Laurel.* Stein and Day. New York. 1980. Print.

Haight, Raymond. "Indicted! How a City Political Gang Got Its Man." *Scribner's Magazine.* March, 1934. Print.

Hallberg, June. *Fitts/Palmer Campaign for District Attorney.* M.A. Thesis, UCLA, 1939. Print.

Hart, Jack R. *The Information Empire.* University Press of America. 1981.

Heimann, Jim. *Out With Stars, Hollywood Nightlife in the Golden Era.* Abbeville Press. New York. 1985. Print.

Kahn, Ada, P. & and Fawcett, Jan. *The Encyclopedia of Mental Health,* Facts on File, 2000. Print.

Knight, Bernard. *Legal Aspects of Medical Practice*, 4th edition, 1987. Print.

Lacey, Robert. *Little Man, Meyer Lansky and the Gangster Life.* Little, Brown and Company. New York. 1991. Print.

Larson, Arnold B. *Newspaper Reporting in the Twenties: Reflections,* University of California, Los Angeles.. Oral History Program, 1970.

Lasky, Jesse L. with Don Weldon. *I Blow My Own Horn.* Garden City, Doubleday & Company. New York. 1957. Print.

Lawler, Oscar. *Los Angeles Attorney,* UCLA Oral History. 1962. Interviewed by Doyce Nunis. Print.

Lawlor, Richard. *Photoplay*. Feb, 1936. Print.

Leasor, James. *Who Killed Sir Harry Oaks?* Houghton Mifflin. New York. 1983. Print.

Leff, Leonard J. The *Dame in the Kimona*, University of Kentucky Press, 1990. Print.

Lewontin, Richard. "It Ain't Necessarily So: The Dream of the Human Genome and Other Illusions." *The New York Review of Books*. 2000. Print.

Leroy, Mervyn, *Take One*, Hawthorne Books, Inc. New York. 1974. Print.

Lichty, Robert, *Standard Catalog of Ford, 1903-1990*.

Longstreet, Stephen. *All Star Cast, An Anecdotal History of Los Angeles*. 1977. Print.

Lubon, Dorothy. "Movie Men are so Crude." *Motion Picture*, June, 1929. Print.

Maltin, Leonard. *The Great Movie Shorts*. Crown Publishing Group, 1972. Print.

Dwight McKinney & Allhoff, Fred. "The Lid Off Los Angeles.," *Liberty Magazine*, November 11, 1939. Print.

MacQueen, Scott. "Roland West," *In Between Action and Cut: Five American Directors*. Frank Thompson, editor. The Scarecrow Press, Inc. Metuchen, New Jersey and London. 1985. Print.

Marx, Samuel and Vanderveen, Joyce. *Deadly Illusions*. Random House New York, 1990. Print.

McWilliams, Carey. *Southern California: An Island on the Land*. Gibbs Smith, 1973.

Moore, Charles. T*he City Observed: Los Angeles*, Vintage Books. New York. 1984. Print.

Mott, Frank Luther. *American Journalism*. MacMillan, New York. 1962. Print.

Munson, Arthur, C., Architect. *Second Floor Plan, Alterations to Joya's Café Bldg.*" Vellum Overlay. Circa 1934

Muir, Florabel. *Headline Happy*, Holt Publishing. New York. 1950. Print.

Nickolls, Lewis. *The Scientific Investigation of Crime*. Butterworth. 1956. Print.

Olender, Terrys T. *For the Prosecution, Miss Deputy D.A.* Chilton Co. Philadelphia. 1961. Print.

O'Brian and Chafetz, *The Encyclopedia of Alcoholism*, Facts on File, Infobase Publishing, New York, 1982 Print.

Petajan, Jack H. *Survival Responses During Fire Exposure.* (Unknown)

Polson, Gee and Knight. *The Essentials of Forensic Medicine, 4th edition*. 1985. Print.

Powell, Hickman. *Lucky Luciano, His Amazing Trial and Wild Witnesses*. 1975. Print.

Price, Michael H. & Turner, George E. "Remembering How The Bat Whispers." *American Cinematographer*, March, 1986. Print.

Rasmussen Cecilia. "Ramparts Site Was a Noir Landmark," *Los Angeles Times*. Sept. 9, 1999. Print.

Paul Sann. *The Lawless Decade*, New York, Fawcett World Library, New York. 1971. Print.

Shuler, Robert. "The Jacobson Outrage." *Bob Shuler's Magazine*, September, 1927. Print.

Shuler, Robert. "The Strange Death of Charlie Crawford." Los Angeles. 1931. Print.

Simpson, Keith & Knight, Bernard. *Forensic Medicine, 9th edition*, 1988. Print.

Sitton, Tom. "The 'Boss' Without a Machine: Kent K. Parrot and Los Angeles Politics in the 1920s." *Southern California Quarterly*. Vol.67. No 4. Winter 1985. Print.

Skretvedt, Randy. *Laurel and Hardy: The Magic Behind the Movies*. Moonstone Press, Beverly Hills, 1987. Print.

St. Cloud, Vern. "Bombing the Lid Off Los Angeles," *Official Detective Stories*. May 25, 1938.

St. Johns, Adela Rogers. *Final Verdict*, Doubleday & Company, Garden City, New York, 1962. Print.

Spitz, Werner, ed., *Spitz and Fisher's, MedicoLegal Investigation of Death, 2nd edition*. Thomas, Springfield, Illinois. 1980. Print.

Starr, Kevin. *Material Dreams*. Oxford University Press. New York. 1990. Print.

Stepno, Bob. "Staged, faked and mostly naked: Photographic innovation at the Evening Graphic (1924-1932)". School of Journalism and Mass Communication University of North Carolina at Chapel Hill

Story, Harold, H. *Memoirs of Harold H. Story*, UCLA Oral History, UCLA, 1967. Interviewed by Elizabeth I. Dixon. Print.

Sutherland, Vincent. "Raymond Bombing Sequel to Chandler-Shaw Deal." *People's World*, Feb. 2, 1938. Print.

Svensson, Arne & Wendell, Otto. *Crime Detection*. 1955. Print.

Todd, Thelma. "How I Was Groomed for Stardom", *Film Weekly*, June 30, 1933. Print.

Tygiel, Jules. *The Great Los Angeles Swindle*, University of California Press, Los Angeles. 1994. Print.

United Artists Corporation Biography. *Joseph M. Schenck*. July 1, 1927.

Print.

United States Senate, Special Committee to Investigate Organized Crime in Interstate Commerce, United States Senate, HEARINGS, Nevada-California, November, December, 1950, March 1951. United States Government Printing Office. Washington, D.C. 1951. Print.

Vanderbilt, Gloria. *Black Knight, White Knight.* Knopf, New York. 1987. Print.

Van Ziemer. Los Angeles County Superior Court Probate Records, #32984

Viglietta Andrew J. "The Unpublished Truth About the Thelma Todd Extortion Case." *True Detective.* March, 1936. Print.

Webster's Collegiate Dictionary, (based on *Webster's New International Dictionary, Second Edition 1934.*) G & C Merriam Co. Springfield. 1943. Print.

Weinstock, Matt. *My LA.* Current Books. New York, 1947. Print.

White, Leslie. *Me Detective.* Harcourt, Brace and Company. New York., 1936. Print.

Winters, Shelley. *Shelley: Also known as Shirley,* Morrow, New York, 1980. Print.

Wilkerson, Tichi & Borie, Marcia. *The Hollywood Reporter.* 1984. Print.

Wolf, Marvin J. and Mader, Katherine. *Fallen Angels,* 1986 and 2012. Print

Woods, Joseph, Gerald. *The Progressives and the Police: Urban Reform and the Professionalization of the Los Angeles Police.* UMI Dissertation Information Service, Ann Arbor. 1973 Print.

Yankel, J. Heim. "Who Shot Our Buron' . . . And Why?" *Clifford Clinton's Civic Digest.* December, 1939. Print.

Young, Betty Lou, *Where the Mountains Meet the Sea.* Pacific Palisades Historical Society, 1983. Print.

York, Cal. "A Queen of Blondes." *Photoplay,* Aug, 1917. Print.

CHRONOLOGICAL LIST OF TODD SECONDARY PRINT SOURCES THROUGH 2005

1932 "What Hollywood Did to a New England Schoolmarm." *Photoplay.* Feb. 1932: 54-55, 115. Print.

1935 Ames, Richard Sheridan. "Thelma Todd Tells—Twice I Tried the Hollywood: The Inside Story of the Attempt to Foil the Arm and Extort Money." Source Unknown. Pre-December, 1935. Print.

1935 "Discard Murder Hints in Thelma Todd Death." *Daily Variety*. Dec. 17, 1935: 6. Print.

1935 "Thelma Todd, 31, Dies, Monoxide Poisoning; No Mystery Angles." *Daily Variety*. Dec. 18 1935. Print

1935 "Letter from Hitchhiker." *Los Angeles Times*. Dec. 19, 1935. Print.

1936 "Into the Lonely Valley." *Photoplay*. Feb. 1936: 56. Print.

1936 "Secrets of New York's Homicide Squad: The Strange Death of Thelma Todd." *Liberty*. Edited by Anthony Abbot (psued. of Fulton Oursler). Oct. 3, 1936: 34-38. Print.

1937 Haldeman-Julias, Marcet. "The Strange Death of Thelma Todd." *Famous Unsolved Murder Mysteries*. Haldeman-Julias Publications, Girard, Kansas. 1937: 124-128. Print.

1937 Holstius, E. Nils. *Hollywood Through the Backdoor*. Longmans, Green and Company, New York. 1937:40-41. Print.

1937 "Thelma Todd Death Riddle." *Screen Book Magazine*. Aug. 1937. Print.

1939 Chandler, Raymond. *Dime Detectives*. "The Lady in the Lake." 1939. Print.

1944 Collins, Frederick L. "Hollywood's Golden Girls and the Telephone Call After Death. *Homicide Squad: Adventures of a Headquarters Old Timer*. (Fuller story of 1936 *Liberty* article.) G. P. Putnam's Sons, New York. 1944: 220-234. Print

1949 Underwood, Agnes. *Newspaperwoman*. Harper and Brothers, NY. 1949: 229-230 Print.

1949 Thomas, Bob. "Hollywood Still Speculates on Thelma Todd Death in 1935." *Kansas City Star*. Dec. 15, 1949. Print.

1954 Lord, Jonathan. "Locked Out of Life." *Unsolved Murders Magazine*. June, 1954: 80-91. Print.

1955 Skolsky, Sidney. *This Was Hollywood*. "Its Greatest Tragedies." Affiliated Magazines, New York. Vol. 1, No.1. 1955:17. Print.

1961 McCabe, John M. *Mr. Laurel and Mr. Hardy*. Doubleday & Co, Garden City, NY. Print.

1962 Carr, William H.A. "Thelma Todd: The Wrong Time for Death." *Hollywood Tragedy*. Lancer Books, Inc. NY. 1962: 57-64. Print.

1962 Sullivan, Edward S. "Hot Toddy." *Hollywood: The Sin Capital of the World*. Pike Publications, Van Nuys, CA. March, 1962: 57-64. Print.

1965 Neutzel, Charles. *Whodunit? Hollywood Style*. Book Company of America, Beverly Hills, CA. 1965: 76-99. Print.

1966 Maltin, Leonard. "The Films of Thelma Todd." *Film Fan*

Monthly. Sept. 1966. Print.

1967   Autori, Degli and Opere, Delle. *Film Lexicon.* 1967: 291-292. Italian, Print.

1970   Austin, John. *Hollywood's Unsolved Mysteries.* Ace Publishing, NY. 1970. Print.

1970   Maltin, Leonard. *Movie Comedy Teams.* Plume Publishing. 1970, revised 1985: 5. Print.

1971   Austin, John. "Hollywood Murder: Thelma Todd's Bizarre Death: Murder or Suicide?" *Citizen News.* Sept. 9, 1971. Print.

1972   Maltin, Leonard. *The Great Movie Shorts: Those Wonderful One- and Two-Reelers of the Thirties and Forties.* Crown Publishing, NY. 1972. Print.

1973   Smith, Allen L. "Mysterious Death of Blond and Beautiful Thelma Todd." *Hollywood Studio.* Sept. 1973: 31-34. Print.

1975   Anger, Kenneth. *Hollywood Babylon.* Straight Arrow Press, San Francisco, CA. 1st Ed.: Paris, 1960. USA, 1975: 201-207. Print.

1976   Horden, Nicholas. "The Death of Thelma Todd: Hollywood's Strangest Unsolved Case." *Los Angeles Magazine, Los Angeles Times.* Oct. 1976. Print.

1978   Zolotow, Maurice. "The Big Schlep." *Los Angeles Magazine. Los Angeles Times.* Sept. 1978. Print.

1979   Parrish, James Robert. *The Funsters.* Arlington House, New Rochelle, NY. 1979: 633-642. Print.

1979   "Aspects of Expressionism: Roland West." *Monthly Film Bulletin.* July 1979. Print.

1979   Stewart, John. "Thelma Todd: Queen of Comedy." *World of Yesterday.* Aug. 1979. Print.

1980   Stump, Al. "The Beautiful and the Dead: Hollywood's Unsolved Mysteries." *Los Angeles Herald Examiner.* Feb. 3, 1980. Print.

1980   Guiles, Fred L. *Stan: The Life of Stan Laurel.* "Stan Rebels." Stein and Day, New York. 1980. Print.

1982   Scott, Tony. "Southern California Landmarks are Rich in Showbiz History." *Daily Variety Forty-Ninth Anniversary Issue.* Oct. 26, 1982. Print.

1983   Nash, Jay Robert. *Murder Among the Mighty: Celebrity Slayings that Shocked America.* Delacorte Press, NY. 1983: 252-253. Print.

1983   Nash, Jay Robert. *Open Files: A Narrative Encyclopedia of the World's Greatest Unsolved Crimes.* McGraw Hill, NY. 1983: 118-127. Print.

1983   Young, Betty Lou. *Pacific Palisades: Where the Mountains Meet the Sea.* Pacific Palisades Historical Society. 1983. Print.

1983   Kaplan, Margaret Hall. "Actress' Death Remains a Mystery After

48 Years." *Los Angeles Times, Sunday: Westside.* Dec. 18, 1983. Print.

1984 Jacobson, Laurie. "Thelma Todd: Who Killed Hot Toddy?" *Hollywood Heartbreak: The Tragic and Mysterious Deaths of Hollywood's Most Remarkable Legends.* Simon & Schuster, NY. 1984: 93-100. Print.

1984 McKenna, Kristine. "Enquiring Into More Hollywood II." *Los Angeles Times.* Nov. 29, 1984. Print.

1985 MacQueen, Scott. "Roland West." *Between Action and Cut: Five American Directors.* Ed. Thompson, Frank T. Scarecrow Press, Metuchen, N.J. 1985. Print.

1986 Wolf, Marvin J. and Mader, Katherine. *Fallen Angels: Chronicles of Los Angeles Crime and Mystery.* Facts on File Publications, NY. 1986: 127-133. Print.

1987 Mader, Katherine & Wolf, Marvin J. "Thelma Todd's Murder: Solved!" *Los Angeles Magazine, Los Angeles Times.* Dec. 1987. Print.

1987 Munn, Michael. "Case 4: Thelma Todd: The Ice Cream Blonde." *The Hollywood Murder Casebook.* St. Martin's Press, NY. 1987: 67-78. Print.

1987 Skretvedt, Randy. *Laurel & Hardy: The Magic Behind the Movies.* Moonstone Press, Beverly Hills. 1987. Print.

1988 Cohen, Daniel. *Encyclopedia of Unsolved Crimes.* Dodd, Mead & Company, NY. 1988: 177-181. Print.

1988 Crivello, Kirk. *Fallen Angels: The Lives and Untimely Deaths of Fourteen Hollywood Beauties.* Citadel Press, Secaucus, NJ. Print

1989 Kohn, George C. "Thelma Todd: Murder, Suicide, or Mishap?" *Encyclopedia of American Scandal.* Facts on File, New York. 1987: 324-325. Print.

1989 Edmonds, Andy. *Hot Toddy: The True Story of Hollywood's Most Sensational Murder.* William Morrow & Company, New York. 1989. Print.

1989 Slatzer, Robert. *Celebrity Plus* magazine. "Hollywood Mystery Deaths: Thelma Todd — Tinseltown's Ice Cream Blonde — A Mob Victim?" Feb. 1989: 52-55. Print.

1990 "Murder & Scandal & Blood, Oh My!" *The Hollywood Reporter.* Oct. 12, 1990: 11-12. Print.

1990 Nash, Robert J. *Encyclopedia of World Crime.* Crimebooks, Inc., Wilmett, IL. 1990: 2960-2963. Print.

1991 *White Hot: The Mysterious Murder of Thelma Todd.* Dir. Paul Wendkos, Writ. Andy Edmonds, Perf. Loni Anderson, Maryedith Burrell, Robert Davi. Neufeld-Keating Productions. 1991. Television Movie, DVD.

1991 Thomas, Kevin. "Anderson Believable as 30's Start Thelma Todd." *Los Angeles Times, (TV Movie Review).* May 4, 1991. Print.

1991 Sanello, Frank. "Murder of 30's Starlet Thelma Todd No Longer a Mystery." *Chicago Tribune, TV Week.* May 5, 1991. Print.

1992	Austin, John. "The Strange and Unsolved Death of Thelma Todd." *More of Hollywood's Unsolved Mysteries.* Shapolsky Publishers, Inc. NY. 1992: 69-85. Print.

1995	Mitchell, Glenn. *The Laurel and Hardy Encyclopedia.* Batsford, London. 1995: 185, 269-270. Print.

1995 Hamann, G.D. *Thelma Todd in the 30s.* Filming Today Press, Hollywood. 1995. Print.

1996	Donati, William. *Ida Lupino: A Biography.* University Press of Kentucky, Lexington, KY. 1996: 37-42. Print.

1996	Thompson, Frank T. "Unsolved Los Angeles Mysteries: Thelma Todd." *Los Angeles Uncovered.* Wordware Publishing, Inc. Plano, TX. 1996: 64-66, 134. Print.

1997	Gordon, William A. The Ultimate Hollywood Tour Book. North Ridge Books, El Toro, CA. 1997. Print.

1997	Lynn, Kenneth S. *Charlie Chaplin and His Times.* Simon and Schuster, NY. 1997: 385. Print.

1997	Lovett, Anthony R. and Maranian, Matt. *L.A. Bizzaro: The Insider's Guide to the Obscure, the Absurd, and the Perverse in Los Angeles.* St. Martin's Press, NY. 1997: 113. Print.

1998	"The First Sex-Slay Mysteries: Did Mob 'Ice' the Ice Cream Blonde?" *National Enquirer.* March 3, 1998. Print.

2002	Wright, David G. *Joyita: Solving the Mystery.* Aukland University Press, Aukland, New Zealand. 2002. Print.

2005	Fleming, E.J. *Carole Landis: A Tragic Life in Hollywood.* McFarland & Company, Inc., Jefferson, NC. 2005. Print

INDEX

Abernathy, R. J., 89, 100, 227, 228
Agua Caliente, 196
Ainsworth, Helen, 84, 85, 96, 243, 245
alcohol, 26, 27, 32, 61, 64, 66, 69, 71, 73, 96, 99, 114, 116, 122, 127, 146, 147, 149, 155, 158, 163, 222, 223, 226, 227, 229, 237, 243, 244, 245, 246, 252, 254, 255, 256, 259
Alperson, Joe (Prince Omwah), 66
Anderson, Loni, 149
Anderson, Robert, 13, 42, 46, 54, 57, 59, 60, 174, 175, 188, 189, 190, 192, 250, 251
Andrews, Robert, 150
Anger, Kenneth, 143, 144, 148, 154, 169, 171, 172, 203, 204, 212
apartment, 36, 132, 176, 182, 183
Arbuckle, "Fatty", 115, 119, 120, 195, 219
Ardell, Sonia, 52, 239
autopsy, 15, 20, 26, 27, 48, 49, 50, 89, 90, 98, 139, 140, 141, 145, 173, 207, 219, 220, 222, 223, 224, 225, 226, 252, 254, 259
Baker, George, 22, 43, 48, 190, 233, 234
Bann, Richard, 147, 173, 174, 176
Barrymore, John, 195
Basquette, Lina, 146, 147, 151, 255
Bechtel, Gene, 21, 25
Bennet, Joan, 12
Berger, Gustave, 85, 86, 99, 100, 168
Bern, Paul, 119
Billings, Elton, 61
Blackton, Greg, 8
Blalock, Eugene (Deputy District Attorney), 54, 56, 74, 75, 87, 95
Blanchard, A. R., 67, 79, 86
blood, 2, 3, 19, 20, 23, 26, 27, 33, 44, 48, 49, 60, 86, 89, 90, 95, 99, 110, 122, 135, 142, 143, 145, 146, 219, 220, 221, 222, 223, 225, 226, 228, 248, 252, 253, 254, 255, 256, 258, 259
Bompensario, Frank "the bump", 160
Bonelli, William G., 160, 261
boudoir, 36, 37, 41, 42, 94, 183
Bowron, Fletcher, 160, 162
Brocolli, Albert, 81
Brown, Rough-house, 162
Brown, Thad, 51, 52
bruises, 19, 89, 145, 146, 219

Bruneman, Les, 160, 165
Bush, James, 150, 151
Button, A. Ronald, 57, 66, 76, 84, 92, 93, 95, 203, 204
Cafe Trocadero, 5, 16, 17, 18, 20, 26, 27, 29, 30, 31, 32, 33, 34, 42, 44, 48, 50, 53, 54, 55, 56, 61, 71, 72, 74, 76, 78, 79, 80, 81, 88, 90, 91, 95, 96, 99, 124, 132, 133, 135, 137, 138, 139, 140, 143, 144, 168, 169, 176, 177, 184, 185, 190, 203, 213, 214, 218, 226, 227, 234, 238, 242, 246, 252, 254, 255, 256, 257
Cagney, James, 123
camellia, 1, 16, 32, 33, 48, 135, 218, 226, 227
Carberry, Jack, 115, 116, 163
carbon monoxide, 3, 15, 16, 19, 20, 24, 26, 27, 32, 43, 44, 47, 48, 49, 50, 51, 57, 58, 59, 60, 61, 69, 70, 74, 89, 90, 99, 110, 135, 143, 146, 163, 170, 171, 176, 212, 216, 220, 221, 222, 223, 224, 226, 228, 229, 240, 243, 246, 249, 250, 251, 252, 253, 254, 256, 258, 259
Carmen, Jewel, 11, 35, 51, 52, 53, 58, 59, 62, 63, 65, 66, 72, 75, 84, 123, 192, 194, 195, 203, 207, 215, 227, 239, 240, 251
Carter, Earl H., 91, 175
Carter, Sara Kane, 62, 65, 175, 227, 238, 239
Castellammare, 13, 18, 50, 52, 90, 130, 131, 134, 136, 144, 172, 175, 176, 179, 180, 193, 206, 213, 258, 259
Castillo Del Mar estate, 12, 14, 52, 90, 130, 131, 144, 213, 215
Cavett, Tom, 54, 57, 60, 90, 219, 220, 256
Chandler, Harry, 31, 112, 113, 162, 264
Chandler, Raymond, 134, 135, 136, 155
Chaplin, Charlie, 56, 195, 198
Chase, Charley, 6, 10, 57
Chez Roland, 192
Chicago, Illinois, 139, 205, 209, 210, 276
Christmas, 7, 16, 23, 36, 55, 61, 63, 67, 73, 75, 80, 85, 89, 90, 92, 96, 98, 210, 211, 219, 230, 236, 239, 245
Clark, Bruce, 1, 2, 3, 15, 19, 25, 48, 50, 57, 94, 95, 137, 138, 160, 191, 218, 219, 220, 224, 225, 251
Clark, William, 15, 21, 51, 160, 167
Cohen, Micky, 209

Cohn, Harry, 158, 261
Coleman, Ronald, 150
Cooper, Gary, 9
Cooper, Grant, 162, 166, 167
Cooper, Robert, 42, 46, 47, 59, 162
Cornero, Tony, 159, 164
Corsair, 11, 35, 52, 56, 88, 192
County Board of Supervisors, 116
Cox, Frank, 161
Craig, Gavin, 165
Crawford, Charles, 114, 157, 158, 162, 163, 165
Crosby, Bing, 12, 76
Cryer, George E., 164, 165
Cummings, J. E., 63, 75, 239
D'Este, Patricia, 66, 67
Davis, Betty, 24, 56
Davis, E. P., 81
Davis, James, 159, 163, 165
Davis, Marion, 9
Dewey, Thomas E., 210, 261
DiCicco, Pasquale "Pat", 11, 12, 13, 17, 30, 44, 45, 55, 56, 72, 73, 76, 79, 80, 81, 82, 84, 86, 97, 128, 129, 148, 149, 150, 168, 169, 170, 171, 172, 181, 205, 207, 229, 242, 245, 246, 255, 257, 260, 261, 276
Dix, Richard, 9
dogs, 19, 29, 38, 41, 93, 94, 135, 159, 165, 186, 187, 189, 192
dresses, 1, 23, 32, 43, 47, 48, 57, 62, 63, 64, 93, 136, 143, 190, 218, 226, 232, 234, 238, 239
Earl, Edwin T., 91, 115, 159
Eddy, Guy, 156, 157
Edmonds, Andy, 126, 128, 131, 132, 140, 145, 146, 147, 148, 154, 205, 206, 207, 208, 209, 210, 212
Edwards, J. E., 63
Eidam, Lew, 150
Eilers, Sally, 57
Emerson, O. R. (Deputy District Attorney), 32
extortion, 27, 28, 29, 37, 61, 87, 92, 98, 132, 163, 164, 181, 205, 229, 245, 246
Faberow, Norman, 244, 261
Fairbanks, Douglas, 195
Famous Players, 7
FBI, 27, 28, 98, 163
fingerprints, 16, 91, 218
Finnegan, Patrick (Lord Lansdowne), 77, 79, 86

First National Pictures, 10, 11
Fisher, Robert E., 64, 238, 239, 262, 264
Fitts, Buron (District Attorney), 54, 68, 74, 81, 85, 86, 91, 115, 136, 167, 262
Foley, Andy, 159
Ford, James, 10, 151
Ford, Martha, 20, 21, 22, 23, 25, 26, 43, 47, 48, 50, 55, 57, 62, 63, 65, 70, 72, 75, 77, 78, 81, 87, 150, 170, 172, 190, 227, 230, 231, 232, 233, 234, 235, 236, 237, 238, 239, 241, 246, 261, 263
Frank Meline, Inc, 180
Furthmann, Charles, 10, 150
Gable, Clark, 66
Galer, Robert, 85, 96
Gallery, Don, 171, 193
gambling, 17, 54, 56, 91, 92, 93, 94, 121, 132, 154, 155, 156, 157, 158, 159, 163, 164, 165, 166, 167, 180, 195, 196, 198, 203, 204, 205, 206, 209, 210, 211, 212, 255
gangsters, 29, 110, 113, 132, 133, 148, 197, 208, 209, 229
Gans, Bob, 165
garage, 1, 2, 3, 12, 13, 14, 15, 16, 19, 20, 22, 23, 24, 25, 27, 29, 30, 31, 32, 39, 40, 43, 44, 46, 49, 51, 55, 56, 57, 58, 59, 60, 61, 69, 70, 90, 91, 94, 95, 97, 98, 114, 129, 130, 131, 132, 134, 135, 136, 137, 138, 140, 143, 144, 146, 147, 166, 169, 170, 171, 172, 173, 174, 175, 176, 177, 186, 189, 191, 193, 207, 213, 215, 216, 217, 218, 219, 222, 224, 226, 227, 229, 234, 243, 245, 246, 248, 249, 250, 251, 252, 253, 256, 257, 258, 259, 260
Gargan, Eddie, 26, 233, 234
Garrigues, Charles, 160, 262
Garvin, Anita, 10
Geisler, Jerry, 162, 195
Gompert, Frank, 91, 136, 138, 172
Gordon, Alex, 171, 177, 192
Graham, Virginia, 123
Granger, Dorothy, 6, 10
Grauman Sid, 16, 18, 32, 38, 57, 61, 71, 72, 99, 170, 254, 255
Grier, John, 63
Griffith, Corrine, 195
Griffith, D. W., 195
Grimes, Callie, 161, 162
Gruidl, Wanda, 96

Hall of Justice, 15, 31, 32, 67, 72, 74, 79, 81, 222
Hall, Al, 10
Hall-Mills murder, 111
Hammond, Anita, 18, 76
Hancock, Peter, 26, 233, 234
Hanlon, Robert, 192
Hardy, Oliver, 6, 10, 56, 57
Harlow, Jean, 10, 66
Harmsworth, Alfred, 110
Hays board, 119, 120
Hearst, William Randolph, 25, 69, 110, 113, 123, 140, 141
Hellman, Marco, 165
Hendry, W. P., 31, 122
Hickman, William, 68, 160
Hill, Virginia, 17
Hollywood Baptist Church, 11, 56
Holzman, Harry, 87, 98
Hopper, Hedda, 123
Horden, Nicholas, 126, 127, 128, 131, 169, 170, 171, 172, 203, 204
Hot Springs, Arkansas, 209, 211
Hounie, Alex, 61, 90
Howatt, Douglas, 91
Hunter, Catherine, 76, 79, 92, 96
Hupmobile, 2, 42, 97, 189, 217, 252, 256, 257
Ince, Thomas, 119
Jacobsen, Carl, 161, 162, 163, 264
Jacoby, Norman "Jake", 114, 167
jewelry, 2, 3, 32, 37, 44, 45, 64, 83, 122, 127, 128, 129, 207, 218, 231, 258, 260
Johnson, George (Deputy District Attorney), 32, 33, 41, 42, 43, 44, 45, 54, 57, 63, 67, 73, 74, 75, 79, 87, 89, 95, 219
Jornier, Georges, 96
Joyas, 93, 206, 214
Karr, Horace, 157, 163
Kauffman, Lazar, 150
Keating, Fred, 17
Keaton, Buster, 195
Kelly, Patsy, 1, 6, 10, 12, 21, 56, 57, 78, 97, 128, 207, 232, 242
Kennedy, Edgar, 10
Kennedy, John F., 133, 205
Keyes, Asa, 111, 165
King, Dennis, 150
Kynette, Earl E., 159

Lane, Lola, 130, 192, 194, 195, 213, 214
Langdon Harry, 10
Larson, Arnold, 109, 114, 115, 262
Lasky, Jesse, 7, 262
Laurel and Hardy, 1, 10, 11, 264
Laurel, Ruth, 147
Laurel, Stan, 1, 6, 10, 11, 21, 26, 47, 56, 57, 147, 233, 264
Lavine, Morris, 114
Lawrence, Massachusetts, 6, 7, 9, 10, 129, 150, 151, 174, 206, 276
Lebedeff, Ivan, 10, 57, 150
Lindsay, Margaret, 30, 55, 56, 72, 80, 81
Los Angeles, 1, 2, 4, 11, 12, 15, 16, 17, 19, 21, 22, 25, 26, 28, 31, 48, 50, 54, 55, 56, 57, 60, 61, 65, 69, 72, 79, 80, 86, 93, 97, 98, 109, 111, 112, 113, 114, 115, 118, 119, 121, 124, 126, 139, 145, 153, 154, 155, 159, 160, 161, 162, 165, 166, 170, 171, 174, 203, 205, 207, 208, 209, 210, 211, 212, 213, 222, 237, 240, 262, 263, 264, 265, 276
Los Angeles Athletic Club, 180
Los Angeles City Hall, 31, 158
Los Angeles Mountain Park Company, 180
Los Angeles Police Department, 2, 3, 4, 12, 13, 15, 16, 19, 20, 22, 23, 25, 26, 29, 30, 31, 34, 44, 46, 47, 48, 50, 51, 52, 54, 55, 57, 58, 59, 60, 61, 62, 63, 65, 66, 73, 75, 77, 78, 83, 84, 89, 90, 91, 93, 94, 95, 97, 109, 110, 113, 114, 115, 116, 117, 122, 126, 127, 128, 132, 133, 134, 135, 137, 138, 139, 140, 141, 145, 154, 155, 156, 157, 158, 159, 160, 161, 162, 163, 165, 167, 168, 170, 172, 174, 176, 177, 180, 185, 186, 187, 191, 206, 207, 209, 210, 211, 216, 220, 227, 229, 231, 235, 238, 239, 241, 243, 248, 249, 250, 251, 252, 256, 260
Los Angeles Police Department Ang: Vice Squad, 156, 159
Lowell Normal School, 9
Lucas, Dick, 160, 162
Luciano, Charles "Lucky", 145, 154, 164, 203, 204, 205, 206, 207, 208, 209, 210, 211, 212, 262, 264
Luden, Jack, 57
Lupino, Constance, 80
Lupino, Ida, 16, 17, 32, 57, 74, 75, 76, 78, 79, 80, 82, 96, 242, 243, 255

Lupino, Stanley, 16, 17, 18, 30, 32, 57, 61, 74, 75, 76, 79, 80, 81, 82, 90, 96, 124, 141, 177, 242, 243, 245, 255
Luttermoser, Erwin, 196, 197
Lyman, Abe, 27, 28, 150
MacFadden, Bernarr, 110
MacQueen, Scott, 169, 170, 171, 173, 177, 197
Mader, Kathleen, 169, 170, 171, 172, 173, 174, 175, 177
Madonna, 149, 150
Mahoney, Vincent, 22, 23, 50, 193
Malibu walk, 34, 181
Mannix, Eddie, 56, 57
Marco, Albert, 159, 162, 163, 165
Martin, Dr. Harry, 192
Marx brothers, 1, 11, 57, 263
Mayer, Louis B., 166
McAfee, Guy, 164, 165, 166
McCormick, Robert, 110
McLean, Evalyn Walsh, 192
McPherson, Aimee Semple, 111, 114
Menninger, Karl, 247
Mesa Unit Castellammare, 180
Mesa Unit Trust, 180
Miami, Florida, 209, 210, 211
Mocambo, 5
Monroe, Marilyn, 119, 133, 149, 150, 205
Monroe, Russel, 15, 48
Morris, Chester, 11, 114, 171, 177, 192
Mother Grey, 53, 66
Muni, Paul, 56
Munn, Michael, 203, 204
Mystery man, 52, 53, 55, 63, 75, 79, 239
Nance, Frank (Coroner), 20, 26, 27, 32, 33, 35, 36, 37, 38, 39, 40, 41, 46, 48, 55, 184, 219, 220, 223, 228, 235, 236
Nash, Jay Robert, 126, 145, 146, 147
Nealis, Eddie, 160
Neutzel, Charles, 126, 147
New York, 7, 8, 9, 11, 28, 55, 73, 76, 79, 80, 81, 82, 87, 92, 97, 110, 111, 113, 150, 151, 195, 204, 205, 209, 210, 211, 255, 261, 262, 263, 264, 265, 276
Norvell, Mahlon, 65, 66, 110
O'Hare, Mary, 164
Ogden, Utah, 126, 127, 129, 152
Orsatti, Vic, 56, 164, 166
Otis, Harrison Gray, 112, 113
Page, "Farmer", 165, 166

Paramount Pictures, 7, 8, 9, 10, 13, 73, 151, 254
Parker, Austen, 150
Parrot, Kent Kane, 57, 158, 161, 164, 165, 166, 264
Parsons, Louella, 11, 52, 84, 123, 192
Patterson, Joseph, 110
Paulist Fathers, 213
peas and beans, 27, 90, 139, 140, 141, 152, 178, 207, 226, 227, 229, 248, 255
Persson, W. F., 26, 62, 63, 64, 75, 227, 238, 239
Peters, Claude, 76
Peters, Ernest, 16, 17, 18, 29, 33, 34, 36, 37, 39, 40, 56, 71, 72, 73, 91, 99, 132, 133, 135, 170, 185, 218, 227, 254, 257
Pickford, Mary, 195
Pidgeon, Walter, 9
Pinker, Ray, 57, 58, 89, 90, 91, 110, 138, 220, 249, 250, 251
Pitts, ZaSu, 1, 6, 10, 57, 75, 76, 85, 96, 143, 144, 151, 171, 193, 242
poison, 24, 27, 49, 70, 89, 220, 224, 227, 228, 246, 251, 258, 259
Post, Wiley, 12, 68
Powell, William, 9
Priester, Harvey, 10, 13, 17, 32, 44, 50, 56, 57, 78, 87, 88, 129, 150, 242, 255
Prince, Arthur, 18, 95, 96
psychiatrist, 85, 95
Raft, George, 17
Rappe, Virginia, 115, 119
Raymond, Harry, 160, 162, 163, 166, 264
Redondo Beach, 160
reporters, 3, 12, 15, 17, 19, 20, 22, 25, 27, 29, 46, 47, 52, 53, 54, 55, 58, 65, 71, 72, 74, 75, 77, 79, 80, 81, 82, 83, 84, 86, 87, 88, 90, 92, 94, 97, 98, 99, 109, 110, 111, 113, 114, 115, 116, 117, 120, 131, 133, 134, 138, 141, 154, 157, 163, 164, 166, 169, 176, 182, 186, 198, 204, 208, 216, 228, 231, 232, 233, 239, 242, 250, 252, 256, 257
Roach, Hal, 5, 6, 10, 11, 22, 39, 57, 85, 97, 125, 147, 152, 170, 171, 172, 173, 174, 175, 176, 177, 178, 203, 204, 206, 213, 233, 245
Robert Goldie (Goldberg), 92
Rochester, George, 30, 54, 55, 57, 64, 67, 73, 74, 75, 76, 77, 79, 80, 81, 86, 87, 88, 89,

90, 91, 92, 93, 94, 95, 99, 100, 109, 134, 136, 139, 140, 141, 227, 228, 229, 238, 239, 252
Rogers, Will, 12
Romero, Eddie, 21, 25, 51, 54, 131
Roosevelt Highway, 3, 34, 88, 130, 180, 187, 206, 257
Rose, A. Brigham, 165, 166
Rose, Gertrude, 91, 137
Roselli, A. S., 2, 3, 159, 209
Roselli, Johnny, 158
Rowland, Richard A., 10
Rowland, William, 18, 255
Sampson, Dr. Phil, 13, 15, 89, 207, 219, 220
San Diego, 85, 99
San Francisco, 75, 76, 78, 79, 92, 96, 119, 140, 229, 230, 276
San Juan, Arthur, 63, 239
Santa Anita, 75
Santa Barbara, 213
sardonyx ring, 128
Sauer, Florian "Jack", 13, 193, 195, 219, 255, 259
Schafer, Alberta, 2
Schafer, Rudolph, 2, 13, 43, 44, 54, 57, 68, 85, 87, 94, 146, 147, 185, 187, 191, 193, 215, 219, 220
Schenck, Joseph, 17, 19, 35, 39, 43, 57, 122, 125, 164, 166, 192, 195, 196, 197, 264
Schiffert, Edward, 28
Schimanski, Harry, 28, 98
Schneiderman, Edwin, 244, 246
Seattle, 157
Sebastian, Charles, 115, 157
Shannon, Eileen (Queenie), 194, 195
Shaw, Frank, 159, 163, 264
Shaw, Joe, 158, 162
shoes, 13, 32, 57, 64, 91, 130, 135, 136, 137, 138, 139, 140, 141, 144, 152, 178, 207, 238, 248
Shuler, Robert "Fighting Bob", 154, 161, 162, 163, 165, 264
Shultz, Dutch, 208, 210
Siegel, Benjamin, 159, 164, 209, 211
Skolsky, Sidney, 92, 123
Skouras, Spyros, Charles and George, 38, 42, 43, 246
Smith, Charles, 2, 13, 46, 54, 57, 58, 59, 73, 172, 174, 215, 251, 259

St. Johns, Adela Roberts, 116
Steed, Blaine, 26, 51, 52, 69
steps, 130, 136, 152
Stewart, Robert P., 77
Stokes, Warren, 26, 233, 234
Strickling, Howard, 122
Stump, Al, 129, 203, 204
suicide, 3, 23, 25, 29, 44, 74, 95, 96, 97, 126, 136, 143, 150, 153, 154, 184, 191, 229, 242, 243, 244, 245, 246, 247, 248, 252, 260
Swan, Merle, 66
Swanson, Gloria, 195
Sweetnam, Sidney, 159
tabloids, 110, 111, 113, 124, 142, 146, 147, 148, 150, 151, 152, 163, 210, 260
Talmadge, Norma, 19, 35, 195
Taylor, Joe, 25, 26, 54, 119, 131, 160, 231
Taylor, William Desmond, 68
Temporary Tooth, 15, 23, 24, 67, 145, 173, 219, 221
The Combination, 31, 53, 54, 111, 114, 120, 147, 149, 154, 155, 156, 157, 158, 160, 163, 197, 205, 209, 211
Thelma Todd's Sidewalk Cafe, 2, 3, 12, 13, 16, 17, 18, 23, 24, 27, 28, 29, 33, 34, 35, 36, 38, 39, 40, 42, 43, 46, 48, 53, 54, 55, 61, 68, 69, 74, 84, 85, 86, 87, 88, 91, 92, 93, 94, 95, 96, 98, 130, 131, 132, 133, 136, 140, 143, 144, 146, 149, 154, 166, 168, 171, 172, 174, 176, 177, 179, 181, 182, 183, 184, 187, 188, 189, 190, 192, 193, 194, 195, 196, 197, 203, 204, 205, 206, 207, 211, 212, 213, 214, 215, 217, 229, 233, 234, 245, 246, 248, 250, 252, 257, 258, 259, 260
Thomas, Bob, 153
Todd, Alice, 1, 7, 13, 16, 18, 25, 28, 32, 33, 75, 84, 87, 88, 95, 97, 98, 99, 132, 148, 173, 174, 185, 229, 261, 276
Todd, John, 7, 148, 206
Todd, William (brother), 206
Todd's apartment, 3, 6, 9, 14, 16, 17, 18, 19, 22, 25, 26, 28, 29, 31, 33, 34, 36, 37, 38, 39, 41, 42, 43, 46, 51, 53, 57, 58, 59, 60, 73, 76, 77, 84, 88, 91, 94, 137, 143, 144, 161, 168, 169, 170, 172, 174, 176, 177, 178, 179, 181, 182, 183, 184, 185, 186, 187, 190, 191, 213, 214, 215, 217, 232, 246, 248, 251, 252, 254, 257, 259

Todd's automobile, 1, 2, 3, 5, 6, 8, 9, 12, 13, 15, 16, 19, 20, 22, 23, 24, 25, 26, 27, 30, 32, 33, 34, 36, 39, 40, 42, 44, 46, 47, 51, 52, 53, 56, 57, 58, 59, 60, 61, 62, 63, 65, 70, 89, 90, 91, 94, 96, 97, 98, 110, 114, 133, 134, 137, 143, 144, 145, 146, 162, 166, 169, 171, 172, 174, 175, 176, 186, 188, 189, 190, 191, 192, 193, 203, 207, 213, 215, 217, 218, 219, 220, 221, 223, 224, 227, 229, 239, 240, 243, 246, 248, 249, 250, 251, 252, 253, 254, 256, 257, 258, 259

Todd's heart condition, 9, 15, 20, 27, 51, 98, 147, 220, 223, 225, 244, 253

Tramonto Drive, 12, 181

Trinity Methodist Church, 161

Utley, James, 159

Valentino, Rudolph, 111

Vanderbilt, Cornelius, 111

Vanderbilt, Gloria, 12, 265

Vendome, 5, 30, 61, 81, 124

Wagner, A. F., 15, 16, 20, 27, 48, 49, 50, 51, 55, 59, 60, 89, 90, 98, 99, 140, 141, 145, 160, 173, 219, 220, 221, 222, 223, 224, 225, 227, 229, 249, 252, 255

Wallis, Captain Hubert J., 3, 4, 16, 23, 25, 28, 29, 31, 60, 66, 73, 94, 102, 160, 161, 162, 163, 185, 186, 220, 251

Wertheimer, Al, 164

Wertheimer, Lew, 166

West, Mae, 66

West, Roland, 2, 3, 11, 12, 13, 14, 15, 16, 18, 19, 22, 29, 31, 34, 35, 36, 37, 38, 39, 40, 41, 42, 43, 44, 45, 46, 52, 54, 56, 57, 58, 59, 61, 66, 68, 71, 72, 73, 76, 77, 78, 81, 82, 83, 84, 85, 86, 87, 88, 89, 91, 92, 93, 94, 95, 97, 98, 99, 123, 124, 125, 130, 132, 137, 143, 144, 148, 149, 150, 164, 166, 168, 169, 170, 171, 172, 173, 174, 175, 176, 177, 178, 179, 180, 181, 182, 183, 184, 185, 186, 187, 188, 189, 190, 191, 192, 193, 194, 195, 196, 197, 198, 203, 206, 207, 212, 213, 214, 215, 216, 217, 219, 227, 229, 230, 233, 234, 239, 242, 245, 246, 248, 253, 254, 255, 256, 257, 258, 259, 260, 263

Whitcomb, E. R., 76

White Spot, 166

Whitehead, Joe, 57, 58, 250, 251

Whitehead, Mae, 1, 2, 3, 13, 16, 19, 20, 23, 25, 26, 32, 33, 36, 37, 41, 54, 55, 57, 58, 60, 65, 73, 129, 131, 132, 135, 138, 144, 173, 174, 175, 182, 185, 191, 207, 215, 216, 217, 218, 219, 220, 224, 225, 226, 233, 235, 236, 237, 242, 258, 260

Wilkerson, Billy, 17, 96, 124, 265

Williams, Rusty, 159, 162

Winchell, Walter, 123

Windsor, Claire, 32

Winn, Jess, 54, 67, 85, 89, 92

Winters, Shelly, 192

Wolf, Marvin, 170, 171, 172, 173, 174, 175, 177, 262

Wollcott, Harold, 64

Woodall, J. L., 75

Woodman, Frederick, 157

Wynn, Ed, 9

Yacht Joyita, 11

Yarrow, Lloyd, 54, 67, 85, 89, 92

York, Charles Duke, 76, 77, 79, 86, 230, 265

Zwillman, Longy, 209

NOTES

Key to major sources:

CT	Chicago Tribune
CIT	Coroner's Inquest Testimony on Death of Thelma Alice DiCicco
HCN	Hollywood Citizen-News
IDN	Los Angeles Illustrated Daily News
LAT	Los Angeles Times
LAE	Los Angeles Examiner
LAR	Los Angeles Record
LA H&E	Los Angeles Herald and Express
LET	Lawrence Evening Tribune
NYT	New York Times
NYDN	New York Daily News
SMEO	Santa Monica Evening Outlook
SFC	San Francisco Chronicle

ONE: MONDAY MORNING

1. *LA H&E*, 12/21/35.
2. Description developed from various photographs Todd's body and of Wallis with Todd's body, printed in *SMEO*, 12/17/35; *LAT*, 12/17/35; *LA H&E*, 1/4/36; *LAE*, 1/4/36; *CIT*, 110.
3. Coroner's Register (effects of decedent Thelma Todd); *CIT*, 105-106.
4. The description of the garage is taken from various photographs published in the papers at the time of Thelma's death, from photographs in the LA County Coroner's file, and from the inquest testimony of Anderson (*CIT*, 90) and Whitehead. See *LAE*, 12/23/35 and 1/4/36, particularly.
5. The estate comprises lots 7, 8, 13, and 14 of block 14 of the Castellammare tract. West purchased lots 7 and 14 in 1926, on which he built Castillo Del Mar. In late 1928, he purchased lot 8 and probably lot 14–the latter was in his name by 1931, at any rate. The two additional lots, to the east of the estate, have never been developed. West purchased the café building in 1935 from his landlord, the Residential Land Corp. It is now owned by the Paulist Fathers, who received it as a bequest from Lola Lane, West's widow. [Los Angeles County Assessment Records, Books 270, 921, and 4416; West Collection, American Academy of Motion Picture Arts and Sciences, check stub of 11/14/28].
6. *IDN*, 12/19/35, *CIT*, 75; from the 1930s map, Posetano seems always to have dead-ended up the hill just south of the garage. To reach Revello, Mae had to head north on Posetano and connect with Revello just before it dead-ends into Castellammare. If, when heading up to the garage, Mae took her wrong turn at Breve Way and Castellammare (probably the easiest place to miss the turn), she and Roland probably approached the garage along Posetano (rather than up from Stretto).
7. *CIT*, 75.
8. The ignition button was separate from the ignition key lock.
9. *CIT*, 78 West testified he later found the "very valuable robe" in Thelma's apartment.
10. *CIT*, 76 and 110 West notes the dust while he describes himself looking at the gas gauge, an action he performed prior to Clark's arrival. He does not verbalize Clark's conclusion about the significance of the dust.
11. Clark does not specifically address the issue of how the blood came to be on Thelma's face. Wagner first suggests wounds resulting from the head falling onto the steering wheel in his preliminary autopsy report Monday at 7:00 p.m. [*IDN*, 12/17, *SFC*, 12/17], but it is likely that the police must have first concluded this and suggested it to Wagner.
12. *CIT*, 107.
13. Interview with Coy Watson, 2002.
14. "All murders are immediately reported to the Central Homicide Squad." (*The Guardian*, 1939) Interview with A. T. Nelson; *CIT*, 107 Clark would have called them before, but the switchboard operator at the West Los Angeles Division, where he was chief detective, had not told him why he was needed at the Sidewalk Café when Schafer had phoned from the private office of a print shop in Santa Monica and asked for a detective. *CIT*, 102.
15. Interview with Florian Sauer; *LA H&E*, 12/17/35.
16. Underwood, Agnes. *Newspaper Woman*, New York: 1949. Harper and Bros. 108-110.
17. *LA H&E*, 5/14/59. Wallis was born in Marden, Wiltshire and joined the LAPD in 1914 at the age of 35. He had served with the London police for six years.

TWO: QUEEN OF THE LOT

1. While many specific facts about Thelma's life are sourced below, much of the material in this chapter is derived from a series of articles written in the *Lawrence Evening Tribune* shortly after her death.
2. *Washington Post* 12/22/35.
3. *SFC* 12/17/35.
4. Quoted in Skretvedt, Randy. *Laurel and Hardy: The Magic Behind the Movies*. Moonstone

5. *LA H&E*, 12/17/35; *LAE*, 12/22/35.
6. Dorothy Lubon, "Movie Men are so Crude," *Motion Picture*, June, 1929.
7. *LET*, 12/17/35.
8. Ireland Civil Registration, Births Index, FHL # 255825
9. *Lawrence, Mass. City Directory 1901, 1902,1904,1905*
10. *Lowell Sun*, June 22, 1900
11. *LET*, 7/30/26, 8/2/26, 12/17/35.
12. Interview with William Todd, July, 1985; *LAE*, 12/17/35.
13. In early 1925, she was selected as the Lawrence Winter Carnival Snow Queen, and on June 1 of the same year won the Elks Club's "Miss Lawrence" contest. Two weeks later in Swampscott she was crowned "Miss Massachusetts". Interview with William Todd; *LET*, 6/16/25. There is some evidence she acted in two locally produced films, *The Life of St. Genevieve* and *Tangled Hearts*.
14. *LET*, 6/2/25, 6/16/25, 12/17/35.
15. Lasky, Jesse L., with Don Weldon. *I Blow My Own Horn*. Garden City, NY: Doubleday & Company, 1957. 193-4.
16. "*Fascinating Youth*, Screen Scrapbook".
17. Dorothy Lubon, "Movie Men Are So Crude," *Motion Picture*, June, 1929 37:78.
18. Thelma Todd, "How I Was Groomed for Stardom", *Film Weekly*, June 30, 1933
19. Except as otherwise noted, Jesse Lasky is the source for the account of the school and the film product in the following paragraphs.
20. *LET*, 5/3/26, 12/17/35.
21. "*Fascinating Youth*, Screen Scrapbook".
22. *LET*, 5/17/26, 5/18/26, 5/19/26. *Boston Globe*, 5/6/26
23. *LET*, 5/18/26.
24. *LET*, 5/18/26.
25. A dispute with the school's steering committee revealed her high standing among her fellow students. At issue was a new system governing teaching appointments in the local elementary schools. Thelma emerged as the leader of the students, who protested that since they entered the Normal school under the old rules, they should be exempted from the provisions of the new. After she appeared before the committee to argue the students' view, the committee members praised her skill in advocating her position, though their minds were not changed. Undoubtedly, her appearance played its part in impressing the committee members: it was the wisdom of the times that beauty rarely accompanied intelligence as it did in Thelma's case. The unusual combination of the two in Thelma would become a mainstay of press coverage of her career. Recalling the incident at the time of Thelma's death, the *LET*, observed "Thelma gave evidence of that supposedly rare combination of beauty and brains that was ultimately to carry her to the heights." [*LET*, 12/17/35]
26. *Dorothy Lubon.*
27. Interview with Lina Basquette, 1984.
28. *LAT*, 2/24/28; *LAE*, 2/20/28.
29. Llewellyn Carrol, "What Hollywood Did to a New England Schoolmarm." *Photoplay*. Feb. 1932: 54-55, 115.
30. The introduction of sound complicated film making in the late twenties. Many of the films of the period were shot in both silent and talkie versions, including all features Thelma worked on in 1929.
31. *LET*, 12/17/35.
32. *Dorothy Lubon.*
33. *LAT*, 8/27/28, 9/18/28.
34. *Llewellyn Carrol*, 115; interview with William Todd.

35. Grace Kingsley, "Thelma Todd Signs Two", *LAT*, 4/25/29.
36. In April, 1927, she recorded "Let Me Call You Sweetheart," If I Had You," and "Honey" for Victor. http://victor.library.ucsb.edu/index.php
37. Maltin, Leonard. "The Great Movie Shorts," in *The Series*, 85.
38. Parsons, Louella. *LA H&E*, 12/17/35.
39. Llewellyn Carroll, "What Hollywood Did to a New England Schoolmarm," *Photoplay*, February, 1932.
40. *LAE*, 12/18/35.
41. Items in the West Collection at the Academy of Motion Picture Arts and Sciences Library suggest West and Jewel Carmen may have separated in early 1932. West's secretary, Helen Hallet, wrote to Jewel on Jan. 30, 1932, asking her to pay for toll calls made earlier that month and to forward any mail for West, who, the letter implied, was out of town. On February 7, 1932, Hallet again wrote to Jewel, alluding to Jewel's request to the *LA Examiner* previously delivered to the house on Revello. On April 29, West requested discontinuance of service of his telephone at Castillo Del Mar, and for several months Hallet wrangled with the phone company about non-payment of a bill, pleading she had not been able to get the present occupants of the house to pay for their charges. On June 15, 1932, West requested the post office to send all mail addressed to him at Castillo Del Mar to the United Artists Studios on Formosa in Hollywood.

    During some of the winter and spring of 1932, West was in Coronado with the *Joyita*, which was undergoing repairs between 2/16 and 4/17. It is conceivable West had simply gone to San Diego with the yacht while Jewel stayed behind awaiting summer and better weather before she joined him on a voyage. The West Collection material grows sparse as 1932 advances and ends entirely in early 1933.
42. Interview with Lina Basquette; LET, 12/28/35.
43. The title "Broccoli King" may have had more sinister implications in 1935. Food racketeering had long been a staple of New York's Italian mobsters, and DiCicco's father's title suggests he may have been involved in this underworld enterprise. Less than one week following Todd's death, in fact, after a pair of buglers had trumpeted his arrival in what UPI called "medieval pageantry," the pugnacious mayor of New York City, Fiorello La Guardia, climbed on the back of a truck to proclaim to a crowd of 300 produce dealers in the Bronx city market that the "sale, display and possession" of artichokes, would be prohibited in the city after Christmas. La Guardia had singled out the "Artichoke King," Cirro Terranova, who controlled artichoke wholesaling in the city, as the initial target in his war against food racketeering. Terranova forced artichoke growers to sell their crop to Terranova's company, and retailers, intimidated through violence, "either bought artichokes from [Terranova] or they didn't have artichokes for sale."

    Despite the sinister connotations of his appellation, the elder DiCicco, who died in 1924 [*NYT*, 12/12/41], may have been nothing more than a Long Island farmer who made it big. He came to the United States in 1886 and established a "large scale truck farm in Queens. See Gloria Vanderbilt, *Black Knight, White Knight*, Knopf, New York. 1987 112.
44. Interview with William Todd.
45. *LAE*, 4/28/33.
46. *IDN*, 1/1/36.
47. *LAE*, 2/24/34, 12/17/35.
48. *LA H&E*, 12/19/35.
49. *LET*, 12/28/35.
50. Interview with William Todd.
51. *Gloria Vanderbilt*, 142-5. Vanderbilt also reports that a friend of her mothers, who claimed to have been a close friend of Thelma Todd, declared that "everybody knew he was the one who killed Thelma." 38-39.
52. *LAE*, 9/6/34; according to West; *LET*, 12/28/35 (TT wanted to patch it up).
53. Interview with William Todd. Todd stated that Thelma realized she was getting older and would

54. eventually age out of demand in Hollywood.
55. Pat DiCicco claimed that he first heard of Thelma's death while he was at Paramount studios. He must have heard fairly early in the afternoon, as, according to Phil Sauer, he reached the garage before Wallis did.
56. The descriptions of these scenes are based on news photos taken at the garage in the early afternoon of December 16, 1935. See for example, *LAE*, 12/16/35; *LA H&E*, 12/16/35; and the *LAT*, 12/16/35. Additional photos upon which this reconstruction is based can be found at the Los Angeles Public Library in the *LA Herald and Express* Collection and in the Bettmann Archive.
57. Interview with Florian Sauer, 11/30/84.
58. *CIT*, 5.
59. *LAE*, 12/18/35.
60. A photo taken at the scene shows him so attired and disposed. Bettmann Archive.
61. Photo, *LAE*, 12/17/35.
62. Photos, Bettmann Archive.

THREE: MONDAY AFTERNOON

1. Interview with William Clark, July 10, 1986.
2. While most the details described in this chapter were reported in the newspapers on Monday, December 16 and Tuesday, December 17, 1935, some were taken from later testimony or recollections by the investigators and witnesses, especially at the Coroner's Inquest of December 18, 1935.
3. *CIT*, 116.
4. *LAE*, 12/29. Sampson probably based this surmise on West's statement that Thelma had a weak heart and medical knowledge that cardiac arrhythmia is associated with carbon monoxide poisoning.
5. *LAE*, 12/17/35.
6. *LAE*, 12/17/35.
7. *CIT*, 107.
8. During 1935, Thelma lost a front tooth—the upper left lateral incisor, to be precise. This is a very public tooth, especially for an actress, and Thelma was wearing a temporary bridge—a false tooth. She had been to the dentist on the previous Saturday.

   A bill from Dr. Ralph J. Arnold, Todd's dentist, in the Probate records does not give specific dates of service, but describes services rendered from "1934 to Dec. 14 1935," so the tooth may actually have been removed in 1934.

   LA Times [12/17/35] describes the tooth as a gold inlay; *LA Herald and Express* [12/17/35] describes it as a "gold cap."

   Thelma's Saturday dentist visit is confirmed by Whitehead's Inquest testimony as well as Arnold's bill and other sources. But, contrary to press reports—e.g., *LA Times* [12/18/35], which says "a temporary front tooth placed by her dentist last Saturday had been loosened"—the bridge does not seem to have been installed on this visit. According to the bill, Dr. Arnold surgically removed the real tooth, installed a temporary bridge and made "occasional adjustments" to it. This implies that the bridge, installed "for a period of bone regeneration," had been in place for a while, maybe since the summer, maybe even earlier.

   The December 14 appointment may have been made for another "occasional adjustment" or, since construction of a permanent bridge is among the last services listed on the bill, perhaps Dr. Arnold fit the permanent tooth. This would explain the Times description of it as a "gold inlay"—which sounds like a permanent false tooth.

   In reporting this discovery, *Illustrated Daily New* [12/17/35] places the dislodged item in Thelma's mouth and describes it as a "temporary shell" and "temporary cap." On 12/17, the *LA Examiner* calls it an actual tooth "which Miss Todd has had filled Saturday," but by 12/29, it became a "false tooth" that was found in Thelma's throat.

Though Wagner does not mention the tooth in his Inquest testimony, Nance does confirm the dislodging of it while disclosing autopsy results to the press. *LAT*, 12/18/35.

In *Stan*, it was claimed that Thelma referred to her false tooth as her "peg tooth"; this implies that she may have had the artificial tooth, or a series of artificial teeth, for some time

9. *CIT*, 120.
10. *CIT*, 116.
11. *HCN*, 12/27/35.
12. Underwood, Agnes. *Newspaperwoman*, 112-113.
13. *IDN*, 12/17/35.
14. *SMEO*, 12/17/35, *LAT*, 12/18/35; *LET*, 12/18/35, *LA H&E*, 12/17/35.
15. *CIT*, 108.
16. *CIT*, 108.
17. Probate records of Todd's estate
18. *LAT*, 12/20/35; *LAE*, 12/31/36.
19. *Out With the Stars*, Jim Heimann, 100-106.
20. *IDN*, 12/17/35.
21. *LA Evening Post Record* 12/17/35.
22. *LAE*, 12/24. *LAE*, 12/25/35 reports Grauman's statement that Todd left about 3:00.
23. *IDN*, 12/18/35; *LAE*, 12/18/35.
24. *SMEO*, 12/17/35; *LAT*, 12/17/35; *LA H&E*, 12/17/35.
25. *LAE*, 12/17/35. He told the Coroner's Inquest Jury that she was "quite sober." (47).
26. *IDN*, 12/17/35.
27. *IDN*, 12/17/35, quoting West.
28. *CIT*, 61.
29. Interview with Norman "Jake" Jacoby.
30. *NYDN*, 12/17/35 (late edition).
31. Serial #05964, contained in File # 6510, Los Angeles County Department of The Chief Medical Examiner-Coroner.

The following is an approximation of the document:

    Form R-144   Serial No. 05964
    Los Angeles Police Department
Suicide (strike over)
Homicide
Dead Body found   Division: West

Filed: Captain Bruce Clark
4:45 p.m. December 16, 1935   Found: Dec. 16, 1935 10:30 AM

On Scene: Capt. Wallace, Detectives W.J. Clark, Eddie Romero answered call with Captain Bruce Clark

Body found in garage at 17531 Posetano Road. Deceased identified as Thelma Todd.

Small amount of blood from mouth and nose. No other visible bruises.

The body was sent to the County Morgue where an autopsy showed deceased died of Carbon Monoxide Poison.

Witnesses: Roland West Mae Whitehead

32. *NYT*, 12/17/35.
33. *IDN*, 12/17/35.
34. *IDN*, 12/17/35. The idea makes no sense, really, as carbon monoxide kills people through bonding with oxygen in the blood, not through replacing oxygen in the air. A motor would not die as long as there was oxygen in the air. Wagner may have been thinking that, in an air-tight atmosphere, the oxygen would have depleted as a result of the motor running over a period of time. In any case, carbon monoxide is not capable of killing an engine unless it somehow replaces all the available oxygen in the air.
35. *NYT* and *LAT*, 12/17/35.
36. *NYT*, 12/17/35; *HCN*, 12/26/35.
37. *NYT*, 12/17/35.

FOUR: TUESDAY

1. *LA H&E*, 12/17/35
2. *LAE*, 12/17/35.
3. *LA H&E*, 12/17/35; *EPR* 12/17/35.
4. *LAE*, 12/17/35, *HCN*, 12/17/35, *NYT* 12/17/35; *LA H&E*, 12/17/35 reported Ford having numbered the guests at 471.
5. *EPR*, *LAE* and *LAT*, 12/18/35; *CIT*, 95.
6. *LAE*, 12/18/35.
7. *The Guardian*, 287.
8. *IDN*, 12/17/35.
9. *IDN*, 12/17/35.
10. *IDN*, 12/17/35.
11. *LAE*, 12/17/35.
12. *LA H&E*, 12/17/35.
13. *IDN*, 12/18/35.
14. *LAE*, 12/18/35.
15. *HCN*, 12/17/35; *NYT* 12/17/35; Ford was said to be "positive, beyond all question" that she talked with Thelma; *LAE* [12/17/35] quotes her similarly as "positive beyond all doubt."
16. *LAT*, 12/18/35. *LAE* [12/18/35] quotes Ford.
17. *LAE*, 12/18/35.
18. *LAE*, 12/18/35. The caller's use of the phrase *hot toddy* is also reported by *LA Times* [12/18/35] and by *LA Examiner* [12/18/35]. *LA Times* [12/18/35] adds Ford describing the nickname as one Thelma liked; the other *LA Examiner* story states that she described it as "a nickname no one but Thelma ever used."
19. *LAE*, 12/18/35.
20. *LAE*, 12/18/35.
21. *EPR*, *LAT*, *LAE*, 12/18/35; *LA H&E*, 12/17/35.
22. *NYT*, 12/17/35.
23. *LAT*, 12/18/35; *IDN*, 12/18/35.
24. *LAT*, 12/18/35.
25. *LA H&E*, 12/17/35.
26. *IDN*, 12/17/35.
27. *LAE*, 12/17/35.
28. *SFC* 12/18/35; *LA Times* 12/18/35.
29. *LAT*, 12/18/35.
30. *LAT*, 12/17/35.
31. *HCN*, 12/18/35.
32. *LAE*, 12/18/35.

33. *HCN*, 12/18/35.
34. *LAE*, 3/7/35.
35. FBI file #9-675, Thelma Alice Todd DiCicco, Letter from R. Whitley, Special Agent in Charge, New York City, to Director, FBI, May 14, 1935.
36. Daniels, Bebe and Ben Lyon, *Life with the Lyons: the Autobiography of Bebe Daniels and Ben Lyon* London: Odhams Press Ltd., 1953, 194-5; LeRoy, Mervyn and Dick Kleimer *Mervyn LeRoy: Take One*, New York: Hawthorne Books, Inc., 1974; *LA H&E*, 12/26/35.
37. Richard Sheridan Ames and Thelma Todd, "Twice I Tried to Trap the Hollywood Extortionist"; unidentified published manuscript in the Thelma Todd folder of the Dorothy Herrick Library, Academy of Motion Pictures Arts and Sciences; date unknown, but probably Fall of 1935.
38. *LAT*, 12/17/35; Viglietta, Andrew J. "The Unpublished Truth About the Thelma Todd Extortion Case," *True Detective*, March, 1936.
39. *Viglietta*.
40. *LAT*, 12/17/35.
41. *NYT* 12/18/35.
42. The FBI compared Schimanski's handwriting samples to those found on the notes directed to other extortion victims following Todd's death, including her mother, Alice, who received a threatening letter from "Ace" on the day after Thelma's death. FBI file #9-675, Thelma Alice Todd DiCicco, Memorandum for Mr. Coffey, Sept. 25, 1944.
43. *HCN*, 12/17/35; *NYT* 12/18/35; *NY American* 12/18/35.
44. *NYT*, 12/17/35, *HCN*, 12/18/35; *LAT*, 12/17/35; FBI file #9-675, Thelma Alice Todd DiCicco, Telegram from Hanson to J. Edgar Hoover 1/2/36.
45. *NYT*, 12/18/35; *SFC* 12/18/35; *LAE*, 12/18/35, *Lawrence Telegram* 12/18/35; *SMEO*, 12/18/35.
46. *LAE*, 12/18/35.
47. *IDN*, 12/17/35.
48. *IDN*, 12/18/35; *LA H&E*, 12/17/35.
49. *LAE*, 12/18/35.
50. *HCN*, 12/17/35, *NYT* 12/18/35, *IDN*, 12/18/35; *EPR* 12/17/35.
51. Agnes Underwood statement in the "Entertainment Tonight" episode
52. *LAT*, 12/18/35.
53. *LAE*, 12/17/35.
54. Finch, Christopher and Linda Rosenkrantz, *Gone Hollywood: The Movie Colony During the Golden Age* New York: Doubleday, 1979, 365.
55. *NYT*, 12/29/41.
56. Internet Movie Database.
57. *LA H&E*, 12/17/35.
58. *LAE*, 12/18/35.
59. *LAE*, 12/18/35.
60. *LAE*, 12/18/35.
61. *IDN*, 12/18/35 (photo, 9).
62. *IDN*, 12/21/35.

FIVE: WEDNESDAY MORNING

1. *LAE*, 12/18/35.
2. *CIT*, Coroner's Subpoena.
3. This description is aided by Charles Moore's in *The City Observed: Los Angeles*, Vintage Books. New York, 1984. 14.
4. Interview with T. A. Nelson, June 20, 1986.
5. Olender, Terrys T., *For the Prosecution, Miss Deputy D.A.*, Philadelphia: Chilton Co., 1961.

6. *LET*, 12/18; *LAE*, photo (12/19) shows Captain Jess Winn and Investigator Lloyd Yarrow attending Coroner's Inquest; *LA H&E*, 12/18/35.
7. *HCN*, 12/18/35.
8. Weinstock, Matt. *My LA*. Current Books. New York, 1947. 95. Olender, Terrys T. *For the Prosecution, Miss Deputy D.A.* Philadelphia: Chilton Co., 1961. 103. Interview with Norman "Jake" Jacoby. The jurors were L.M. Preston, A.V. Swartz, George H. Gray, Fred Ballin Jr., Harry Hausman, C.S. Bertschy, William Concannon, Frank E. Fay, and D.D. Miller [*CIT*, Coroner's Subpoena].
9. *LET*, 12/18/35.
10. *LAE* [12/17/35] listed Alice Todd, Roland West, Sid Grauman, Mae Whitehead, Ernest Peters, Ida Lupino, R. W. Schafer, Robert Anderson, E.H. Carter, Robert H. Cooper, and Martha Ford; the *LA Times* [12/18/35] listed, in addition to others, Stanley and Constance Lupino. The *Illustrated Daily News* [12/18/35] describes Alice Todd's breakdown as does the *Los Angeles Herald and Express* [12/18/35].
11. Interview with Lina Basquette; Carroll, Llewellyn, "What Hollywood Did to a New England Schoolmarm," Photoplay, February, 1932. *LA H&E*, 12/18/35.
12. *History of Hollywood*, 279-80; *Who's Who in Los Angeles, 1929*; *LAE*, 3/23/35.
13. *CIT*, 6; The precision in Priester's description of Todd's clothing and jewelry that evening may have reflected the fact that he had seen them again Tuesday afternoon, when the coroner had given him Thelma's personal effects to deliver to Thelma's mother.
14. *CIT*, 11-14.
15. *IDN*, 12/19/35; *LAE*, 12/19/35.
16. *LAT*, 12/19/35.
17. *CIT*, 18-19.
18. *CIT*, 19.
19. *CIT*, 42 Mrs. Whitehead assented to the description offered by Deputy District Attorney George Johnson that Todd "was sitting back of this wheel in the normal position of a person who was about to start the car or drive."
20. *CIT*, 18 and 43.
21. *CIT*, 32-33.
22. *CIT*, 43.
23. *CIT*, 18-19.
24. *CIT*, 44-53.
25. The previous day, citing Peters, the papers reported her statement a little differently: "Never mind, Peters, I'll look after myself" (*IDN*, 12/17/35). *SMEO*, 12/17/35 and *LAE*, 12/17/35 also use the phrase "look after [my]self."
26. *Chicago Herald and Examiner* 12/19/35.
27. *IDN*, 12/19/35.
28. *IDN*, 12/19/35.
29. *LAE* [12/19/36] has photograph of West testifying: He holds a cigarette in his right hand and wears a broad-collared suit. An overcoat is draped over his lap.
30. *LAE*, 12/24/35.
31. MacQueen, Scott, "Roland West," in *Between Action and Cut: Five American Directors*, Frank Thompson, editor, The Scarecrow Press, Inc., Metuchen, New Jersey and London, 1985 108; "*Biography West*", in West collection, AMPAS.
32. *NYT*, 9/22/18, 5/19/29.
33. *NYT*, 9/22/18, 5/19/29.
34. *NYT*, 9/22/18; MacQueen, 114-116.
35. *smiling genially IDN*, 12/19/35.
36. *CIT*, 34.

SIX: WEDNESDAY AFTERNOON

1. *CIT*, 122.
2. *CIT*, 70.
3. *CIT*, 70-2.
4. *CIT*, 72-3.
5. *CIT*, 73.
6. *CIT*, 85.
7. *SFC*, 12/19/35.
8. *LAE*, 1/3/36.
9. *CIT*, 80.
10. *CIT*, 80.
11. *CIT*, 87-88, 90.
12. *CIT*, 91.
13. *CIT*, 91; *LAT*, 12/18/35; *IDN*, 12/18/35.
14. *CIT*, 93.
15. *LA H&E*, 12/19/35.
16. *CIT*, 98.
17. *IDN*, 12/19; *CIT*, 94, 98, 99. Mrs. Ford remembered the phone call as occurring about 4:30, but she accepted the recollection of other guests who placed it closer to 4:10.
18. *CIT*, 94-5.
19. *CIT*, 95.
20. *CIT*, 106, 121.
21. *CIT*, 96; *SFC* 12/20/35.
22. *CIT*, 111-12.
23. *CIT*, 112.
24. *CIT*, 113.
25. *CIT*, 114.
26. *CIT*, 115.
27. *CIT*, 115.
28. *CIT*, 115-116; *IDN*, 12/19/35; Mahoney fixed the times as 10:00 a.m., 4:00 a.m., and 10:00 p.m., miscalculating by one half hour.
29. *CIT*, 117-118.
30. *CIT*, 118.
31. *LAT*, 12/19; *LA H&E*, 12/21/35.
32. *LA H&E*, 12/19/35.
33. "Verdict of Coroner's Jury," attached to *CIT*.
34. Cal York, "A Queen of Blondes," Photoplay, Aug, 1917. Her origins, like that of many early film figures, were somewhat clouded by myth and perhaps the publicity machinery of the studios. According to one report in a fan magazine of the time, she was a native of Danville, Kentucky who came to Los Angeles with her parents shortly after finishing grammar school. A film studio lured her away from her studies in a Los Angeles convent before her seventeenth birthday and for several years she earned "pin money" playing bit and extra parts at Pathe, Keystone, and finally Fine Arts studios until Douglas Fairbanks discovered her one day on the set.

    Another biographical sketch, offered by a rival fan magazine and supplemented by testimony in a civil suit Carmen would bring against several studios in the middle 20s, fixed her birth in 1897 in Portland, Oregon. Jewel's real name was Florence Levina Quick. Her father, Amos William Quick, owned several restaurants in Portland and as a little girl Jewel ran the cash register. How she got to Los Angeles is not clear from this history but, quoting Carmen herself, D.W. Griffith discovered her on the lot of his epic *Intolerance*, in which she had an extra part as a slave girl. After three months of waiting on a bench from nine in the morning until four in the afternoon, Griffith featured her in *Sunshine Dad* and *Children in the House* in the spring of 1916.

Supported by courtroom affidavits and quotations from Carmen herself, the second story is the likelier of the two. In either case, after appearing opposite Douglas Fairbanks in four features made in the summer and fall of 1916, she signed with Fox Studios in early 1917. Fox's version of *A Tale of Two Cities*, in which she played opposite William Farnum as the weeping Lucy Manette, established her as a star. Before the decade was over she had enjoyed top female billing in at least seven Fox and Frank A. Kenney Pictures. She had also married Roland West.

When and how Carmen and West met is somewhat murky. According to Louella Parsons, writing in 1935, their romance blossomed after Jewel starred in West's stage hit, "The Unknown Purple." Contemporary accounts, however, do not list her in the cast. Certainly, Jewel herself declared years later that she and West had married in New York City on June 1, 1918, several months before the play opened at the Lyric Theater in New York, and the play's lead female role was evidently named for her. Elizabeth Peltret's article on Jewel in the November 1918 edition of *Motion Picture* did not mention West, however. In fact, the first public acknowledgment of their relationship seems to have come in an article in *Stars on View* in 1921, after the release of *Nobody*, the second West film for Joe Schenck's Metro Pictures in which Carmen was cast as the female lead. Previously, Carmen had starred in *Silver Lining* for her husband/director.

Except for starring in West's *The Bat* in 1926, a Mary Roberts Rinehart thriller that was also Joseph Schenck's first United Artists' production, Carmen's movie career ended in the early twenties, probably out of her own desire. West's prodigious income and an award of $59,406.21 in a civil action Carmen brought against Fox studios may have made working unnecessary. In 1929, following a radio version of West's hit *Alibi* in which "her voice proved all that it should be," she seems to have considered returning to the screen to star in West's next picture opposite *Alibi* star Chester Morris. [Grace Kingsley, *LAT*, 4/25/29]

On 4/27/25, Jewel sued Fox in the New York State courts for conspiring with Frank A. Keeney Pictures Corporation to prevent her from working. She alleged that her contract with Fox was void because she signed it while under age and did not affirm it on reaching age 21. Fox argued that her contract was valid because she made it while over 18 and, though 21 is the age of majority for women in New York, women reach majority at age 18 in California. The whole matter hung on Jewel's actual age. Her father's deposed that she was born in 1897 despite an entry in the family Bible that placed her birth year as 1895. According to the elder Quick, the original family Bible was burned. When a new one was bought, Jewel's birth year was mistakenly entered at 1895. However, the mistake was corrected as soon as it was noticed. (*NYT*, 4/28/25)

Jewel's age is of interest for another reason. According to Anita Loos, Peg Talmadge, explaining her worries over daughters Norma and Constance, told her of "the dire fate of little Jewel Carmen."

> A couple of years ago Jewel was the hottest bet in Hollywood. She could have stashed away one year's salary in tax-free bonds and been independent for life. But through sheer lack of will power, Jewel started giving in to every man on the lot. And then, because she was under the legal age of consent, the entire company was forced to cross the border into Mexico to keep several higher-ups from being sent to jail. For Jewel, that was only the beginning. One day when they were filming on the streets of Tijuana, Jewel spotted a Mexican bullfighter and walked right out of her million-dollar contract. She's still down there, hustling at bargain rates and being paid off in pesos!

Movie historian Anthony Slide rejects this tale as "a vicious character assassination" and the story is probably apocryphal. Certainly, it's difficult to figure out the timing: California's legal age of consent was 18. Jewel turned 18 on 7/15/15 according to her father's deposition, while she was still just a cut above an extra, not a star. The plot has much in common with other anecdotes told about different people and could well be a Hollywood Myth. On the other hand, it could be true in some parts and false in others. Certainly, Jewel didn't wind up hustling tricks in TJ. Still, it is interesting to note that Anita Loos was the writer of a number of Carmen's films and did not question the truth of Peg Talmadge's anecdote.

[35] Where this interview took place is unclear. *LA Herald and Express* [12/18/35] states that it took

place at her apartment, but *SFC* 12/20/35 citation of Carmen as telling Police Captains Blaine Steed and Thad Brown that she had not told them of her sighting on Tuesday because "some newspaper men were at police headquarters" implies that she was interviewed there.

36. *LAT*, 12/18/35.
37. *LAE*, 12/18/35 as told to Louella Parsons.
38. *LET*, 12/19/35; *Times* 12/18/35, 12/19/35; *SFC* 12/20/35.
39. *LAE*, 12/19/35; another version [*LET*] of Miss Carmen's statement places her on Sunset when she initially sighted Todd's automobile; a third [*LAT*] specifies that the hat Miss Todd wore was "saucer-shaped."
40. *LAT*, 12/19/35; Ardell confirmed the story *CT*, 12/19/35.
41. *SFC*, 12/20/35.
42. *LAT*, 12/18/35.
43. *LA H&E*, 12/19/35.
44. *LAE* 12/18/35.
45. *LAE*, 12/18/35; Katherine LaHue, citing Jack Sauer.
46. *LA H&E*, 12/19/35.
47. *LAE*, 12/20/35, *LAT*, 12/20/35, and *LA H&E*, 12/19/35 all focused on the hat issue.
48. *LA H&E*, 12/19/35.
49. *HCN*, 12/19/35; *LA H&E*, 12/19/35.
50. *LA H&E*, 12/19/35.
51. *LAE*, 12/19/35.
52. *LA H&E*, 12/19/35.
53. *LAE*, 12/20/35; *NYT*, 12/19/35, 12/20/35.
54. *IDN*, 12/21/35.

SEVEN: THE FIRST WEEK ENDS

1. *LA H&E*, 12/19/35.
2. *NYT*, 12/19/35.
3. *NYT*, 12/19/35.
4. *LAE*, 12/21/35 states that the order to return Miss Todd's body to the county morgue for removal of the vital organs was issued on Wednesday at 10:00 a.m.; also see *LAE*, 12/19/35; *NYT*, 12/20/35; *SMEO*, 12/19/35; *IDN* 12/19/35.
5. *LA H&E*, 12/19/35.
6. *SMEO*, 12/19/35; *LAT*, 12/19/35; *LAE*, 12/19/35, 12/20/35; *SFC* 12/19/35; *HCN*, 12/20/35.
7. *LAE* and *EPR* 12/19/35.
8. *LAE*, 12/20/35.
9. *LAE*, 12/20/35.
10. *CIT*, 26, 55.
11. *SFC* 12/20/35.
12. *SFC* 12/20/35; *NYT*, 12/20/35; *LAE*, 12/20/35.
13. *IDN* 12/21/35.
14. *IDN* 12/21/35; *SFC* 12/21/35; *HCN*, 12/20/35.
15. *CT*, 12/20/35.
16. *LA H&E*, 12/19/35.
17. *IDN*, 12/21/35; *LAT*, 12/21/35; *LAE*, 12/21/35.
18. *HCN*, 12/21/35.
19. *HCN*, 12/21/35; *LAE*, 12/22/35.
20. *CIT*, 10, 18.
21. *LA H&E*, 12/19/35; *SMEO*, 12/19/35; *LAE*, 12/21/35; *Chicago American* 12/19/35;

22. *HCN*, 12/19/35.
   LAE, 12/20/35; *LAT*, 12/20/35; *LA H&E*, 12/19 and 12/20/35; *IDN*, 12/19/35; *HCN*, 12/19/35; Thelma's friends and relatives gathered at the grey colonial Todd homestead for private services in Lawrence that day as well *LA H&E*, 12/19/35; *SFC* 12/20/35.
23. *CIT*, 106, *LA H&E*, 12/20/35.
24. *LAE*, 12/21/35.
25. *CT*, 12/21/35; *LAE*, 12/21/35, 12/22/35.
26. *LAT*, 12/23/35; *Daily News* 1/8/36.
27. *LAE*, 12/23/35, 1/8/36; *NYT* 12/24/35, *LAT*, 12/23/35, 1/8/36.
28. *LAE*, 12/20/35; *CIT*, 61, *LET*, 12/20/35.
29. *LAE*, 12/20/35.
30. *HCN*, 1/7/36; *LAE*, 1/8/36; *LAT*, 1/8/36. Although the use of the throttle is only mentioned in the last attempt, undoubtedly the phaeton's choke was utilized in some way in the initial trial.
31. *HCN*, 1/7/36; *IDN* 1/8/36.
32. *IDN*, 12/17/35; *HCN*, 1/7/36; the strong winds of that night would have forced a stronger draught through the slight openings at the top and bottom of the sliding garage doors.
33. *IDN*, 12/18, which notes that the shut off could happen even if the car had been running a long time.
34. *CIT*, 93.
35. *LAE*, 12/23/35; *LAT*, 12/23/35.
36. *LAE*, 12/23/35.
37. *LAT*, 12/23/35; *LAE*, 12/23/35; *NYT* 12/24/35; *CIT*, 87
38. *LAE*, 12/21/35, 12/29/35, 1/4/35; *LAT*, 12/21/35; *IDN* 12/21/35.
39. *LAT*, 12/24/35; *LAE*, 12/21/35; *NYT* 12/22/35.
40. *HCN*, 12/26/35; *SMEO*, 12/26/35; *IDN* 12/26/35; *LAT*, 12/26/35; *LAE*, 12/26/35.
41. *LA H&E*, 12/19/35; *LAE*, 12/20/35, 12/21/35.
42. *LA H&E*, 12/20/35.
43. *IDN*, 12/21/35.
44. *LAE*, 12/21/35.
45. *SMEO*, 12/24/35; *NYT* 12/25/35; *SFC* 12/25/35; *HCN*, 12/24/35.

EIGHT: THE PUBLIC CLAMOR
1. Florabel Muir, *Headline Happy*, 73.
2. *LA H&E*, 12/19/35.
3. *LAE*, 12/20/35.
4. *HCN*, 12/20/35.
5. *LAE*, 12/21/35.
6. *LAE*, 12/21/35; *IDN*, 12/21/35; according to the *LAE* the drug store employees were named Hamilton Wimscott and Irving Hamilton
7. *LA H&E*, 12/20/35; according to *IDN*, 12/21/35, Martha Ford had already speculated that "Miss Todd probably was calling from somewhere on Sunset or Hollywood boulevard between Laurel Canyon boulevard and Vine street."
8. *SMEO*, 12/21/35; *LAT*, 12/21/35. The times given in the various newspapers for the alleged visit by Todd and her gentleman friend to the Christmas tree lot are inconsistent. The *LA Times* [12/21/35] reports the visit occurring "long after" Thelma's estimated time of death and "just a few hours before her body was found," while the *Santa Monica Outlook* [12/21 & 12/24/35] reports the visit as occurring at 3:00 a.m. Monday morning. A few days later, describing the threats to Cummings and San Juan, the *Herald Express* [12/24/35] reports the visit occurring at 3:00 p.m. Sunday afternoon, while the *SFC* [12/25/35] says "Jerry Cummings...claimed he saw Thelma Todd Sunday, December 15, hours after police believed she died..." The *Chicago*

Tribune [12/25], under a "[special]" byline, said the Todd visit happened "several hours after detectives believe she died of carbon monoxide fumes."
9. SMEO, 12/24/35; LAE, 12/24/35; IDN, 12/24/35.
10. LAT, 12/25/35.
11. IDN, 12/12/35; LAE, 12/23/35.
12. LAT, 12/26/35; LAE, 12/26/35, 12/27/35; SFC 12/26/35.
13. LAE, 12/18/35
14. LAT, 12/24/35, 12/25/35; HCN, 12/23/35; SMEO, 12/23/35; IDN, 12/24/35; LAE, 12/24/35; NYT, 12/24/35; CT, 12/24/35
15. SMEO, 12/23/35.
16. HCN, 12/26/35.
17. LAE, 12/28/35.
18. LAE, 12/21/35, 12/22/35, 12/23/35, 12/28/35; LAT, 12/28/35; The woman who spoke for Carmen probably was Mother Grey, her live-in spiritualist [LA H&E, 12/19/35]
19. LAE, 12/25/35.
20. LAE, 12/27/35.
21. LAT, 12/26/35; LA H&E, 12/25/35.
22. IDN, 12/30/35.
23. IDN, 12/30/35; the newspaper checked the records of other drugstores in the Sunset/Laurel area but found that the Sunset/Laurel area and the section of North Hollywood where the Fords lived were in the same zone, which meant no handwritten operator log of calls to Ford's home would be available.
24. LA H&E, 12/23/35.
25. LA H&E, 12/20/35, 12/23/35.
26. HCN, 12/21/35; Alperson was acquitted of the disturbing the peace charge [LA H&E, 12/27/35].
27. LA H&E, 12/20/35; the term "gorilla man" was used at the time to denote a brutish, thug-like man, often a sexual psychopath. See LA Record 8/2/27.
28. LA H&E, 12/21/35.
29. LA H&E, 12/21/35.
30. LA H&E, 12/26/35; IDN, 12/27/35; HCN, 12/26/35, 12/27/35; LAE, 12/27/35; SMEO, 12/26/35.
31. LA H&E, 12/19/35.
32. IDN, 12/25/35, "Voice of the People," from "Voter and Taxpayer." The letter mainly attacked Fitts.
33. HCN, 12/19/35; FBI File on Thelma Todd DiCicco
34. LAE, 1/4/36.
35. Woods, 100; LAE, 12/20/35, 12/23/35, 1/4/36; HCN, 12/27/35; LAT, 12/28/35, 1/4/36; IDN, 1/4/36.
36. LAE, 12/21/35, 12/23/35.
37. LA H&E, 12/23/35.
38. LA H&E, 12/21/35.
39. LA H&E, 12/20/35.

NINE: GENTLEMEN FROM OTHER TOWNS
1. LA H&E, 12/19/35.
2. LA H&E, 12/22/35; HCN, 12/23/35.
3. LA H&E, 12/23/35; LAE, 12/24/35.
4. LAE, 12/23/35; IDN, 12/23/35; LAT, 12/23/35.
5. George Rochester the Hynes, California publisher, who headed the 1935 Grand Jury, is often

6. *LAT*, 12/23/35; *LAE*, 12/23/35.
7. *SFC*, 12/20/35.
8. *NYT*, 12/24/35; *LAT*, 12/24/35; *SFC* 12/24/35.
9. *LAT*, 12/24/35.
10. *LAE*, 12/24/35; *SMEO*, 12/23/35; *IDN*, 12/24/35; *LAT*, 12/24/35; *HCN*, 12/25/35; *SFC* 12/24/35.
11. *SMEO*, 12/23/35; *LAT*, 12/24/35.
12. *LAE*, 12/24/35; 12/25/35.
13. *HCN*, 12/27/35, 12/30/35; *LA H&E*, 12/27/35, 12/28/35; *LAE*, 12/31/35; The press reported that two other intimate friends of Todd, Catherine Hunter and Marion Wilkerson were also to be questioned about the "Gentleman from San Francisco," but, if they were, there is no record of their responses. Both were also called before the Grand Jury. Although the newspapers did not specifically state that they had denied knowledge of the "Gentleman from San Francisco," it is likely that, had they been able to identify him, the papers would have played it up, which they did not.
14. *HCN*, 12/26/35; *SMEO*, 12/26/35; *LAE*, 12/26/35.
15. *LAE*, 12/26/35.
16. *LAE*, 12/25/35.
17. *LAE*, 12/20/35; *LA H&E*, 12/20/35.
18. *IDN*, 12/30/35; *LAE*, 12/29/35; *LA H&E*, 12/29/35; *LAT*, 12/29/35. On 12/30, the *LAT* disclosed that three long distance calls from the Trocadero were being checked as were three others to the Trocadero, one of which originated in New York.
19. *LAT*, 12/30/35.
20. *LAT*, 1/5/36, 1/7/36; *LAE*, 1/5/36, 1/7/36.
21. *LA H&E*, 12/27/35. The *Los Angeles Examiner* quoted York as claiming that Thelma had phoned him on *Saturday* to tell them that "she had talked to Mrs. Ford on the telephone that morning and told her she was bringing some surprise guests to the party." *LAE*, 12/28/35.
22. *LAE*, 12/28/35; despite this demand, York and Lansdowne admitted that they had waited another four days before going to police.
23. *LA H&E*, 12/27/35; *LAT*, 12/28/35.
24. *LAT*, 12/28/35.
25. *LA H&E*, 12/28/35.
26. *HCN*, 12/30/35; *SFC* 12/31/35; *LAT*, 12/31/35.
27. *LAE*, 1/1/36; *HCN*, 1/1/36.
28. *SMEO*, 1/2/35; *HCN*, 1/2/36; *LAE*, 1/3/36.
29. *LAE*, 12/23/35.
30. *LAE*, 12/31/35.
31. *LAE*, 12/23/35.
32. *LA H&E*, 12/23/35 reports substantially the same story
33. Catherine Hunter, "Blonde Menace", *ScreenPlay*, February, 1932.
34. *CT*, 12/28/35. Although he did not elaborate on what was nonsensical in the two actors' story, York had given the investigators several hard facts that could be checked, including his claim that Thelma had called him Saturday morning. As the investigators had already checked the call records of her apartment's phone as part of their investigation of Mrs. Ford's claims and the Gentleman from San Francisco, they might easily have tested York's claims by inspecting them again. Perhaps they did—and perhaps York failed the test.
35. *EPR*, 12/31/35.
36. *NYT*, 12/29/35; *SMEO*, 12/28/35. It appears that such gags as York and Lansdowne

described were commonplace at Hollywood parties. On 12/19, Harrison Carol had reported in his *Evening Herald and Express* column that another event was planned for the Ford party. "By narrowest margins . . . a grisly gag was not pulled at the Wallace Ford's party, at which Thelma Todd was supposed to be present. Vince Barnett had plotted to arrive at the party with three other men playing poker in a hearse. The gag was abandoned at the last minute when he couldn't find a hearse with . . . windows."

37. *LAE*, 12/24/35.
38. *LAT*, 12/24/35; *LAE*, 12/24/35; *IDN*, 12/24/35; one report placed this encounter in front of the Hollywood Legion Stadium. *LAT*, 12/29/35.
39. *IDN*, 12/24/35, 12/25/35; *LAE*, 12/24/35; *LAT*, 12/24/35; *LA H&E*, 12/24/35.
40. *LAE*, 1/3/36, 8 "Ida Lupino Star Witness Before Todd Death Jurors".
41. *LAE*, 1/3/36.
42. *IDN*, 12/24/35, 12/25/35; *LAE*, 12/24/35; *LAT*, 12/24/35; *LA H&E*, 12/24/35.
43. *LAE*, 12/24/35.
44. *LAE*, 1/3/36.
45. *LAT*, 12/24/35; *IDN*, 12/24/35; *LAE*, 12/18/35, 12/24/35, 1/3/36.
46. *LAT*, 12/24/35.
47. *LAE*, 12/18/35.
48. *IDN*, 12/24/35.
49. *IDN*, 12/24/35, 12/25/35; *LAE*, 12/31/35.
50. *IDN*, 12/24/35; *LAT*, 12/24/35; *Chicago Tribune* 12/24/35.
51. *LA H&E*, 12/27/35.
52. *LA H&E*, 12/27/35.
53. *LAE*, 12/28/35.
54. *LAE*, 12/25/35, 12/28/35; *LAT*, 12/27/35, 12/28/35; *HCN*, 12/27/35; *IDN*, 12/28/35.
55. *LAE*, 12/28/35; *IDN*, 12/28/35.
56. *LAE*, 12/28/35.
57. *LAT*, 12/28/35; *Los Angeles Examiner* 12/28/35; as in almost every aspect of this case, there is some disagreement between reports as to whether DiCicco claimed that he and Todd spoke briefly and "pleasantly" (*LAT*) or "merely nodded" (*LAE*).
58. *LAT*, 12/28/35.
59. *LAE*, 12/28/35, 1/2/36, 1/3/36, 1/4/36, 1/5/36; *IDN*, 12/28/35, 1/2/36, 1/6/36; *LAT*, 1/5/36, 1/8/36.
60. For instance, Miss Lupino she declared before the Grand Jury that neither she, her parents, nor her Japanese butler had received a message from DiCicco on the day of the party that he would not attend the dinner party. *LAE*, 1/3/36.
61. *IDN*, 12/26/35.

TEN: WEST TAKES THE STAND
1. *LA H&E*, 12/28/35.
2. *LA H&E*, 12/28/35.
3. *LA H&E*, 12/21/35.
4. *LA H&E*, 12/19/35.
5. *LA H&E*, 12/21/35, 12/25/35; *LA H&E*, 12/28/35.
6. *San Pedro News Pilot*, 12/30/35; *LA H&E*, 12/31/35.
7. Interview with William Todd.
8. From anonymous letter sent to LAPD, dated 12/17/35.
9. Helen "Cupid or Kewpie" Ainsworth was an actress and later an agent and producer of B-movies. She was Marilyn Monroe's agent in 1946.

10. *IDN*, 12/25/35; *LAE*, 12/25/35; the *LAT* and *Hollywood Citizen-News* reported that Ainsworth quoted Todd as referring to New Year's Day as the date by which the change in her life would take place.
11. *LA H&E*, 1/2/36.
12. *LA H&E*, 1/2/36.
13. Although some members of the Grand Jury wanted to interrogate Todd's psychiatrist after hearing of Ainsworth's comments, there is no evidence that, if he existed, he was ever identified [*LAE*, 12/26/35]
14. *Milwaukee Journal* 11/17/35, 40, Sara Day, "For a New Outlook on Life—Get a Hat".
15. *LAT*, 12/25/35; other reports specified that the check Thelma wrote was on her account, not just for the hat. The amount of the check was $21.
16. *LAT*, 12/26/35; *CT*, 12/25/35; *LAE*, 12/26/35.
17. *LAT*, 12/28/35; *SMEO*, 12/27/35; *LAE*, 12/27/35, 12/28/35; *HCN*, 12/27/35; *IDN*, 12/27/35.
18. *LA H&E*, 12/28/35.
19. 'As a matter of fact,' [DiCicco] insisted, 'West is a total stranger to me. I never met him. I would hardly know him by sight.'[*LA H&E*, 12/28]
"West admitted . . . that he never had met DiCicco." [*LA H&E* 12/27]]
20. *IDN*, 1/9/36.
21. *LAE*, 12/23/35, 1/9/36; *LAT*, 1/10/36.
22. *IDN*, 12/26/35; *LAE*, 12/26/35; *LA H&E*, 12/27/35.
23. *LAE*, 1/8/36.
24. *LAE*, 12/31/35.
25. MacQueen, 127-133; *Theatre Magazine*, 4/10/29; *NYT*, 4/9/29
26. *LAE*, 12/30/35, 1/3/36.
27. Interview with Florian Sauer.
28. *LA H&E*, 12/30/35.
29. *LA H&E*, 12/28/35; *LAE*, 12/28/35.
30. *HCN*, 12/30/35; Interview with Rudy Schafer 12/1/2000
31. *LAE*, 1/4/36.
32. *LAE*, 1/16/36.
33. Telegram to J. Edgar Hoover, Jan. 2, 1936, FBI file # 9-675, Thelma Alice Todd DiCicco.
34. *LAE*, 1/4/36.
35. *LAE*, 12/31/35.
36. *LAE*, 12/31/35; *LA H&E*, 12/31/35.
37. *LA H&E*, 12/28/35.
38. *LA H&E*, 12/31/35; *LAT*, 12/31/35.
39. *LA H&E*, 12/28/35.
40. *LAE*, 12/31/35. The day after West's first stand before the Grand Jury, reports reached newspapers that Thelma often stayed over at the apartment of her close friend Catherine Hunter, Charlie Chaplin's secretary, when she was out late and did not want to return all the way to the Sidewalk Café.
41. *IDN*, 12/31/35; *LAE*, 12/31/35, 1/1/36; *SFC* 12/31/35; *LAT*, 12/31/35, 1/1/36; *LA H&E*, 12/31/35, 1/1/36.
42. *LAT*, 12/31/35, 1/1/36; *LAE*, 12/31/35.

ELEVEN: MURDER, SUICIDE OR ACCIDENT?
1. *Evening Post Record* 12/17/35.
2. *LA H&E*, 12/25/35, 12/26/35, 12/31/35; *LAE*, 12/26/35, 12/27/35, 1/1/36; *LAT*, 12/26/35; *NYT* 12/26/35; the identity of the person who noticed the throat lacerations was

never established, but members of the press and police were present at the autopsy and the report could have come from one of them [Underwood, Agnes. *Newspaperwoman*, 112-113.]

3. *LAT*, 12/21/35; *IDN*, 12/21/35; *LA H&E*, 1/7/36, 12/21/35 (the paper dramatized the murder possibility of the running board stain in this earlier edition; it is possible that the Grand Jury investigator the paper quoted on 1/7 may have been prodded into the speculation by the paper's reporter); *HCN*, 1/7/36.

Pinker raised one new issue while on the stand that Tuesday. He reported that he had discovered a blood-stained handkerchief monogrammed with the letter "S" in the car when he arrived at the scene early in the afternoon of December 16. However, West had already testified that he had asked Rudolph Schafer to cover Todd's face from photographers with the latter's handkerchief.

4. *LAE*, 1/1/36; *SFC* 1/1/36.
5. *SFC* 1/1/36.
6. *IDN*, 1/1/36.
7. *LAE*, 12/28/35; *IDN*, 12/28/35; *HCN*, 12/27/35.
8. *LAE*, 12/31/36.
9. *LAT*, 12/19/35, 1/1/36; *LAE*, 12/21/35, 1/1/36, 1/7/36; *LA H&E*, 1/3/36, 1/7/36; *IDN*, 1/1/36; *SFC* 1/1/36; *HCN*, 12/31/35, 1/1/36.
10. *HCN*, 1/7/36; *LAE*, 1/8/36.
11. *LAE*, 1/3/36; 1/5/36; *Chicago Herald and Examiner* 12/21/35.
12. *NYDN* 12/18/35.
13. *SMEO*, 12/19/35; *LAT*, 12/19/35; *LAE*, 12/19/35, 12/20/35; *SFC* 12/19/35; *HCN*, 12/20/35.
14. *LAT*, 12/23/35; *IDN*, 12/23/35. It was curious that the detectives were able to find out so little about the gambling plans, since a story in the *Herald Express* had described them in detail on December 20. *LA H&E*, 12/20/35.
15. *LAE*, 12/25/35; *LAT*, 12/25/35; *HCN*, 12/25/35; *LA H&E*, 12/25/35.
16. *LAE*, 1/4/36.
17. *LA H&E*, 12/20/35.
18. *LA H&E*, 12/20/35; *LAT*, 1/4/36.
19. *HCN*, 1/3/36; *IDN*, 1/4/36; *LAE*, 1/4/36; *LA H&E*, 1/3/36.
20. *LAE*, 1/4/36.
21. *HCN*, 1/5/36.
22. *LAE*, 1/4/36; *HCN*, 1/3/93; *LAT*, 1/4/36.
23. *IDN*, 1/4/36; *LA H&E*, 1/4/36; *LAE*, 1/4/36; *LAT*, 1/4/36.
24. *LAE*, 1/4/36.
25. *LAE*, 1/3/36; *LAT*, 1/3/36; *SFC* 1/3/36; *IDN*, 1/3/36.
26. *HCN*, 1/4/36; *LAE*, 1/5/36; the interest in Todd's life insurance policy surfaced was related to the impending opening of her safe deposit box. Earlier, A. Ronald Button had testified that the actress did not carry life insurance.

One paper reported that Johnson and Blalock had denied reports that prominent witnesses were being sought to expand their testimony to give more evidence of suicide.

27. *LA H&E*, 12/20/35, 12/30/35; *HCN*, 12/30/35; *LAE*, 12/25/35.
28. *LAE*, 12/26/35.
29. *LA H&E*, 1/2/36; *LAE*, 1/3/36; *HCN*, 1/2/36; *LAT*, 1/3/36; *SMEO*, 1/2/36; *Washington Herald* 1/2/36.
30. *HCN*, 12/25/35.
31. *SFC* 12/21/35.
32. *LAE*, 12/22/35, 1/5/36, 1/7/36; *IDN*, 1/7/36; *LAT*, 1/5/36, 1/7/36; *LA H&E*, 12/17/35.

33. *LAT*, 1/4/36.
34. *LAT*, 1/5/36; *LAE*, 1/7/36.
35. Since completing their report on the case, the police had assisted the Grand Jury's investigation only in a peripheral, advisory capacity. Detective Bruce Clark told the jury on January 6 that the police had been certain since the day her body was found that Todd had not been murdered. A few days later, Captain Wallis also testified before the Grand Jury. Without a suicide note or any clear motive for suicide, one had to conclude the death was accidental, Wallis explained. Officially, police records listed the death as "accidental with possible suicidal indications." As far as the LAPD was concerned, the case was closed. *LA H&E*, 1/9/36; *LAT*, 12/20/35, 1/7/36, 1/10/36; *HCN*, 1/6/36, 1/10/36; *IDN*, 1/7/36; *SFC* 1/7/36; *LAE*, 12/23/35; *CT*, 12/24/35.
36. *LAT*, 1/1/36.
37. *LA H&E*, 1/7/36, 1/8/36; *HCN*, 1/6/36; *SFC* 1/7/36; *EPR* 12/31/35. Although West maintained to reporters that he had been grilled by the Grand Jury, the DA told reporters on 12/31 that "We do not intend to question West about any love he may have had for Thelma Todd. We do not feel that enters into the question" [U. U. Blalock quoted in *LA H&E*, 12/31/35]
38. *LA H&E*, 12/27/35.
39. Letter from J.H. Hanson to Director, FBI, Dec. 21, 1935
40. *LA H&E*, 12/26/35, *EPR* 12/31/35. Besides Alice, Margaret Lindsay, Pat DiCicco's consort at the Trocadero, was also a victim of emotional strain during the Todd inquest. On January 8, Warner Brothers studios announced that Miss Lindsay had suffered a nervous breakdown, forcing the studio to replace her as the lead in its upcoming film, "Murder by an Aristocrat." This announcement followed denials by the actress' secretary of rumors that she had secretly married DiCicco. Several days later, the actress denied that she had collapsed emotionally: "Naturally, I have been upset by being drawn into the unfortunate case, but it is not true that I have been or am now ill as a result of it." *LAT*, 1/8/36; *LAE*, 1/8/36; *LA H&E*, 1/7/36, 1/10/36.
41. *EPR* 12/20/35; *LAE*, 12/31/35; *LA H&E*, 12/20/35, 1/1/36; *SFC* 12/31/35.
42. *LA H&E*, 12/23/35; *EPR* 12/23/35; *LAT*, 12/28/35.
43. *IDN*, 12/28/35, 1/3/36; *LAT*, 12/28/35, 1/3/36, 1/7/36, 1/8/36; *LA H&E*, 12/28/35, 1/3/36, 1/8/36.
44. *LAE*, 1/9/36, 1/10/36, 1/11/36; *LAT*, 1/9/36, 1/10/36; *HCN*, 1/10/36.
45. *HCN*, 1/6/36, 1/17/36; *LAT*, 1/10/36, 1/17/36; *LAE*, 1/11/36.

TWELVE: THE REPORTERS

1. Interviews with Catherine Rohrer, Terry Allen, and William Todd.
2. In Los Angeles there were six major dailies: the *Times*, the *Examiner*, the *Herald-Express*, the *Illustrated Daily News*, the *Evening Post-Record*, and the *Hollywood Citizen News*, all of which provided substantial coverage of the Todd case. Westside community papers with smaller circulation, but which provided detailed coverage included the *Santa Monica Evening Outlook* and the *Venice Vanguard*. Other papers of special note in covering the story include the *New York Times*, the *New York Post*, the *San Francisco Chronicle*, and the *Lawrence Eagle Tribune* (Thelma Todd's hometown newspaper.)
3. *IDN*, 12/26/35, *LAT*, 12/26/35, *LA H&E*, 12/27/35.
4. *Webster's Collegiate Dictionary*, 1943 edition, (based on *Webster's New International Dictionary, Second Edition*, 1934), 1014
5. Frank Luther Mott, *American Journalism*, 1962, 666-667.
6. Edwin Emery, *The Press and America*, Allyn and Bacon, Boston, 1997 554
7. Mott, 667; Emery, 555.
8. Mott, 670.

9. Paul Sann, *The Lawless Decade*, Fawcett World Library, New York. 1971 187-191. *Mott*, 670.
10. *Mott*, 672.
11. Sann, 195-202; Bruce Hentsell, *Sunshine and Wealth*, 1984, 95-97.
12. *Mott*, 67; *Emery*, 559. Bob Stepno, School of Journalism and Mass Communication University of North Carolina at Chapel Hill, "Staged, faked and mostly naked: Photographic innovation at the Evening Graphic (1924-1932)".
13. Gottlieb, 117.
14. Gottlieb, 49.
15. Kevin Starr, *Material Dreams*, 102-103; the *Los Angeles Record*, "Story of Harry Chandler," March 4/7, 1924, which details allegations about Chandler's extensive Mexican land holdings and their link to his opposition to the Boulder Dam proposal.
16. Interview with Jack Halstead, 10/28/86.
17. Stephen Longstreet, *All Star Cast, An Anecdotal History of Los Angeles*. 1977, 167.
18. Interview with Norman "Jake" Jacoby, 12/88.
19. Arnold B. Larson, *Newspaper Reporting in the Twenties: Reflections*, University of California, Los Angeles, Oral History Program, 1970. Jack R. Hart, *The Information Empire*, University Press of America, 1981, 72.
20. *Larson*, 113.
21. While reporters might use their positions to make a little extra cash, the papers themselves were playing in a bigger game. When necessary, all the resources of a paper could be brought to bear on a given institution or individual. Larson claims that in 1929, when ex-District Attorney Asa Keyes was indicted for taking bribes during the prosecution of the Julian Petroleum scandal, the *Los Angeles Times* arranged matters so that the indictment of was returned late in the afternoon at the old brown courthouse—not in the Hall of Justice where the beat reporters could cover it. "Everything had been staged-managed to give the *Times* an exclusive beat. People don't understand how the news was stage-managed behind the scenes by the newspapers in those days." Carey McWilliams, *Southern California: An Island on the Land*, 1973, x-xii. *Larson*, 104.
22. Interview with Norman Jacoby, 12/23/87.
23. *The Guardian*, 287.
24. Interview with Norman "Jake" Jacoby.
25. J. Heim Yankel, "Who Shot 'Our Buron' . . . And Why?" *Clifford Clinton's Civic Digest*, December, 1939, 42.
26. Clinton Clifford's *Civic Digest*, "The Life and Ventures of Buron Fitts," November, 1939, 5.
27. *Larson*, 74-5.
28. See, for example, Robert Giroux, *A Deed of Death*, Farrar and Giroux, 1990.
29. Interview with Norman "Jake" Jacoby.
30. *Larson*, 74-5.
31. *Hart*, 80.
32. Adela Rogers St. Johns, 35-36.
33. Mrs. William Clark, recalling what her husband had told her about the circumstances surrounding the Todd investigation, 7/10/86.

THIRTEEN: THE PUBLICISTS

1. Leonard J. Leff, *The Dame in the Kimona*, 1990, 5.
2. *Leff*, 17-32.
3. John Austin, *More of Hollywood's Unsolved Mysteries*, 8.
4. *Austin*, 77.
5. Interview with Emily Tortia, 12/8/87.
6. Samuel Marx and Joyce Vanderveen, *Deadly Illusions*, Random House New York, 1990.
7. Interview with A.T. Nelson.
8. *Marx and Vanderveen*, 163.

9. Ezra Goodman, *The Fifty Year Decline and Fall of Hollywood*, A Macfadden Book, circa 1961, 48.
10. *Goodman*, 48.
11. *Goodman*, 52. Quoting Douglas Churchill, "Hollywood…Gags Candid Press Critics, Studios Threaten Withdrawal of Advertising Unless Newspapers Write kindly—Crisis Seen Near in Press Relations," *Editor and Publisher*, August 10, 1935.
12. Among the sources for this information was the author's mother, Dorothy Croddy, who as a young actress experienced the effect of Miss Parson's negative appraisal in person. She recalled the terror many of her ilk felt when trying to pass muster with the columnist: "If Louella took a dislike to you, she could be most unkind and you never even knew why."
13. *LAE*, 12/18/35.
14. Jim Heimann, *Out With Stars*, 63, 73-77.
15. See Tichi Wilkerson and Marcia Borie, *The Hollywood Reporter*, 1984.
16. *Goodman*, 51.
17. *LA H&E*, 12/21/35 and 12/22/35.
18. *NYDN* 12/17/35, 8, Late Edition.
19. See, for example, Dorothy Lawlor, *Photoplay*, February, 1936, 56. It is also interesting to note that in the book *The Hollywood Reporter* which details the "golden years" of the newspaper, no mention is made of the Todd death. In fact, the "Hollywood Potpourri 1935" section which summarizes the year's events, fails to mention it at all.
20. *Leff*, 77.

FOURTEEN: THE MAKING OF A LEGEND

1. Greil Marcus, *The Dustbin of History*, Harvard University Press, Cambridge, Massachusetts, 1995, p. 37
2. Nicholas Horden, "The Death of Thelma Todd Hollywood's Strangest Unsolved Case, *Los Angeles Magazine*, October, 1976.
3. Anthony Abbot, "The Strange Death of Thelma Todd," *Liberty Magazine*, circa 1940, 38. William Carr, *Hollywood Tragedy*, 1962; Charles Neutzel, *Whodunit? Hollywood Style*, 1965, 76-99; Jay Robert Nash, *Murder Among the Mighty*, 1983, 127; Jay Robert Nash *Open Files*, 1983, 253-254; Jody Jacobson, *Hollywood Heartbreak*, 1984, 100; Andy Edmonds, *Hot Toddy: The True Story of Hollywood's Most Sensational Murder*. William Morrow & Company, New York. 1989, 276-277.
4. "Sender of Todd Death Wire Found," *Los Angeles Examiner*, 3/29/36.
5. *Horden*, 178.
6. *Jacobson*, 100.
7. *Edmonds*, 285.
8. *Liberty Magazine*, 35, *Horden*, 172, and *Stump*, 8.
9. *SFC* 12/17/35; *LAT*, 12/17/35.
10. In the Matter of the Estate of Thelma Alice Todd DeCicco [sic], Inventory and Appraisement, No. 155,304, 2. Also see Schedule "A". The appraisal was conducted for the administration of Todd's estate by Elizabeth Kenny.
11. L. Allen Smith, *Hollywood Reporter*, "Mysterious death of blond and beautiful Thelma Todd," September, 1973, 34.
12. Tony Scott, *Variety*, Forty-Ninth Anniversary Issue, "Southern California Landmarks Are Rich in Showbiz History, October 26, 1982, 86.
13. Al Stump, *Los Angeles Herald Examiner*, CALIFORNIA LIVING, "The Beautiful and the Dead: Hollywood's Unsolved Mysteries," 9. Most articles on the Todd funeral remark upon the soft organ music played by Irene Robinson, one of Thelma's friends, one identifying it as Dvorak's *New World Symphony*, followed by Tchaikovsky's "Andante Cantabile." [*IDN*, 12/19/35]. One reporter noted that the music and setting "wasn't 'Hot Toddy's' kind of a party—she loved

14. sunshine and brilliance—laughter and happiness." [*LA H&E*, 12/20/35] Another, contradicting other reports slightly, declared that "the last music they played for Thelma was not a dirge, but a soaring, singing organ melody, filled with the voices of chiming bells." [*LAE*, 12/20/35].

14. "The Sunshine Of Your Smile" Lilian Ray & Leonard Cooke, 1915; sheet music collection at the University of Wisconsin, Milwaukee.

15. For example, for those giving 270 as the number of steps, see, *Liberty Magazine*, circa 1940, 34; *Sullivan*, 57-64; *Neutzel*, 76-79; *Horden*, 172; *Stump*, 8; *Scott*, 36; and Daniel Cohen, *The Encyclopedia of Unsolved Crimes*, 1988, 179. Mader and Wolf, "Thelma Todd's Murder Solved!," *Los Angeles Magazine*, December, 1987, 223, claim 271 steps; Jacobs claims 208; and Maurice Zolotow, "The Big Schlep," *Los Angeles Magazine*, September, 1978, 252, states 280.

16. *LAT*, 12/17/35, 1. Also see AP Wirephoto, *Wideworld Photo*, TB 22125. Actually, there are 70 steps in three segments of 24, 22, and 24.

17. *LAE*, 12/19/35. This story was reported in the *LA Examiner* three days before the picture and caption noting the "270" had been "inspected minutely by investigators" appeared in the same paper.

18. *Horden*, 105; *Stump*, 8.; *Nash*, 123; *Wolf and Mader*, 129; and *Edmonds*, 17

19. *Horden*, 179.

20. *Edmonds*, 275.

21. *CIT*, 18-19, 76.

22. Edward S. Sullivan, *Hollywood: the Sin Capital of the World*, 1962. Also see *Stump*, 8, Jacobson, 122-123, *Cohen*, 179, and *Edmonds*, 251.

23. *NYT* 12/18. The same information without the quote is contained in the *LA Examiner* [12/18/35] and in the *Venice Evening Vanguard* [12/18/35].

24. *SFC*, 12/18/35; however, the *Santa Monica Evening Outlook* had reservations about Peter's claim, calling it an "eleventh hour statement." *SMEO*, 12/18/35.

25. *CIT*, 49.

26. *CIT*, 47.

FIFTEEN: THE PATINA OF MYSTERY

1. *LA H&E*, 12/23/35.

2. Secondary sources reporting and/or commenting on the story of the unscuffed slippers include: "The Strange Death of Thelma Todd," *Liberty Magazine*, 36; *Sullivan*, 57-64; *Neutzel*, 76-99; *Horden*, 173; *Zolotow*, 251; Parrish and Leonard, *The Funsters*, 641; *Stump*, 9; *Kaplan*, 37. *Nash, Murder Among the Mighty*, 124-125; *Jacobson*, 100; Scott MacQueen, *Between Action and Cut: Five American Directors*, "Roland West," 156; *Cohen*, 180; *Mader and Wolf, Fallen Angels*, 130; and *Austin, More of Hollywood's Unsolved Mysteries*, "Thelma Todd," 83.

3. *SMEO*, 12/20/35; *Chicago Daily Tribune* 12/21/35.

4. *LA H&E*, 12/19/35. Fitts' involvement began after the Coroner's Inquest had rendered its verdict. As the legal advisors to the Grand Jury, the district attorney's office began an independent investigation in conjunction with that body. See *HCN*, 12/19/35; *SFC*, 12/20/1935.

5. See *NYT*, 12/23/35 and the *LET*, 12/21/35 for substantially the same report.

6. *LA H&E*, 1/3/35.

7. *LA H&E*, 1/4/35.

8. *LA H&E*, 1/4/36.

9. *HCN*, 1/4/35.

10. This argument is forcefully made by Maurice Zolotow in "The Big Schlep," *Los Angeles Magazine*, September 1978, 250-253. Also see, Patrick Jenning, "The True Story," *Los Angeles Magazine*, which discusses the parallels between *Lady and the Lake* and the 1940 murder prosecution of the Santa Monica physician, Dr. George Dazey.

11. Raymond Chandler, *Lady and the Lake*, Vintage Books Edition, 1976, 151-153, 195.

12. *Horden*, 105; *Zolotow* citing *Horden*, 252; and *Jacobson*, 100.
13. *Edmonds*, 20-21.
14. *Parrish and Leonard*, 641.
15. *Zolotow*, 252.
16. *Scott*, 85-86.
17. *CIT*, 106-107.
18. *LAE*, 1/4/36.
19. *LAE*, 1/8/36.
20. *HCN*, 1/7/36.
21. *HCN*, 1/7/36.
22. *CIT*, 34.
23. International News Photos, Los Angeles Bureau 12/26/35, UPI/BETTMANN.
24. See, "The Strange Death of Thelma Todd," *Liberty Magazine*, 36; *Sullivan*, 57-64; *Neutzel*, 76-79; *Horden*, "almost virginal," 105; *Stump*, "appeared new," 9, and *Scott*, 85.
25. *SMEO*, 12/20/35.
26. *HCN*, 12/20/35.
27. *NYT*, 12/23/35; *LET*, 12/21/35.
28. *LAE*, 12/22/35.
29. *NYT*, 12/23/35; *LET*, 12/21/35.
30. "The Strange Death of Thelma Todd," *Liberty Magazine*, 37.
31. Agnes Underwood, *Newspaperwoman*, 1949, 230.
32. See for example, *Sullivan*, 57-64, *Nash, Murder Among the Mighty*, 125, *Scott*, 85, MacQueen, 156 and Edmonds, 27.
33. *Edmonds*, 263.
34. *IDN*, 1/1/36.
35. *SFC* 1/1/36; *LAE*, 1/1/36.
36. *SFC* 1/1/36.
37. *SFC* 1/1/36.
38. *SFC* 1/7/36.
39. *LAT*, 1/1/36.
40. *HCN*, 12/31/35.
41. *HCN*, 12/24/35.

SIXTEEN: FRAUDS AND SLANDERS

1. Kenneth Anger, *Hollywood Babylon*, 1975. While the American edition was published in 1975, there was apparently any earlier version published in France in 1960. Also see, *Neutzel*, 76-79 and *Sullivan*, 57-64.
2. *Anger*, 206.
3. *Anger*, 206.
4. While a number of creditors are listed as making claims against the estate, Pitts is not among them.
5. *Anger*, 201-206.
6. *LAT*, 1/4/36; *LAE*, 1/4/36.
7. While Anger claimed inside knowledge of the events he covered, he did not provide sources for his information. As *Los Angeles Times* writer Kristine McKenna reported after interviewing Anger, his methods are unusual:
    "Often rumored to be a disciple of British mystic and magician Aleister Crowley, Anger is a devout advocate of extrasensory perception and his beliefs in telepathic communication play a big part in shaping his books. In fact, that is his central research tool." [Kristine McKenna, "Enquiring Into More 'Hollywood II," *LAT*, 11/29/84.]
    In the late 1960s, when the interest in magic and mysticism were at a peak, Anger became a fixture in certain rock music circles, including that of the Rolling Stones. He reportedly claimed

to be adept at the black arts of Satanism and convinced more than a few hangers-on of his powers.[Christopher Anderson, *Jagger, Unauthorized*, 172-173]
8. *Edmonds*, 21 and 27.
9. Nash, *Murder Among the Mighty*, 123.
10. *Nash*, 124.
11. See, for example, *Stump*, 8, Margaret Hall Kaplan, "Actress' death remains a mystery after 48 years," *LAT*, Westside Section 12/18/83, and *Cohen*, 180.
12. "Airtalk," an interview and call-in show hosted by Larry Mantel featuring Andy Edmonds, KPPC Radio, Pasadena, 4/89.
13. Interview with Richard Bann.
14. Interview with Rudy Schafer, 12/1/2000.
15. Fred Lawrence Guiles, *Stan, The Life of Stan Laurel*, 163.
16. *Neutzel*, 76-99.
17. Frank Sanello, "Murder of 30s starlet Thelma Todd no longer a mystery," *Chicago Tribune*, TV Week, May 5, 1991, 5.
18. Also see Kevin Thomas, "Anderson Believable as '30s Star Thelma Todd," *LAT*, May 4, 1991, F9.
19. In an interview conducted near the airing of White Hot, Andy Edmonds also indulges in trying to find a popular, modern analogy to the situation of Thelma Todd. She is quoted as likening the actress' supposed relationship to the mobster as a "Fatal Attraction." See Ira Letofsky, *LAT*, Orange County Edition, May 5, 1991, 7.
20. Interview with Lina Basquette.
21. Llewellyn Carrol, "What Hollywood Did To A New England Schoolmarm," *Photoplay Magazine*, 54-55 and 116.
22. *Dorothy Lubon*.
23. *Carrol*, 116. Thelma's experiences with Hollywood's casting couch were also confirmed in the interview with William Todd, Thelma's cousin.
24. *Carrol*, 116.
25. Bob Thomas, *Kansas City Star* 12/15/49.

SEVENTEEN: KEEPING THE LID ON

1. "The Jacobson Outrage," *Bob Shuler's Magazine*, September, 1927, 152.
2. *Edmonds*, 283.
3. *LAE*, 1/3/36; 1/5/36; *Chicago Herald and Examiner* 12/21/35.
4. *LA H&E*, 12/21/35, 1/1/36; *LAE*, 1/5/36, 1/6/36.
5. *Woods*, 67.
6. This group replaced an older vice establishment that dated back to the gold rush days–in the 1870s, four hundred gambling dens had crowded about Olvera Plaza [*The Guardian*, 1937]–but came crashing down in 1908, when Deputy DA Thomas Lee Woolwine told the *LA Express* that the present mayor, Arthur Harper was in cahoots with vice czars to protect organized gambling and prostitution in a "segregated zone" a few blocks east of City Hall. After much political wrangling, a Grand Jury investigation discovered numerous brothels in full operation along with evidence that Harper and some of the police commissioners owned rental property and hotels in the area. Also in on the act was Police chief Kern, who had sold fire insurance to licensed businesses in the area.

The revelations led to a suppression of the segregated district. This did not end vice in LA, but it did relieve the city of its most open and obviously protected form for a few years. Prostitution was dispersed throughout the city and the whores and panderers became more discrete. Gambling was also hard hit, and afterward was confined mainly to betting on Pacific Coast League baseball games and horse races in Mexico. In 1913, the city's virtuousness was enough to gall at least one writer, who complained that the city had become "chemically pure" in a story in the nationally distributed magazine, *Smart Set*. [Willard Huntington, "Los Angeles: The Chemically

Pure", *Smart Set*, March, 1913; *Woods*, 87, 90]

A burgeoning wartime economy soon brought an influx of young unmarried navy men and construction workers eager for entertainment. In addition, successive charter reforms, prohibiting political parties in municipal elections and establishing civil service in the place of patronage, had stripped politicians of traditional sources of campaign funds. As elections neared, the politicians found that only panderers and gamblers, who were eager to buy influence on the administration of the vice laws, had a reason to provide campaign funds.

7. Garrigues, Charles H. *You're Paying for It! A Guide to Graft*. New York: Funk & Wagnalls, 1936, 128-136; Garrigues, *IDN*, 3/2/34; "Patterns of Vice Protection", 6; Interview with A.T. Nelson, June 19, 1986; James, Thomas H., *Chief Steckel Unmasked* (LA, 1931), 33.

8. Interview with A. T. Nelson, June 19, 1986; Garrigues, 136.

9. Adela Rogers St. Johns, *Final Verdict*, Doubleday & Company, Garden City, New York, 1962, 461-8. Alfred Cohn and Joe Chisholm, *"Take the Witness"*, New Home Library, New York, New York, 226-36; See Robert Shuler, "The Jacobson Outrage", *Bob Shuler's Magazine*, September, 1927, 146-148 for accounts of several other similar "frame-ups" of anti-vice crusaders.

10. Also indicted in the plot were a vice squad sergeant and two black patrolmen. After Karr and Brown were granted immunity, they testified against the mayor, who was defended by former DA John Fredericks. The disappearance of a crucial notebook from Woodman's home and a key witness, last seen at the train station in the company of a police officer, scuttled the prosecution's case. [Cohn, Alfred and Chisholm, Joe, *"Take The Witness!"*. The New Home Library. New York, 1934. 226-227; *Liberty Magazine*, I. 9; Dave Clark, who killed Charles Crawford and Herbert Spencer, was rumored to have been blackmailed by Spencer over "wild party photograph" [Chamberlain, Joseph, "Fitts and the 'Gangsters'", 32; FBI report of 1/16/37, title "UNKNOWN SUBJECTS; MRS. NANCY MALONE CLARK - VICTIM. DAVID HARRIS CLARK–VICTIM"]; *Woods*, 46-48; St. John, 488-90; *Richardson*, 79-103].

11. *IDN*, 3/18/52. *Liberty Magazine*, I, 9.

12. Briggs, Arthur E., *Southern California Renaissance Man*, UCLA Oral History, 1970, interviewed by Elizabeth Dixon; Lawler, Oscar, *Oscar Lawler, Los Angeles Attorney*, UCLA Oral History, 1962, interviewed by Doyce Nunis, 624-626; Harold H. Story, *Memoirs of Harold H. Story*, UCLA Oral History, UCLA, 1967, interviewed by Elizabeth I. Dixon; Finney, *Angel City in Turmoil*, 99-100; *McKinney and Allhoff*, III, 22.

13. "Memo for Richardson" in Roselli file in *Herald* morgue.

14. "Memo for Richardson", *LA Examiner*, morgue "John Roselli" file; "Cops and Robbers", *IDN*, 3/26/52; Police Commission minutes, 10/25/27, 11/15/27, 11/29/27, 12/13/27, 12/20/27; *Richardson*, 222; letter from Bob Coyne to Fletcher Bowron, 3/21/41.

15. Siegel, perhaps the most overrated figure in US criminal history, first came to California after he visited Las Vegas in the early thirties to look over the area for future operations. He was active in Los Angeles vice from 1936. In 1937, at the time of his arrest for the murder of "Big Greenie" Greenburg, his personal papers indicated that he had invested heavily in gambling operations in Redondo Beach and Hermosa Beach; cancelled checks to Eddie Nealis, Farmer Page, and Tony Cornero were found in his files.

After the shakeup of 1938, Siegel moved in on the vacancy created by the departure of the Combination leaders, but his enterprises were small scale by comparison and somewhat unsuccessful. His much heralded move to Las Vegas, where he muscled out restaurateur Billy Wilkerson, former owner of the Trocadero, from the Flamingo Hotel, ended in failure and his death.

EIGHTEEN: THE BIG FIX

1. *Garrigues*, 214.
2. Interview with William Clark; Unpublished, untitled manuscript in the *J. Shaw* collection detailing Raymond's career.
3. *Woods*, 367; *LAE*, 3/15/39;

According to a letter from FBI Special Agent J.H. Hanson to J. Edgar Hoover (1/6/36), a police detective who claimed widespread corruption existed in the LAPD and Los Angeles in general told Hanson that "Taylor ... is absolutely honest, is not in with the click that controls things, with the result that Taylor is shoved around the police department and is not permitted to investigate cases, as he should properly do.

On the other hand, Edgar Dudley, an investigator for the Minute Men, wrote that "protection money is divided up between the Secretary to Mayor Frank Shaw, the Chief of Police, Jim Davis, the Chief of Detectives, Joe Taylor and among four out of five county supervisors." ["Memorandum on the Evasion of Federal Income Taxes in Los Angeles City and County", May 1934]

4. *St. John*, Cecilia Rasmussen, "Ramparts Site Was a Noir Landmark," *LAT*, 9/29/99.
5. Wallis' early LA residences and occupations are charted in the annual *LA City Directory*, 1908-1914.
6. *Woods*, 562 fn; *The Record* 8/6/27.
7. *St. John* III, 24; *White*, 125.
8. *LA Record*, 8/6/27 through 8/14/27, *passim*; *McKinney & Allhoff*, II, 22
9. Robert Shuler, *Bob Shuler's Magazine*, Sept. 1927, 148. 166; *Woods*, 251-55; Gotlieb, Robert and Irene Wolf, *Thinking Big: The Story of the Los Angeles Times, Its Publishers and Their Influence on Southern California*. G. P. Putnam & Sons, 1977.
10. *Bob Shuler's Magazine*, August 1927, 134; *LA Record* 8/6/27; *LAT*, 4/27/29
    One vice squad member available for duty—in fact, sitting in the squad room with nothing much to do—was A.T. Nelson, a recent and still untrusted member of the department. Shortly after the Jacobson incident, Nelson transferred to the Wilshire Division. [Nelson interview, June 19, 1986].
11. St. Cloud, Vern. "Bombing the Lid Off Los Angeles," *Official Detective Stories*. March, 1938. III, 43.
12. *LAT*, 4/3/29; according to St. Cloud and the *Illustrated Daily News*, Raymond afterward refused reinstatement into the LAPD, claiming that his "enviable reputation he had earned as an officer of the law had been tarnished." However, his reputation was anything but enviable. Raymond's culpability in the Jacobson case was demonstrated thoroughly during the trial, despite the fact that he and his co-defendants were not convicted. A witness who was waiting for his girlfriend near the Beagle Street house testified that Raymond had told him to "beat it." Additionally, Raymond was identified as the man who had rented an apartment on 6th Street several weeks before, which Wallis, Lucas and several unidentified females visited frequently. The prosecution claimed the apartment was the planned locus of the frame-up. [*LAT*, 3/30/29, 4/4/1928]; "Sample of Monday Night Radio Hour [October 31, 1927]" *Bob Shuler's Magazine*, December, 1927; "Is Our Police Department Full of Cheap Crooks," *Bob Shuler's Magazine*, October, 1927.
13. From FBI report of 1/16/37, title "UNKNOWN SUBJECTS; MRS. NANCY MALONE CLARK - VICTIM. DAVID HARRIS CLARK - VICTIM.
14. Unpublished, untitled manuscript in the *J. Shaw* collection detailing Raymond's career.
15. "Sixty Friends Honor Schenck" *LAT*, 12/27/28; West also attended; Bob Coyne correspondence in Clifford Clinton papers.
16. Parrot's name had been prominent in three vice scandals during 1935 alone. In January, he had been called before the Grand Jury during an investigation of gambling conditions. In July, during an investigation conducted in Los Angeles by a special state legislative committee looking into liquor license racketeering, he had been accused of making secretive telephone calls to the chief of a local liquor control division. In October, two proprietors of a raided Santa Monica Boulevard gambling club subpoenaed Parrot, Fitts, the entire Grand Jury, and numerous other law enforcement and local organized crime figures to testify about gambling payoffs *LAE*, 1/11/35, 1/12/35, 7/11/35, 7/12/35, 7/13/35, 7/14/35, 10/4/35 & 10/9/35.
17. Tom Sitton, "The 'Boss' Without a Machine: Kent K. Parrot and Los Angeles Politics in the 1920s," *Southern California Quarterly*, Vol. 67, No. 4, Winter 1985, p. 367. Parrot was born on May 22, 1883 to Joseph Parrot of New York and Georgia Grubb of Pennsylvania [Certificate

18. Sitton, 380-4.
19. June Hallberg, *Fitts/Palmer Campaign for District Attorney*, M.A. Thesis, UCLA, 1939:
    During the eight years of George Cryer's administration as mayor of Los Angeles from 1921-28, his campaign manager, Kent K. Parrot, gradually moved into the position of political boss and coordinator of local gambling (with the invaluable aid of gossiping newspapers accusing him of great secret power and thus adding to it). Parrot brought Guy MacAfee, former policeman, Bob and Dave Gans, slot machine owners and operators, and others into the gambling picture and during the three years, 1924-27, of his hand-picked Chief of Police, R. Lee Heath (listed on Buron Fitts roster of endorsers [when he ran against Palmer], big time gambling was at its height. Under the Shaw administration, Parrot played no such dominating role, but his police methods for protecting only the 'legitimate' rackets were continued and, with Joe Shaw, he still was of great significance in Los Angeles gambling and prostitution. Mr. Parrot, as a very astute behind-the-scenes politician, has in full the 'passion for anonymity' as the author can well testify after extensive and exhaustive unsuccessful attempts to secure an interview.

    On 1/12/35 Parrot was subpoenaed by Grand Jury looking into gambling. He was also named as a key figure in LA vice by Charles Stoker, *Thicker'n Thieves* [2] and William G. Bonelli *Billion Dollar Blackjack* [54], among others.
20. A. Brigham Rose, "Personnel of the Syndicate," Radio Talk July 1, 1938.
21. *IDN*, 11/15/29.
22. A. Brigham Rose, "Personnel of the Syndicate," Radio Talk July 1, 1938. Interview with Grant Cooper, May, 1989.
23. "Kent Parrot Admits Debt", *LAE*, 12/25/35.

NINETEEN: THE CASE AGAINST ROLAND WEST

1. Anger, 206. Anger's version of the story was subsequently retold by Jay Robert Nash in *Murder Among the Mighty* in 1983, 127; by Munn in 1987, 75, and Cohen in 1988, 180. The latter two writers apparently never ran across the work of Horden, MacQueen or Mader and Wolf.
2. Nicholas Horden, 1976 *Los Angeles Magazine*, 176. While Horden's parenthetical was apparently added to give the story greater veracity, DiCicco's comment about West teaching Todd a lesson is interesting given DiCicco's purported violence against women, as described by his second wife, Gloria Vanderbilt in *Black Knight, White Knight*.
3. MacQueen, 158.
4. MacQueen, 158.
5. Mader and Wolf, 226.
6. Mader and Wolf, 226.
7. Mader and Wolf, 228.
8. Mader and Wolf, 226. Scott MacQueen had already reported this particular story and cited Alex Gordon as the source. It is likely that Mader and Wolf used this lead to confirm with Gordon.
9. MacQueen later confirmed that his rendition of the story was attributable to Hal Roach through others who had heard it.
10. See *Los Angeles Magazine*, January, 1988
11. Phone contact with Hal Roach residence, December, 1987.
12. Phone interview with Richard Bann, December 1989.
13. These telephone interviews were conducted between December, 1989 and February, 1992. While the authors were anxious to interview Hal Roach personally, they were never able to arrange an appointment.
14. The substance of the Roach story as reported here was based on our inquiry as to what exactly the law enforcement personnel told Roach. The interview was conducted with Bann on May 15, 1991.

15. Anderson, *CIT*, 59.
16. *CIT*, 38.
17. *LAT*, 12/30/35.
18. That he was not employed by the West property is found in the *LAE* [12/28/35]; his observation is found in *LAT*, 12/18/35.
19. Phone interview with Alex Gordon 12/6/89.

TWENTY: THE MYSTERY OF ROLAND WEST

1. Betty Lou Young, *Where the Mountains Meet the Sea*, 1983, 125, et seq. The information about its intended use was confirmed in a phone interview on 10/21/86 with Robert Hanlon, the widowed husband of Lola Lane who stated that even during his tenure in the building from 1953-1973 the words "Castellammare Community Center" appeared on several walls. A representation of the café building appears on a promotional add for the Castellammare development printed in the *Los Angeles Times* on October 4, 1925. (Young, 132). The Community Center is designated on plans drawn up for the Los Angeles Mountain Park Co. by Wilkie Woodward Engineer, dated May 1926.
2. *Scott*, 36, quoting Fr. Kieser, who as head of Paulist Productions took over the building from Lola Lane, the widow of Roland West. Also see Young.
3. *Scott*, 36.
4. Floor plans, "Sheet No.1, Present Building".
5. Interview with Michael Rhodes, 3/12/86.
6. *Scott*, 36. Also see Young.
7. *LAT*, October 4, 1925; Los Angeles County Tax Assessment Records, Books 113, 270, 921 and 4416.
8. West may have acquired the building at an earlier date, but the first record of his ownership appears in September 1932 under the name of the Residential Land Corp, one of his companies. Los Angeles County Assessor Records, Book 270.
9. Floor plans, Joya's Café Building, 17571 To 17601 Malibu Road, Los Angeles, Sheet No. 1, Present Building. Also see photo reproduced in *Young*, 125.
10. Los Angeles County Assessor Records, Book 270. See note: "Right of way for the public walk has been vacated." Also plans for the replacement stairway were among those at the café.
11. A comparison of the plans designated "Sheet No.1 Present Building" and "Sheet No.2 Proposed Alterations" reveals the scope of the work on the second floor drawn up in May, 1934. These appear to be part of major renovations undertaken in 1934. For example, plans dated 3/24/34 citing Raymond Spalding, Engineer affect Store 1, Lot 13 (N) and 12 (S) Block 12.
12. Phone interview with Robert Hanlon, 10/26/86.
13. Floor plan, "Second Floor Plan, Alterations to Joya's Café Building," Circa 1934.
14. Robert Hanlon Interview. Also see, Damon Runyon, "The Brighter Side," a newspaper column in which the writer reviews West's later establishment, Chez Roland. *LAE*, 5/2/43.
15. Interview with Florian "Jack" Sauer, 11/30/84.
16. Robert Hanlon interview. A number of renderings for the interior details are included in the café's floor plan collection. Circa 1934.
17. Floor plan, "Second Floor Plan, Alterations to the Joya's Café Building, Arthur C. Munson Architect." Circa 1934.
18. *LAE*, 8/23/35, *LAT*, 12/17/35.
19. *LAE*, 12/17/35.
20. *LA H&E*, 6/27/35, *LAE*, 12/17/35.
21. *CIT*, 30-31, 27-33 and 1-6.
22. *CIT*, 54-55, 24-32 and 1-3.
23. *CIT*, 69, 19-24.
24. No element of West's testimony about the living arrangements was more confusing than his use

of the term, "boudoir." According to the 1934 Webster's New International Dictionary the term referred at the time to a "small private room, esp. one belonging to a lady." West's description, however, apparently referred to a large space which is hardly private. Word usage aside, he contradicted himself and totally obscured the reference, at one point claiming he had no key to the "ladie's boudoir", [*CIT*, 57, 3-4] at another that he "went to the lady's boudoir, opened it with my pass key and examined the huge couch in there because she had slept on that couch and there was what I considered an impression on that couch, thought she had slept there because no one else could have done that." [*CIT*, 69, 24-25] To make matters worse, when discussing the running water, he referred at one point to "the other lady's boudoir." [*CIT*, 68, l. 15]

One wonders if part of the problem lies in the transcription. The court reporter had no way of distinguishing "lady's" from "ladies'," the first signifying a private area West claimed was reserved for Miss Todd, and the other referring to the ladies' restroom on the second floor of the café, some 20 feet down the hall from the interior entrance of the apartment. If this is the case, West may have been trying to distinguish two quite separate areas, both of which he referred to as a boudoir. Unfortunately, this interpretation still fails to account for West's contradiction about the keys. While at one point he claimed he did not have a key to at least one of the areas, he clearly did, and opened it to examine the couch, which he claimed retained the impression of a sleeping body.

It is interesting to note that one set of the 1934 floor plans show a small alcove area in the ladies' restroom designated for a "couch." [Floor plan, "Second Floor Plan, Alterations to Joya's Café Bldg., Arthur C. Munson-Architect," Vellum Overlay. Circa 1934.] If this is indeed where West went to investigate, then he was maintaining that it was the bathroom from which he heard the water running, and the one Thelma used as a matter of course. Perhaps, then, West was claiming that Miss Todd's apartment, as distinguished from his own, consisted of the main room outside his bedroom, the lobby area, and the bathroom down the hall.

Again, on a practical basis this makes little sense, and would offer the actress no privacy. The restroom lies off the main hallway on the second floor; across the way were the main doors to the nearly opened Joyas dining room. Right next to the lobby/boudoir was the entrance to the hallway leading to the second floor private dining rooms already in operation. There was also a small cocktail bar and gaming area nearby. It is difficult to believe that Thelma Todd would share her bedroom with patrons waiting to be seated in the restaurant, or with women freshening up before dinner.

Given the absurdity of this arrangement, and the fact that there was no other place for her, it is very clear that Todd was domiciled in the actual apartment. Mae Whitehead certainly knew, and testified, this to be the case. West, in his testimony, admits that he too was living in the café and used the same apartment. Why was West trying to make one apartment into two apartments, actually three, his, Thelma's and the alcove in the ladies' lounge?

[25]. *IDN*, 1/3/35; *HCN*, 1/3/35
[26]. *SFC* 1/7/36.
[27]. *NYT*, 12/18/35.
[28]. *IDN*, 12/18/35.
[29]. *CIT*, 56.
[30]. *CIT*, 67.
[31]. *CIT*, 51, 12-13.
[32]. *CIT*, 20.
[33]. *CIT*, 56.
[34]. *CIT*, 56.
[35]. *LA H&E*, 12/17/35.
[36]. *IDN*, 12/17/35.
[37]. *IDN*, 12/18/35.
[38]. *CIT*, 58.
[39]. *CIT*, 58.

40. *CIT*, 82, 20-32.
41. *CIT*, 85-6.
42. *CIT*, 85.
43. *CIT*, 61, Also 70, 25-28.
44. *CIT*, 70-l, 32.
45. *CIT*, 81.
46. *CIT*, 86.
47. *CIT*, 82, l, 11.
48. *CIT*, 83, 7-10.
49. *CIT*, 73, 2-4.
50. *CIT*, 69, 28-31.
51. *LAE*, 12/18/35.
52. *CIT*, 104.
53. *CIT*, 104.
54. *CIT*, 42-43.
55. Phone Interview with Robert Hanlon, 10/21/86.
56. Winters, Shelley, *Shelley: Also known as Shirley*. Morrow. Parsons, Louella, *Waterloo Daily Courier*, May 16, 1957.
57. *MacQueen*, 146-147.
58. *MacQueen*, 108.
59. *MacQueen*, 108-109.
60. Interview with Don Gallery, 6/29/94.
61. Interview with Rudolph Schafer, December 1, 2000.
62. Interview with Jack and Mary Sauer, 11/30/84.
63. *LAE*, 1/8/36; *IDN*, 12/19/35.
64. Movie Picture World, 11/15/16.
65. *LAT* and *LAE*, 9/3/39. Also see, *IDN*, 10/27/39. There is disagreement over the date of the original separation. The 3/31/34 date was cited in Carmen's suit according to the *LAT* of 9/3/39. The *Los Angeles Examiner* of 11/28/40 mentions that they parted in 1930. There is other evidence contained in the Roland West Collection (AMPAS) that West and Carmen were living separately by January 1932, as West's secretary was sending Carmen's telephone and newspaper bills to her for payment.
66. *LAT*, 11/29/40.
67. *LET*, 12/27/35, *LAE*, 12/31/35.
68. *HCN*, 12/26/35, *LAT*, 12/26/35.
69. *LAE*, 4/1/52.
70. Los Angeles County Superior Court Probate Records, Van Ziemer, #32984
71. Interview with Katherine La Hue, 9/10/84.
72. *LAE*, 6/26/52. Also see, Los Angeles Superior Court Probate Records, Van Ziemer # 32984.
73. Biography, Joseph M. Schenck, United Artists Corporation, July 1, 1927. Also see, "Pix Pioneer Joe Schenck Dies at 83....," *Daily Variety*, 10/23/61.
74. *Daily Variety*, 10/23/61.
75. Biography, United Artists Corporation, 1927.
76. *Daily Variety*, 10/23/61.
77. *LAT*, 3/19/41, Reston, 220-222, *HCN*, 3/12/41.
78. *Allvine*, 162-167.
79. *NYT*, 6/4/40, *LAE*, 1/10/40, *LAE*, 6/4/40. Also see, McWilliams, *The Education of Carey McWilliams*, 86-92.
80. *LAE*, 3/18/41.
81. *LAE*, 3/20/41.

82. *HCN*, 3/19/41 and 3/20/41. Also see, *LAE*, 3/20/41.
83. *LAT*, 12/28/35.
84. *LAE*, 1/3/47. The announcement of this pardon by a "Justice Department spokesman" was made a year and three months after the pardon was granted.
85. MacQueen, 118.
86. Michael H. Price and George E. Turner, "Remembering How The Bat Whispers," *American Cinematographer*, March, 1986, 34.
87. *Price*, 43.

TWENTY-ONE: THE PRINCE OF DARKNESS

1. C. C. Colton, Lacon, Longmon, Hurst, Rees, Orme, and Brown, London, 1823, p 178
2. Anger, *Hollywood Babylon*, 204-206.
3. Horden, 175.
4. *Stump*, 8.
5. Michael Munn, "Thelma Todd: The Ice Cream Blonde," *The Hollywood Murder Casebook*, 67-78.
6. *Munn*, 77.
7. *Munn*, 77.
8. *Munn*, 78.
9. Interview with Richard Bann.
10. For a discussion of the Kennedy claims, Gerald Posner, *Case Closed*; and Anthony Summer, *Goddess* who claimed that Monroe's death was engineered by organized crime. Also note that Luciano himself had been named as the killer in the mysterious death of Sir Harry Oakes, a leading citizen of the Bahamas in the 1940s. James Leasor, *Who Killed Sir Harry Oakes?*
11. *Edmonds*, 9.
12. *Edmonds*, 9.
13. *Edmonds*, 9.
14. *Edmonds*, 283.
15. *Edmonds*, 56; interview with William Todd.
16. *Edmonds*, 64.
17. *Bergreen*, 31.
18. *Edmonds*, 95.

None of the standard works on Luciano and Capone mention this connection or any relationship between the two mobsters until much later in life. Indeed, it is doubtful. While Luciano grew up on the Lower East Side, Al Capone continued to live and cavort in Brooklyn until he moved to Chicago, Illinois when he was 22 years old. And as one of Capone's biographers, Laurence Bergreen writes, that in spite of the myth: "None of the Capones would ever have much to do with Manhattan; nor would Manhattan and its racketeers have much to do with them, except to condescend to them."

In fact, the only documented meeting between the two men in their early years occurred when Capone was in his late teens. Lucania, only two years older than Capone, but clearly his senior in the rackets, mediated a dispute between Al and another man. Al had made an indecent comment to the man's sister and got slashed across the cheek with a knife. While this incident led to Capone's nickname "Scarface," the decision of the senior mediators that Al should forget the whole thing because he started it, seemed to have settled the matter. [*Bergreen*, 28, 45, 50; Fox, 45]

Much of Edmond's telling of underworld context of the Todd death is pure fancy. For example, she claims Al Capone had three murder "raps" by the time he left Chicago: two committed by Luciano, for which Capone took the blame and bribed his way out of, and one committed in a bar room fight when Capone got his scars. In fact, there is no evidence that he was ever arrested for the murder of anyone, although he did once crack a man's skull with a pool cue during a bar fight (the victim lived) and reportedly killed one Tony Perotta, in a quarrel over gambling, but was never arrested. No one was killed in the incident of Al's scarring. In any case, none of these incidents had anything to do with his decision to move to Chicago, which was instead prompted by the chance to make big money under the tutelage of his gangster/mentor Johnny Torrio. [*Edmonds*, 96-98. *Bergreen*, 46, 50, 58]

19. *Edmonds*, 113.
20. *Edmonds*, 113-114.
21. See, for example, Dewey, *Twenty Against the Underworld*, Fox, *Blood and Power*, and Lacey, *Little Man*.
22. *Lacey*, 96.
23. *NYT*, 4/2/36.
24. See, for example, Campbell, *The Luciano Project*, Feder, *The Luciano Story*, Gosch, *The Last Testament of Lucky Luciano*, Powell, *Lucky Luciano, His Amazing Trial and Wild Witnesses*.
25. *Gosch*, 231-232. There is significant reservation about the accuracy of much of the material in Gosch's book, the purported authorized biography of Luciano, because many of the incidents described do not comport with known facts bearing on the mobster's career, as noted in Robert Lacey's source notes. While it is known that Gosch knew Luciano and conducted significant interviews, it is difficult to sort out the truth of the matters asserted from the fiction of later additions. While the authors did not rely on its contents for specific background on Luciano, the statement quoted is consistent with other sources and is anecdotal rather than dispositive on a specific incident. In a query to Lacey on the matter, he agreed with the authors that this particular statement was probably genuine and had the ring of truth to it.
26. See *Edmonds*, 218, 207-208 and 225, and 239. While such cross country travel was theoretically possible in 1935, it would have been relatively rare. The fastest air travel of the time for a one-way trip would have taken between 18 and 24 hours, even longer depending on the weather. The fastest airliners of the time flew at only 200 M.P.H. and required three or four fueling stops along the way. Yet, Edmond's has Luciano making the trip on a regular basis.
27. The sources for this basic scenario are too numerous to list in any comprehensive way. See for example, *Anslinger*, 103; *Dewey*, 190 et seq.; *Fox*, 158-169; *Lacey*, 92-96; and *Sondern*, 107-109. Also see, *NYT*, 4/2/36.
28. *NYT*, 6/4/36.
29. *NYT*, 11/3/35, 4/12/36, and 4/24/36. Also see, *Hickman*, 215-216.
30. *Hickman*, 215-216.
31. *Hickman*, 267-268.
32. *Hot Springs Sentinel Record*, 4/2/36, 4/3/36, and 6/19/36.
33. *Hot Springs Sentinel Record*, 4/3/36.

TWENTY-TWO: LET THE EVIDENCE SHOW

1. Rudyard Kipling, An Interview with Mark Twain, p. 180, *From sea to sea: letters of travel*, 1899, Doubleday & McClure Company.
2. Interviews with Robert Hanlon and Mike Rhodes.
3. Phone Interview with George Diestel, 6/29/94.
4. *CIT*, 18.
5. *LAT*, 1/1/36.
6. *CIT*, 31.
7. *CIT*, 30, 41; *LAT*, 1/1/36.
8. *CIT*, 19.
9. *CIT*, 19, 42-43.
10. *CIT*, 19, 31-32.
11. *CIT*, 180; *LAT*, 12/18/35. Also, examination of the many photos of the scene reveals the actress wearing the coat.
12. Coroner's Register; *CIT*, 180.
13. *CIT*, 106. By the time these items reached the morgue, they had been clipped to the collar of Thelma Todd's dress (*CIT*, 121).

14. *LAE*, 12/24/35.
15. *LAE*, 12/26 and 12/27, specifically mentions the girdle, but the item is not listed on the coroner's register. It is possible that the coroner's office garbled the reference to the stockings, meaning two stockings, rather than two pairs.
16. *CIT*, 108. A *LAT* report also listed gloves as items found on the seat, but they are not mentioned by Clark, or any other witness, nor are they among the items registered by the coroner. Neither do pictures of the interior of the auto reveal any gloves, only a handkerchief, presumably removed by Clark. It is probable that no gloves were found and that the reporter merely mistook the handkerchiefs for gloves.
17. All of the witnesses are united in this observation. Also see, *CIT*, 110.
18. *CIT*, 110. Photos taken at the scene from the right side of auto clearly show a thick covering of dust on the seat and on its back.
19. *LAE*, 1/7/36. The *Daily News* also reports on the print but claims it came from the side of the car. Contemporary photos seem to indicate a smudge on the back of the seat, so it is likely that the *Examiner* version is more likely.
20. *LAE*, 12/17/35.
21. The trip to the dentist is confirmed by the Coroner's Inquest testimony of Mae Whitehead. The nature of the dental work is noted in a bill submitted by Dr. Ralph J. Arnold to the estate of Thelma Todd and is contained in the probate records. Arnold's services were rendered from "1934 to Dec. 14, 1935, so it is possible that Thelma had the temporary bridge for some time. According to the description of the services in the bill, the dentist had surgically removed the real tooth, installed a temporary bridge "for a period of bone regeneration" and made "occasional adjustments." [See note 8, Chapter 3.]
22. *LAT*, 12/18/35.
23. Initial reports in the *LA Examiner* [12/26/35] and *LAT* [12/26/35] place the marks on the throat, not inside it. Other reports, add the notion that the cause might be a bottle or pipe, thus implying that the injury was inside the throat. *NYT* and *SFC*, 12/26/35.
24. *LAE*, 12/26/35; *NYT*, 12/26/35; and *LAT*, 12/26/35.
25. *NYT*, 12/26/35.
26. *LAT*, 12/26/35 and *LAE*, 12/26/35.
27. *CIT*, 48.
28. *CIT*, 75.
29. *CIT*, 106 and 110.
30. *LAT*, 12/21/35; *NYT*, 12/22/35; *IDN*, 12/21/35; *LAE*, 12/21/35, 12/29/35, 1/4/36.
31. The descriptions of distance can be found in *IDN*, 12/21/35 and the *LAT*, 12/21/35.
32. *LAT*, 12/21/35; *IDN*, 12/21/35.
33. *LAT*, 1/2/36; *HCN*, 1/7/36; *LAT*, 12/26/35; *LAE*, 12/27/35.
34. *CIT*, 115.
35. *CIT*, 111-112.
36. *LAE*, 12/29/35.
37. *LAE*, 12/29/35.
38. *HCN*, 12/17/35; *NYT*, 12/17/35.
39. *CIT*, 114.
40. *CIT*, 114.
41. Svensson and Wendell, *Crime Detection*, 1955.
42. According to probate records, Todd had five treatments for the condition between 10/9/35 and 11/4/35. Creditor's Claim No. 144,304, In the Matter of the Estate of Thelma Alice Todd DiCicco. April 2, 1936.
43. *LAE*, 12/26/35.
44. *LAE*, 12/30/35.

TWENTY-THREE: THE CAUSE OF DEATH

1. For a brief period in the afternoon of December 16, 1935, the lifeless body of Thelma Todd rested in the Todd and Leslie Mortuary on Arizona Avenue and Seventh Street in Santa Monica. The mortuary, a two-story structure of modern and functional architecture with an attached chapel, served as a temporary holding place for police cases. Bodies entered and left the mortuary by way of a loading area off an alleyway on the east side of the chapel building.

    The loading area was sealed off in the mid-1980s remodeling of the building, but up to that time the initials "T & L" could be seen on the cement threshold of side entry door. The mortuary continued in that capacity until the early 1970s when it was converted into a women's' health clinic. It was remodeled in the 1980s with a new facade and the chapel area was reworked. It suffered damage in the January 1994 earthquake and was torn down in March 1995.

2. Wagner testified as to the time he began the procedures. (*CIT*, 114). It can be inferred that he completed his work the next day because a press conference was held at 7:00 p.m. that evening at which a report of an "incomplete" autopsy was made public. (*IDN*, 12/17/25 and *SFC* 12/17/35). A complete autopsy awaited examination of the brain (*LAT*, 12/17/35) and the liver and stomach (*LET*, 12/17/35). By the time of Wagner's testimony on Wednesday afternoon, he had examined all of these organs.

3. Authorities ordered the release of the body for the removal of unspecified vital organs to be analyzed for the possibility of evidence of poisoning. (*LAE* and *NYT* [12/19/35]). It is possible that these steps were prompted by Martha Ford's claimed phone call and the various sightings which might have cast doubt on Wagner's time of death estimates and the police theories.

4. The substance and sequence of Wagner's findings appear in his *CIT*, 111-112.

5. *CIT*, 117, 111.

6. Both statements were made before the inquest. Wagner was quoted by the *SMEO*, 12/17/35 and Nance's statement was made to reporters of the *LAT* [12/18/35].

7. *LAT*, 12/18/35. Also see, *LAE*, 12/18/35 and 1/1/35.

8. *LA H&E*, 1/1/36.

9. *HCN*, 12/17/35.

10. *CIT*, 115. Wagner stated that he was calculating the autopsy from Monday evening.

11. *Morland*, 68; *LAT*, 3/19/95.

12. *Morland*, 68. Today, forensic pathologists take the temperature of the liver, the consistency and internal placement of which provides the most accurate readings.

13. Simpson and Knight, *Forensic Medicine*, 9th edition, (1988), Butler & Tanner Ltd., London, 6. Experts vary as to when a body would seem cold. Morland, for example, states that it could feel cold within six to 12 hours after death (page 69); Dieckmann, a former Detective Lieutenant and commander of the San Diego Homicide Squad claims it would indicate that the victim had been a cadaver for 18-24 hours. (9). It is interesting that Dieckmann, who seems to have worked as a homicide detective from 1936 to 1947, would make this observation. Clark, who reported that Todd's body was cold, may have been relying on the same perception and thus assumed that Todd had been dead for 18 hours or more.

14. Spitz and Fisher, *Medicolegal Investigation of Death*, 2nd edition, (1980), Thomas, Springfield, Illinois, 14.

15. *Morland*, 70-71; Svensson and Wendel, 220-221.

16. *Morland*, 70-71; Pena, 240-241, Svensson, 220-221.

17. *CIT*, 118.; see also Polson, Gee and Knight, *The Essentials of Forensic Medicine*, 4th edition, (1985), Pergamon Press, Oxford.

18. Svensson and Wendel, 220-221.

19. *CIT*, 106.

20. *CIT*, 118; Bernard Knight, *Legal Aspects of Medical Practice*, 4th edition, (1987), Churchill Livingstone, Edinburgh, 123.

21. Lividity is apparent from between 20 minutes to 4 hours after death, and is complete at an average

of 8-12 hours after death. When lividity is first appearing, up to around 3 hours after death, if the medical examiner presses firmly against the discolored flesh, it will "blanch," or turn white temporarily (in the manner that you can get a spot on your hand to turn white by pressing firmly). With the passage of 6-8 hours from the time of death, blanching will no longer occur, because the blood congeals in place. Once the blood has congealed in the lower parts of the body, "fixed lividity" is said to have occurred.

22. *Morland*, 70; *Pena*, p 237.
23. *CIT*, 117; Nance as quoted in *LAT*, [12/18/35]; he made an estimate of six to eight hours for the stomach to empty itself.
24. Interview with Dr. Joseph Choi.
25. Wagner made this observation in his Coroner's Inquest testimony. [*CIT*, 117]. The author's confirmed it in a series of interviews conducted with Dr. Joseph Choi, Senior Deputy Medical Examiner, Los Angeles County Coroner's Office, November/December, 1988.
26. Edward A. Dieckmann, *Practical Homicide Investigation*, 13.
27. *CIT*, 117-8.
28. *SMEO*, 12/19/35; *NYT*, 12/20/35.
29. *NYT*, 12/20/35; *HCN*, 12/29/35.
30. Interview with Dr. Joseph Choi.
31. Nickolls, *The Scientific Investigation of Crime*, 359. London, 1956
32. *IDN*, 12/19/35.
33. David Fisher, *Hard Evidence*, 31 and 42.
34. Interview with Dr. Joseph Choi.
35. James V. Vandiver, *Criminal Investigation*, 196; Pena, 241.
36. *HCN*, 1/17/35; *LAT*, 1/17/35.
37. Los Angeles County Coroner File # 6510.
38. Interview with Dr. Joseph Choi.

TWENTY-FOUR: THE SIGHTINGS

1. "It Ain't Necessarily So: The Dream of the Human Genome and Other Illusions", *The New York Review of Books*, 2000, 151-2.
2. *NYT*, 2/10/66, 6/11/66; *Internet Movie Database*, "Wallace Ford Biography"; "I've Been Married 14 Years and I'm Still Courting My Wife", Paramount Studios publicity file, Herrick Library, Academy of Motion Picture Arts and Sciences clipping file.
3. Lou Delahanty, "The Real Wallace Ford," *Shadowplay*, June, 1934, 46; obit., *NYT*, 2/10/66.
4. As reported by Harrison Carol in the *Evening Herald and Express*.
5. *LA H&E*, 12/17/35, 12/19/35; *LAE*, 12/24/35; *IDN*, 12/19/35.
6. *CIT*, 94.
7. *LAE*, 12/18/35, 12/25/35; *LAT*, 12/25/35.
8. *NYT*, 12/17/35; *LAE*, 12/17/35, 12/25/35; *LAT*, 12/18/35; *LA H&E* 12/17/35, 12/25/35.
9. *CIT*, 94-5.
10. *NYT*, 12/17/35; *LAE*, 12/17/35, 12/18/35; *IDN*, 12/17/35; *LAT*, 12/18/35; *HCN*, 12/17/35; *LA H&E*, 12/17/35.
11. *LAE*, 12/25/35; *LAT*, 12/25/35.
12. *LAT*, 12/18/35; *NYT*, 12/17/35; *LAE*, 12/17/35, 12/18/35.
Ford also speculated that "Miss Todd probably was calling from somewhere on Sunset or Hollywood boulevard between Laurel Canyon boulevard and Vine street" when she made the call. Whether or not she tried to reconcile this idea with her claim that the call came from Santa Monica is not clear. *IDN* 12/21/35.
13. *CIT*, 95.
14. *LAE*, 12/18/35; *LA H&E*, 12/17/35; *CIT*, 94-5.

In her testimony before the Coroner Jury, Ford did not mention any corroborators other than George Baker, and only implicitly referred to her comments to the party attenders after the phone call.

Baker told police that the man he spoke to over the phone had told him that Todd hadn't been at the café all day; West does not mention this element and says only that he told Baker that "Miss Todd will be here in a little while." Baker testified before the Grand Jury, but not the Coroner's. None of the other corroborators testified, but newspapers reported that they had confirmed Ford's story (see *LA H&E*, 12/27/35).

15. Ford's comment to reporters that café employees answered Todd's line when the actress did not do so first supports her claims of their somewhat infrequent phone conversations. *LA H&E*, 12/17/35; *SFC*, 12/18/35; *LAE*, 12/18/35.

According to her Coroner's testimony, about a dozen guests had arrived when the phone rang that afternoon. How many were in the room where she answered the phone is unclear; she states that the guests were "divided between the living room and the various places outside." [*CIT*, 99] As she referred to "places" outside instead of "outside" as a whole, one would assume that at least four persons, two pairs, were standing outside, leaving perhaps eight in the living room. One of the guests in the living room was probably Ed Gargan, who had just arrived at the house and probably would not yet have passed from the reception area in the living room to the outside; Peter Hancock was also probably there, as Ford seems to have announced Todd's impending arrival to them at the same time. On the other hand, Warren Stokes was probably not among this group of eight, and may not have even been at the party yet, since he seems to have learned that Todd was coming a bit later. The same goes for George Baker.

17. Ford testified that the phone had two extensions, but did not suggest that she picked up the call in another room—such as a bedroom.
18. *CIT*, 95.
19. *CIT*, 97.
20. *CIT*, 25.
21. *LAT*, 12/18/35; *CIT*, 24-25.

It is hard to imagine how there could have been so much confusion over the identity of callers and receivers. Certainly, Roland West forthrightly states that he always answered Todd's apartment phone as Mr. Schafer, for reasons that he never stated, but which one might have had to do with his desire to keep his intimate relationship with Todd from being a gossip item. But, one wonders, how could Martha Ford not have known whether she was speaking to Alice Todd or Todd's maid when she called to invite the actress to her Sunday afternoon party, how Todd's maid could have thought she was talking with Martha Ford when she was actually speaking with Ford's maid when she called to convey Todd's acceptance, and how Ford's maid could have assumed at the same time she was speaking with Todd, when she was actually speaking with Todd's maid? Poor phone service might account for some of this, but it is hard not to guess that some other factor was involved.

22. *LA H&E*, 12/20/35.
23. *LAE*, 12/21/35; *IDN*, 12/20/35, 12/21/35; unfortunately, there is no record of the police interrogating the drugstore employees, although it is likely that they did so.

As the Ford home and the Sunset Boulevard area directly east of the Laurel Drugstore were both in the same telephone zone, police could not reference manual operator records.

24. *LAT*, 12/24/35 It is interesting in light of the controversy over Todd's shoes that, on viewing the actress' evening clothes, one cigar store customer declared that the woman in the cigar store wore different shoes from those Todd had died in.

Persson's claim that the number Todd had him dial ended in 7771 must have launched some investigatory effort, although there is little evidence of it from newspaper records.

25. *LAT*, 12/19/35; Ardell confirmed the story *Chicago Times* 12/19/35; Carmen explained she hadn't told police about the sighting because of reporters at police headquarters when she was first interviewed.
26. "I couldn't possibly be mistaken" *LA H&E*, 12/19/35; "I could not be mistaken" *SFC*

12/19/35; "could not positively identify Miss Todd" *LAT*, 12/19/35.
27. *LAE*, 12/19/35; *LA H&E*, 12/19/35.
28. *LAT*, 12/19/35.
29. *LAE*, 12/19/35.
30. *LA H&E*, 12/19/95.

TWENTY-FIVE: SUICIDE?
1. Siegfried Sassoon, "Suicide In the Trenches", *Counter Attack and Other Poems*, E.P Dutton, New York, 1918
2. It is unclear exactly how many jurors believed in a suicide finding, but one paper reported that the panel was almost evenly divided between suicide and murder theories, with few accident believers. *LAT*, 1/4/36.
3. *CIT*, 8.
4. *CIT*, 21 and 23.
5. *CIT*, 59.
6. Phone Interview with Ann Reynolds, 6/29/35.
7. *LAE*, 12/29/35.
8. Until the 1960s seven states had statutes making suicide a felony. Stephan A. Flanders, *Suicide*, Library in a Book, New York, 1991, 41.
9. Glen Evans and Norman L. Faberow, *The Encyclopedia of Suicide*, Facts on File, New York, 1988, 70.
10. *LAE*, 12/25/35; *IDN*, 1/8/36.
11. *Evans and Faberow*, 254.
12. *Evans and Faberow*, 230.
13. *Flanders*, 30-31. Also see, Kahn and Fawcett, *The Encyclopedia of Mental Health*, 361.
14. *Flanders*, 31.
15. *Flanders*, 31-32.
16. Interview with Cole Johnson 12/10/95.
17. *Evans and Faberow*, 87.
18. *Flanders*, 34; *Evans and Faberow*, 58.
19. *Evans and Faberow*, 153-154.
20. *Flanders*, 33-34.
21. *Flanders*, 20.
22. *In the Matter of the Estate of Thelma Alice Todd DiCicco*, No. 155,304, Creditors Claim of T.A. Meyers, Contractor, 2/7/36.
23. *Flanders*, 32.
24. *Evans and Faberow*, 58.
25. *Evans and Faberow*, 135.
26. *Evans and Faberow*, 71.
27. *Evans and Faberow*, 3.

TWENTY-SIX: AN ACCIDENTAL CONCLUSION
1. *SFC*, 12/20/35.
2. *CIT*, 61-62.
3. The VIN of Todd's phaeton was KB1008.
4. Robert Lichty, *Standard Catalog of Ford, 1903-1990*, 122 and 326-327. Also see, *Griffith Borgeson*, 223-225.
5. *LAT*, 12/18/35.
6. *HCN*, 1/7/36; *IDN*, 1/18/36.
7. *IDN*, 12/18/35.
8. *CIT*, 92-93.

[9]. These tests were conducted on 12/22/35, but the press did not report them until Whitehead testified before the Grand Jury on 1/7/35. *HCN*, 1/7/35. Also see, *LAE* and *LAT*, 1/8/35.
[10]. *LAT*, 1/8/36.
[11]. *LAE*, 12/21/35.
[12]. *LAT*, 12/23/35; Also see *IDN*, 1/8/36.
[13]. See *LAE*, 12/23/35; *NYT*, 12/24/35; and *LAT*, 12/23/35.
[14]. *LAT*, 12/30/35.
[15]. *CIT*, 110.
[16]. *CIT*, 89.
[17]. *HCN*, 1/7/36.
[18]. *LAE*, 12/23/35; *LET*, 12/20/35.
[19]. *LAE*, 12/20/35.
[20]. *LAE*, 12/23/35.
[21]. *LAT*, 1/1/35; *LAE*, 1/1/35.
[22]. Svensson and Wendel, 260-261.
[23]. Robert H. Dreisbach and William O. Robertson, *Handbook of Poisoning*, 1987, 259.
[24]. *CIT*, 113.
[25]. Petajan, Jack H., *Survival Responses During Fire Exposure*, 107-110.
[26]. Svensson and Wendel, 260-261.
[27]. Svensson and Wendel, 260-261; James V. Vandiver, *Criminal Investigation*, 196, 1983.
[28]. These figures were arrived at by actual measurements at the garage and by estimating the amount of displacement based on photographs and descriptions of the scene.
[29]. The garage had a volume of approximately 3840 cubic feet. A 20 percent reduction would take the volume down to 3072 cubic feet. Thus, .5 percent is 15.35 cubic feet; .4 percent is 12.288; .2 percent is 6.144; and .15 percent is 4.6. Note that the volume of displacement is higher than 20 percent, the amount of carbon monoxide needed to reach these levels would be less.
[30]. *Dreisbach and Robertson*, 259. Also see, *Svensson and Wendell*. Given the relatively primitive state of filtration and the condition of the phaeton's engine, we have added 6 percent for our calculations.
[31]. Interview with Dr. Joseph Choi.
[32]. O'Brian and Chafetz, *The Encyclopedia of Alcoholism*, Facts on File, New York, 1982 50, set the rate at .015 percent; Choi used .020 percent.
[33]. *O'Brian and Chafetz*, 50.
[34]. The following table shows roughly the progress of Todd's intoxication on that night:

Time	Event	Add	Subtract	Net BAL
08:45	Cocktail	.0406		.0406
10:30	1 3/4 hours oxy		.02625	.01435
10:30	Champagne	.0406		.05495
11:00	1/2 hour oxy		.0075	.04745
11:00	Champagne	.0406		.08805
11:30	1/2 hour oxy		.0075	.08055
11:30	Brandy	.0406		.12115
12:00	1/2 hour oxy		.0075	.11365
01:00	1 hour oxy		.0150	.09865
01:00	Champagne	.0406		.13925
01:45	3/4 hour oxy		.01125	.12800
01:45	Champagne	.0406		.16860
03:00	1 1/4 hour oxy		.01875	.14985
03:30	1/2 hour oxy		.0075	.14235
04:00	1/2 hour oxy		.0075	.13485

05:00	1 hour oxy	.0150	.11985
06:00	1 hour oxy	.0150	.10485
07:00	1 hour oxy	.0150	.08985
08:00	1 hour oxy	.0150	.07485

Additional calculations using a standard formula for deriving blood alcohol level, Widmark's, show roughly the same figures.

[35]. Basquette claimed in an interview to have had a strange interaction with Todd either at the Trocadero or Mocambo shortly before her death. Thelma was at a table with three or four gentlemen, "very, very drunk" and behaving very dramatically—"dancing around." At some point, on the dance floor, Thelma grabbed Lina and said, "Help me. You've got to help me." Lina was with Lyle Talbot, whom she described as a notorious drinker and a bad drunk, but a pure, self-righteous prude when on the wagon. And that night he was on the wagon with a vengeance. He was upset by Thelma's behavior, her public drunkenness, and indignantly insisted that Lina have nothing whatever to do with her. When she heard of Thelma's death a day or so later, "in the papers, on the radio," she felt badly. Perhaps Thelma wasn't just over dramatizing, perhaps Thelma really did need her help that night. Perhaps if she'd intervened. While, at first, Basquette claimed that this event happened on the night Todd died, in subsequent conversations she was unsure whether it was nights days before.

[36]. *LAT*, 12/28/35; *LA H&E*, 12/28/35 12/31/35; Grauman's count varies in the papers; the *Los Angeles Times* quotes him as saying Todd only a half a glass, while the *LA Examiner* cites him for a "couple of glasses"

[37]. Interview with Dr. Joseph Choi.

[38]. *LAT*, 12/21/35; *IDN*, 12/21/35.

[39]. *LAT*, 12/21/35 published Cavett's explanation, but the *LAT* of that date argued that the blood could mean that the actress was killed outside the garage and presumably planted in the car.

[40]. Interview with Florian Sauer.

Printed in Poland
by Amazon Fulfillment
Poland Sp. z o.o., Wrocław